200 mi

200 km

D0786857

Russian Federation

Hopa

Trabzon

PONTIC MTS.

Georgia

★Tbilisi

Azer.

Yerevan
★

Armenia

Erzurum

Mt. Ararat

Elazig

EASTERN TAURUS

Van

Lake Van

Diyarbakir

Iran

Euphrates River

...ntep

...n

Tigris River

...ria

Iraq

Baghdad
★

**ASIA
(MIDDLE EAST)**

Euphrates River

Saudi Arabia

N

1. Antalya. Muammer Kaylan was born in 1925 in this town on the Mediterranean coast.

2. Isparta. Kaylan spent his childhood in this provincial capital nestled in Anatolia.

3. Gallipoli. An Allied campaign during World War I was fought on this peninsula in an unsuccessful bid to capture the Dardanelles. The Turkish and Allied casualties numbered more than 500,000. Gallipoli is still a bitter memory for many Turks, Brits, Australians, and New Zealanders.

4. Istanbul. The headquarters for Kaylan's influential newspaper *Hürriyet* (*Freedom*), Istanbul now houses several statues of Mustafa Kemal Atatürk, one of which overlooks the Bosphorus Strait.

The Kemalists

Muammer Kaylan

The Kemalists

*Islamic Revival
and the Fate of
Secular Turkey*

 **Prometheus Books**

59 John Glenn Drive
Amherst, New York 14228-2197

Published 2005 by Prometheus Books

Inquiries should be addressed to
Prometheus Books
59 John Glenn Drive
Amherst, New York 14228–2197
VOICE: 716–691–0133, ext. 207
FAX: 716–564–2711
WWW.PROMETHEUSBOOKS.COM

09 08 07 06 05   5 4 3 2 1

Library of Congress Cataloging-in-Publication Data

Kaylan, Muammer.
The Kemalists : Islamic revival and the fate of secular Turkey / Muammer Kaylan.
p. cm.
ISBN 1–59102–282–7 (alk. paper)
1. Kemalism. 2. Islam and secularism—Turkey. 3. Turkey—History—20th century. I. Title.

DR590.K378 2005
956.103—dc22

2004029911

Printed in the United States of America on acid-free paper

To the memory of Kemal Atatürk, who was a revolutionary teacher of enlightenment much more than a warrior and a statesman.

Contents

Acknowledgments

This book might not have been written without the encouragement and enthusiasm of my wife, Magrid, and the suggestions of Bob Abramson of Bonita Springs, Florida. Thanks are due to them.

I would also like to thank the staff members of the Office of the Press Counselor of the Turkish Embassy in Washington, DC, for their help in providing the historical pictures you see in this book.

Special thanks are due to Mike Hirsch, the president of the Whitehall Printing Company in Naples, Florida; Steven L. Mitchell, editor in chief; Christine Kramer, production manager; and Heather Ammermuller, assistant editor, at Prometheus Books for their invaluable help.

My sons, Ali and Mike, have helped greatly with their computer expertise during the development of the book and on the Turkish fonts seen in *The Kemalists*. Thanks are due to them as well as to my daughter, Nilüfer, who provided background information for the chapter on Polonezköy and on recent social developments in Turkey.

The 1st and 2nd Articles of the Turkish Constitution

1. The Turkish state is a republic.
2. The Turkish Republic is a secular, social, law-and-order state.

It is not necessary to see my face in order to see me. If you understand my thoughts and are touched by my feelings, that is enough.

Kemal Atatürk

From *The New York Times*, June 14, 1999, with Celestine Bohlen reporting:

ISTANBUL, Turkey, June 12—When the Foreign Minister of Kyrgyzstan met with her Turkish counterpart at a recent international gathering, she asked him a question so painful and so blunt that it ended up making front-page news here in Turkey.

"When we got our independence, you gave us inspiration," said Rosa Otunbaeva, the official from the Central Asian country. "Turkey was our horizon. When we looked at Turkey, we thought we would one day be like you."

And then with tears in her eyes, she blurted out, "What has happened to you?"

Some Notes on Turkish Spelling and Pronunciation

c—*j*, as in John. *Can*—life

ç—*ch*, as in chain. *Çene*—jaw

g—a hard *g*, in go. *Gel*—come

ğ—a soft *g*, as in oghlu. *Oğlu*—son of

i—*i*, as in in. *İlkbahar*—spring

ı—*e*, as in dozen. *Basmacı*—raider

o—*o*, as in order. *Osmanlı*—Ottoman

ö—*i*, as in bird. *Ördek*—duck

ş—*sh*, as in pasha. *Paşa*—general

u—*oo*, as in hoot. *Un*—flour

ü—*u*, as in cute. *Ümit*—hope

Introduction

elcome to my world, a world rich in adventure and unforget-
table experiences! It is a world also of indelible memories—
but not all of them fit the description of Turkish delight.

When I think about the present conditions in Turkey, I remember the painter Abdülcelil Levni. Born in Thrace, in the city of Edirne, late in the seventeenth century, Levni was the Ottoman Empire's greatest painter of the *Lale Devri*, the Era of the Tulip. As the chief court painter, Levni preferred to use soft colors in his paintings of joyful scenes, like the fantasyland garden parties of that period. He worked together with the poet Vehbi, illustrating his two-volume book of poetry called *Surname-i Vehbi* (Vehbi's Letter of Destiny), which now is on display in Istanbul's Topkapı Palace Museum.

Levni was a man of humor. He witnessed the sumptuous times of the Ottoman Empire's dreamy elite when that empire's fortunes were already declining. Levni's words spoken in Ottoman Turkish almost three hundred years ago reflect the present conditions in Turkey:

> Of a confused duck, which forgets where its head is,
> They say that it dives into the lake butt first.

The incremental revival of the Islamic reactionary movement in Turkey over the past decades reminds me of the poetry of Kul Nesimi, who rebelled against the Ottoman radical Islamists. He was a *melami*, a member of a Sufi dervish sect that disregarded the external rites of religion and lived without vanity and worldly care.

For his liberal views on Islam, Kul Nesimi was executed. He wrote this poem three hundred years ago.

> Sometimes I rise in the sky
> And watch the world,
> Other times I come down
> And people gaze at me.
> Sometimes I teach in a *medrese*
> In the name of God,
> Other times I am in a tavern
> Imbibing wine for love.
> It is no one's business what I do,
> For I've chosen to wear
> The cloak of a melami dervish,
> And I've smashed on a stone,
> The bottle said to contain honor and shame.

In difficult times the Turks are known to say, "Little wit in the head makes much work for the feet," and "When the wise fall, the fool profits." These expressions are usually followed by poet Tevfik Fikret's words: "We laugh when our conditions should make us cry."

This book is not meant to be a cri de coeur about my own life, however. My purpose is to explain the impact of Turkey's secular reforms of the 1920s and 1930s, imposed on a defeated, backward nation ruled for centuries by the Shariah, Islam's version of canon law. It is to explain how through political irresponsibility and greed the nation's clock later was turned back. This game of darkness and ignorance goes on despite a multitude of potential danger signs caused by a militant Islamic reactionary movement.

The Turkish Republic's secular reform laws prohibit *tarikats*, Islamic brotherhoods such as Qadiriyah, Nur, the Light Sect, and the Nakshibendi. Yet they exist openly, even inside the secular state itself, and promote fundamentalist Islam in the political and social life of the nation.

Since the 1950s, forty thousand new mosques have been built in Turkey at a time when more secular schools were needed to educate the people. Meanwhile, ideological clashes and social and political corruption have destroyed the well-being of the country.

It would be wrong solely to blame my nemesis Süleyman Demirel, who was prime minister seven times and president once, for all of the misfortunes that befell Turkey's citizens. Surely, he played a leading role in causing the present economic, social, moral, and political misfortunes. It is a fact that the policies of Demirel's ruling Justice Party in the late 1960s and in 1970 caused disunity and a near civil war between right- and left-wing extremists. His party cleared the way for a legitimate Islamic revival, which later opened up a floodgate of corruption as offshoots of the Justice Party emerged.

Demirel returned to power repeatedly and in 1991 even promised to fight corruption. Demirel's words *Verdimse ben verdim* famously represent his views on accountability: "If I gave it, I gave it myself." The breakdown in the Turkish state's administration began with Demirel's regime. As a result, the functions of the state collapsed, and the plunder of the state's wealth became commonplace.

Others also played destructive roles that have been instrumental in changing the destiny of the Turkish nation, and they are responsible for a powerful fundamentalist movement. They mishandled a Kurdish separatist revolt and caused deep poverty as well as moral decline. They are morally and legally responsible for Turkey's instability and for its institutional collapse.

Adnan Menderes, who was prime minister between 1950 and 1960, had a favorite vote-getting slogan, "We will create a millionaire in every district." Turkey was a country of millionaires and billionaires until January 2005, when the Turkish government eliminated six zeros from the lira. Just before the election of November 3, 2002, Tansu Çiller, Turkey's first female prime minister (1993–96), surpassed the predictions of Menderes. During her election campaigns, she promptly declared her intention to create trillionaires in every district. At that time, one US dollar was worth 1.65 million Turkish liras.

Süleyman Demirel's first political organization, the Justice Party, is considered to be the nucleus of a corrupt yet powerful triumvirate of politicians, businesspeople, and members of the media who later dominated the country. This dominance changed the elite's attitudes and altered time-honored moral values. A great majority of Turks stricken in fall 2002 by deep poverty did not believe in their political leaders, their political parties, their parliament, or their media. They were taken in by lies and false election promises prevalent through the past five decades. Adnan Menderes once told the electorate, "Finally, we have achieved comfort." And Süleyman Demirel claimed that, "Turkey has become great." In his election campaigns, he promised pie-in-the-sky—to every family a house and a car.

Turgut Özal, former premier (1983–89) and president (1989–93) and a leading member of the religious order Nakshibendi Brotherhood said, "We have been transformed into a little America." His words were true only for an elite group he had created—a corrupt class of wealthy people, who are still known as Özal's Princes. Some of Özal's famous words included, "Nothing will happen to the constitution if only a little hole is punched in it." He also said, "Let's not create a distinction between black and white money," meaning stolen money was just as good as earned money. These quotations are repeated regularly in the Turkish press.

Özal's policies opened the door to widespread corruption and led to tax evasion and swindling to receive government grants with false documents, causing huge losses to the state. The swindling was done through bogus documents that showed the export of locally produced goods when nothing was actually exported. The owner of the fake documents received a government grant intended to encourage the export of Turkish goods. A privileged class of scoundrels, protected by the old-guard political elite, looted the state's treasury and the nation's banks of billions of dollars. They got away with it because of bribery, an inadequate judicial system, and scared prosecutors. The words *Adalet mülkün temelidir*—"Justice is the foundation of the state"—displayed in each Turkish court had lost their meaning.

Turkey in fall 2002 was a country with over sixty political parties and a dysfunctional government of looters. Suffering under the weight of severe poverty and corruption, the nation had lost sight of its political future and its own identity. While a great number of have-nots were being alienated from the secular reforms established many years earlier, the elitist class protected the status quo and felt no need to maintain moral values. The merchants of Islam, those exploiters of religion, along with the Communists, the Fascists, and thieves and looters embedded in the state and the media, used every means to manipulate the country's future. The Kemalism that had grounded modern Turkey with its firm belief in a single state, a single nation, a single language, and a single flag was aggressively assaulted by the powerful revival of Islam and a disastrous Kurdish separatist movement. The nation was led away from its foundation in secular reform and ended up in total confusion about its destiny. Turkish voters became such a bewildered lot that they repeatedly brought back to power the same looters, habitual liars, scoundrels, criminals, and Islamic bigots.

New records for false promises were established in the political campaigns for the crucial election of November 3, 2002. Politicians promised instant solutions to the country's ills, including the quick reduction of the nation's debt of more than $200 billion. Others promised to kick out the International Monetary Fund, which had paid over $31 billion in loans over four years to Turkey, becoming the country's biggest creditor.

The judgment of history on Turkey's old-guard political bosses shall not be kind. It is a fact that their policies, their corruption, their lies, and their lack of accountability led the nation into potential dangers that would include the complete deterioration of its overburdened, inefficient, and unfair judicial system and repeated blunders in policy, which have no equal in the history of the secular republic. Before the election of

November 3, 2002, Turkey's government had changed twelve times in thirteen years.

According to Fuat Miras, the chairman of the Turkish Chambers of Commerce and Stock Exchanges (TOBB), millions of Turks in spring 2002 were at the threshold of starvation. The official figures showed at the time that 43 percent of the population of more than seventy million was living below the poverty line. In January 2005, a family of four with two schoolchildren needed a monthly income of about $1,250 in order not to be considered poor.

The people's anger and frustration finally erupted on November 3, 2002. Hoping for salvation from their misery, the Turks voted for a new party with powerful Islamic roots. This was *AK Partisi*, the Justice and Development Party, its abbreviated name *AK* signifying a clean and unblemished political organization. This claim proved to be uncorroborated as scores of party members were in the courts at that time on charges of corruption. Only the social democrat *Cumhuriyet Halk Partisi* (CHP), the Republican People's Party, was able to enter parliament in inconspicuous opposition. Other mainstream parties, including those on the center-right, had collapsed and their oligarchic leaders eliminated.

It was a momentous event, a vengeful, silent revolution against the status quo, the secular state, and its strict Kemalist dogma. The election results shook the foundation of Turkey's secular republic, and many wondered whether the modern reforms of the 1920s and 1930s had become totally obsolete in a country where Islam had suddenly taken a new and powerful hold. Some columnists even cheerfully declared that Kemalism was dead. Five months later, in March 2003, Mehmet Nuri Yılmaz, the chairman of the state's Department of Religious Affairs, resigned. In a statement to the press, he gave as the reason for his resignation the involvement of religion in politics. Yılmaz warned: "Letting everyone talk politics in the 72,000 mosques of the country would be asking for chaos."

In truth, during the last fifty-four years, the secular legacy of Mustafa Kemal Atatürk has been betrayed. After the death of its founder, fearing unwanted or dangerous outside influences, Kemalism isolated Turkey. It later remained a rigid dogma that discouraged change. When Kemalism's most remarkable objective, the spirit of Western reforms, was neglected, its inspiration vanished, leaving peasants and subsistence farmers, 43 percent of the population, uneducated and ignorant. The growing trend of economic globalization was also ignored. That betrayal turned the Turkish clock back to the days of the Ottoman Empire.

Mustafa Kemal Atatürk was a soldier and statesman but above all an extraordinary reformer. Following the collapse of the Ottoman Empire after World War I, he led a successful war of independence against the Allies, who were occupying Turkey. Atatürk founded modern secular Turkey in 1923 and introduced sweeping new reforms, mainly during a ten-year period. He modernized Turkey's legal and educational systems and adopted the European way of life for the people. Perhaps one of the most remarkable of his reforms is the total elimination of writing Turkish in the Arabic alphabet, which had prevailed for centuries. Atatürk adopted the Latin alphabet, thus completely overhauling the country's educational system.

Another of his extraordinary reforms was the establishment of a secular republic by eliminating the role of the Islamic religion in the affairs of the state. The Ottoman Empire had been ruled throughout centuries by the Shariah, the canon law of Islam. Shariah rule, however, was often seen as an obstacle to modernization and progress. These reforms separated Turkey from other Islamic countries, as none of their leaders was able to follow in Atatürk's footsteps.

I was a child of Mustafa Kemal Atatürk's revolution and one of his pupils. He changed us, the Young Turks. We called ourselves Kemalists then and took solemn oaths to protect his secular legacy. Some of us turned out to be Janus-faced opportunists.

This is their story as well as mine.

The Time
of Troubles

If you throw a stone in the sewer, expect to get covered with muck.

Turkish proverb

he Time of Troubles—also known as the Time of Chaos—is forever in my mind and I remember it all, even after so many years. I remember it because it had such an impact on my life and because it drastically changed the destiny of Turkey. I remember those days vividly when the greed for power turned the streets into killing fields and opened up Pandora's box, from which sprang the specter of the Islamic reactionaries. I vividly remember the bloody demonstrations of both left- and right-wing extremists. And I still hear their wild slogans while they clashed on the campuses and in the streets.

The Time of Troubles began in 1970. In the spring of that year, after a four-year stint at the United Nations in New York as a correspondent, I was recalled to the headquarters of the influential newspaper *Hürriyet* (*Freedom*) in Istanbul. The recall was for consultations to improve the general news content of the paper. Soon the real reason of my recall was made clear. I was appointed *Hürriyet*'s editor-in-chief.

I found that a great deal had changed in the country as well as at the newspaper itself, which was struggling with serious circulation problems. Nineteen hundred seventy was a terrible year in Turkey. The Soviet Union's cold war efforts to destabilize the country and destroy its fragmented democracy were starting to pay off. Large shipments of arms were being smuggled into the country from Bulgaria and Syria, where Turkish extremists were being trained as terrorists.

The left-wing Turkish Labor Party harbored militant radicals who, like the extreme right, had infiltrated political parties, the government, the military, the police force, and the National Intelligence Agency (MIT). Student unrest had plagued the university campuses since 1968, and by 1970 the student associations, the labor unions, and the political parties had divided the country into two radical camps. On one side were the Marxists-Leninists and Maoists of the far left, and on the other side stood the extreme right with its two highly determined factions. The first was the reactionary pro-Islamists, who wanted a return to the Shariah (Divine or Canon Law), and the Caliphate (the temporal and spiritual leadership of the Islamic world). The others were the ultranationalists, who dreamed of *Kızıl Elma*, the Red Apple, pan-Turanist or pan-Turkic unity—the unification of all Turkic peoples between the Balkans and western China.

The political parties were turning into lawless outlets for mobsters and adventure-seeking opportunists. Mass demonstrations and violent clashes between supporters of extremist factions were a prelude to widespread bloodshed. The armed street battles that followed left their mark on modern Turkish history as the "Times of Chaos."

The radical left, specifically, the Federation of Revolutionary Youth of Turkey (*DevGenç*), founded in 1969, adopted terrorist methods to achieve a Soviet-style bloody destabilization of the existing government. A Soviet clandestine radio station called *Bizim Radyo* (Our Radio), which broadcast from Romania and East Germany, falsely represented itself as the real voice of the nation, and spread disinformation about the policies of the Turkish state, such as membership in NATO. A violent leftist outfit, the Turkish People's Liberation Army was organizing a terrorist campaign that would include the kidnapping of foreigners, particularly Americans. Ironically, the danger from Communism became a bogeyman serving corrupt right-wing politicians who used it to scare the nation while unscrupulously robbing the state institutions.

It was summertime. From my office window on the third floor of the *Hürriyet* building at Cağaloğlu, then Istanbul's press district, I was watching a noisy leftist demonstration below on Babıali Street. The demonstration was against my newspaper, its publisher, and its journalists. The demonstrators were shouting Maoist slogans: "Damn the Freemasons!" "Down with the compradors, agents of the Americans." The word *comprador* represented a Chinese agent engaged by foreign capitalists in China in charge of their Chinese employees and acting as an intermediary. The word *kompradorlar*, plural in Turkish, implied that we were considered to be the agents of the Americans. The Freemasons, too, were viewed by most Turks to be members of a secret society with powerful foreign links and wicked designs against the country. It was believed that the Freemasons' aim was to divide the country.

My office door opened and an aide walked in carrying a small box. He placed the box on my desk and said: "The main doors are secured, chief." Several years earlier, I had worked on Babıali Street consecutively as the chief news editor of three different newspapers, and the title *chief* had stuck to me.

"Good," I said. "What is the box for?"

"A pistol," he answered. "It's a locally made one by *Kırıkkale*. Erol Simavi Bey figured you might need it for protection. Who knows, some wild-eyed extremist might try to kill you."

A gun sent by a worried newspaper publisher, a member of the local lodge of Freemasons? He sends me a gun to protect myself? *Is he kidding?* I thought. *He may be concerned about a government action against the newspaper, but I am a sitting duck, fair game for any wild-eyed assassin, including the agents of the regime.*

"Thank you," I said, "but I won't carry a gun. Please take it away."

As another roar of "*kompradorlar*" filled the room, he left with the gun. I looked out and watched the demonstrators. For two decades, Marxists had infiltrated the government and gradually gained solid ground in

Turkey. Agitators organized by *Darzhavna Sigurnost* (DS), the Bulgarian Secret Service, surrogates for the Soviet KGB, had agents at the universities. They were spreading disinformation about the state for being a NATO member and pro-American with anti-Western propaganda. Now capitalism was out and Marxism had become fashionable among the pro-Soviet intellectuals. The Marxists, whom we used to call *tatlı su solcuları* (sweet water leftists) because they hoped to hold high positions in a pro-Soviet government, believed that the time was right to create martyrdom of a few leftists in the final push.

Several pro-Soviet newspaper columnists played a pivotal role in creating this crisis. For years they had been sowing the seeds of self-doubt in the minds of their readers. According to these journalists, NATO was bad, as was the imperialist United States of America. Turkey should get out of NATO. Their goal was to join the Soviet camp and become a Soviet satellite like Bulgaria. These columnists reinvented the word *komprador* and stood against their common enemy, the Islamic reactionary movement.

The Turkish regime's handling of the crisis was ineffective. *Adalet Partisi* (AP), the Justice Party in power, headed by Prime Minister Süleyman Demirel, was unable to stop the bloodshed resulting from the civil unrest. In fact, the Justice Party government had opened the way for a retreat from Kemal Atatürk's secular reforms by starting the politicization of the Islamic issue. Demirel believed that the way to counter Communism's advance was to reduce the secular institutions of the state, the main legacy of Atatürk since the 1920s. Demirel often spelled out his views in the face of the danger from the Soviet Union: "Let my citizens go hungry, but be free." The right-of-center regime of Demirel had joined forces with the Islamic reactionary movement, which had been marginalized during Kemal Atatürk's secular reforms. Atatürk was the man who in 1923 had built a new nation from the collapsed Ottoman Empire. Now his secular reforms were being eased to secure a following among the religious segment of the population. Qur'an schools along with Islamic brotherhoods and their dervish converts were allowed to mushroom. For some people, supporting the Islamic revival turned out to be a golden opportunity; it was used as a vehicle to help advance political careers and to gain wealth.

The pro-Islamic policies of Justice Party's regime changed Turkey's destiny in 1972; a strictly secular, reformist party had to form a ruling coalition with another that directly opposed secular reforms. This was *Cumhuriyet Halk Partisi* (CHP), the Republican People's Party, which had been the main vehicle of Atatürk's pro-Western reforms less than five decades earlier. When the Republican People's Party formed a coalition with Necmettin Erbakan's pro-Islamic National Salvation Party (MSP) in 1972, it started a chain of events that would prove to be highly destructive to Atatürk's secularist legacy. Thus, Bülent Ecevit, then the leader of the left-of-center Republican People's Party, by forming a coalition with Necmettin Erbakan's Islamists, presented the latter with its best opportunity to gain political legitimacy.

These developments in the early 1970s helped to bring *Refah* (the Welfare), an Islam-oriented party, to power in 1996. It was the first time in the history of the secular republic that Necmettin Erbakan, the Islamist prime minister in power, was actually able to reverse secular reforms with the aim of establishing an Islamic state.

A serious situation in the summer of 1970 caused doubts about the legality of Süleyman Demirel's Justice Party regime. Demirel as the prime minister was pushing laws through parliament that were deemed to be unconstitutional. These laws were aimed to silence the opposition Republican People's Party (CHP), to prevent demonstrations of the university students against the regime, and to restrict freedom of the press. The Constitutional Court annulled these laws and asked for the formation of a parliamentary commission to investigate Demirel's actions. Demirel simply ignored the decision of the Constitutional Court.

Other serious issues occurring in the 1970s would play a crucial role later in undermining the country's stability. On February 10, 1970, *Hürriyet*'s colorful rival newspaper *Günaydın* (*Good Morning*) had printed a news article alleging that Süleyman Demirel and his brother businessman Şevket Demirel had exploited their influential positions to get rich. On March 12, 1970, Ismet Inönü, highly respected elder statesman, publicly accused Süleyman Demirel of using the Islamic religion for political gains. Demirel had permitted the opening of *imam-hatip* (imam-cleric) schools, which under Atatürk had been returned to the training of clerics. Now these schools were open for general education, and people with a religious background rushed to enroll their children. These schools mushroomed and provided a fertile foundation for the growth of Islamic fundamentalism.

Around the same time, eight members of a high-level parliamentary commission investigating allegations of corruption against the Demirel brothers were fired. The Justice Party as the majority in parliament blocked the parliamentary investigation on corruption against Süleyman Demirel himself. The Constitutional Court intervened on May 21, 1970. The Court ruled that blocking the investigation in parliament was unconstitutional and that the high-level commission was duty bound to continue its investigation.

Consulting with other editors of *Hürriyet* during that fateful summer, I had decided to run an editorial against Süleyman Demirel, which accused the prime minister of acts against the constitution. Remarking on the prime minister's attempts to ignore the decision of the Constitutional Court, we wrote in that editorial:

> The existing conditions leave now a single way out for the prime minister, namely to resign and await the formation of a commission to investigate his assaults on the constitution.
> The honorable Süleyman Demirel should resign not only to protect his esteem but also not to cause additional turmoil in Turkey which is already struggling in a sea of unrest.

Hürriyet boldly printed this editorial on June 19, 1970, on its front page with the headline *Başbakan İçin Tek Yol: İstifa*—The Only Way Out for the Prime Minister: Resignation. It was a timely warning that might have prevented events that were to follow: a near civil war, a Kurdish separatist revolt, the looting and plundering of the nation's resources, poverty, the revival of a highly assertive and militant Islamic reactionary movement, two coups d'etat, and one behind-the-scenes military intervention that toppled a government.

A terrific uproar followed my editorial, and I was at once put in the hot seat. Some rowdy supporters of Süleyman Demirel, encouraged by Nezih Demirkent, an employee of *Hürriyet*, burned copies of the newspaper in Eskişehir in western Turkey. Demirkent lacked journalistic abilities but was a man of great ambition. He wanted to own *Hürriyet* even though he didn't have the financial means to buy the newspaper.

The burning of the papers, as expected, shocked Erol Simavi, the publisher of *Hürriyet*, whose character bordered on timidity. He became concerned about a government action against the newspaper.

Demirel's supporters denounced me as a CIA agent, an American lackey, and a traitor. The situation reminded me of an encounter with an American journalist in the 1960s when attempts at coups d'etat were numerous; particularly a few efforts by Colonel Talat Aydemir were significant. The journalist had come to ask for some background information at a time when I was in charge of *Haber Ajansı*, an affiliate news agency of *Hürriyet*. She told me, "I bet your passport is in your desk drawer."

"No," I said. "My passport is not here, and I have no intention of running away."

I don't think she believed me, considering the fact that I was then also reporting to the international news agency Reuters. She must have known, as I did through experience, that this was a connection that could trigger visions of espionage in suspicious nationalistic minds in countries like Turkey.

In 1970, my situation was a bit more complicated. *Hürriyet*, which decreased in circulation to about three hundred thousand in order to compete aggressively, needed exceptional news coverage as well as new web-offset color printing presses. *Günaydın*, a major competitor that had spun off from *Hürriyet* a year earlier, was printing in color and gaining circulation. *Hürriyet*, too, had been expecting a government permit to import similar presses. Demirkent complained that the permit would never be issued now because we had made Demirel angry. It was common knowledge at the time that Turkish governments could be notoriously stingy with newsprint supplies to newspapers critical of their policies.

A four-year stay in America clearly had affected my general outlook on life. Yet, Turkey was not America, and there were limits to such things as freedom of the press and free speech, as well as the right to criticize the wrongdoings of the high and mighty in office. I had been in trouble with other regimes in Turkey before and was even threatened with jail by Adnan Menderes, who did not like my reports to Reuters. Menderes had been the prime minister between 1950 and 1960. He was overthrown on May 27, 1960, and later hanged by the armed forces.

This time, my troubles were much more serious than a mere jail term. I was hearing reports that extremists on both the left and the right would kill journalists of whose conduct or writings they didn't approve. There were other warnings as well. Kemal Biselman, a journalist friend, told me that since I had come out so strongly against Demirel, whose friends and supporters included disreputable people, I had better watch my step. Cüneyt Arcayürek, *Hürriyet*'s bureau chief in Ankara, a man who was extremely pro-Demirel in his writings, told me: "It was improper to call for Mr. Demirel's resignation, before you wiped the dust off your shoes so soon after arriving from America!"

I believed that my observations were accurate, and the proof would come later. During the Times of Chaos, 5,250 young Turks, mostly far-right and far-left extremists, were killed as a result of clashes on the university campuses and in the streets. The Islamic reactionary movement advanced and again the generals got involved in politics, toppling governments on occasion.

Süleyman Demirel did not resign. Instead he held on to power until March 1971, when the military moved in and forced him out of office and dissolved the parliament.

Meanwhile, during that summer of 1970, the upheaval throughout the country along with the suspense and the pressure on me escalated. One day in my office, as I listened to the roars of compradors rising from the street, my phone rang. I picked it up and heard clicking sounds. Someone was listening in again. Constant monitoring of my calls had started since the publication of the editorial.

The caller was Turhan Aytul, a journalist and trusted friend. A well-informed editor, he had worked in newspapers such as *Milliyet* (Nationality), *Cumhuriyet* (Republic), and *Yeni* (New) *Istanbul*.

"What's up, Şeytan?" I asked Aytul. I used to call him "Devil" because of his sharp mind and agility. He used to call me "Mayk," a nickname he had given me because I worked for Reuters in the past, and Mayk was the name of his favorite fiction character Mike Hammer, the detective in the Mickey Spillane novels.

"Bad news," he said, "I hear people talking about some plan to kill you. Watch out—you too may become a victim of a staged accident!"

I had been noticing signs of surveillance of my activities since the editorial. I was being tailed and my mail was always tampered with and my phone calls monitored. I was receiving threatening phone calls: *Hey, you cuckold, and son of a cuckold, we will kill you!*

The life of a journalist in Turkey in those days could only be expected to be precarious if he had enough nerve to publicly call for the prime minister's resignation. Only a decade earlier, during the regime of Adnan Menderes, journalists had become jailbirds for much lesser offenses.

It had started raining and the rain was pounding on the window, drowning out the shouts of the demonstrators.

And the rain brought back vivid memories. When it rained during my childhood years in Isparta, my hometown in the heart of Anatolia, floods poured down from the surrounding mountains into the town. Between walls, which had been built to protect the town, the waters roared through. The walls crossed the whole town and cut through our neighborhood. I remember our house facing the walls and beyond the walls a gigantic plane tree (also called buttonwood or sycamore). There was a ditty then about the rain and the flooding:

> It's raining and the floods are flowing.
> The black girl is looking from the window.

We would sing it as we played and danced in a room-size hollow inside the trunk of that tree.

☪

The boy sat on top of a concrete alcove next to the living room of the house, munching a *simit*, a large, pretzel-like ring covered with sesame seeds. He had a bird's-eye view of his mother's dental clinic and could hear all the painful sighs of the patient, an old peasant. She was extracting a tooth, and the boy saw blood. He felt sorry for the peasant, for only recently he himself had known pain. Three days earlier, the boy had fallen off a wall and a sharp stone had cut his upper lip. The wound was stitched at the hospital in Isparta. Now he walked into the living room, listening to the chimes of the grandfather clock his father had built before he died.

The living room was simply furnished. There was the clock standing next to a wall and above it a handwoven wall carpet depicting the Şahmerdan, a tigerlike animal with a human face that was supposed to keep the snakes out of the house but never did. The wooden floor was covered with handwoven carpets, and in a corner stood the divan where the boy enjoyed sitting. Because of his injury, he had not been to school for three days, and staying home bored him.

It was a critical time in the young republic's history, and the boy had heard about a Kurdish rebellion raging in eastern Anatolia. He knew that his mother constantly worried about this revolt.

The boy's mother in a white coat entered and sat beside him.

"Are you all right?" she asked, touching his face.

Looking at his mother's light brown hair and brown eyes, the boy wondered: *How can she stand other people's pain and the sight of their blood?* His own pain was still there, especially when he bit into his *simit*, but he answered, "Fine, Mom, I guess."

She held the boy's face in her hands. "The politics in our country can be dangerous," she said. I want you to promise me that you will have nothing to do with politics and political parties when you grow up."

"I promise, Mom," the boy said.

I would remember that advice many years later. *How right she had been,* I thought. I knew that I was under surveillance. It had been like that for several weeks. They had been watching me and keeping me in suspense all this time. Why? Why would they not kill me now? If I were killed in the street so soon after the publication of the editorial, my murder would point a finger at the prime minister's henchmen. Later, in the existing chaos, who would care about a journalist having been assassinated? I would be just another unsolved murder case.

There is a difference, I thought. I was a well-known, well-liked journalist. Eliminating me openly by a ganglike shooting in the street might have serious repercussions.

How about an accidental death when things cooled down a little, the editorial all but forgotten? Now, remember what Turhan Aytul said. *Watch out—you, too, may become a victim of a staged accident!* They could poison my food or arrange an accidental drowning in the Bosphorus.

Do you remember how Osman Nuri Tepe, Nazmiye Demirel's shoemaker, died?

How did he die?

Poor man, he was the victim of a traffic accident.

God bless him in the hereafter and may his soul be happy.

Nazmiye Demirel was the wife of Prime Minister Süleyman Demirel.

Why, then, did Ali Tepe, a hotel owner and brother of the dead man, make what seemed to many to be an outrageous notarized statement? His statement, printed in *Günaydın* on November 15, 1969, alleged that Osman Nuri Tepe, the shoemaker, was killed because *he was a close friend of Nazmiye Demirel, and he knew too much about the Demirels' guests*—and because he had talked. Now the hotel owner was scared of being killed, and in order to protect himself, he wrote the notarized statement, signing at the same time his last will and testament.

Come, come now, who would believe such an accusation without any proof? People die in accidents all the time.

Having made enemies however, I had to watch *my* step. And I trusted nobody.

I left the newspaper building and drove around with my clunky car. As I rode through the back streets, I frequently checked the rearview mirror for any sign of surveillance. Where would I go? West Germany?

There were supporters of the regime there, including Islamic reactionaries among the Turkish guest workers.

America! I could be safe there.

A cat jumped over a dirt puddle and disappeared in an alley between old wooden houses. The stray cats were always a problem for drivers in the narrow streets. The Turks considered killing a cat to be a sin, even if it were an accident, for this would bring misfortune.

A big car with powerful headlights passed me. I noticed the driver staring at me. Who is he and why did he look at me like that?

I slowed down and saw the taillights of the speeding car disappear before steering the car into a dimly lit side street. Passing a small mosque, I heard the call of the *müezzin* for evening prayers and sped toward the beach road, and then on a sudden decision, I turned back.

Leave the car with the keys in the ignition at the newspaper's parking lot. Then walk to the Hippodrome in the Sultanahmet Square. You will have to watch out for surveillance. Take a taxi and go home.

I had experience in avoiding surveillance. Once I had helped a young, stunningly beautiful singer to escape from Baghdad. *An escape plan has to be simple*, I thought. I would get up early in the morning as I had done in Baghdad, get out of the apartment building with my wife, and take a stroll to Yeşilyurt's train station. Once there, I would hire a horse-drawn buggy and go to the international airport, which was only a couple of miles away.

Arriving late at home, I told my wife what we had to do. "There is an early plane tomorrow for Vienna," I said. "We will board the plane at the last minute."

She was a young Austrian with blue eyes and an unusual name, Magrid.

"Good," she answered. "Vienna, then what?"

"America," I said.

So this is it, I thought.

Fearing for my life, I must now flee from the country where I had grown up as an Anatolian.

Exile was to become my destiny.

Thinking about my destiny reminded me of the words of Ahmet Muhip Dranas, the poet who once wrote:

> Our souls fly like butterflies,
> In this peaceful garden called destiny.

I was in body and soul an Anatolian, and I didn't feel at all like a butterfly floating in a peaceful garden.

2

The Anatolian

The wolf catches the sheep without a shepherd.

Turkish proverb

$\mathcal{I}$ am an Anatolian, someone born and bred in *Anadolu*, Turkey's heartland, and I speak the Anatolian dialect. Anatolia is the whole of Asian Turkey. Also called Asia Minor, it reaches from the Aegean and Marmara seas to the borders of Syria, Iraq, Iran, Armenia, and Georgia. It is a land mass comparable to the Eastern seaboard of the United States from Maine down to the Carolinas. From the Neolithic to the Ottoman times, it has seen civilizations and cultures come and go. It has been a crossroads for transmigrations of peoples going in both directions.

Prehistoric man brought agriculture and animal husbandry from the Fertile Crescent through Anatolia to Europe. Waves of Hittite and other cultures rolled back and forth in conquest and defeat. Alexander the Great's Greeks crushed the Persian Empire on his march through Anatolia. Roman armies later ruled and protected the Eastern provinces of their empire. Finally, the Seljuks and Ottomans united the fragmented land, while crusading Europeans still poured through it wielding their swords until the Ottoman Empire grew stronger through its conquests.

The Seljuks, one of the several Turkish tribes that had moved into Anatolia out of central Asia, ruled over a great part of western Asia between the eleventh and thirteenth centuries before the Ottomans, one of the other tribes, became more powerful and started uniting them all.

Every Anatolian male is a *Mehmetçik*, a man born to be a soldier. The *Mehmetçik*, a Turkish version of the American G.I., is the backbone of the Turkish armed forces.

One might also describe the Anatolian as a tough, obstinate country bumpkin; dynamic traditionalist; and hard-nosed individual. A long-distance walker with a hard body, the Anatolian is usually a preferred candidate to become a *piyade*, or foot soldier, in the army. There are songs about him: "I am in the army as a soldier of the infantry, Oh my sweetheart, I am burned, I am done for."

S. F. Abasıyanık, a well-known writer, identified an Anatolian with these words: "From his speech, it was obvious that he was an Anatolian."

According to my birth certificate, I was born in 1925 in Antalya, on the Mediterranean coast. Then, Antalya was a struggling provincial town, where people used mosquito nets around their beds at night and checked their yards and basements regularly for poisonous snakes, and trips to the market were often made on the backs of donkeys. Now, Antalya is a vital center of tourism, with beautiful beaches and orange groves thronging with German, Russian, and British visitors.

I was given the name Muammer Ali, which means a long, exalted, and happy life.

When I was about a year and a half old, my father, Ali Rıza, manager of the state bank *Zıraat Bankası* (the Bank of Agriculture in Antalya), died of typhoid fever. Born in 1877, he had been a dentist, a clock maker, and finally a banker. During the Turkish War of Independence (1919–23) against the occupying forces of the Allies and the invading Greek armies, my father had supported and given financial aid to the provisional government of Mustafa Kemal (later known as Kemal Atatürk).

Ali Rıza had been my mother's second husband. Her first husband, the father of my oldest brother, Hilmi, had died in the early 1920s after falling out of a mulberry tree. When Ali Rıza and my mother were married, my father, who was considerably older than my mother, told her: "You have a choice to learn one of the skills I can teach you—dentistry or clock repair. You must learn one of them so that you can support yourself should anything happen to me."

Mother chose dentistry. After my father died, mother took her three sons and moved back to Isparta, her and father's ancestral town in the lake district north of Antalya. Isparta is renowned for its handwoven rugs, rose gardens, apple and apricot orchards, and vineyards.

My maternal grandfather, Nuri Ergun, was an illiterate man of substance who owned vineyards, gardens of roses, carpet looms, a mill, and a grain store in the marketplace. A medium-sized man of few words, with white hair and a white, round beard, wearing black baggy trousers and a colorful sash, grandfather had made the pilgrimage to Mecca. Thus he had earned the honorific label of *hacı*, or pilgrim, and was universally addressed as Hacı Nuri.

In spite of owning a fine Tatar horse cart (the long, four-wheeled rural wagon of the steppes of southern Russia and Anatolia), and employing a driver named Veli, grandfather preferred to visit his properties riding a donkey. There were days when I would follow him to the marketplace on the dusty road, he riding the donkey and I walking behind, carrying a stick cut from a cornelian cherry tree. We would reach the marketplace amid voluminous braying. The market was always crowded with the townspeople and peasants from surrounding villages who would extol their goods and produce in front of their stalls or their stores in a veritable human cacophony. There was the constant aroma of shish kebab or oven-roasted lamb or goat in the air mixed with the pungent smell of spices.

Because my mother, Hacer (whose name meant meteorite), wanted to live closer to her parents, she had a house built across from her father's. A widow at age thirty-two, she lacked the formal education to practice dentistry. When I was about two years old, Mother wrote a letter to the government in Ankara that explained her predicament. A telegram instructed her to apply to the Faculty of Dentistry at the University of Istanbul, where a course was due to start.

It was a peaceful period in Turkey, following a time of wars and turmoil that had destroyed the Ottoman Empire. The First and Second Balkan Wars in 1912 and 1913, World War I and the battles of Gallipoli (1915), followed by the Turkish War of Independence (1914–23), had destroyed the youth of the nation. Too many professionals had been killed in the wars, and the young republic was hard at work reforming, rebuilding, and modernizing.

Thus it was that mother, having left us three boys in the care of our maternal grandparents, departed for the University of Istanbul.

My grandparents' house was already crowded. Now the three of us joined grandfather's three sons, along with their wives and offspring. A stable housed the horses and the donkey. Grandmother Feride stored the grains, vegetables, and fruits, which she raised in her garden, in a root cellar. Because of that root cellar, we always had fruit during the winter.

When grandfather decided to modernize his water-powered mill on the outskirts of town, he ordered a turbine from Italy, and soon it arrived with an Italian engineer in attendance. The Italian owned a brand new car and was showing it off—automobiles were rare in Isparta at the time. My uncle Enver persuaded the Italian to let Veli, our horse-cart driver, drive the automobile.

"Veli is experienced," he told the Italian.

Veli took the wheel and drove the automobile straight into the wall, causing considerable damage to the front end. Grandfather was angry when he received the bill for this escapade.

I remember in the spring watching Grandfather supervise the process of boiling rose petals in large containers in order to extract rose oil and rose water. When the roses blossomed, Grandfather's precision work, as he called it, would start. All he needed were patience, a steady hand, and keen eyes. Using an eyedroper, he would pick up drops of rose oil swimming on the surface of the fresh rose water in the container. He would collect the oil drops in glass tubes and prepare them for export.

During winter evenings by the warmth of a charcoal-burning brazier,

Grandfather would sit on a divan covered with colorful rugs. He usually had a sheepskin coat over his shoulders. My grandfather had never attended school and could not even sign his own name. He always carried a bronze seal with his name engraved on it and kept the seal in a velvet purse tucked into his multicolored sash.

During the summers, I used to ride horses bareback performing errands for my grandfather. My reward was usually homemade ice cream, made with ice brought down from the summit of Mount Davras, the tallest peak of a mountain range that surrounds Isparta on three sides.

Because I had no father, Grandfather treated me kindly and tried to take my father's place. Therefore, when I misbehaved, he would not hesitate to teach me a lesson. My punishment would be several painful strikes on my rear with the hard wood of a cornelian cherry stick.

One day, Grandfather decided that it was time for all the boys in the household to be circumcised. A circumciser was engaged; rice pilaf was cooked in large cauldrons; lambs and goats were roasted whole; *baklava* and Turkish pastries called *börek* were prepared on round brass trays. Our neighbors were invited for the circumcision feast. We were dressed in loosely fitting gowns and white circumcision hats lettered in gold with the word *Maşallah*, God Bless. It was also common for parents to give their children *Maşallah* charms to wear to avert the evil eye.

I sneaked away and hid in a large cupboard in a guest room. My hiding place was discovered and I was carried away, giving full vent to my distress. I was held down by several pairs of hands in front of the circumciser, my legs were pulled apart while one of my uncles stuffed my mouth with a piece of *lokum*, or Turkish delight. I normally loved the tasty treat because it was rich in roasted pistachio nuts, but it didn't ease the pain of the cut.

I was not very keen on fasting between dawn and sunset during the month of Ramadan, the ninth month of the Muslim year. I remember the deep sounds of the *davul*, a large drum that was used to wake people up just before dawn each morning for the meal before the fast. The fasting would last for a whole month. Like everyone else, I would get up to the sound of the neighborhood drum, eat my meal, and drink fruit juices.

Each evening those who fasted would wait for the sound of the artillery shot to end their fast. That was the sign for the beginning of a feast that included *pide*, a delicious flat bread baked with tasty toppings.

Despite the alluring evening feast, my fast would never last longer than until lunchtime. Yet I was not the only violator of the fast in my grandfather's household. My uncles Ali and Enver would also violate the fast and, like us children, would not hesitate to enjoy the evening feast. My grandfather knew all about our mischievous behavior but never complained, although he was very concerned about the lifestyles of my two uncles.

Ethem, the eldest of my three uncles, was a quiet rather religious man who prayed every day. He was a rug designer. My other uncles, Ali and Enver, were not religious. Ali was known as *Çolak Ali* because he had lost one of his arms in the battles of Gallipoli. He loved horses and riding. A womanizer, he always carried a loaded gun and disappeared every night to some ill-famed house to get drunk on *rakı* or the powerful alcoholic drink arrack, while being entertained by belly dancers.

At last Mother returned in 1930. She had become the first female dentist in Turkey. My presents from the big city were a mechanical bird and a box camera with film.

We moved to our new house beside Grandfather's, where Mother began her practice of dentistry. Through the years, I would see many patients from the town and peasants from nearby villages. The peasants, wearing baggy pants that were oftentimes patched, were dirt poor. They could hardly afford a simple tooth extraction, let alone regular dental care or major dental work. For my mother's dental services, they would bring a chicken, a caged partridge, or a rabbit. Mother used to tell her patients, whom she had just newly fitted with a set of false teeth: "You can bite apples and eat roasted chickpeas now." The Turks love *leblebi*, double-roasted chickpeas.

I attended the Independence Elementary School in an old, wooden building. The classrooms were crowded, and the books were printed in the Latin alphabet for the first time in the thousand-year history of the Turkish people. My daily walk to the school was a four-mile round trip on a dirt road, alongside walls built the length of a dry stream to prevent flooding in the rainy season.

It was a time of reforms. A secular republic had been declared on October 29, 1923, and the reforms were being imposed on my generation. The reformer was Mustafa Kemal Atatürk, the war hero who had been elected as the republic's first president. Intent on pulling his nation into the twentieth century, he abolished Arabic writing and introduced the Latin alphabet in 1928. He put a check on the power of religion to interfere in government and secular matters. He suppressed the *tarikats*, or Islamic brotherhoods, and renounced the Sultanate. Turkey would no longer be ruled by despotic sultans not elected by popular vote. The Caliphate, the temporal and the spiritual leadership of Islam in Turkey, was abolished on March 3, 1924. Old teaching methods and religious schools such as *medreses* were dropped in favor of European ways of teaching. Teachers were retrained, and attendance at secular schools became compulsory. Religion classes were abolished in schools.

In less than a decade, Turkey's legal, social, economic, and political systems were modernized; the Gregorian calendar was introduced; and a new sense of national identity was created. President Atatürk's policy of rejuvenating the nation with a new understanding of the Turkish identity was intended to erase the ancient *Osmanlı* (Ottoman), Persian, and Arabic influences. He aimed to eradicate the bigotry of religious intolerance. It was a ruthless reform movement based on fervent nationalism and the heroic militant characteristics of the Turks. Atatürk wanted to energize a backward nation.

Reforming a nation that neglected modernization and enlightenment for centuries, however, was not an easy task. There was powerful opposition from the fundamentalists and established conservative traditionalists. The radicals resisted the reforms and caused bloodshed by killing secular officials. There were clashes between secularist officials and fundamentalists who demonstrated against the regime, shouting, "We don't want infidel reform!" In order to accomplish what he set out to do, Atatürk used force when necessary or tried to be an example to his people. He stood in front of a blackboard like a schoolteacher and showed how to write the

Latin alphabet. He wore a European hat and told the people that they too should wear it instead of the fez.

My generation and the generations that followed no longer learned how to write and read Turkish in the Arabic alphabet. The writing and reading of Arabic script, which had been the written characters of Ottoman Turkey for centuries, now became a specialty. For people who wished to do research in old Ottoman library books or study historical documents of the empire, it was like learning a foreign language. The Qur'an, Islam's holy book, was later translated into Turkish and printed in the Latin alphabet. Turkish replaced Arabic in the call of the *müezzin*, who announces the hour of the five daily prayers from the gallery of minarets throughout the country.

The Turkish word for God, *Tanrı*, was substituted for the Arabic word *Allah*. This, along with the call to prayer in Turkish, caused resentment among devout Muslims. Even among the secular elite, *Tanrı* could not gain ground against the word *Allah* throughout the reform years and for decades thereafter. Finally, in 1933 public resentment of the changes in devotional practices brought back the Arabic language to the *müezzin*'s call to prayer.

The fez (actually named for the city of Fes, in Morocco), a brimless, cone-shaped, flat-crowned hat made of red felt, was outlawed in 1925. The fez had become a symbol of Ottoman incompetence and had been used in the West to ridicule the Turks. It was replaced by the *şapka*, or European hat.

The new laws brought about women's emancipation and their right to vote in 1934. Women were discouraged from wearing a *peçe* or veil. Religious marriage ceremonies performed by an imam and religious divorce were outlawed. By law a man could no longer marry four women. Monogamy became the rule, and divorce was possible only through legal proceedings in a secular court.

Western dress replaced the veil and the *çarşaf* or *chador*, the black garment that covered women from head to toe. Mother hated this garment and never wore it. "A woman should be proud to show her face to the world," she used to say.

The educated class in the big cities quickly adopted the new ways, but the countryside was slower in accepting the overthrow of age-old customs. In the first year, following the decree of Western dress codes, my mother often experienced some unease when walking in the streets. She even refused to cover her head with the traditional headscarf of Muslim women (a practice that was resurrected as a hot political issue in the 1990s). Because Mother preferred to wear Western dress, children chased her in the streets shouting, "*Tango fiyanga*," meaning a loose woman with a bow tie. These children only did, of course, what their Islamic reactionary families encouraged them to do.

It became an obligation to adopt a surname when the titles of nobility were dropped. This caused confusion, and my own family ended up with three different surnames. Prior to this reform, people had no surnames in Turkey, except for the nobility, who sometimes sported the name of a locality attached to the word *zade*, short for the Farsi word *zadegan*.

Kemal Atatürk's political organization was the *Cumhuriyet Halk Partisi* (CHP), or Republican People's Party. This party organized the *Halkevi*, a People's House, in every town. Most of these People's Houses had a library and a theater, where performances were regularly staged, and could also be used for sporting events. The People's House was a revival of the *Türk Ocağı* (Turkish Hearth) clubs that were organized in 1912 to raise the educational standards of the Turkish people. Halide Edib Adıvar (1883–1964), a novelist and educator, was a leading organizer of the *Türk Ocağı* clubs and a pioneer in the emancipation of Turkish women. Adıvar wrote that Atatürk deserved to be placed on a pedestal in the heart of every Turk, "even among those who have been irretrievably wronged by him." The present revival of the specter of the Islamic reactionary movement shows that her views are not universally shared.

The library of the local People's House in Isparta was my favorite place because it provided me with knowledge about early Ottoman history. I read many books there, including one called *The Turkish Pirates*. It was a history of the Turkish maritime wars during the glorious times of the Ottoman Empire, but mostly about Barbaros Hayreddin Pasha, the Barbary corsair who was appointed admiral-in-chief of the Ottoman

Empire in 1533 during the reign of Süleyman the Magnificent. The admiral is better known in the West by the name of Barbarossa, or Redbeard, although the color of his beard was not red. His older brother Oruç Reis actually had the red beard.

Barbarossa was born in 1466 on the island of Lesbos and, like his three brothers, took to the sea at an early age. His brother Oruç Reis was to distinguish himself in North Africa. Oruç was killed there while fighting against the Spanish. Barbarossa died in 1546, but the powerful Turkish navy that he had helped establish remained intact until the Battle of Lepanto on October 7, 1571, which came as a crushing defeat to Ottoman might.

In that library in Isparta I first learned the meaning of the Turkish word *sıngın*, a terrible defeat or a rout. The Turks considered the outcome of the Battle of Lepanto a rout. Lepanto clearly showed the vulnerability of Ottoman power and delivered a great blow to the idea of Turkish invincibility.

When the Turks invaded the island of Cyprus in 1570, the Venetians formed an alliance with Pope Pius V and Philip II of Spain. Philip ordered his half-brother Don Juan of Austria to command the alliance's fleet. A total of 487 ships, of which 245 were Turkish, took part in this historic naval battle. After about four hours of fighting in the Gulf of Patras near Lepanto, Greece, the alliance sank two hundred Ottoman galleys and took thousands of prisoners. That battle had a great moral impact on both the Europeans and the Ottomans and became a subject for painters like Tintoretto, Titian, and Veronese.

Sokollu Mehmet Pasha, the distinguished Ottoman grand vizier, rebuilt the Ottoman navy once again. It is interesting to note that Sokollu, a Serb by birth, appointed a Calabrian (Italian) renegade, Kılıç Ali Pasha, as grand admiral. The second in command was Piyale Pasha, a Hungarian, and the rearguard squadron commander and paymaster of the fleet was Hasan Ağa, a Venetian.

Still, Barbarossa's death is considered to be the beginning of the end of Ottoman naval power. His tomb is located in the Beşiktaş district of Istanbul.

The book about the Turkish maritime wars was generally based on information provided by the historian Katip Çelebi, who died in Istanbul in 1657. Katip Çelebi had been an army clerk (*katip*) and had taken part in many campaigns. He wrote several books, among them *The History of the Maritime Wars of the Turks* and *Cihannuma* (*A View of the World*), a geographical study. For the first time in Ottoman history, this book made use of European atlases. Katip Çelebi warned the Ottoman regime of the importance of the "science of geography" and said, "By making use of geography the infidels have discovered America and become masters of India." The Ottoman dignitaries ignored his timely warning.

The secular reforms of the 1920s and 1930s and that little library in Isparta shaped my own life at an early age. Yet, when I was attending middle school, there was another guide who helped me to understand my heritage as a Young Turk.

The Colonel

One can always find a way to cross even the tallest mountain.

Turkish proverb

knew him as the Colonel. My mother had rented the top floor of our house to this army fellow. He looked huge on horseback and quite smart in his uniform and cap, although he was short and bald.

According to his wife, the Colonel suffered from hallucinations and nightmares, stemming from his wartime experiences. He had been in several World War I battles, including those at Gallipoli against the Allies. During the War of Independence, he had fought against the invading Greek armies at Inönü, a crucial battleground.

Television, of course, had not yet been invented, and we did not have a radio at the time. The Colonel had a hand-cranked Victor Gramophone, *Sahibinin Sesi*, His Master's Voice, with the familiar picture of a Jack Russell terrier listening to the voice of its owner. This Victor Gramophone was state-of-the-art at the time and the envy of the town. I think nobody else in town had anything like this record player.

53

The Colonel used to play three records over and over again without getting tired of them. As a result, they are forever in my memory. The one I liked best was Valencia, while the other two were Turkish songs that served as reminders of the horrible war years. One of them was a *gazel*, a chant of a lyric poem performed by a singer:

> Every place is in darkness
> Only where he stands
> There is brightness.
> What will be will be for my lover,
> Will it be Maghreb or the grave?

Maghreb (generally meant to refer to Morocco but also used for Yemen), north Africa, and various Arab countries south of Anatolia, were among the sites in World War I where a great number of Turkish soldiers died.

The third song from the War of Independence was about the poplar trees of Izmir and an irregular militia commander named Çakıcı Efe. Its subject was his notorious band's torching of mansions.

When the Colonel was in a good mood and we neighborhood children were bored of zapping black flies with rubber bands on the dirt street, he would tell us stories about Turkish history and his wartime experiences. He would talk about the suffering of the troops in the trenches with hardly any medicine and little food consisting of mostly beans and bulgur. The Colonel considered the 1920 Treaty of Sevres that divided Turkey among several foreign powers a terrible humiliation for the Turks and complained about the atrocities committed by the invading forces.

"Our women," the Colonel would say, "carried heavy artillery shells on their backs or on two-wheeled ox-carts to the front during the War of Independence. There were wicked criminals who hoarded food for black-market profits. There was anarchy. Many armed bands of outlaws popped up all over the country; some were patriots, others robbers and murderers."

Famine spread during the war. The economy and agriculture were ruined because of the repeated drafting of men and pack animals.

The Colonel's voice grew bitter when he spoke of the Greeks, British, French, and Italians—the foreign forces that occupied Turkey after World War I. They all killed or tortured people. "The local Greeks were expecting that Greece would invade Anatolia," he used to say. "They told their Turkish neighbors 'Our uncles from Athens will come soon and make you wear red shirts.' Indeed, Greek soldiers caused many civilian Turks' shirts to turn red with blood. Later, Greek irregulars known as *Mavri Mira* or Black Fate, murdered villagers, including children, and ransacked and burned many Anatolian towns and villages."

The Colonel could not forgive the Arabs, co-religionists with the Turks, for their betrayal of the Ottoman Empire during World War I by collaborating with the British forces. He said, "The Arabs stabbed us in our backs!"

The Colonel was a good storyteller. The best of his fables and legends were about central Asia. I used to listen to them with awe. Among them was the story of *bozkurt*, a mythical gray she-wolf.

According to the legend of *Ergenekon*, the Turks in central Asia descended from the mating of a Turk with a she-wolf named *Asena*. They were called the *göktürk*—Sky Turks or Blue Turks, and they spoke *Orhon* Turkish. There are even Chinese fables about this early nation in central Asia. The wolf guided the Turks in their early history out of a drought-stricken valley surrounded by high mountains. This valley is known as the legendary land of Turan. The wolf then became the symbol of the Turks and later the fable gave rise to *Kızıl Elma,* or Red Apple, a pan-Turanist or pan-Turkic ultranationalist movement that started just before World War I.

Dating back to the heroic age of the *Oğuz* (or Oghuz) Turks, who inhabited a great part of Asia, *The Tales of Dede* (Grandfather) *Korkut*, a great epic written in the fifth and sixth centuries CE, tells the stories of Turkish mythology. My favorite was "Bamsi Beyrek and His Gray Horse" from the *Legend of Alpamish*.

I was to learn from the Colonel about the treachery that caused the Turks to enter the Great War that was to end all wars, on the wrong side, resulting in the collapse of the Ottoman Empire. In the center of that treachery was the battle cruiser *Yavuz* (*The Inflexible*), dearly loved by the Turkish people.

The walls of coffeehouses in Isparta, our hometown during the 1930s, were plastered with color posters of this warship, and there was even a song about her:

> Here comes *Yavuz* cutting through the sea.
> Hey, girl, I'll marry you by hook or by crook.
> You will see.

Some years later when I visited the battle cruiser in Istanbul as a high school student, I was impressed with her size. She had five turrets, each with a pair of long guns capable of firing eleven-inch shells.

Originally, *Yavuz* was the notorious German warship *Goeben* that altered the course of history. She was built by Bloom & Voss at Hamburg and launched in March 1911 as a Moltke class battle cruiser. In 1914, when the war started, the *Goeben*, escorted by the light cruiser *Breslau*, was under the command of Wilhelm Souchon, a ruthless German Rear-Admiral. The Germans eluded the British warships in the Mediterranean and entered the Dardanelles.

In July 1914, the Turks were very angry with the British, who refused to deliver two warships built in England, which had already been paid for with Turkish public donations. They were Dreadnaught class and named *Reşadiye* and *Sultan Osman I*. The battleships were state-of-the-art at the time, and the Allies feared that their presence in the Ottoman navy would alter the balance of power. This dispute over the delivery of these ships, a dispute created by Winston Churchill, First Lord of the Admiralty, would play a crucial role in the course of World War I and, disastrously for the Turks, would cause them to change their wartime strategy.

The Colonel said, "With the connivance of some Ottoman officials, Souchon was able to involve a sick Ottoman Empire in the war."

The Colonel blamed Enver Pasha, a brigadier general and a member of the triumvirate of the Committee of Union and Progress (CUP), or the Young Turks, that ruled the country between 1913 and 1918. "Enver was the minister of war," the Colonel said. "He signed a secret agreement with the Germans. Souchon made a fool of Enver by bombarding the Russian coast. For two German warships and economic aid of two million Turkish pounds in gold, we entered a war and lost an empire."

The Turkish involvement in the war began when the *Goeben* and the *Breslau*, freshly painted and sporting their Turkish names *Yavuz* and *Midilli* (*Mitilini*), sailed into the Black Sea. Rear-Admiral Wilhelm Souchon, newly appointed commander-in-chief of the Ottoman fleet, was aboard the *Goeben*. Both warships had German crews wearing fezzes and the ships were flying the colors of the Ottoman Empire.

At dawn on October 29, 1914, the *Goeben* launched a surprise attack on Sevastopol in the Crimea, the base of the Russian Black Sea fleet, and simultaneously so did the *Breslau* at the Russian Black Sea port of Novorossiysk. The cruiser *Hamidiye* first warned the people of Feodosia in the Crimea and then bombarded the town. That fateful morning, which changed the world, the Turkish destroyers *Muavenet* and *Gayret* bombarded Odessa.

It was the first attack on Sevastopol from the sea since the Crimean War (1854–56). This attack surprised even Enver Pasha, who had instructed Souchon to attack only Russian vessels in the Black Sea if they entered Turkey's territorial waters. Yet Souchon had his own plans, namely, to force the Ottoman government to enter the war on the side of Germany. Thus he disobeyed Enver's order.

Enver Pasha and other leading members of the CUP had earlier been fearful of British and Russian plans to dismember the Ottoman Empire after the war. Enver speculated that in the case of the Allies' defeat by Germany, the Ottoman Empire could expand into central Asian territories now occupied by Russia. In this way, he hoped, his dream of a pan-Turanist empire could be realized.

On November 2, 1914, Russia declared war against the Ottomans, whose sultan and caliph, Mehmet V, proclaimed a jihad. The war spread and a great number of Turkish soldiers died in places like the Caucasus, Gallipoli, and the Arabian deserts.

The Colonel used to tell me that it had been a terrible mistake to defend places like Yemen, which had no strategic importance. He would sing a song that is still very much alive in Anatolia:

> This place is called Yemen,
> And its rose looks like grass.
> But I wonder why whoever goes there
> Never returns.

After the war, the *Goeben*, still called *Yavuz*, was left idle, its hull rotting until 1927, when a French company began extensive repairs. She sailed again in 1930 as the flagship of the Turkish fleet. When Atatürk died in 1938, the battle cruiser carried his mortal remains. I would visit the cruiser again in later years when it was a floating museum before she was sold for scrap in the early 1970s.

The Colonel had despised Enver Pasha and had belittled his World War I military strategies. Still, he had sort of a grudging respect for this flamboyant Ottoman officer's later life and for the way he died. He said, "The only thing that was good about Enver is that he died on a battlefield, fighting against the Russians in central Asia. It was a fitting death for a Turk." In the early 1920s, Enver Pasha had indeed led the *Basmacı* rebellion in central Asia against the Russian Bolsheviks.

Under the spell of the Colonel's stories, I became quite fascinated with the history of central Asia, the cradle of the Turkish people. I used to study the maps and see towns, mountains, and rivers with Turkish names from the borders of Afghanistan to parts of Siberia and throughout Kazakstan, Turkmenistan, Kyrgyzstan, Uzbekistan, and Xinjiang in western China, where fifteen million Uygurs (or Uigurs) live. The Altai Mountains, located in West Siberia and Mongolia, were one place that intrigued my young mind.

This fascination with the Turkic peoples would haunt me in later years. As a newspaper editor, I would attempt to send reporters to central Asia and the Caucasus but would meet stiff resistance from the Soviet officials when requesting visas and when trying to interview Kazan and Crimean Tatars. The Soviets did not wish us to get close to the Turkic people then living under Soviet rule. Ahmet Uran Baran, our staff correspondent in Moscow, was under constant surveillance, and the press packages he sent us were always opened and inspected by the Soviet KGB.

The Altai (or *Altay*) is a twelve-hundred-mile long mountain system, which extends from the Gobi Desert to the West Siberian plain in Chinese, Russian, Mongolian, and Kazak lands. The Altai is a watershed from which the waters of great rivers like the Ob flow northward to the Arctic. The highest ridges of the mountain system tower more than thirteen thousand feet. The name *Altai* is derived from the Turkic-Mongolian word *Altan* or *altın*, which means golden. Altai means also red foal. (The word *Altaic* stems from this mountain system as in Altaic languages, principally the Turkic languages and two other subgroups: Mongol and Manchu-Tungus).

The language spoken by the Oghuz Turks of Siberia and central Asia was pure Turkish. The Orhon inscriptions—the oldest extant Turkish writings and literary legacy discovered in 1889 in the valley of the Orhon River in northern Mongolia—are believed to be referring to the Oghuz Turks. Two large monuments erected in 732 CE and 735 CE are carved in a script used also for inscriptions found in other parts of Asia, including Siberia and western Turkestan. The polished style of the inscriptions, deciphered in 1893 by the Danish philologist Vilhelm Thomsen, suggests much earlier development of the language. Thomsen called them "Turkish runes."

These monuments, relating to the legendary origins of the Turks, were erected in honor of an emperor named Bilge Hakan (The Wise Emperor) and his brother Prince Kul Tekin. A part of the inscriptions says in epic and forceful language that if the sky and the earth did not collapse, who would be able to destroy the Turkish nation? Bilge, also known as Pijia, ruled Mongolia from 716 until his death in 734. He decimated a Chinese army and forced the Chinese to seek peace in 721.

In the summer of 2001, Turkish and Mongolian archaeologists discovered thousands of silver and gold artifacts near this memorial located 270 miles west of the Mongolian capital Ulan Bator. Among them was a gold crown decorated with a bird, gold plates and bowls, and two silver figurines of deer. The treasure is believed to have belonged to Bilge Hakan.

A result of the tenth-century westward migration of the Turkish peoples from central Asia and Siberia was the *Selçuk* (Seljuk) Empire. This ruling family of the tribes of Oghuz Turkmen created an empire stretching from the Amu Darya, a sixteen-hundred-mile-long river that serves as part of Afghanistan's northern border, to the Mediterranean Sea. The advance of the Seljuk dynasty marks the beginning of Turkish power in the Middle East. Still, the Anatolian Turk considers central Asia the cradle of his people, his ancestral homeland—the land of the Gray Wolf.

The Colonel had great respect for another general of the Ottoman Empire. His name was Osman Nuri Pasha, the hero of the siege of *Plevne* (Pleven) in Bulgaria in the 1877–78 war between Russia and Turkey, which was sparked by Bulgaria's rebellion against Turkish rule. Surrounded by superior Russian forces, Field Marshal Osman Pasha would not surrender. He fought four battles between July 20 and December 10, 1877, with a force of twenty-three thousand soldiers and fifty-three cannons. He repelled the Russian force of fifty thousand soldiers and 184 cannons in three battles but suffered severe losses. Later the Russians captured him while he was being treated for his wounds near the River Vit, situated in northern Bulgaria. The fighting cost the Russians thirty-five thousand lives and their allied Romanians an additional five thousand troops.

Finally, Turkish resistance crumbled under continuous enemy advances, and in February 1878, the Russian armies stood at the gates of Istanbul. Only the threat of British intervention by its Mediterranean fleet anchored in the Dardanelles stopped the Russians from attacking the city. In July 1878, the Congress of Berlin along with British pressure, forced the Russians to withdraw. For saving the Ottomans from the Russian menace, the British rewarded themselves by occupying the island of Cyprus off the Turkish coast.

The Colonel had a doleful voice, and when he was in a good mood, he would sing a song about the bravery of Osman Pasha:

> I struck the stone with my sword,
> The stone cracked from end to end.
> Glorious Osman Pasha keeps his word,
> I will not leave Plevne till the end.

The Colonel hated the word *hanedan*, or the Ottoman dynasty, the House of Osman. The origin of this dynasty dates back to a Turkish tribe leader in central Asia named Oğuz, who, according to some legends, was the grandson of Noah (of the famous biblical ark). The dynasty actually began with the rule of Osman I (1258–1324), the leader of a Turkmen principality in northwestern Anatolia. Osman was a descendant of the *Kayı* branch of the Oghuz tribe and is considered the founder of the Ottoman dynasty and the Ottoman Turkish state.

Osman I extended his control over Byzantine fortresses in northwestern Anatolia and captured the great city of Bursa before his death. This was the beginning of the great Ottoman Empire, which flourished until 1683, when the failed second siege of Vienna signaled its decline. The Colonel's hatred of this dynasty was based on the historic failures of incompetent and often mad sultans who squandered glory achieved by Süleyman the Magnificent.

Then there was the case of Vahdettin, also known as Mehmet VI, the last Sultan, whose rule, according to the Colonel, was a total disgrace. "Vahdettin, Abdulhamid the Damned's brother," he said, "opposed the Nationalists and on August 10, 1920, ordered the signing of the shameful Treaty of Sevres. This treaty, never ratified, aimed to dismember the Ottoman Empire. The Nationalists, despite this betrayal, were able to free the Turkish heartland from the invading forces. I am hopeful that members of this dynasty will never show their faces in this country again."

The attitude of others against the House of Osman was often worse.

When the subject of expelling members of the royal family was debated in the Grand National Assembly on March 3, 1924, some members had expressed the view that the women should stay. It was a feeling of compassion. Ihsan Eryavuz, a former member of the Committee of Union and Progress (CUP) stood up and shouted: "The bones of their dead in graves even ought to be thrown out." Years later, when, as a young reporter, I met an Ottoman princess (one of Vahdettin's granddaughters) in Istanbul's Park Hotel, I remembered the Colonel's words.

Often the Colonel would talk about the Turkish casualties of World War I: "We buried over eight hundred fifty thousand young Turkish officers and soldiers during World War I," he used to say, his voice still overwhelmed with grief. "Over three hundred seventy thousand were wounded. Almost ninety thousand were killed at Gallipoli alone.

"Now you must remember this—at Gallipoli a watch in Mustafa Kemal's breast pocket stopped a piece of shrapnel that could have killed him. The Gray Wolf survived and won our freedom."

The Gray Wolf

The wolf's guest keeps his dog by his side.

Turkish proverb

*T*he man who was my teacher and inspiration when I was a child died in 1938. As a child in Isparta in the 1920s and 1930s, I would see his pictures everywhere. In one black-and-white picture I well remember, he appeared dressed in Western civilian attire, standing by a blackboard and teaching the intricacies of this new and foreign phenomenon, the Latin alphabet. He was fair both of complexion and hair and had steely blue eyes and bushy eyebrows. In that particular photograph, there was nothing of the dictator about him; he represented only a teacher to us Young Turks.

I was an eager participant in his reforms. When he died, only fifteen years after he had proclaimed a secular republic and created a new nation from the ashes of the Ottoman Empire, I was a thirteen-year-old middle school kid in Istanbul. It was the morning of November 10, 1938, a school day.

People don't usually cry when a dictator dies. But we did—a nation cried.

Western writers called him the Gray Wolf, the symbol of the Turks. I knew him as a ruthless but enlightened dictator determined to change his countrymen. He had to be ruthless in order to modernize a backward nation at a time when its illiterate people considered any reform the work of the infidel.

I knew him first by his given name, Mustafa Kemal. As his reforms progressed, he took on a new identity like everyone else and called himself Atatürk, Father of the Turks.

On summer family outings to the sandy beach of Florya in Istanbul, we would often see him on the terrace of the presidential villa at the end of a pier that jutted into the Sea of Marmara. He would stand there after a swim, looking at a scene unthinkable in Turkey not too many years before: women in bathing suits, playing on the beach or swimming in mixed company. By force when needed, by gentle persuasion when appropriate, he had accomplished an enormous change in Turkey. He had freed some, if not all, of the people from the restrictions of Islam and had given them a secular life.

I remember that his reforms in the 1920s and 1930s were not accomplished without bloodshed. Three Kurdish revolts during his rule—in 1925, 1930, and 1937—were basically rooted in Islamic fundamentalism rather than in Kurdish nationalism. Sheik Said for instance, who led a Kurdish revolt against the state in 1925, hated the secular reforms and considered them the work of a government of infidels. Sheik Said declared himself *Emirülmücahidin*, the Leader of the Warriors of the Islamic Faith. He belonged to the strictly orthodox Nakshibendi (Nakshibendiya) Brotherhood.

Sheik Said wanted to restore the Shariah, the canon law of Islam. The Independence Tribunal in Diyarbakır, eastern Anatolia, sentenced him and his fifty-six disciples to death. The uprising claimed thirty thousand lives. The revolt, like other Kurdish uprisings, were suppressed for two important reasons—to stop Islamic radicalism and to protect Turkey's unity and territorial integrity. The Independence Tribunals were political courts established to try and, if found guilty, to punish opponents to the regime

as well as army deserters and traitors. Called *Istiklal Mahkemeleri*, the courts were finally dissolved in March 1927. Some of the judges of the three-member tribunals were known as "hanging judges."

One of the best-remembered events of those years of reform is the *Menemen Incident*, when a young, secular second lieutenant named Mustafa Fehmi Kubilay was brutally murdered by Islamic reactionaries. It happened in 1930 as a second and eventually unsuccessful experiment to create an opposition party. The opposition group was named the Free Republican Party, and it had the blessing of Kemal Atatürk. This was a move to develop democratic institutions in the country at a time when women were given the right to vote and to hold elected office. Politicians of both parties as well as government officials had no experience in democracy, and some of them combined religion with politics. The trial ended in disaster when mobs stoned the offices of the ruling People's Party in Izmir, western Turkey. The rioters tore up the pictures of Ismet Inönü, who was then prime minister.

On December 23, 1930, Islamic fanatics rioted in Menemen near Izmir, and a dervish named Mehmet, a member of the banned Nakshibendi religious order, unfurled the green flag of Islam. The turban-wearing dervish claimed that he was the *Mahdi*, or Muslim messiah, who had arrived to deliver the faithful and to overthrow the godless government. Dervish Mehmet announced to a crowd in a mosque that anyone who wore the *şapka*, or European hat, was a *kafir*, an unbeliever, an infidel, and that the Shariah would soon be reinstated. He said that he had a "Caliphate Army" of seventy thousand soldiers behind him and that anyone who stood against the Shariah would be killed. "I am immune to bullets," he declared, and some people applauded and others joined him.

A company of soldiers led by the twenty-four-year-old second lieutenant Kubilay arrived. Kubilay, a teacher in civilian life, left his troops behind and approached the reactionaries alone. He asked them to surrender their arms. He was shot and wounded. Two other security personnel were killed. Dervish Mehmet cut off the wounded officer's head in the mosque's courtyard and stuck it on a pole. The reactionaries drank Kubilay's blood and shouted: "We are the army of the Shariah."

Reinforcements from the town arrived at the scene, killing Dervish Mehmet, five of his supporters, and dispersing the mob. On February 3, 1931, twenty-eight leading members of the Islamic mob were hanged.

I remember that Kubilay became a national hero. Kubilay's bravery became a subject of study in schools, and a memorial for him and two others was built in Menemen. A tablet on the monument reflects their bravery: "They were believers, they fought, they died. We are the guardians of their legacy." Claims that the members of the opposition Free Republican Party, which had been dissolved, were involved in a conspiracy could not be proved.

Mustafa Kemal Atatürk was not a saint but a man with a vision who was determined to drastically alter the destiny of his people. He knew that many efforts to reform the sick man of Europe, the Ottoman Empire, like the *Tanzimat* (a reform period between 1839 to 1876), had failed in the past because of despotism, ignorance, and religious intolerance. He took lessons from these experiences and from the Young Turk Revolution of 1908—when the CUP seized power—in which he had participated. He knew that it was not easy to teach new ways to a backward people. For years the Shariah had firmly withstood his attempts at reform. It had ruled the lives of the Turks for a millennium, and Turks obeyed its rules: the finger severed by the Shariah does not hurt.

It took tremendous courage, patience, and determination to discard an outdated system of Islamic law in 1926 and adopt the Italian penal code, the Swiss civil code, and the German commercial code. At the time, no modern laws existed because Shariah had been the law during the Ottoman Empire. Italian, Swiss, and German codes were used because their adoption was the quickest way to overhaul the justice system. Benito Mussolini's Fascist code, however, was later used against free speech and freedom of the press. Several writers and poets were jailed; others had to escape from the country.

Much has been written about Atatürk in the past. *Atatürk: The Rebirth of a Nation* by J. P. D. Kinross; *The Gray Wolf, Mustafa Kemal: An Intimate Study of a Dictator* by H. C. Armstrong; *Atatürk* by A. L. Macfie; and a recent one also titled *Atatürk* by Andrew Mango are only some of them.

The British historian H. C. Armstrong wrote, "[Atatürk's] dictatorship—a benevolent, educating, guiding dictatorship—was the only form of government possible at the moment." Andrew Mango wrote, "Atatürk was a competent commander, a shrewd politician, a statesman of supreme realism. But above all he was a man of the Enlightenment. And the Enlightenment was not made by saints."

Alan Moorehead in his book *Gallipoli* described Atatürk's crucial role as an Ottoman officer during the Dardanelles War (February 1915 to January 1916).

"I do not command you to obey me," Atatürk told his troops at Gallipoli in 1915. "I command you to die." And much has been said about Atatürk, from his womanizing to his excessive drinking of *rakı*, which he loved. (*Rakı* was the cause of his death from cirrhosis of the liver.)

When I was growing up in Anatolia, we heard many rumors about his later life, including how he had become a man of the night surrounded by flatterers commonly known as "the usual companions." He would finally get to bed at dawn and wake up late in the afternoon for another nightly session of drinking and card playing. He began to neglect the reform movement, and only one man, Hikmet Bayur, his chief secretary, dared to criticize him.

Kemal Atatürk, however, was a man of principles, which are easily summed up in six fundamentals: republicanism, populism, secularism, reformism, nationalism, and statism. The Kemalist reforms represent a total political, social, and secularist revolution. To Atatürk secularism meant the separation of state and religion as well as the separation of Islam from educational, cultural, and legal affairs. This was a complete reversal for the Shariah-based Ottoman state. Secularism now granted to the individual independence of thought from the dominance of Islam and its institutions. The reforms of the 1920s and 1930s did away with the traditional institutions of the Ottoman Empire and replaced them totally by secularist and modern institutions.

Kemal Atatürk's nationalism was meant to protect the unity and independence of the nation and had nothing to do with racist, fascist, or communist ideologies. I think we may begin to understand Atatürk's views on nationalism through this statement: "We Turks are a people who, throughout history, have been the very embodiment of freedom and independence." Atatürk also said: "I have been able to teach many things to this nation, but I haven't been able to teach them how to be lackeys."

Kemal Atatürk can be counted among the most eminent personalities of the world. Contrary to the claims of Islamic fundamentalists, he was not a fascist or a communist. His contemporaries in Europe were Adolf Hitler of Nazi Germany, Benito Mussolini of fascist Italy, and Francisco Franco of Spain. But Atatürk stood out in contrast to these European leaders as a reformist who was able to modernize his nation and whose revolution changed the role of Islam in a modern state.

Years later, John F. Kennedy said that Atatürk was one of his century's greatest men, whose leadership and farsighted comprehension of the modern world embodied the power and high courage of a military leader. But perhaps *Le Temps* newspaper of Paris described him best: "Atatürk has shown the miracle of modernizing a people within a few years."

In her book *One Lifetime Is Not Enough*, published in 1991, Zsa Zsa Gabor claimed that Atatürk had been her lover. She was then married to Burhan Belge, a Turkish diplomat and writer. She had met Belge in Budapest and asked him to marry her.

According to her account, Gabor saw Atatürk one night in a restaurant in Ankara and met him regularly thereafter in a secret hideaway. "Atatürk knew how to please a young girl," she wrote.

The romance lasted six months. During the lovers' trysts, she would inform Atatürk of her husband's secret meetings with some alleged Young Turks every Tuesday in their home. Burhan Belge was supposedly the leader of these ambitious men, and she would inform Atatürk about their various allegiances.

I met Gabor's first husband, Burhan Belge, in the 1950s at the editorial offices of the newspaper *Vatan* in Istanbul. He was working at the time as the lead writer for *Zafer*, the official newspaper of the Democratic Party. I do not believe that Belge had any intention to conspire with other Young Turks against Atatürk's regime. I knew him as a Kemalist who totally believed in the reform movement. Belge rarely wanted to discuss his life with his famous ex-wife.

The Islamic fundamentalists always saw Atatürk and his followers as their primary enemy—and they still do. These extremists, who opposed secular reforms and wanted the Sultanate, the Caliphate, and the Shariah restored, called him many names: cross-eyed Kemal, *Kefere* (unbeliever) Kemal, and *Deccal*, an evil liar who, in religious belief, will appear before the end times to mislead the Muslims. Because he had been promoted to marshal after the Battle of Sakarya, during the War of Independence, and given the title *Gazi* (hero warrior), others called him *Gazoz Pasha*. The French word *gazeuse* is widely used in Turkey as *gazoz* for lemonade.

By adopting children like a little girl named Ülkü, he wanted to show the nation the importance of educating children. This was another reason for his enemies to spread malicious rumors. One of Atatürk's adopted daughters was Sabiha Gökçen, who later became Turkey's first woman military pilot. She died in March 2001 at the age of eighty-eight. A year earlier, Gökçen, disturbed by the Islamic reactionary movement, had told an interviewer from the *Anatolian News Agency*: "Attacks on Atatürk have increased recently. There are enemies today who wish to destroy that great individual. They are inhuman." Gökçen, a symbol of Turkish women's emancipation, was involved in bombing raids during the Kurdish uprising in the 1930s in eastern Turkey under Atatürk's regime and flew in barnstorming publicity runs through the Balkans.

According to the Islamic reactionaries, Atatürk was an atheist. I do know that during his regime, no one was told not to pray or not to attend prayers in a mosque. The doors of the mosques were always open to the public for prayers during the reform years, just as they are today. The existing historical documents and his speeches prove that Atatürk believed religion to be a personal matter between a man and his god. In his speeches, Atatürk warned people against the merchants of religion who exploited their religious feelings. According to the *Belgelerle Türk Tarihi Dergisi* (Periodical of Documented Turkish History), Atatürk said in 1930: "Religion is a necessary institution. States cannot survive without religion."

But Atatürk also said, "It is shameful for a civilized nation to expect help from the dead." The occasion for this was the closing in November 1925 of all the *tarikats* (or Islamic brotherhoods), their dervish convents, and the tombs of a number of men believed to be holy. It was a long-established custom for people to visit these tombs to pray and ask for help from these holy men for the realization of their dreams.

Atatürk said in his speeches that the Turkish republic could not be the country of sheiks and dervishes and their disciples. "The best and true *tarikat*," he added, "is the order of civilization." He warned, "Resistance to the flood-tide of civilization is in vain: she is pitiless toward those who ignore or disobey her." Some of these words, spoken in 1927, are note-worthy because of the present revival of Islamic sects and dervish convents and their sheiks and a number of charlatans who claim holiness. Atatürk said, "How can a civilized nation tolerate people who allow themselves to be led by the nose by sheiks, dervishes and the like . . . and who entrust their faith and their lives to fortune-tellers, witch doctors, and amulet-writers?" I remember that by the 1950s, even in Istanbul, regular visits to the tombs of Islamic holy men had increased once again—just two decades after Atatürk's reforms took hold.

The best-known shrine of an *evliya* (a saint or a holy man) in Istanbul is the one of Eyup Sultan, located at the Golden Horn, an estuary that divides Istanbul. It is the tomb of Eyup Ansari, the disciple, the companion, and the standard-bearer of Prophet Muhammed. Eyup had been killed during the Arabs' siege of Constantinople in 670 CE. This shrine and its mosque are one of the most popular places where people go, hoping for help from the dead. Colorful Iznik tiles with flower designs cover the walls of the tomb in the mosque's courtyard. Old trees shade the courtyard, where storks and herons have nests. The visitors, walking by fluttering pigeons, approach the tomb's window, pray, ask favors, and tie pieces of rags to the windows' iron bars. Unmarried women request to meet marriage-minded men; others, to get rid of bad husbands; barren women, to be able to have children; students, to pass tough exams; and poor people, to get rich. Atatürk's words about not expecting any help from the dead were all but forgotten only twenty-five years later.

Atatürk, unlike other dictators, did not steal the state's resources or rob its treasury. The state provided for his needs, including the use of a yacht named *Savarona* purchased in March 1938 for $1.25 million. He enjoyed this luxury yacht for only six weeks before he was carried one night to his bedroom in the Dolmabahçe Palace, where he died. *Savarona* was later transferred to the navy to become a training ship.

Atatürk left no fat bank accounts in Turkey or abroad. Most of his savings were invested in model farms. In his will he bequeathed all his property to the Republican People's Party, leaving some funds for his adopted children, for the Historical and Language Societies, for his sisters, and for the education of his colleague Ismet Inönü's children. This, too, was a reflection of his character. Years earlier he had said, "Gentlemen, our face was always spotlessly clean and pure and always will remain spotlessly clean and pure." Atatürk as a strongman had every opportunity to steal public funds and receive bribes for government tenders. Compared with the incredible corruption that spread after his death, he was a true example of an honest public official. When he died, he left no Swiss bank accounts, and his limited savings were used to help others.

This extraordinary leader was born probably in 1881, the same year as his rival, Enver Pasha, in Salonica (Thessaloniki) in northeastern Greece, then a thriving port of the Ottoman Empire. The exact date of Atatürk's birth is uncertain but he chose May 19, an important date of Turkey's independence movement, for his official birthday. Ali Rıza, his father, was a soldier who served as an Ottoman army lieutenant during the Russo-Turkish War of 1877–78 and wanted Mustafa to become a military officer. So he hung his sword on the child's cradle to influence his son's personality through the years. He told the boy stories about Ottoman military campaigns, and the boy became interested in military uniforms. When Ali Rıza died, Mustafa was seven years old. His mother, Zübeyde, moved to a relative's farm and later remarried.

The name *Kemal* means excellence. His mathematics teacher at a secular middle school in Salonica called him Kemal because the teacher's name was also Mustafa. The secular reform movement is known as Kemalism. The word *Kemalist*, a follower of that movement, originates from that name. Known as Mustafa Kemal from middle school on, he graduated first from a military school in Monastir, in present-day Macedonia, then the War Academy in Istanbul in 1905.

At the War Academy, he got involved in the political dissident movement against the despotic rule of Sultan Abdul Hamid II. In 1905, he graduated as a captain from the General Staff College, where an informer had discovered his and others' clandestine activities. They were all banished to remote posts of the empire. Mustafa Kemal ended up in Damascus with the 5th Army, where, having seen the treatment of the local people by corrupt Ottoman officials, he helped organize a short-lived revolutionary society called the Fatherland and Freedom.

The young officer was transferred to Salonica in 1907 and in February 1908 joined the Committee of Union and Progress (CUP). The leading figure of the CUP was his rival Enver Pasha, who would become the hero of the Young Turk Revolution of 1908.

5

The Adventures of
Enver Pasha

"We have cured the Sick Man."
Enver Pasha, July 23, 1908, in Macedonia

The state funeral ceremonies in August 1996 for the mortal remains of Enver Pasha in Istanbul serve as a good example of the present nostalgia for the Ottoman times. Once Enver Pasha was reviled as the man who had caused the Ottoman Empire in its dying days to enter World War I on the side of Germany and brought about its collapse. I remember from my childhood years that Enver Pasha was considered a nonperson during the times of Kemal Atatürk. Now he is rehabilitated and being made into a national hero.

This new admiration for Enver Pasha is due to some of his actions. He was a leading figure of the CUP, which brought about the Young Turks Revolution of 1908. The CUP aimed to end the despotic rule of Sultan Abdul Hamid II and to restore a parliamentary constitution. Enver had joined Mahmut Şevket Pasha's Army of Deliverance in Salonica, advancing on Istanbul from the Balkans to depose the sultan, who favored the country's return to absolutism.

Mahmut Şevket Pasha, also a leader of the Young Turks reform movement, was the commander of the 3rd Army in Salonica. The CUP was successful in deposing the Sultan but failed in its other objectives, which aimed to curb the sultan's power in order to modernize the country through secular reforms. It's clear that the initial source of the modern Turkish reforms accomplished during the 1920s and 1930s is in the founding of the CUP. The party's slogan was "Freedom, Justice, and Equality." The CUP won the general election and deposed the sultan in 1909 but could not stop the disintegration of the Ottoman Empire.

In 1909, Mahmut Şevket Pasha marched with an army from Salonica to Istanbul and crushed the powerful Islamic fundamentalist uprising against the reforms brought about by the CUP. This conflict is known as the 31st March Incident, or the Revolt of Dervish Vahdeti.

Dervish Vahdeti, an Islamic extremist from Cyprus, was the publisher and editorial writer of the newspaper *Volkan* in Istanbul. He had received his education in a medrese as a child and memorized the Qur'an, thus becoming a *hafiz* (or *hafez*)—one who can accurately recall all passages from the sacred text.

The soldiers, unhappy about their living conditions and encouraged by Dervish Vahdeti, rebelled and rioted in the streets. Several army officers and members of parliament were called infidels and were subsequently murdered. Dervish Vahdeti, along with other Islamic fundamentalists and soldiers who took part in the uprising, was court-martialed and hanged. Dervish Vahdeti was forty years old when he was executed in a public square near St. Sophia in Istanbul. Despite the squelching of the uprising, the Islamic reactionaries were able to assassinate Mahmut Şevket Pasha in 1913, when he was the grand vizier of the CUP government.

My secular education in the 1930s opened my eyes to the destructive role Islamic fundamentalists had played in the history of the Ottoman Empire. Since the French Revolution of 1789, and the proclamation of the *Tanzimat* reforms in 1839, there had been a movement for freedom among

Ottoman intellectuals and officers of the armed forces. Later, the nationalistic revolts against the Ottoman regime, particularly in the Balkan territories, and the regime's inability to deal with the empire's ills also incited young officers and intellectuals. The *Tanzimat* had created an Ottoman intellectual class known as the Young Ottomans. In 1865 some of these Young Ottomans were involved in a secret revolutionary society. It was called the Patriotic Alliance, and the poet Namık Kemal was its most outspoken representative figure.

Mithat Pasha, an Ottoman administrative reformer, highly influenced by Namık Kemal's writings, had initiated in 1876 the first constitution of the Ottoman Empire. This constitution, called the *Kanunu esasi*, had guaranteed a broad range of democratic freedoms, including, according to its article 12, the freedom of the press. Mithat Pasha, twice the Ottoman grand vizier, was later banished to At-Ta'if in present-day Saudi Arabia, where he was murdered in 1883. He is believed to have been strangled by an agent of Sultan Abdul Hamid II.

The members of the Ottoman Union, another secret society, had adopted Mithat Pasha's constitution and the words "Freedom or Death" as their slogan. Enver Pasha, a member of this society, later helped to develop it into the CUP, the vehicle of the Young Turk Revolution.

I always considered the life of Enver Pasha fascinating, despite the disasters he had brought upon the Ottoman Empire.

Enver was born on November 23, 1881, in Istanbul and given the name Ismail Enver. His father, Ahmet, was a bridge keeper in Monastir, Macedonia. An ancestor of his father was a member of the minority group called the Gagauz. Enver secretly began reading revolutionary publications and the poems of Namık Kemal while a lieutenant at the military academy in Istanbul. His uncle Halil (Kut), two years younger than Enver, was also a lieutenant at the academy and very protective of him.

One night they were both arrested and taken to a special court in Sultan Abdul Hamid's Yıldız Palace. Judge Kadri was the sultan's chief of intelligence. He accused the young officers of acts against the regime. The judge, exasperated with Halil's denials on behalf of Enver, shouted at them: "Is this man [Enver] a goose?"—meaning, is he unable to defend himself. Eventually, both were released. Enver graduated a staff captain with excellent grades and was posted to the 3rd Ottoman Army in Macedonia to fight the nationalist rebels.

The trial of Enver and his uncle at the Sultan's palace had been a turning point in their lives. Halil was the first to become a member of the Ottoman Union and later initiated Enver's membership. By then a sense of Turkish identity had developed in Enver's mind: he began having doubts about the Ottomans as leaders of a nation and the Ottoman Empire as the fatherland. His dream of uniting all Turkic people, the ideology of pan-Turanism, began to take shape.

Enver's uncle, known in Turkish history as Halil Pasha, was the Ottoman commander who trapped a British army of seventeen thousand troops in Kut al-Amarah in eastern Iraq on December 3, 1915. Lord Horatio Herbert Kitchener, the British war secretary, offered him a bribe of £1 million to let the al-Kut garrison go free. Halil Pasha refused, and on April 29, 1916, he captured more than ten thousand British and Indian troops, along with their commander, Major General Charles Townshend. Halil Pasha, who took the surname Kut, died in 1957.

Unlike his uncle, Enver Pasha was not a gifted military leader and had severe weaknesses in strategizing, logistics, and organizing. The Turks still remember the annihilation in January 1915 of a Turkish army of about one hundred thousand soldiers at Sarıkamış, in eastern Anatolia. When World War I started, Enver, dreaming of conquests in the Caucasus, central Asia, and even in India, led this army personally against the Russian forces, who were well established in the mountains. Because of deep snow, Enver left his artillery behind. The Turkish soldiers died in an epidemic of typhus or froze to death without tents and winter uniforms in the mountain passes.

I recall that the Colonel, my mentor in Isparta, blamed Enver Pasha for wasting the lives of soldiers in order to win glory in distant Ottoman lands that had no strategic value. The journalist Falih Rıfkı Atay, writing in his book *Zeytindağı* (*Olive Mountain*) about the soldiers who died during World War I, said: "We have wasted the Turkish soldier not in battle but in gambling." Atay was a young reserve officer during World War I.

The lives of Mustafa Kemal Atatürk and Enver Pasha overlap closely during the final years of the collapsing Ottoman Empire. Enver Pasha had attended the same military academies as Mustafa Kemal. Enver had married into the *hanedan*, the Ottoman dynasty, thus becoming *damat*, a bridegroom of the House of Osman. After the CUP Revolution of 1908, Enver, now a major, was appointed inspector general of the CUP in the Balkan territories. The two officers, both CUP members, disliked each other intensely. Because of their rivalry, Enver, in his early years in power, played a crucial role in Mustafa Kemal's future by denying him promotions.

In 1911 Italy attacked Libya, then an Ottoman province. Enver organized the Ottoman resistance there and was appointed the governor of Benghazi. Mustafa Kemal, also fighting the Italians in Libya, was sent to Vienna in 1912 with eye problems and malaria, and while he was there, the First Balkan War broke out. His mother, Zübeyde; his sister; and his stepfather became refugees and escaped to Istanbul when the European territories of the Ottoman Empire were lost. After the short-lived (two summer months of 1913) Second Balkan War, Mustafa Kemal, then stationed in Gallipoli, was promoted to lieutenant colonel and transferred to Sofia as the military attaché.

Enver Pasha had other plans. He returned to Istanbul from Benghazi and participated in the political activities of the CUP. This led to a coup d'etat on January 23, 1913, that brought the CUP to power. During the Second Balkan War, Enver had been chief of the general staff and had recaptured Edirne from the Bulgars. After the coup d'etat, Enver became the leading figure in the triumvirate of three revolutionaries, Enver, Mehmed Talat, and Ahmed Cemal. This triumvirate ruled the Ottoman Empire through the First World War until 1918.

Mustafa Kemal predicted a German defeat. He criticized Enver and Talat for having close ties with the Germans. They were now ministers of war and the interior, respectively. Talat, known as the *Telgrafcı* because he had worked earlier as a telegraph operator at the post office, had sided with the Allies at first. Later, under Enver's influence, he supported the Germans.

British intelligence meanwhile wrongly believed that the leaders of the CUP were members of a German and Jewish conspiracy.

After the disaster in Sarıkamış, Enver was able to recover his prestige in 1916 only when the Allied forces withdrew from the Dardanelles. Mustafa Kemal had shown his military prowess at Gallipoli by thwarting the Allies' attempt to advance and forcing their retreat. Because of his success in Gallipoli, Mustafa Kemal became known as the Savior of Istanbul.

Enver Pasha was a reformist but a self-centered and vain adventurer. Still wanting to establish a pan-Turkic empire, Enver considered the Russian Revolution of 1917 to be his opportunity. He occupied Baku in Azerbaijan in 1918, when the Ottoman Empire was on its knees.

When the war was lost, the Allies occupied Turkey. In the interior of Anatolia, there was communal strife and increased brigandage. In order to prevent total chaos in Anatolia, Mustafa Kemal was appointed inspector general of the 9th Army, receiving from the sultan's government broad civil and military powers.

May 19, 1919, the date Mustafa Kemal landed at the Black Sea port of Samsun, is considered the beginning of the struggle for an independent Turkish nation. For only five days before he arrived in Samsun, the Greek troops, with British and American naval support, had landed in Izmir on the pretext of preserving order. They began a drive into the Anatolian interior, the Turkish heartland, killing people and ravaging the countryside. To avoid dismissal, Mustafa Kemal resigned from the army, and at Erzurum in eastern Turkey, he persuaded General Kazım Karabekir, the commander of the 15th Army Corps of eighteen thousand men, to join him in a fight against the Allies. A provisional government was formed in Ankara, and this angered Sultan Mehmet VI (Vahdettin), who was cooperating with the Allies to protect his throne. A reactionary government in Istanbul declared Mustafa Kemal and his associates infidels who were to be shot on sight.

This didn't work, and many prominent officers, including Ismet Inönü and Fevzi Çakmak, the sultan's war minister, joined Mustafa Kemal in Ankara. An election was held and a parliament, the Grand National Assembly (TBMM), was established, which elected Mustafa

Kemal president and commander-in-chief. Kemal defeated the Greek forces at Sakarya and pushed them into the Aegean Sea at Izmir. This victory caused the collapse of the Allies' plans to divide up Turkey among themselves. Author R. E. Ünaydın would later write: "[The Allies] intended to annihilate us in our own country."

After the victory, Mustafa Kemal, addressing the armed forces, declared: "You have not only overcome the enemy but also the perversed luck of this nation." The Treaty of Lausanne, signed on July 24, 1923, fixed the present Turkish borders.

Having saved the country from foreign occupation, Mustafa Kemal and his associates began the reform movement. During Ottoman times, reforming the ailing empire had been impossible because of the sultans' despotism, the ignorance of the reactionary forces, and the concerns of Janissaries—the Ottoman Empire standing army—about their privileges. When they were opposed to change, the Janissaries took to the streets and shouted, "We don't want the infidel's reform." The Janissaries were able to depose rulers, capturing and garroting with a silken cord anyone they opposed. A good example of their unruly behavior is the fate of Osman II, known as Genç (Young) Osman.

Born in 1603, Genç Osman became sultan at the age of fourteen and ruled between 1618 and 1622. He was intelligent, ambitious, and coura-geous, and he understood the need for reform. He wanted to break the power of the degenerate and undisciplined Janissaries by secretly recruiting a new army in Syria and Egypt. The Janissaries became suspi-cious of his activities and revolted. Genç Osman was deposed and stran-gled in 1622 at the age of eighteen.

Enver Pasha missed the reform movement in Turkey soon after World War I. All three members of the triumvirate fled to Odessa in November 1918, then Enver and Talat traveled to Berlin, where an Armenian assas-sinated Talat. Enver, having met Karl Radek (Karl Sobelsohn), one of the leaders of the German Communist Party in his jail cell in Berlin, was impressed by Radek's proposal, that Enver travel to Moscow, meet Vladimir Ilyich Lenin, and persuade the Russian Bolsheviks to sign an agreement with the Turkish nationalists.

Enver's German friend General Hans von Seeckt, who had served as chief of staff of the Turkish army when the war was coming to an end, was now the commander of the limited German army. Seeckt arranged a private airplane for Enver's journey to Moscow, but the plane had to make an emergency landing in Lithuania. Eastern Europe was in turmoil as a result of the Russian civil war. Enver, fearing arrest, was hiding his true identity and traveling with false papers. The Lithuanians, at war with the Soviets, suspected that Enver was a spy and kept him as a prisoner for two months. Enver had to return to Berlin. There he received the false identity papers of a German Communist Jew named Altman. In Latvia, he was arrested again and jailed on suspicion of spying. He finally arrived in Moscow in the summer of 1919, more than ten months after he had first started out from Berlin.

In Moscow, Enver Pasha, once the finest fencer in the Ottoman Empire and an expert in political intrigues, worked in the Russian foreign ministry between 1920 and 1921. I remember that the Colonel, my childhood mentor, had been disgusted with Enver for working for the Russians in Moscow. Any Turk serving the Russians was considered an outright traitor. Russia and Turkey had fought ten wars between 1676 and 1878. "He had to, I guess," the Colonel had told me. "Enver couldn't come back to Turkey to be hanged. Mustafa Kemal surely would have hanged him."

In September 1920, Enver attended a Bolshevik congress in Baku, Azerbaijan, still behaving as the Turkish leader despite Mustafa Kemal's nationalist movement in Anatolia. He was met there with strong opposition from a Turkish Communist delegation. Enver remained an attraction in the streets of Moscow; he was a small man with a large, black, curved Kaiser Wilhelm II moustache, wearing a *tarbuş*, a tall red hat similar to the fez.

Regarding Turco-Russian relations, he was not successful, as the Bolsheviks preferred to deal with the Kemalists. After a period in Batum in Georgia, Enver returned to Moscow again and there made a proposition to the Bolsheviks: he would deliver British India to the Russians, if the Bolsheviks helped him overthrow Mustafa Kemal's regime in Ankara. He wanted to seize Chinese Turkestan and establish a Turkic republic with the local Uigur and Kazak populations. From there, Enver proposed, he could start the jihad, a holy war with the help of other Turkic people and drive the British forces from India. The Soviet government was not interested.

He later came up with a new plan that fooled Lenin. If Lenin sent him to central Asia, he would pacify the Basmacı rebels of Turkish origin, end their revolt against the Bolsheviks, and spread among them the gospel of Marxism-Leninism. Even though the Bolshevik leaders were suspicious of the dapper Turk's motives, they accepted the offer and dispatched him to Bukhara with his staff of loyal Turkish officers. Enver arrived in Bukhara on November 8, 1921, and by the time the Bolsheviks realized their mistake, it was too late.

Now Enver was in the historic homeland of the Turks. In Bukhara, a major city in Uzbekistan, he met reformist Turkic leaders such as Zeki Velidi Togan, a Bashkiri. Bukhara was under Bolshevik control, and Enver tricked the Russian administration by saying he was going out to hunt. He rode out of town with other Turkish officers and some local supporters. This wily pasha, who at age thirty-two had become minister of war of the once mighty Ottoman Empire, then joined the Basmacı rebels in the hills of eastern Bukhara. He inspired them to jihad and was successful in uniting them to a degree. He received aid from Abdul Said Mir Alim Khan, the former emir of Bukhara, a fugitive from the Russians, and later from Amanullah, the king of Afghanistan.

The word *Basmacı* comes from the Turkish verb *basmak*, meaning to raid or to conduct a surprise attack. A Basmacı is a raider. The Basmacı bands in Turkestan during Lenin's rule, speaking different dialects of Turkish, knew the central Asian terrain well. They fought the Russian occupiers effectively but lacked a leader who could unite them into a single force. That was the vacuum Enver Pasha tried to fill. It is believed that at one point in the Basmacı rebellion, the spring of 1922, Enver Pasha commanded a force of three thousand poorly armed soldiers. He had a command structure with former Turkish army officers and succeeded in controlling much of the former kingdom of Bukhara.

Enver Pasha announced that he was commander-in-chief of all the armies of Islam and, because of his marriage to the Ottoman sultan's young niece Naciye, he was entitled to a special title. Enver wanted to be known as Kinsman of the Caliph, the Prophet's Representative on Earth.

In February 1922, Enver captured the town of Dushanbe. Two months later, he was in control of a large area surrounding Bukhara. He made a crucial mistake, however, by calling himself Emir of Turkestan, thus alienating Mir Alim Khan, the Emir of Bukhara. By losing a critical battle on June 14, 1922, his luck changed, and the support he had enjoyed disappeared. The King of Afghanistan, nervous about rumors that Lenin was sending a huge army to crush Enver's forces, cut off his aid. Other factions also deserted.

Six weeks later, on August 4, 1922, Enver received word in the village of Abiderya, in present-day Tajikistan, that a Soviet force of about three hundred soldiers was approaching. It was the Muslim Festival of Sacrifice, a holiday that commemorates Abraham's sacrifice, and Enver was celebrating with his few remaining men. As they were exchanging gifts, gunfire was heard. Enver, holding his pocket Qur'an, drew his sword and rode his horse, Dervish, toward the Bolshevik troops. Only about twenty-five riders followed him. According to Şevket Süreyya Aydemir, Enver's Turkish biographer, it was a suicidal onslaught against machine-gun fire. He was shot seven times and fell. His horse died with him. He could have escaped to Afghanistan with his remaining forces, but he did not—instead, he died fighting.

The Soviets did not realize for some time that they had actually killed Enver Pasha, and they left his decapitated body on the battlefield with others, where local citizens buried him. Enver Pasha's grave under a walnut tree beside a river became a shrine for the Turkic people of central Asia. Seventy-four years later, his mortal remains were returned to Turkey from Abiderya and buried in Istanbul in a state ceremony in August 1996. Süleyman Demirel, president at the time, led the military and religious funeral.

This was the story of two rival Ottoman army officers whose lives through the reform years and later had impressed and left a mark on many young Turks, including myself.

Mustafa Kemal Pasha, a brilliant strategist who created a modern state, became a marshal and left a secular legacy. In his speeches he said, "My humble body certainly one day will turn to earth, but the Turkish Republic will endure forever." Enver Pasha, an adventurer who gambled away an empire, died in a battleground in central Asia. A few years after Enver Pasha's death in central Asia, a new generation of Young Turks was at the center of a great reform movement and the birth of a new nation. The chains of the Islamic bigotry and darkness that afflicted the Ottoman Empire were finally being broken by the members of this new generation.

I was one of them.

6

Islam versus Secularity

It is better to have a wise enemy than a mad friend.

Turkish proverb

I remember how the railroad came to Isparta and how as students we marched to the station to see the train. Most of us had never seen a train before, so it was an awesome experience to see this giant engine huffing and puffing. We welcomed Ismet Pasha, Kemal Atatürk's gifted colleague and eventual successor, who arrived in town aboard the train. He had taken the surname of İnönü, a battleground in western Anatolia where he had defeated the invading Greek armies in 1921.

The middle school I attended was a long way from home, so I had to walk there and back each day on unpaved rural roads. Our principal's first name was Hilmi, but he was better known as the dog handler because of his habit of dissecting dogs in the classroom. The principal was a strong disciplinarian, but he rarely hit children to enforce order. He preferred twisting their ears instead, accompanied by fearsome facial expressions. Once he had grabbed the ear of the misbehaving student, he would twist it hard and wouldn't let go. The pain would last forever.

Life was simple in our provincial town, and deaths, like births, were visible daily occurrences. Anatolian Turks have no use for fancy, elaborate coffins, so rich and poor alike end up in the same simple pine boxes. The best example for the Turkish mentality on death and dying was expressed long ago in a folktale involving Nasreddin Hoca, the satirist mullah of Ottoman times. The word *hoca* means teacher and is used as an honorific for clerics.

"At a funeral, where should one stand," a friend one day asked Nasreddin Hoca. "In the front of the coffin, beside it, or right behind it?"

The hoca answered, "Anywhere is fine. Just try not to be inside the coffin itself."

We had two religious holidays. One was the Muslim Festival of Sacrifice that the Arabs call *Eid al-Adha*, when the whole town would turn into a giant slaughterhouse as people celebrated Abraham's sacrifice of the ram as a substitute for his son. During the second holiday at the end of Ramadan, people served candy to their guests.

I remember one Festival of Sacrifice very well because of the grief it caused me. I was about seven years old. I had a little black lamb as a pet, which I had named *Kirpik* because of her long eyelashes. Before the festival, my mother had bought a ram for the early morning sacrifice on the first day of the holidays. A butcher was hired and instructed to distribute the meat to poor families in our neighborhood.

Unfortunately, on that occasion, the ram had found a sack of wheat in the basement of our home where it was kept. The ram ate it all and drank plenty of water. The next morning, we found the ram's body in the basement blown up and tight as a drum. Our holidays were ruined. Mother didn't have any choice but to sacrifice my lamb. I begged and cried, "Please don't kill my little lamb, Mom," but it was no use. I stayed away not to see it slaughtered but could not avoid hearing its bleats as it was taken away.

As the first generation of Anatolian schoolchildren educated under Atatürk's new reforms, our lives fluctuated between Islamic Ottoman traditions outside school and a secular education in the classroom. Members of the older generations, who had studied in a medrese or religious school, were superstitious and prone to believe in things like haunted houses and fortune-tellers. "The genies are playing ball there" was an expression often used for a house near my old elementary school, where people kept hearing strange noises. According to the tales told around town, genies were stoning the roof of that house almost every night! This house would later always remind me of author Hüseyin Rahmi Gürpınar's writing: "That is a place where demons and fairies are plotting mischief."

A *muska* was a Muslim religious amulet that contained a verse from the Qur'an. It was worn like a necklace in the expectation that it would ward off evil. Another amulet prepared by a mullah was even supposed to improve a woman's beauty with the result of attracting an eligible man's attention, thus leading to marriage.

In school, we were told not to believe in superstition and fortune-tellers, but outside school we would hear people talking about the magic healing breath of a certain imam. He could simply blow away whatever was ailing a sick person with his breath. Another imam had the magic of causing pregnancy in barren women by writing religious verses in Arabic on their naked bellies. Uncle Enver used to laugh and say that he knew all about that imam's potent magic and that there was a little more to it than mere writing on the belly.

In school, the revolutionary ideas of Ziya Gökalp (1875–1924), a former member of the CUP and chief ideologist and spokesman of the nationalist movement, became our guiding light. Gökalp, a sociologist, writer, and poet, had espoused pan-Turanism, the unification of all Turkic peoples, while a secret member of the CUP in his early years. He was later concerned with modernizing the nation and influenced politicians and writers of his generation with his ideas. Gökalp's book *Kızıl Elma* (*Red Apple*) is a collection of his verses about pan-Turanism.

After the collapse of the Ottoman Empire, Ziya Gökalp described the beginning of the struggle for the Turkish reforms: "We were defeated because of our backwardness. To take revenge, we shall adopt the enemy's science. Learn his skills and steal his methods." Through Gökalp's teachings, we children adopted many of the ways of Western civilization while still being aware of Turkish history and traditions.

I was an elementary school student on October 29, 1933, when we celebrated the tenth anniversary of the secular republic. We were a proud nation then; we trusted our government, our leader, our state, our media, and our institutions; and, most of all, we had pride in ourselves. We believed that our chests were the bronze shield that protected our young secular republic. And to prove our belief we sang a song that announced the achievements of a young generation: We were fifteen million young who came out of ten years of struggle with pride, with heads held high. With a song adapted from a Swedish tune, we expressed the love for our land. Long before our generation, this had been the theme song of the young officers who fought in the War of Independence:

> The mountain's top is swathed in smoky mist,
> The sparkling stream flows ever on.
> Now the sun rises from the horizon,
> Let us march, friends.
> Let earth, sky, and water listen to our voice,
> Let the ground groan under our powerful steps,
> Let us march, friends.

We voiced the slogan *Ne mutlu Türküm diyene*—"How happy is the one who can say I am a Turk." It came from a speech of Atatürk and was meant to unite us all regardless of our ethnic and religious differences.

When I was still in the first grade of middle school, Mother declared one day that she wanted to move to Istanbul. She was very good in her dental profession and wanted to increase her practice. At the same time, she was concerned that Isparta in those years lacked higher education for her children. Our move to Istanbul would therefore benefit the whole family. My mother had a half-sister in Istanbul who would help us get settled in the big city.

As we were preparing to relocate, the Charleston, that lively ballroom dance, was sweeping through our provincial town, and many people were singing and dancing to this tune:

Bring beer, waiter,
Bring wine, waiter,
Bravo Charleston.

Soon the preparations for our move were completed and to make a clean getaway, we went to the Turkish bath in town, where the bath attendants gave us a spirited rubdown with a mittenlike washcloth made from rough material. In the steaming heat of the Turkish bath, a rubdown would create a miraculous revival of one's body. Layers of dead skin were rubbed off, opening the pores. Red all over, you would feel so clean and fresh. Afterward, I remember drinking cooled *gazoz*, a carbonated soft drink of lemonade, which came in old-fashioned bottles with bulky, wired porcelain caps.

I met the Colonel for the last time before we left. He came in uniform, riding his horse, a gray Arabian stallion, and sat beside me on the steps leading to our home. "How lucky you are," he said, "to be off to the big city. That's a wonderful chance for you to study and become somebody."

Lately, the Colonel had been entertaining the neighborhood with new phonograph records. These included songs by Safiye Ayla, a colored woman, who had a soft, velvety voice. When he played Ayla's song— "We spent hours together every night—My crazy heart remembers those sweet moments"—we would all listen, quite mesmerized.

As he shook my hand and wished me luck, the Colonel said: "Will you promise me one thing?" I answered, "You name it, my Colonel." He replied: "Promise me that you'll always protect the republic and its secular Kemalist reforms."

"I promise, my Colonel," I said, even though there was no need for such a promise. I was a child of the revolution, and Kemalism had molded me.

Since first grade, my days in school, as for all other children, had begun with a ceremonial oath: "I am a Turk, I am honest, I am industrious. My primary duty is to protect Turkish independence and the Republic of Turkey. . . ."

Besides, Kemal Atatürk's injunction in his speech to the youth of the country was always in my mind: "Your primary duty is to protect and defend forever the Turkish independence and the Turkish republic. This is the sole foundation of your existence and your future. This foundation is your best treasure."

The next day, we visited the cemetery where father was buried in a typical Anatolian grave with headstones and footstones shaped like columns. After saying our prayers and goodbyes, we took a horse-drawn buggy to the railroad station and boarded the train for Istanbul with much trepidation about our future.

It was 1937, and I was a twelve-year-old Young Turk, completely different in mind, manners, and appearance from an *Osmanlı*, a citizen of the collapsed Ottoman Empire. Kemal Atatürk was my teacher, and I considered myself a Kemalist.

Early Days
in Journalism

Not to know isn't shameful, not to ask is.

Turkish proverb

*I*n 1937 Istanbul was an orderly city. This center of Levantine culture* had in earlier times been the capital of the eastern Roman and subsequently the Byzantine and Ottoman empires. The city's old buildings are an amazing blend of architectural styles, masterpieces from many different periods of history. Among its most noticeable treasures are the Byzantine walls that still surround the city. The famous Byzantine church, the Hagia Sofia (Saint Sophia), is a museum, as is the Church of Chora with its beautiful mosaics.

One of the many mosques, whose minarets make the skyline of Istanbul so enchanting, is the Blue Mosque, built between 1609 and 1616 for Sultan Ahmet I at the eastern end of the Hippodrome of Byzantium.

---

* The term *Levantine* is historically used for countries along the eastern Mediterranean shores and for Anatolia and as a synonym for the Middle or Near East. The word describes an inhabitant or a native of the Levant. A *levanter* is a powerful Mediterranean wind.

Another, the Süleymaniye Mosque, was built for Süleyman the Magnificent, who is also known as *Kanuni*, the Lawgiver. It took seven years between 1550 and 1557 to complete this mosque. Its builder was the great Ottoman architect Sinan. Once, as a young reporter, I climbed its central cupola that stands 174 feet high. I was there to write a story about the restoration work that was in progress. Looking at the Golden Horn, the Bosphorus Strait, and the Sea of Marmara from the edges of that huge dome made for a spectacular view. There is an odd little room with holes in its interior walls near the dome, overlooking the prayer hall. This room was the collection center for soot produced by the lamps and candles below in the prayer hall before the dawn of electricity. The soot flowing through the holes was collected and used to make ink.

The stained-glass windows of the prayer hall, with floral motifs by the artist known as Ibrahim the Drunkard, create a somber atmosphere in the vast interior. Outside the mosque, there are two impressive mausoleums with interior walls covered with beautiful Turkish faience, wall tiles with flower designs. These mausoleums house the mortal remains of Süleyman the Magnificent and his Russian wife, Roxelana. While visiting the Capitol building in Washington, DC, years later, I was to see the image of Süleyman the Magnificent in its rotunda among the images of other noted historical lawgivers.

The air was clean in Istanbul in 1937. The Bosphorus and the Marmara Sea were bountiful with swordfish, mackerel, bluefish, and bonito. The only pollution I remember was in the Golden Horn, caused by centuries of discharges from shipbuilding and factories. Making one's way about the city, which sprawls widely over seven steep hills, was easily accomplished on the trams that were still running in those days. Crossing the Bosphorus between the European and Asian shores was possible only by ferryboat until recently, when two suspension bridges were built. Ferryboats are still the only way to get to the Princes Islands in the Marmara Sea. These small, rocky islands are popular summer resorts with a very Mediterranean atmosphere, lovely summer houses, and gardens with showy bougainvilleas, as well as pine trees and gorgeous views.

The ferryboats were moored at the old Galata Bridge, an iron construction floating on pontoons across the Golden Horn and connecting the old and new sections of the city. The old bridge was recently replaced. It was a place teeming with fishermen, vendors, and traffic. People used to fish from the lower level of the bridge, and vendors fried fish over charcoal, advertising their merchandise with melodious jingles, while noisy trams rambled to and fro on top. On the bridge, the aroma of fried fish was mixed with the smell of the sea, the smell of *lakerda* (delicious salted bonito), along with the aroma of spices coming from the Egyptian Spice Market, an enclosed bazaar nearby on Eminönü Square. There were always children on the bridge diving into the Golden Horn to recover coins thrown by tourists. On Sundays the bridge and the ferries were crowded with people speaking many different languages.

Traffic congestion was unheard of, and traffic lights were nonexistent in those days. There were very few motorized vehicles then in all of Turkey compared with the five million now. Still, Istanbul was a lively city with the vibrant noise of the Orient.

Muhallebici eateries were at every corner, especially since the Turks, who created baklava, yogurt, pastrami, bulgur pilaf, and shish kebab, have a notorious sweet tooth. A *muhallebici* is a special type of restaurant where only sweets made from milk products are served. The *muhallebi* itself is a kind of rice flour pudding usually flavored with rose water or orange blossom water. In addition, there were pickle shops all over the city, some no larger than a cubicle with a window, selling nothing but pickles of every kind. These stores carried the most varied pickled vegetables and fruits imaginable, including eggplant. I used to frequent the one near Çemberlitaş, the Hooped Column built by Byzantine Emperor Constantine with ten drums of purple porphyry stones. Iron hoops have been placed around the column for protection after part of it was blown down by a gale in 1105.

The Turks call compotes and freshly squeezed fruit juices *şerbet*, which emigrants have spread as sherbet all over the world. Tiny *şerbet* stands were an important part of the ancient city.

Istanbul's population has grown tremendously the last two decades. Now with a population of twelve million, this city is fast approaching the country's population of fourteen million in 1927.

Babıali was then Istanbul's street of the press. Located on a steep hill, it connects the district of Cağaloğlu with Sirkeci Square below in the old city. That square has become synonymous with the great railway station, the old terminus of the Orient Express. The street ends on top of the hill. Babıali is actually two words: *Bab* in Arabic means door or portal and *Ali*, high or sublime. During the Ottoman Empire, this location was the center of the Ottoman government known as the Sublime Porte. The actual portal that led to the prime ministry still stands nearby. The Ottoman interior and foreign ministries and the Council of State were also located in the same compound gated by the Sublime Porte. This high gate, with its huge flowing eaves across the Gülhane (Rose Chamber) Park near the Old Seraglio (a palace), continued to be a side entrance to the office of the city's governor.

The middle school and high school I attended were nearby, but to my surprise both lacked the friendly atmosphere of my old school in Isparta. The teachers were stern men who imposed discipline either with a ruler's slap on the hand or banishment of the misbehaving pupil to a corner. The culprit was often ordered to stand on one foot for a long time. My best grades were in history, geography, literature, and composition. I did not do as well in math, biology, chemistry, and physics. This would portend my later becoming a newspaper reporter.

In high school during World War II, one of my teachers was Nihal Atsız, a blond man who was proud of his Aryan looks. He used to comb his hair just like Adolf Hitler but was very careful with his words in class. Atsız had been in trouble with the regime of Ismet Inönü for his racist and ultranationalist activities. He was the author of books grouped under the title *Bozkurtlar*, the Gray Wolves. As a leader of the ultranationalist pan-Turkic movement, Atsız had been involved in attacks against the Communists. He had been sentenced to a jail term for insulting Sabahattin Ali, a well-known left-wing writer and teacher. Another of my teachers was a young Armenian who had studied in America. He taught the fine art of penmanship, making us trace and retrace the ovals, loops, and humps. This cursive writing with perfected ascenders and descenders is now being erased by the computer age.

Shortly after our arrival in Istanbul, Mother moved into an apartment building on top of the hill. In this building, several professors from Istanbul University's medical faculty had their clinics. The building across the street from the local branch of the ruling Republican People's Party had ornate doors, a marble entrance hall, central heating, and an elevator and was home to several eminent doctors. It was built for those professionals who wanted to have their homes and their medical clinics in the same building. For twenty-five years, Mother was to live and practice at that location.

There were two houses between this building and the nearby high school for girls. In later years, *Hürriyet*, the leading newspaper, would buy the houses and construct a modern building for its printing plant and editorial offices. I had no idea then that this daily newspaper would play a vital role in my later life.

One of the most vivid memories I have of my youth is of the day in 1938 when Kemal Atatürk died. It was morning recess in school, and we were all playing in the courtyard. Someone lowered the school's flag to half-mast, and we all knew at once what had happened. Although it was common knowledge that Atatürk had been ill, his death came as a tremendous shock. All of us began to cry. A few days later, we visited the Dolmabahçe Palace on the Bosphorus, where Atatürk had died in his bedroom, and like thousands of other people, we paid our last respects to his remains.

His body lay in state in the palace's throne room. Military officers with drawn swords were guarding the catafalque as we passed rows of wreaths. Outside, the daylight reflected on the Bosphorus, while inside the palace, the mourners sobbed. The air was rich with the smell of fresh flowers. The date and time of his death is still a national anniversary. There was a ditty in those days:

> At five minutes past nine,
> My Pasha closed his eyes at Dolmabahçe,
> And the whole world wept.

Each year at 9:05 a.m. on November 10, the sirens of trains, ships, and factories blare, and the whole country freezes in its tracks for a minute in Atatürk's memory.

Atatürk, known as the Eternal Leader, died just before World War II, leaving the country in the hands of his colleague, Ismet Inönü, also known as Ismet Pasha. Ismet Inönü had unimpressive looks, but, as Atatürk had often described Inönü's shrewdness, he was a man in whose belly many foxes danced.

I remember an interesting quote by this old fox. Once Inönü was asked about his country's relations with America, and he answered: "To conduct politics with big states is like sharing the same bed with a tiger." Did he say tiger or bear? After so many years no one is sure.

Inönü was the statesman who secured the present boundaries of Turkey in the Treaty of Lausanne in 1923, which canceled the Treaty of Sevres imposed by the Allies on a defeated Ottoman Empire in 1920. But, like Atatürk, Ismet Inönü was a dictator.

During Ismet Inönü's repressive regime, the brutality of his police was well known. I personally had a bad experience with Inönü's police when I was about sixteen. The incident happened during the early days of World War II. One afternoon, I was standing on a sidewalk in Istanbul, killing time, when a policeman ordered me to move. I smelled the strong odor of *rakı* on his breath, and since I had done nothing wrong, I refused to leave. Being young and foolish, I told the uniformed officer that he had been drinking on the job. He got angry and took me to the local precinct, where he pushed me into an upright box in which I could hardly move while standing up. I had already heard about the existence of these unique wooden boxes at the police stations. They were called *tabutluk*, and, true to their name, each one resembled a coffin.

A second policeman, a giant of a man, who was also in uniform, appeared and without saying a word began punching me brutally with his fists. There was nothing I could do in that tight box to protect myself but stand still and take the beating. Finally, when he decided that I had had enough and had learned respect of authority, he stopped. The policemen had the audacity to force me to sign an affidavit if I wanted to get out of that hellhole. It stated that during my stay at the police station I had been treated well and that I had no complaints!

Ismet Inönü's unique qualities as a statesman came in handy during World War II, when the Turks were subjected to tremendous pressures from both Hitler and the Allies to enter the war on their side. Inönü, known as the national leader, was able to spare the Turks the devastation of World War II by keeping the country out of the war until 1945. He also prepared the Turks after the war for free elections. I guess he had to, being under pressure from the Allies to establish a democracy. In 1950, the Democratic Party (DP) of Adnan Menderes won the first free parliamentary elections in the young republic's history with 408 seats in the Grand National Assembly against the Republican People's Party's sixty-nine. The population had become unhappy with Inönü's dictatorial regime.

I was too young during the war years, being still in school, to be drafted into the army. My older brother Hilmi had finished his army service before we left Isparta, and that should have been the end of that, but the war changed everything. When World War II began, my brother was conscripted once again, and after another stint in military training, he was discharged. Throughout the war years, this would happen to him several times.

We all felt the effects of the war, in spite of Turkey's neutrality. There were nightly blackouts, shortages of consumer goods, and the rationing of bread and coal. Coffee was scarce; people created ersatz coffee by roasting and then grinding chickpeas. I had learned to play the accordion, which displeased our neighbors and the eminent doctors and professors of the medical faculty, who often complained to my mother not only about my lack of musical expertise but also about my constant stomping.

By the war's end, I had already graduated high school, completing the final exams with barely a passing grade because of the poor marks I received in math, physics, and biology. I was not yet sure what I wanted to be.

My Armenian girlfriend, Seta, unlike most Armenians, was very fair and had long, blonde hair. Seta's aunt had a dress store at the Grand Bazaar, which was a shopping mall long before an American thought he invented the idea. It was located right across from Uncle Enver's carpet store. We would meet, go to a coffee shop in that medieval covered bazaar, have a lemonade or ice cream, and talk about things that interested us. Knowing how fond I was of photography, she kept suggesting that I become a professional photographer.

One day, almost two years before the Truman Doctrine of 1947, which sought to combat Joseph Stalin's expansionist plans against Greece and Turkey, Seta said, "The Russians are going to come here." That was shocking news to me, and it would soon become a real threat when the Soviets demanded territory from Turkey. Seta later moved to Argentina with her family.

A year after the war ended, Mother suggested that I go to England to join my brother Aziz, who was studying shipbuilding on a scholarship from the Marine Bank. She wanted me to follow in her footsteps and study dentistry, despite my poor grades.

In the fall of 1946, I sailed to Marseilles aboard the *SS Ankara*, which used to make regular runs between the ports of the Mediterranean as a passenger liner for the bank. Europe was just beginning to recover from the devastation of the war, and signs of shortages were everywhere. In Piraeus food was short, and in Naples hoards of young street urchins were on the lookout for gullible tourists to swindle or rob, posing as moneychangers. They were infamous for pushing fake rings as genuine diamond.

My brother's family lived in Maidenhead, near London, while he worked as a draftsman for the shipbuilder Vospers, Ltd., in Portsmouth. He dumped me in a boarding house in Maidenhead and went back to his job. During the war years in England, he had become a heavy drinker, a problem that would eventually cause his death. Years later in Istanbul, while walking drunk at night, he was to fall in the street, hit his head on the curb, and die.

While attending an English-language course for foreigners in London, I applied to the University of Bristol to study dentistry, and after interviewing, I was accepted. As students of the medical faculty, we used to meet regularly for parties and dances, drink beer, and sing songs. Despite the fun, I decided that medical school and dentistry were not for me. I began to see myself now more as a future journalist or photojournalist after meeting several reporters from the Bristol newspapers, who often came to the campus in search of human-interest stories.

I took off for London, planning to attend courses in the art of motion-picture photography and in writing. One of the visiting lecturers I met at the British Cinematography Society was the late Alfred Hitchcock, the English film director famous for his skillful use of suspense. He talked about *The Rope*, his new film at the time, demonstrating the techniques he had used to create special effects. Years later I would meet him again by chance in New York on an elevator at the Waldorf Astoria.

I was fascinated with the museums and art galleries of London. The National Gallery, one of the smallest of the great European galleries, was my favorite place. There, the collection of art was divided into schools of national origin such as Italian or Flemish. My favorite was the Spanish school, in particular, the works of Goya and Velasquez. When I had a little extra money, which was not often, I used to go to Albert Hall to listen to the works of Rachmaninoff and Chopin.

Mother was very disappointed with my decision to become a journalist. In her view, journalism could be a dangerous profession in a country still experimenting with democracy. I persisted and promised her that I would not get involved in politics. I don't think she believed me, knowing that journalism would necessarily play an important part in national politics for Turkey's budding democracy. In the spring of 1950, I took the Simplon Express to Istanbul with a second-class ticket.

It was the year the Korean War started, which would last for three years. Turkey's Prime Minister Adnan Menderes of the Democratic Party had sent twenty-five thousand troops to Korea to join the war effort of the United Nations.

Shortly after I arrived in Istanbul, I bought a typewriter, a Smith-Corona, and began writing freelance articles for a morning broadsheet called *Yeni (New) Istanbul*. For several months, I wrote movie reviews for this newspaper. *Yeni Istanbul* was a serious, European-style newspaper that gave much space to national and world news and none at all to glamour shots of girls. This was in contrast to the other newspapers that printed daily pictures of almost nude women. *Yeni Istanbul* was unique in one other aspect never before tried in Turkey—its masthead was light blue while all the other newspapers favored red, the color of the Turkish flag. My job at the paper was not the best, and there was no excitement in writing movie reviews. I wanted to be a reporter, especially one on the Beyoğlu beat, covering the consulates and hotels with notable foreign visitors. But this position in *Yeni Istanbul* was already taken. A young, darkly handsome, and rather shy fellow named Abdi Ipekçi had that beat.

So I began to look for another job and found that *Yeni Sabah* (*New Morning*), an up-and-coming morning broadsheet, was looking for such a reporter. I applied to this newspaper and was interviewed first by Safa Kılıçlıoğlu, the publisher, then by the editor-in-chief, Reşad Feyzi Yüzüncü. Contrary to well-dressed Kılıçlıoğlu's tall, trim, and handsome features and his extreme peevishness, Yüzüncü was an unpretentious fellow with short breath, a large paunch, and a puffy face. He looked and behaved like a teacher rather than a newspaper editor.

Yüzüncü's office was a cramped little place. Two men could barely fit in the tiny office beside the small, smoke-filled newsroom, where the staff members wrote their stories while sitting together at long tables. Everyone lacking a typewriter wrote longhand, while puffing evil-smelling cigarettes and sipping thick Turkish coffee from demitasses.

The older newspapermen, who had gone through school before the secular reforms, were still writing Turkish in Arabic script, which worked for them like shorthand. Their Arabic writing went to Yüzüncü and then to the composing room, where older linotype operators were able to read them and compose the texts in the Latin alphabet.

In that crowded and noisy newsroom, a tall man named Azmi Nihad was listening to news broadcasts from a Paris radio station and writing down in Arabic script whatever news he was able to pick up.

Yüzüncü, sitting by his rolltop desk and I standing by the door, reviewed my qualifications. He then hired me on the spot because he had earlier read some of my articles in *Yeni Istanbul*. My monthly salary would be one hundred Turkish liras, which at the time amounted to something like $40. This was the beginning of my real adventure in the newspaper world. Yüzüncü told me to start work at once, but he did not give me a specific assignment. He said: "Go out there and get me news stories, human-interest stories about foreigners."

He didn't say where and how I would find these stories, and I didn't ask. I was so happy to get the job that I did not want to give him the wrong impression. Excited, I left the smoke-filled newsroom and ran down the stairs. I should have remembered a story going around in Babıali in those days. Kılıçlıo lu had a bad temper and used to bring his dog, a German shepherd, to the newspaper building. One day, Alaeddin Berk, a reporter on the police beat, known as the Captain because of his rank in the army, had stepped on the dog's foot as he ran down the staircase. The dog, howling in pain, had rushed into his master's office. Kılıçlıo lu loved the dog and was very upset. He could not control his temper. He ran out of his office and shouted, "Which animal stepped on my dog's foot?"

Luckily, the German shepherd wasn't around as I rushed out of the building, hoping to meet the world and report my findings.

8

Dimo of the Pera Palace and Other Stories

A hungry bear won't dance.

Turkish proverb

*I*n order to find and interview famous and interesting foreigners, my strategy was to comb the international airport, then call Yeşilköy Airport, the port area, the railroad stations, airline offices, the press offices of the consulates, and the best hotels in the city.

In the summer of 1950, Istanbul had three of what one might call major hotels. The Konak Hotel (Tokatlıyan), although located on Istiklal Street, a busy and fashionable thoroughfare in the Beyoğlu district, was run down and had little action. The Pera Palace, with its majestic view across the Golden Horn to the old town's historic mosques, also was old but still an imposing building. It was a relic of the belle epoque, an era of elegance. It was built in 1888 with impressive marble columns inside and stood next to the old building of the US Consulate.

The Pera Palace has some historical and literary claims. Agatha Christie, the British murder mystery author, used to stay in room 411, where she wrote the book *Murder on the Orient Express*. In her memory, there is a silver plate engraved with the novelist's name on the door of 411. Agatha Christie was a regular visitor to Istanbul between 1926 and 1932. There is even a mystery about her life there. One time she had disappeared for twelve days in Istanbul without any explanation. It is believed that she stayed at a Bosphorus *yalı* belonging to Misbah Muhayyeş, at the time the eccentric owner of the Pera Palace Hotel.

The hotel owes its name to the Beyoğlu district in which it is located, known as Pera during the Ottoman Empire. It is in the European quarter across the Golden Horn from the old city. The word *pera* is derived from the Greek *peran*, meaning opposite. The Pera Palace, with its musty corridors, had been a home away from home for many international figures. They include Margaretha Zelle, the Dutch-born dancer and notorious World War I German spy, better known as Mata Hari. During World War II, the hotel was a center of activity for British espionage. A conspiracy by pro-Nazi saboteurs was exposed in March 1941 when a bomb exploded in the hotel's lobby. I remember the sensation the trial of the conspirators created during the war years. Sarah Bernhardt, Ernest Hemingway, Jacqueline Kennedy Onassis, and the Russian Communist revolutionary Leon Trotsky were among the notables who stayed at this hotel over the years.

The Pera Palace is well known for its turn-of-the-century bar on the street level, its antique chandeliers, and its slow-moving, creaking antique elevator with a decorative, wrought iron door. It was still a busy place in 1950, but the third hotel, the Park Hotel, near Taksim Square, was more fashionable and more popular.

The Park Hotel was built on a hill with an unobstructed view of the Bosphorus and the Marmara Sea. Its manager, a local Armenian named Kazas, was quite charming and a smart dresser. The front desk clerks were local Greeks who spoke foreign languages. Hanging around for a story, I got along well with all of them. Kazas was a friendly, entertaining storyteller. My favorite one was about a stunning Romanian princess and some of the details of his love affair with her.

Kazas would show me the hotel register, and I would peruse the daily guest list in order to spot a potential subject for an interview. Thus through the years, I met and interviewed many international figures, famous movie stars, writers, politicians, scientists, and international criminals. Some of the famous individuals I recall meeting include Somerset Maugham, the British author who wrote *Of Human Bondage*, who himself was also a World War I spy; James A. Michener, the prolific author of *Hawaii* and many other works; and Harold Lamb, a writer not well known today but in his time famous for his historical works on the Mogul empires of central Asia and India. One of his books was titled *Tamerlane: The Earth Shaker* and was a history of the Mongol conqueror Timur the Lame. When I met him in the Park Hotel, he was returning to the United States after a trip to Afghanistan and India to research the life of Babur the Turk or Babar. Babur the Turk was a descendant of Tamerlane and Genghiz Khan and the founder of the Indian Mogul Empire.

The late Michener liked to stay at the Park Hotel because of the hotel's spectacular view of the Bosphorus and the Marmara Sea. He was in his forties then and regularly frequented the Grand Bazaar, looking for a good deal on carpets. Michener collected Oriental rugs.

I remember the ruffled hat and the casual sport jacket worn by Robert J. Oppenheimer, along with his sharp, piercing eyes. The American physicist had led the Manhattan Project, which developed the atomic bomb in Los Alamos. Because of his left-wing friendships, he was labeled a security risk in 1954 as a result of Senator Joseph McCarthy's televised hearings. Oppenheimer always claimed that his goal was the peaceful use of atomic power.

Another man with piercing and lively eyes like Oppenheimer's was James V. Forrestal, the secretary of defense under President Harry S. Truman. President Truman had the foresight to aid Greece and Turkey in 1947 to combat Communist terrorism with the Truman Doctrine.

In those days, Yahya Kemal Beyatlı (1884–1958) was Turkey's national poet, and he used to stay at the Park Hotel, but he kept mostly to himself. Beyatlı was widely known for this poetic line: "Row gently not to awaken the moonlight."

The poet had a problem with an inguinal hernia, which had developed into a large growth that affected his walk. He would leave his room in the hotel to take a walk in the neighborhood, but it was a real struggle for the man. Often I would see him laboriously cross the hotel's lobby; I would rush to hold his arm and help him along on his walk.

Beyatlı was a gentleman with gentle manners. Often remembering his words, "Man lives in this world as long as he is able to dream," I knew that his dreams were coming to an end. He died in 1958.

In the 1950s, as a result of the Truman Doctrine and the Marshall Plan to aid Europe, the relations between the United States and Turkey were rapidly expanding. The US naval fleet visited Turkish ports regularly. Military bases and listening posts were being developed for the North Atlantic Treaty Organization (NATO) against the growing Soviet threat. One of them, the huge Incirlik Air Base near Adana in southeast Anatolia, played a vital role in the Middle East then and continues to do so now. US and British air force jets on Northern Watch, patrolling the northern no-fly zone in Iraq outside of Saddam Hussein's control to protect the Kurds, were based in Incirlik.

Turkey was experimenting with liberal economics in the early 1950s. Turkish journalism was in a highly progressive state, and fast-growing local newspapers fiercely competed with each other. *Hürriyet* was the leading national daily, and *Yeni Sabah* had high hopes of catching up with it in circulation. *Hürriyet* had its own plant, but *Yeni Sabah* did not. *Hürriyet*'s Beyoğlu reporter was Necati Zincirkıran, a fast-talking, chubby, dark, short fellow who had a funny nickname. We called him *Pıt Pıt* because of his rapid movements.

There was great admiration for America in Turkey in the 1950s, and the people had warm feelings for the visiting Americans. I remember the visit of the great battleship the USS *Missouri* when she was anchored at the Bosphorus. As journalists we were invited to tour the ship on which the Japanese had surrendered to General Douglas MacArthur, ending World War II.

One of the sailors I met aboard the USS *Missouri* was unusual in that his father had been a Turkish barber who had gone to the United States as a young man and married an American woman. The young sailor didn't speak any Turkish, and this was his first visit to the old country. I saw tears in his eyes when he talked about his father, who had died only recently.

We would see American sailors having a high old time, as sailors are wont to do, in *Abanoz*, the red-light district, and drinking beer at the lively *Çiçek Pasajı*, the Tavern of the Flower Passage.

For a long time as a cub reporter on the Beyoğlu beat, I had a problem with Dimo, the concierge, manager, and jack-of-all trades at the Pera Palace Hotel. Dimo, a local Greek and no slouch, had caught on to the competition for scoops among the reporters and figured out a way to benefit from it. A potbellied man with little hair, Dimo generally positioned himself near the reception area, which became his domain. Since he had exclusive control of the hotel's register, only he could give access to the names of the guests. Each time I asked him about important guests, Dimo would give me the same answer: "Nobody is here worth writing about." He refused to show me the hotel's guest register. I learned that Abdi Ipekçi, a competing reporter who had switched from *Yeni Istanbul* to the influential newspaper *Milliyet*, was somehow gaining a lot of information from the same hotel.

One day I confronted Dimo with this knowledge. Well, he said, Abdi Ipekçi is good to me. "How is he good to you?" I asked. Dimo pointed to the pastry store across the road and said, "He buys cakes for me from that pastry shop, so I let him see the guest book."

From then on I also started sending the valets of the Pera Palace to the pastry store to satisfy Dimo's sweet tooth. Other reporters, no doubt, figured out how to compete in this arena and eventually, like me, caught on to the trick of making Dimo give up his secrets. Just scanning the hotel register was not good enough, however. As a reporter, you had to know and recognize the names listed. One way to achieve a general knowledge about who was who in the world was to read local and foreign newspapers, magazines, and books.

The cost of the cakes Dimo ate came out of my pocket because the Armenian accountant of *Yeni Sabah* would not accept them as legitimate expenses. "How do I know you didn't eat the cakes yourself," he told me. The man was a real miser with the newspaper's money. Once I was sent to Athens on assignment for a single day, and he refused to pay me for the taxi fare to the Hellenikon Airport from Omonoia Square in Athens. "Why didn't you take the bus?" he asked. Trying to explain to him that I had to catch a plane to Istanbul before press time was a waste of time.

During my rounds as a cub reporter on Istanbul's hotel circuit, I kept meeting many unusual men and women. Colonel Robert R. McCormick, the bombastic publisher-editor of the *Chicago Tribune*, impressed me as a forceful and fearless journalist. McCormick knew that journalism was about the news.

Among my rivals on the Beyoğlu beat were the sons of close associates of Mustafa Kemal Atatürk. Nuyan Yiğit's and Altemur Kılıç's fathers had played distinguished roles during Turkey's War of Independence, the establishment of the secular republic, and the reform years. Nuyan's father was Ibrahim Süreyya Yiğit, who, beginning with the north African campaign in Tripoli against the invading Italians, had been with Atatürk for thirty years. Ibrahim Süreyya Yiğit first met Mustafa Kemal in 1909 in the small town of Yenice in Bulgaria, where he was the *kaymakam* (head Ottoman official in town). One cold winter when the snowfall was heavy, Mustafa Kemal, accompanied by an aide, rode his horse into town. Looking for shelter for the night, he threw snowballs at the windows of the government house, waking up Nuyan's father, who was a young man at the time. They kept each other company that night by sharing a half-empty bottle of *rakı*. Food, like everything else in the collapsing Ottoman Empire, was scarce. According to Nuyan Yiğit's book *Thirty Years with Atatürk*, published in Istanbul in 2004, that meeting was the beginning of a lifelong friendship.

Altemur's father was Kılıç Ali (Ali the Sword), whose guerrillas had fought against French forces in eastern Cilicia* in the early days of the War of Independence. Both Ali the Sword and Ibrahim Süreyya remained loyal supporters and confidants of Atatürk until his death in 1938.

The early 1950s were a time when Turkey, under the Democratic Party regime of Adnan Menderes, was experimenting with the notion of freedom of the press. Yet we were still highly concerned about official reaction to our reports on sensitive subjects. There were events we could

---

* Cilicia is the ancient district of southeastern Anatolia by the shores of the Mediterranean. The Taurus mountain range in the north and west and the Anti-Taurus in the east bound the region. Cilicia was a Roman province in the first century BCE. In 1515 it fell to Ottoman Turks and was occupied by the French during World War I. Severe Turkish resistance forced the French to leave the area in 1921.

not report—for instance, one involving Sukarno, Indonesia's first president. Sukarno had been the architect of his country's independence movement, *merdeka*, against the Dutch.

Sukarno had replaced Indonesia's parliamentary system with his own system of a "guided democracy." A Muslim, he was known in his country as *Djago*, the Rooster, because of his radiant personality and sexual prowess. Istanbul's upscale madam in those days was a young, notorious blonde named Benli Belkis (Belkis with the Mole). A black mole on Belkis's cheek enhanced her beauty. We used to see Benli Belkis often in luxury hotels. She was a resourceful woman. Once while visiting London, Benli Belkis introduced herself to British journalists as Turkey's most famous movie star. A London tabloid published a story about this "famous movie star" with her picture.

Sukarno, while on a state visit, had requested female company from the Turkish officials. A young woman was introduced to him with Benli Belkis's help. Unfortunately, this woman was infected with venereal disease before her encounter with the distinguished guest. There followed a big official fuss and a search for a scapegoat, and Benli Belkis was dispatched to jail on charges of promoting prostitution.

Another colorful individual of those days was known as Ingiliz Kemal because he looked like an Englishman. As a tour guide, Ingiliz Kemal had lots of stories to tell. They were about his adventures during World War I as a young agent of the *Teşkilatı Mahsusa* (the Ottoman Intelligence Service). Enver Pasha had established this spy organization in August 1914 and named it the Special Service.

Ingiliz Kemal's best stories were about his encounters with Thomas Edward Lawrence, better known as Lawrence of Arabia, and how Ingiliz passed himself off as an Englishman while tracking down Lawrence in order to assassinate him. Ingiliz Kemal published books about his incredible adventures, one of which was titled *Ingiliz Kemal against Lawrence*, which was made into a movie.

For John Hyde, the information officer at the British Consulate, any mention of Ingiliz Kemal's adventures was an opportunity for a bellyful of laughs. Hyde, who spoke excellent Turkish, didn't believe Ingiliz

Kemal's stories about Lawrence of Arabia. He was sure they were all the idle talk of a braggart.

Ingiliz Kemal was an older, heavyset man, small in stature, with thinning, natural blond hair. A bulbous nose stood out prominently on a pinkish face with green-blue eyes. He could have passed as an Englishman if he had kept his mouth shut. His English betrayed a heavy accent.

Ingiliz Kemal's real name was Ahmet Esat Tomruk. Born in Istanbul in 1887, Tomruk was orphaned at the age of five. His uncle adopted and educated him. While Tomruk was a student at the Galatasaray High School, the agents of Sultan Abdul Hamid II arrested him. He was blamed for frequent trips to the post office to mail postcards to his friends. Accused of treason, he escaped and ended up as stowaway aboard a British ship, whose captain adopted him. In England, he became a boxer. He returned to Turkey before World War I, fought in Gallipoli against the British, joined the intelligence agency, and served the nationalists in Anatolia during the War of Independence. He died in 1966.

I always listened with interest to his stories told in the lobby of the Park Hotel. Ingiliz Kemal, according to his stories, had done his best to stop Lawrence's guerrilla campaign against the Turkish rail supply lines in the Hejaz. He also had allegedly tried to prevent the capture of Damascus in 1918 by Lawrence and the Arab forces that were receiving aid from Prince Faisal, the father of King Faisal II of Iraq.

Ingiliz Kemal told me one day that Lawrence of Arabia was a liar and a self-promoter, a vain individual. "Lawrence was deceitful about Governor Nahi," he said. "He invented the brutal homosexual rape. Nahi Bey had captured Lawrence in Arab dress briefly in November 1917 in Deraa. I personally knew Nahi as a family man. That officer had no interest in homosexual relationships.

"Actually, Lawrence himself was a homosexual, and Nahi Bey, the Turkish officer, became the scapegoat to explain his homosexual life. In his book *Seven Pillars of Wisdom*, Lawrence wrote that the citadel of his integrity had been irrevocably lost, while he was Nahi Bey's prisoner. Give me a break! The man was an incredible liar."

Ingiliz Kemal said that as a young boy Lawrence had received painful beatings from his mother. Because of these beatings, he said, Lawrence became a sadist. He held Lawrence responsible for the Arabs' slaughter of a Turkish column at Tafas in September 1918 and the massacre of Turkish and German prisoners of war. Ingiliz Kemal said, "Lawrence of Arabia was a psychological basket case, a sadistic, grossly ruthless person. The brutal beatings he had received as a boy from his domineering mother caused him to become a cruel man."

Ingiliz Kemal kept a sharp eye out for wealthy tourists while telling stories in the lobby of the Park Hotel. He would abruptly cut them short to chase a prospective customer. He was happy in those days, as a bigger and most luxurious hotel was soon coming to town. The reporters were also excited about it. Abdi Ipekçi, Ilhan Turalı, and I met American hotel tycoon Conrad Hilton at Yeşilköy airport, and he confirmed the big news. When the high-rise building was completed and the Istanbul Hilton had its opening ceremony, we met a number of celebrities whom Conrad Hilton had brought to town.

One of them was Terry Moore, the stunningly beautiful and delightfully coquettish young Hollywood actress. Because she was so attractive, all the male reporters were trying their best to be noticed by her. I danced with this enchantress during the Hilton's celebrations. I danced with her, but someone else stole the show.

Abdi Ipekçi, who was a secretive reporter always chasing scoops, had somehow managed to create a situation during the day. He helped *Milliyet*'s photographer Ilhan Demirel get an unusual shot of Terry Moore. I remember it so well: Terry Moore near the swimming pool of Istanbul Hilton, sitting in *Playboy*-style pose with that mischievous smile on her face. The trouble was that her skirt did not cover what it was supposed to cover, and she allegedly had on no underwear. *Milliyet* published this picture on its front page the next morning with a minor retouch, and my boss Safa Kılıçlıoğlu hit the roof.

"How did you bunch of fools miss such a juicy photograph?" he kept yelling. "Were you all asleep?" Why wasn't I present with our own photographer when the Hollywood actress bared her bottom, he wanted to know.

Kılıçlıoğlu had a long memory, along with a tongue as sharp as barbed wire. Original news photographs always caused him much grief when they were printed in rival newspapers. He was upset when the United Press International (UPI), started an exclusive picture service to *Hürriyet*, including, for the first time, direct telephoto transmissions from London of pictures relating to international events. The telephoto, the predecessor of today's fax and Internet transmission of digital photography, presented *Hürriyet* with vital supremacy over all other newspapers.

We tried to catch up to *Hürriyet* with exclusive stories and news pictures. One evening we learned from an agency report that a professor from the University of Istanbul had been killed along with his wife in a car accident at the Cote D'Azur. The night editor told Kılıçlıoğlu that he wanted to give wide coverage to the story by obtaining pictures of the accident victims. Our boss answered, "Forget it. The sex life of that woman extends from here to the Cote D'Azur."

And that was that.

Another story I remember well about Kılıçlıoğlu involves the beautiful wife of a second university professor. We knew that this professor's wife had a relationship with our boss. One day, upset with the professor, Kılıçlıoğlu sent him a letter in which he wrote: "If half of your wife is yours, the other half belongs to me." In the end, she took off for America, leaving both her husband and lover behind.

Yeni Sabah, reflecting the character of its publisher, was a notoriously aggressive and conservative newspaper. There was talk about Safa Kılıçlıoğlu's fortunes. Once he had worked for a thread merchant. The merchant was a tax evader, and Kılıçlıoğlu allegedly reported him to the Turkish Internal Revenue Service and collected a reward. That reward money was the financial source of *Yeni Sabah*.

In its early days, the newspaper lacked a printing press but owned a couple of linotypes above the newsroom. The linotypes produced lines of type in solid metal for the compositors. Then the heavy metal pages were carried on the backs of porters almost a mile down the steep hill of Babıali to the plant of the newspaper *Tan* in Sirkeci. One rainy night, a porter slipped and fell, completely destroying the front page. The page had to be redone, thus causing delays in the morning distribution.

Kılıçlıoğlu's biggest ambition in life was to catch up with *Hürriyet* and become the owner of the leading national daily with the largest circulation. One of his quirks, which seasoned colleagues had already warned me about, was his habit of sending reporters abroad on assignments with one-way airline tickets only. He would leave them stranded if they failed in their assignments. The story of the correspondent who had been sent to Tel Aviv without a return ticket was common knowledge in the press district. The correspondent failed in his job and was promptly fired on the spot by cable. The man, lacking funds, had to return to Istanbul aboard a tramp steamer, shoveling coal in the ship's boiler room.

One day we received a telegram from Alaeddin Berk, our police reporter, who had been promoted to war correspondent in Korea. The telegram informed Yüzüncü, the editor-in-chief, about a series of photographs from the war. These were pictures of Turkish troops in battle and were being carried by a passenger aboard a Pan-Am flight. Yüzüncü ordered me to go to the airport and collect the package from the passenger as soon as the plane arrived and rush back to the newspaper. Before I left, one more telegram arrived from Berk. Yüzüncü told me, "Don't go to the airport because the package is not on that plane."

So I didn't, and the next day my world came tumbling down when a rival newspaper printed the war photographs. Faruk Fenik, the old newspaper *Cumhuriyet's* correspondent in Korea, having learned about our man's shipment, had wired the second telegram to *Yeni Sabah* in order to hoodwink our editor. At the same time, he also informed *Cumhuriyet's* editor about what he had done. Thus the package had been picked up at the airport by someone claiming to be from our paper. In later years that someone would become a friend. His name was Zeyyat Gören, who at the time worked for *Cumhuriyet* and also reported to UPI.

There was hell to pay that day in the editorial rooms of *Yeni Sabah*, for these pictures were the first ones to arrive from the Korean War zone. Safa Kılıçlıoğlu yelled his head off; Yüzüncü kept a low profile in his little office; and I tried to be invisible in my corner. There is a Turkish saying for such occasions: "If the blame were a sable coat, no one would wear it."

Anything was fair game for a scoop, including snatching the competitor's photographs. As reporters we constantly played dirty tricks on each other for the sake of grabbing a hot story. One of them was to collect all available pictures of someone involved in breaking news, leaving nothing useful for one's rivals. We would do everything imaginable to make sure the news was exclusive so that our own paper could dominate the subject.

Shortly after the Chinese crossed the Yalu River, wounded soldiers began arriving back from the war zone in Korea. We would wait at the airport for the planes to arrive, interview as many wounded soldiers as we could, and rush to write our stories. The Korean War stories boosted the circulation so much that Haldun Simavi, the publisher of *Hürriyet*, years later would tell me, "We felt the breath of *Yeni Sabah* on our necks."

Yeni Sabah began rolling in money, and the publisher built a large, modern newspaper building across from *Cumhuriyet*'s old headquarters. He bought a new Frankenthal, a German press capable of printing a hundred thousand newspapers in record time. For the first time, we had an organized archive or morgue for the news photographs, a radio listening room with a tape recorder, and a larger and brighter newsroom. The newspapers still did not have telexes and were receiving copies of pages of news from the Associated Press and the semiofficial Anatolian News Agency, delivered by messengers. We had one big, black, ancient Remington typewriter in our newsroom, and the reporters took turns using it. The old-timers still preferred to write their stories in longhand and in Arabic script. The makeup of *Yeni Sabah* also had changed for the better, and new linotype machines produced improved, easier-to-read Latin script.

At about this time, I met Elia Kazan, the American stage and film director whose credits include *On the Waterfront*, *A Streetcar Named Desire*, and *Cat on a Hot Tin Roof*. The son of a Greek rug merchant, Elia Kazan was born in Istanbul on September 7, 1909. His father's second name was Kazancıoğlu, meaning the son of a maker of cauldrons. The family emigrated to New York when Elia was four and changed their name to Kazan, the cauldron.

Elia Kazan was a former Communist Party member who named names before the House Committee on Un-American Activities during the 1950s. I invited him and his wife to the new newspaper building.

Kazan saw the Remington typewriter in our newsroom and said it was a museum piece. Later, I overheard his wife whispering into his ear, "Why don't you take this Young Turk to Hollywood and make him a movie star." Kazan whispered back, "Too bad he is so short."

Well, I was not tall, nor did I have the talent to be a movie actor. This unintentionally overheard exchange hurt my pride, but I consoled myself with the observation that Kazan was even shorter and smaller than I. Because of his short stature he was nicknamed at the Williams College Gadge, short for Gadget. Elia Kazan died in New York on September 28, 2003, at ninety-four.

As time went on, competition between the newspapers became even more fierce, causing much stress in *Yeni Sabah*'s offices. When we missed a major story, which was often enough, Safa Kılıçlıoğlu, who suffered from a back problem, would dress us down in very colorful language. Yet he was a religious man and read the Qur'an regularly. Kılıçlıoğlu used to tell me that at home, when he read the Qur'an aloud, his canaries would sing and accompany his prayers.

The publisher had made the top floor of his new building his penthouse office. The penthouse had a beautiful view of the Bosphorus. He furnished his new office and hired a cook-butler to prepare his lunches. The penthouse door now displayed two light bulbs, one red and one green. When summoned, you had to wait if the red light was on and could go in when the green light came on.

I was summoned there once for a picture that appeared in the newspaper. The photograph showed me interviewing Hulusi Fuat Tugay, the Turkish ambassador to Cairo, who in 1954 had been declared persona non grata by the Egyptian government. Tugay had protested Egypt's land policy since it adversely affected his own Egyptian land holdings along with those of other Turks. Tugay, whose wife was a member of the deposed Egyptian royal family, had an argument with Gamal Abdul Nasser during a reception at the Opera House in Cairo. I had been photographed while interviewing him with my left hand in my trouser pocket, which, according to an old tradition, is considered insulting. By putting my hand in my pocket, the publisher claimed, I had been disrespectful to the ambassador. This was the reason for my summons and his petty lecture to me on the subject of polite behavior.

No one was allowed to use the beautiful main door of *Yeni Sabah's* new building but the publisher himself and his guests. Everybody else had to use the small, unimpressive side door.

Trying to find ways to boost the circulation and thereby to increase the advertising revenues critical to the paper's survival, Kılıçlıoğlu had acquired the services of Esat Mahmut Karakurt, the famous Turkish author of some romance novels with titles like *Blossoming Plum Trees*. The author was also a teacher of Turkish studies at the Galatasaray High School, where instruction was basically in French.

Esat Mahmut Karakurt, a tall, handsome man, used to collect large royalties for the right to serialize his novels in the newspaper, due to his loyal following of housewives. He had a habit of creating the beginning of an exciting scene at the end of each daily episode in order to capture readers' attention and make them buy the newspaper again next day. The hero or the lover of his novels was always modeled after himself. One of Karakurt's novels, *I Loved a Wild Girl*, was about a Kurdish uprising in eastern Anatolia during the rule of Atatürk. As a newspaper reporter, he had been assigned to cover the Kurdish revolt and had gained first-hand experience. The novel was about a love affair between a young Turkish army officer and a beautiful but wild Kurdish woman guerrilla fighter in the mountains.

Since our major rival *Hürriyet* was sending Hikmet Feridun Es, another famous writer, and his photojournalist wife, Semiha, on assignments to exotic countries to write human interest and pictorial travel features, Kılıçlıoğlu decided to trump this with an even better idea, namely, to dispatch Karakurt to the north and south poles. For days he had huge posters hung all over the city, displaying a giant question mark hiding the supposed great mystery. Finally, the question mark was removed and the serialization of the story began.

It was a big flop, for there was no challenge, no adventure, and no interesting photography in Karakurt's stories. This failure disappointed *Yeni Sabah's* publisher, yet his ambition to come up with a big adventure story to clobber the major rival *Hürriyet* did not end.

The Little Governor and Robinson Crusoe

A speaker of the truth is kicked out of nine villages.

Turkish proverb

I first got in trouble with the regime of Adnan Menderes in 1951, during the mass expulsions of ethnic Turks from Bulgaria by Todor Zhivkov, the Bulgarian Communist Party leader and the head of state. Also I was instrumental in creating serious problems for Professor Fahrettin Kerim Gökay, the governor of Istanbul.

A tiny man and a doctor of medicine, Gökay was generally well liked because of his involvement in civic activities such as the *Yeşilay*, the Turkish equivalent of Alcoholics Anonymous. Gökay did his best as governor to aid the poor. He helped to develop cordial relations with Greece by treating the Greek minority in Istanbul well. As reporters, we often used to see Athenagoras, the Patriarch of the Greek Orthodox Church, at the little governor's office having a friendly chat with Gökay. Patriarch Athenagoras was a big man with a long beard. Side by side, the governor and the patriarch presented an amusing sight.

Patriarch Athenagoras's original name was Aristokles Spyrou. He had earlier been the archbishop of the Greek Orthodox Church of North and South America. When he was elected patriarch in 1948, he arrived in Istanbul from the United States and received a warm welcome. The son of a physician, he had attended as a young man the former Greek Orthodox Seminary on Heybeli Island in the Marmara Sea off Istanbul.

Patriarch Athenagoras became known as the Orthodox leader who for the first time in 525 years conferred with the Roman Catholic Church. This happened in Jerusalem in 1964, when Athenagoras met Pope Paul VI and agreed to a revocation of the mutual excommunication degrees of 1054. The Great Schism of that year had split Christianity into the Roman Catholic and Orthodox branches because of cultural and political differences. Due to the Great Schism, there had been no meetings between the two churches since 1439.

Athenagoras died in Istanbul in 1972 at the age of eighty-six, having seen the deterioration of the Turco-Greek relationship because of the Cyprus crisis. Early in the 1950s, we used to cover his activities and report them regularly in the newspapers.

I remember a little verse about Governor Gökay, "Mini mini Valimiz, Ne olacak halimiz?" which means, "Oh, our tiny little Governor/Whatever's to become of us?"

Gökay became the champion of the have-nots and declared war on the neighborhood grocery stores that controlled food prices. He brought the Swiss grocery chain Migros to Istanbul. Soon Migros supermarkets opened up all over the city, angering the local grocers. But people were very happy with the lower food prices. Migros Türk AS is now Turkey's leading supermarket chain, with 240 retail outlets there having Swiss franchise rights. This company also has two retail stores in Moscow; five in Baku, Azerbaijan; and one in Almaty, Kazakhstan, and is still expanding in the Balkans, in Russia, and in central Asia.

Turkish-Bulgarian relations became strained in 1951 because of Zhivkov's policies toward Turkey and his treatment of the ethnic Turks in Bulgaria. These ethnic Turks were the descendants of early settlers from the Ottoman Empire and through the centuries retained their Turkish character and traditions. Zhivkov's regime tried to forcibly assimilate them, making it mandatory for ethnic Turks to assume Christian Bulgarian names. That caused an exodus of ethnic Turks, who flocked into Turkey with kith and kin.

In the summer of 1989, Zhivkov's policy of Bulgarization again caused tremendous problems for Turkey when 330,000 refugees poured into the country. These refugees, accustomed to the social benefits of Communism, could not adjust to their new lives in a democracy, where the state did not totally provide for them. Many ended up going back to Bulgaria. They were not happy there either and once again returned to Turkey. Presently there are about 860,000 ethnic Turks in Bulgaria, about 10 percent of that country's population.

The Bulgarians had a notorious ambassador in Ankara who was named Chobanov. He used to behave more like an agent of the Darzhavna Sigurnost (DS), Bulgaria's Secret Service, than as an envoy. Our persistent reports about his daily activities used to annoy Chobanov, whose name derives from the Turkish word *çoban*, meaning shepherd. One day while leaving Istanbul's Sirkeci railroad station for Sofia, Chobanov spotted us, a group of reporters, standing on the platform next to the window of his railroad car. He angrily stared at us and then directly locked eyes with Abdi Ipekçi and made the vulgar sign of the *mucuk*, the Turkish equivalent of "up yours." When Abdi Ipekçi, as editor-in-chief of *Milliyet*, was shot and killed in Istanbul in February 1979, allegedly by the terrorist Mehmet Ali Ağca, I suspected that the Bulgarian Secret Service might have been involved in his murder.

As relations with the Zhivkov regime further deteriorated in 1951, the flow of Turks expelled from Bulgaria swelled, and the little governor faced a dilemma: how and where to shelter the refugees who kept arriving by the trainloads?

There were some old military barracks in the shadow of the Old Seraglio in Ahırkapı district, where the refugees eventually were housed. When Governor Gökay went to inspect the living conditions of the refugees in those barracks, I happened to hear what he said to the organizers. Gökay took one look at the poor conditions and said, "Even dogs wouldn't stay here if you tied them up." I reported his words promptly, and *Yeni Sabah* printed them on its front page.

The next day there was hell to pay. Prime Minister Adnan Menderes was furious. Concerned about the image of his administration, Menderes, a wealthy landowner from Aydın in the Aegean region, ordered Gökay to deny the report. Even under tremendous pressure from the regime, Governor Gökay stood by his words and refused the prime minister's order. Later, when he was quietly sent away as ambassador to Switzerland, I visited him in Bern, and he invited me to dinner at the embassy. He had no hard feelings toward me, Gökay told me during the dinner. "You were doing your job," he said. "For me to deny what I said would have been improper."

Since my return from England, the Turkish draft board had been warning me regularly that my obligatory military service was long overdue. Finally, I was drafted and shipped to the Reserve Officers Academy in Ankara. After graduating as a second lieutenant, I was posted as English language interpreter to the Turkish Army Staff Officers' Academy in Istanbul. This academy is located on the grounds of Yıldız (Star) Palace, the residence of the notorious despot Sultan Abdul Hamid II, who in 1908 was forced by the Young Turks to restore the constitutional government and was deposed one year later. This sultan was so afraid of an assassination that he used to fire his pistol at shadows in the palace. A few young concubines happened to come into harm's way and were killed on some of those occasions. The despot depended on a vast network of spies. Called the *curnalcı*, they were notorious knaves who reported even on each other to their master on such unspectacular events as visits to a friend's home. The French statesman and journalist Georges Clemenceau, also called the Tiger, once called Abdul Hamid II "that monster of Yıldız, the blood-red Sultan."

Since *Yeni Sabah* was still paying my salary each month as a courtesy, I started working for the newspaper at night, when I was off duty, helping to edit the foreign news. The editor-in-chief of *Yeni Sabah* at the time was a man who preferred to have nothing to do with journalism. Instead of editing the newspaper, he would sleep in his room. One night,

Reşad Mahmut Yanardağ, a night editor, fed up with this aggravation, called the publisher about the sleeping beauty. Kılıçlıoğlu arrived and found the guy sound asleep but did not wake him up. The next morning, the man was fired.

It took me years to receive a promotion at the newspaper. I was appointed chief news editor of *Yeni Sabah* a few years after I was discharged from the army. Apart from editing the news, my job included giving the reporters their daily assignments. However, coming up with creative ideas for lively news coverage in order to boost the circulation was my most important challenge.

The lazy days of summer months following the Korean War were tough for Istanbul's daily newspapers because usually nothing exciting was happening. People flocked to the beaches and did not read newspapers. *Yeni Sabah*'s editor-in-chief then was Osman Karaca, a tall, young fellow. One morning during an editorial meeting, Karaca complained about the current uneventful days. "We need some excitement," he said. "We have a problem with the circulation, and we need to boost it and attract more advertising revenue. Can't any one of you think of something original, which would really get the readers' attention?"

The idea came to my mind that perhaps we could develop our own events or happenings. We could somehow create our own news that would be of great interest to the public. I immediately thought of the book titled *Seven Pillars of Wisdom* by T. E. Lawrence. This book, due to its contents, had not been published in Turkey, and many people were not even aware of its existence. How would it look if we bought the rights for this book and translated it and serialized its contents in the paper with an ingenious advertising campaign? It would be sensational and it would definitely boost the circulation. What if Lawrence's anti-Turkish attitude and writings caused an unfavorable reaction from the public? What if the rival papers took this as an opportunity to criticize us for printing such an anti-Turkish book by Lawrence of Arabia? We could easily lose a lot of circulation instead of boosting it. I gave up that idea rather quickly.

Something else popped into my mind, and when it did, it sparkled like fireworks. This was not an original idea of mine, but it was something that had never been tried in Turkey before. It was simple and related to summertime and it greatly appealed to people who loved to read adventure stories. If well planned, this event could draw hoards of readers.

It was similar to the idea of *Survivor* that was used so successfully in the United States in 2000 to attract TV viewers.

"Let's suppose that we put someone on Sivri Island," I said, getting a little excited as I began to formulate the idea, "without food or water, like a modern-day Robinson Crusoe. We give him a fishing line, a single hook, and only one box of matches. How about a castaway on a barren island? It would be interesting to see how long a person could survive under those conditions."

We decided to have it last seven days and seven nights. We would keep our reporters and photographers around the island on boats and report everything. How that person survives and what he does would be the essence of the story.

The Island of Sivri is a waterless, pointed rock in the Sea of Marmara, uninhabited and barren except for a few wild fig trees. It belongs to a group of islands called the Princes Islands, also known as Red Islands, because of the sparse red soil of the two larger ones, Büyük Ada and Heybeli. During Byzantine times, Sivri Island, like Heybeli, had been used to banish undesirable people. Twice in history Sivri Island was also used as a place to exile thousands of stray dogs from the streets of Istanbul. Stories have been told that some of these dogs were able to swim back to the city, braving the distance and the swift currents of the Sea of Marmara.

The Turks throughout their history never liked to kill stray cats and dogs. Somehow nobody seemed to give a thought as to whether it were cruel to exile the dogs on a barren rock, where there was no food, where they would eat each other and finally starve to death. Under Sultan Mahmud II (1785–1839), whose military and administrative reforms helped to consolidate the Ottoman Empire despite a string of military defeats and separatist revolts, one of these historic banishments of stray dogs is recorded.

In 1918 Sivri Island gained notoriety again when the stray dogs of Istanbul were rounded up, transported by tramp steamer, and banished there. It is said that the sounds of the howling of thousands of dogs could be heard daily in the city. By one estimate, there were about 150,000 street dogs in Istanbul at the end of the nineteenth century. Erol Çakır, the governor of the city, in December 1999 warned of a rabies threat from the dogs.

Karaca liked the idea of a modern-day Robinson Crusoe. We made preparations and in a few days announced our plan on the front page. The response from the public was tremendous, human psychology being what it is. In most people's hearts, there is a love of adventure and a childhood dream of being a Tarzan or a Jane.

We selected a young man from among the applicants because he was big and seemed physically fit enough for this arduous experiment on a snake-ridden barren island with no water or shelter. He survived only one night there and at dawn the next morning begged to be taken out. The cries of the seagulls, the snakes crawling and hissing between the rocks, and the eerie darkness of the night scared the wits out of him. Inexperienced in survival techniques, he was hungry and very thirsty. The reporters, led by Ilhan Turalı on round-the-clock assignment aboard a boat off the island, took him back to the city. We reported on his experience the next day with photographs, and this boosted public interest.

There were no women applicants, and the second young man we selected also did not last long on the island. By that time, there was keen interest in the story as people wondered how this adventure was going to end.

The third man we selected, named Nejat Tözge, was obstinate and wouldn't give up. He caught fish, cooked them with brushwood fire, and ate wild figs and roots to quench his thirst, staying on the island the full seven days and seven nights. As the end of the allotted time was nearing, we announced the day and time of Robinson Crusoe's arrival at Sarayburnu, the Seraglio Point, which juts out into the Bosphorus from Gülhane Park on the European side of the city. The place is called Seraglio Point because it is located near Topkapı Palace, the Old Seraglio, the palace of the Ottoman sultans, now a museum.

I had assigned several reporters and photographers to cover the event there, where a welcoming committee that included the mayor of Istanbul was waiting for the arrival of the survivor. I told Jacket Osman, one of the photographers, to climb a tall tree nearby and take some bird's-eye-view pictures that would show the huge crowd. (We called him Jacket Osman because he preferred to wear long coats despite his short stature.)

Even though we, of course, had hoped for a considerable stir, the tremendous public enthusiasm for the event surprised me greatly. Thousands of people came to see the welcoming ceremony, and Jacket Osman climbed the tree with his camera. The mayor, welcoming the modern-day Robinson Crusoe, declared him a hero and made a speech. Nejat Tözge, looking perfectly healthy, was presented with gifts and flowers and was proud of the outcome. After the ceremony was completed and the crowd dispersed, we all went back to the newspaper building. Jacket Osman, with great excitement, headed to a dark room to develop his film.

I climbed the circular staircase and went to my office. There was the smell of printing ink in the air and the drone of the giant rotary press, printing the Sunday supplement one floor below. Jacket Osman entered my office with a sullen face and gave me a big shock. "Chief," he said, "the film came out blank. Sorry."

We had missed the best shots that could have shown the enormous crowd welcoming our own Robinson Crusoe. Other photographs and the story saved the day. Kılıçlıoğlu, true to his form, yelled from the penthouse at the top of the staircase: "Fire that photojournalist! What he has done is unforgivable. This is crazy. We spent a fortune with Karakurt for the north and south poles story and got nowhere. A nutty idea like this boosts the circulation, and this photographer comes and shits into a sack of figs. Fire him!"

I didn't fire Jacket Osman. I told him to keep a low profile for a few days. Kılıçlıoğlu presented me with a bonus of three hundred liras, about $120 at the time.

This happened over 235 years after Daniel Defoe, the father of the English novel, had written *Robinson Crusoe* in 1719, partly drawing from the experiences of Scottish sailor Alexander Selkirk. Eight years before Daniel Defoe's *Robinson Crusoe* was published, Simon Ockley, a professor of Arabic at Cambridge University, had translated and published in England a book written by an Arab writer named Ibn Tufayl. That book told the story of the life and times of a man living alone on a desert island.

The next summer, however, the rival newspaper *Tercüman (Interpreter)* was quick to grab our story and repeat the adventure on the same island. *Tercüman* too gained circulation through this event and later found a woman who was willing to live like Robinson Crusoe. There was talk at the time in Babıali that local fishermen were secretly visiting the woman and supplying her with food.

Jacket Osman was a creative photo reporter. Once, during one of our more difficult assignments together as cub reporters, he surprised a mysterious character, codenamed Cicero, with his flashlight and shot a rare photograph of the man.

10

Five Fingers Cicero

Ask an Albanian, "Would you like to go to hell?"
And he will tell you: "What is the pay?"

Turkish proverb

While I was still a cub reporter, Muzaffer Kayar, the chief news editor of *Yeni Sabah,* assigned me to research the notorious World War II spy Cicero, to find his address, and to interview him. Later on I was told to cover the court action initiated against him by some merchants, concerning a considerable amount of counterfeit pounds sterling.

From my sources I had learned that Cicero lived at three different addresses in Istanbul. There was even a wild rumor that he kept three women. At any rate, it was difficult in 1950 to find out where and with whom Cicero lived because the man was extremely secretive. He was concerned that British intelligence might still be after him to kill him for his activities during the war.

Finally, I managed to uncover the spy's address in Aksaray, a huge district in the European part of Istanbul, where he lived in obscurity with his family. I went there and knocked at his door on the second floor of an apartment building. A woman appeared, and I assumed that she was Mrs. Bazna.

"May I speak with Mr. Bazna?" I asked. "I am from the newspaper *Yeni Sabah*, and I have an important message for your husband."

"No, you may not speak with him," she answered. "He does not want to speak with you or anyone else. We know what you are after, so please leave. We don't want any trouble, we already have enough of it. Just go away."

During those years, I was an aggressive reporter and would try to do my best to get the story I was assigned to cover. So I didn't give up just because I was refused entry to Bazna's apartment. I began hanging around in the neighborhood, hoping for a chance to catch him and interview him outside.

Cicero's name was given as either Elyesa or Eliyas Bazna. It was actually spelled Ilyas, which is a Turkish name. The first time I met him, his right hand shot up and he attempted to cover his face with his five fingers. He had noticed Jacket Osman, our photojournalist, and he did not like to be photographed. It was a pose that suited him rather well, since Bazna was also known as "Five Fingers Cicero."

He was a short, thickset, swarthy man with dark, shrewd eyes whose favorite color was black—black suits, black overcoats, black hats, and black shoes. On that day, he wore a black overcoat and a black hat, which was pulled down over his forehead, obscuring his face. We had surprised the spy with a powerful flashlight on the staircase of his apartment building.

That initial interview happened about seven years after Elyesa Bazna, a Turkish citizen of Albanian origin, began his astonishing but short career as a spy for Adolf Hitler's Nazi Germany. In October 1943, Bazna had gone to the German Embassy in Ankara, the Turkish capital, in the middle of the night, offering top-secret Allied documents. His price was twenty thousand pounds sterling for the first two rolls of film, a fortune to the man who worked as a valet to the British ambassador in Ankara, Sir Hughe Montgomery Knatchbull-Hugessen. The Germans would have to pay fifteen thousand pounds sterling for each roll of film thereafter, he told them. Bazna's films contained pictures of extremely sensitive Allied documents, stolen from the British ambassador's personal safe and black boxes at his residence. The secret contents of Sir Hughe's dispatch box were also on offer.

The spy was photographing the secret Allied documents even inside the British ambassador's bedroom while Sir Hughe slept, having taken sleeping pills.

Amazed at this serendipitous offer of a potentially huge trove of secret intelligence, the German ambassador, Franz von Papen, dispatched an urgent message to Foreign Minister Joachim von Ribbentrop in Berlin, asking for permission to accept. Berlin, eager to see the documents, forwarded bundles of crisp new ten-, twenty-, and fifty-pound sterling notes by courier, and shortly thereafter the wheels of one of World War II's most incredible espionage operations began to turn.

The Germans referred to this extraordinary spy case by the name Operation Cicero. In order to steal the documents, Bazna, now code-named Cicero by the Germans, had a wax impression made of the key to the British ambassador's safe. The Germans dispatched the wax impression to Berlin, where a better key was made, which perfectly fit the British ambassador's safe.

When Sir Hughe was present, the valet would entertain him by singing arias from well-known Italian operas. While Sir Hughe was away or sleeping, the valet would open the safe and the boxes and photograph their secrets with his camera. The Germans later provided him with a better camera, a Leica. Through Cicero, the Germans learned of important decisions as well as major Allied troop movements and landings and read the top-secret correspondence of the Allied leaders. These included the code word *Overlord*, for the planned invasion of Normandy on D-Day, June 6, 1944.

Ironically, von Ribbentrop, who examined the stolen documents personally, and Adolf Hitler refused to believe that the papers were authentic. They thought the papers seemed too good to be credible. The Germans believed Bazna was a plant used by MI6, the British Secret Intelligence Service, in a game of deception to mislead them. Yet it was not a deception. The secret papers Cicero had supplied to the Germans were genuine and highly valuable.

By the time I met Bazna, Ludwig C. Moyzisch, the German attaché in wartime Ankara who had been the spy's controller, had already exposed him. In 1950 Moyzisch's book *Operation Cicero* disclosed the full details of the stolen secrets. British Foreign Secretary Ernest Bevin had admitted in October 1950 that during the war highly sensitive documents had been lost to the Germans, through a lack of security at the British embassy in Ankara. In 1952 Moyzisch's book was made into a movie called *Five Fingers*, with James Mason as Bazna in the leading role, which was directed by Joseph Mankiewicz.

On first sight, Elyesa Bazna did not look very much like a master spy or what one would expect a spy to look like in the movies. With average height and alert eyes, he resembled more a small shopkeeper from the covered bazaar. Through the years he had gained some weight. I was interested in his side of the story because the world had already heard about the other side. However, he was not talking. According to Moyzisch, the valet had spied for money and also because of his anti-British persuasion. Each time he was questioned by the German attaché, who knew him as Pierre, Bazna told a different story about why he was taking revenge on the British. In one of them, he claimed that an Englishman had shot his father by accident on a hunting trip.

Of Albanian descent, Elyesa Bazna was born in Pristina, Kosovo, in 1904. Kosovo was then still under Ottoman rule. The Serbs occupied Pristina in 1918 and the fourteen-year-old boy's father and mother moved to Istanbul, which was occupied by the Allies following World War I. When he was about sixteen, Elyesa Bazna was employed by a French military unit. In Istanbul at the time there was an active Turkish nationalist underground movement against the harsh Allied occupation. The writer Yakub Kadri Karaosmanoğlu reflects on those occupation years: "The occupying forces [British, French, and Italian] in Istanbul considered all the cruelty and oppression committed by them against the people as lawful."

Bazna claimed once during our talks that he had actually worked as a young agent of the Turkish nationalist movement in Anatolia. He said that he had stolen cars and weapons from the Allies for the Nationalists. At the time, men, especially army officers, and weapons were secretly being transported from Istanbul to Anatolia for the nationalist war effort led by Kemal Atatürk against the Allied occupation.

Bazna was caught stealing and sent to France to serve a prison sentence. Upon returning to Turkey from France, Bazna worked as a driver, a guard, and a doorman for foreign diplomats and embassies. He married and had children while keeping mistresses on the side.

I rather think that he was originally persuaded to be a spy by an organization we will discuss later. Bazna's real spying, however, began when he was employed as a valet by the British ambassador.

Confronted on the staircase of his apartment building, Bazna tried to brush past us without stopping. Although Jacket Osman took his picture, Bazna made no attempt to grab the camera from him. Whenever we cornered him near his apartment or in the law courts, Bazna would keep a tight lip, refuse to answer questions, and try to avoid photographers. I knew that he was still very concerned about his personal safety.

During our first encounter on the staircase, I addressed the spy by his Turkish name. "Why did you spy for the Nazis, Ilyas Bey?" I asked.

He stopped and studied my face with his dark, shifty eyes. He was then about forty-eight years old with black hair and gray sideburns. On other occasions, observing him without his hat, I saw that he was getting bald. Bazna's answer didn't surprise me. "I needed the money," he said. Then, unexpectedly, he added that he was a friend of the Germans, but not a Nazi, and did not like the British.

Then Cicero locked his eyes with mine and said something that shocked me. "There are things that I can't talk about . . . like the Milli Emniyet, for instance. I would suggest that you write nothing about me, if you don't want to get into bad trouble."

The words *Milli Emniyet* alone at the time were enough to scare people. It was the national security agency, better known today as the Turkish Intelligence Service (MIT).

What is he talking about, I wondered. Was Bazna hinting that he had been a double agent for Turkish interests? Or was he trying to scare me? I found his insinuation hard to believe, yet there was some evidence to support such a possibility. During World War II, neutral Turkey was under tremendous pressure from both the Allies and the Axis powers to enter the war. The wartime Turkish government, with wily President Ismet Inönü walking a tightrope of diplomacy, was very concerned about the alliance between the Soviet Union, the Americans, and the British. Czarist Russia had captured large amounts of territory from the Ottoman Empire during the Russo-Turkish wars, and the Soviet Union was also harboring expansionist ideas. The Soviets had adopted Czarist Russia's centuries-old goal of reaching warm waters through Turkish territory to the south. After the war, a victorious Soviet Union would pose the greatest danger to the security of Turkey with its warm-water access through the Bosphorus and the Dardanelles Straits.

The Turkish hesitancy to join the war on the side of the Allies until it was too late caused the occupation of Romania and Bulgaria by the Soviets. Only when Turkey had finally declared war on Germany and Japan in late February 1945 did Ismet Inönü's regime realize the importance of the opportunities missed. These included the claim on the Aegean islands occupied by Greece after World War II. As a result, the Dodecanese and other Greek islands close to the Anatolian coast transformed the Aegean Sea into a Greek lake. The claims regarding the Aegean Sea are now a constant cause for strained relations between Turkey and Greece.

The signing of a nonaggression pact between Germany and the Soviet Union in August 1939 had been bleak news in Turkey for Ismet Inönü's regime. When Hitler launched a massive invasion of the Soviet Union in the summer of 1941, the Turks—always suspicious of Russia's aims—felt relieved.

I remember asking Ismet Inönü a question on this subject when he was the prime minister of a weak coalition government in Turkey in the 1960s. Inönü, then old, deaf, and diabetic, had invited me to his house in the Taşlık area of Istanbul. He had been Kemal Atatürk's prime minister twice, in 1923 and 1937, and after Atatürk's death, he had run the country until 1950 with an iron fist as the second president of the republic. Inönü, a powerful secularist, a man with shrewd eyes, loved to eat cheese despite his doctor's orders not to touch it. His deafness was due to his wartime experiences with artillery fire. I had to shout often to explain myself. I addressed him as *paşam*, my general, despite the memory of the torture I had suffered once from his police. He died in 1973 an unhappy man, having witnessed the extremists' attempts to drag the secular country he had helped create onto the threshold of a civil war and the emergence of a powerful new Islamic fundamentalism.

I said to Inönü, "The Second World War must have been very stressful for your government. Was there a period that you consider worse than the others?"

"The first two years were very difficult," he said, "because of the uncertainty of how the war would affect our own situation. We had no wish to enter another war. Remember, we had lost a whole generation during the First World War and then the Independence War. Through reforms we had been successful in bringing up and educating a new generation of Turks. The safety of this new generation and the integrity of the Turkish borders were foremost in my mind. In addition our armed forces lacked equipment, so we did our best not to enter the war. To answer your question, I have to say that the German invasion of the Soviet Union was the turning point of the Second World War for us."

"How do you explain that, Pasham?" I asked. But he wouldn't go into details. That was understandable, for the Soviet threat was still a factor that had to be seriously considered in the 1960s.

Years later I found the answer to the question I had asked Ismet Inönü in *Anılar ve Düşünceler* (Remembrances and Thoughts), a book written by his elder son, Erdal Inönü. In it, Erdal, also a politician, describes how his father had received the news of Germany's massive invasion of the Soviet Union.

Erdal and his brother Ömer took a message for their father when he received a phone call from a high government official about the German attack. They saw an extraordinary reaction in their father's face when they woke him up with the important news.

Inönü smiled, and when the news had sunk in, he started to laugh. He laughed not because a new and destructive war had started but because he believed that the potential danger to Turkey had been reduced.

But had it really?

Soon the direction of the war would change again and signal disturbing portents of a new world order. This new world order would include a victorious and highly assertive Soviet Union occupying Eastern Europe and the Balkans.

The top-secret papers stolen from the British ambassador's safe contained a clear message of warning to the Germans—the Allies were winning the war; Nazi Germany would be destroyed; the Soviet Union would emerge from the war as a superpower. One possible way out for Adolf Hitler would be to seek peace with the Americans and the British, playing the Soviet threat as a bargaining chip. Hitler could then concentrate on the Eastern Front and halt the Soviet advance.

I believe that this view played an important role in developing Turkey's foreign policy by the wartime Turkish officials.

Were they able to receive intelligence in order to direct their foreign policy in a manner they wished? Did they even do their best to change the course of the war?

One outcome of the war obviously revealed the direction of Russian intentions. Joseph Stalin soon showed his hand by demanding the Turkish Straits and the two eastern provinces of Kars and Ardahan. The Truman Doctrine in 1947, and later NATO, stopped the Russians from achieving their traditional dream, namely, control of the Bosphorus and the Dardanelles, two vital waterways from the Black Sea to the Aegean and the Mediterranean. So when Cicero hinted to me that there were interests besides money involved in his activities, I remembered the shadow car.

During World War II, there were not many cars in the streets of Ankara, especially at night. Yet L. C. Moyzisch had reported that a big, black, mysterious car was following him and the spy in the streets of Ankara while they secretly exchanged money for films. Since the British were unaware of the valet's spying activities at the time and the Germans did not have a car tailing them, who was it that was shadowing them?

Moyzisch was able to elude the pursuer and drop the spy near the

British embassy. He strongly suspected the Turks but never found out for sure who had chased them. There were suspicions that American intelligence had been investigating Moyzisch's nightly activities.

If these suspicions were right and Moyzisch really were under surveillance by the Office of Strategic Services (OSS) or American intelligence, why were his meetings with Cicero not put to an end? Or better still, why was Cicero not turned into a double agent by the Americans to mislead the Germans?

I was to meet Elyesa Bazna many times later while reporting for Reuters from Turkey. By then he was in trouble with the law. Several merchants, to whom Bazna had passed some of the pounds sterling he had received from the Germans, had finally sued the former valet. The pound notes were worthless—Cicero had been paid in counterfeit money, about three hundred thousand pounds' worth. Only the first payment of twenty thousand pounds sterling and some diamonds were genuine, Cicero had told me one day.

Being cheated by Hitler's Third Reich and then charged with fraud in Turkey was a big blow to Cicero. During his trials at the Trade Courts, then located at the Sirkeci docks near the Golden Horn in Istanbul, I saw him as a broken, disappointed man. In the mid-1950s, the Trade Courts ruled against Bazna and ordered him to pay back what he owed. By then the spy was penniless and jobless.

Suddenly his dreams of wealth had collapsed, and he was left without any means to take care of his large family. He tried to earn a living by singing and by doing odd jobs that came along. And he tried to salvage something of Operation Cicero.

In 1952, while the movie *Five Fingers* was being shot on location in Turkey, he applied to play his part in the movie but was rejected. In 1954, he wrote a letter to German Chancellor Konrad Adenauer asking for reimbursement for the counterfeit pounds sterling. He would even have settled for a pension from the German government for his wartime services. There were press reports that he was successful in receiving some funds from the Germans. These reports were not proven, and Bazna told me, "I got nothing."

I offered to write the details of his spying for Turkish newspapers, but he rejected this offer. He was after big money for his memoirs and believed that a fortune would be waiting for him in West Germany. He considered himself the spy of the century.

Finally, he went to West Germany in 1961 and published a book titled *I Was Cicero*. By then it was too late because Moyzisch's book *Operation Cicero* had fully disclosed the spy affair eleven years earlier. In the end, Bazna was allowed to stay in Germany, where he found a job as a watchman. He died in Munich in 1970 at sixty-six and was buried in a German cemetery.

After the war, a number of British sources wrongly claimed that Elyesa Bazna had been a double agent under the control of the British Secret Service. Having known Cicero, I do not believe that British intelligence ever controlled him. The genuine and extremely important top-secret papers he had stolen and supplied to the Nazis, including the code word *Overlord*, are enough to prove that.

I have always suspected that Bazna had been a double agent working for Turkish interests. Now we know that he *was* a double agent who took full advantage of his position in the British Embassy in Ankara.

In an article that was published in the September 1999 issue of *World War II* magazine, I asked the following questions: Was Bazna also reporting to the Turkish authorities on the side while the Germans paid him funny money? If not, who really followed the spy and his handler at night in the streets of wartime Ankara, where wartime security was tight?

Ilyas Bazna, a patriot, might have been persuaded earlier to cooperate with *Milli Emniyet*, the Turkish Security Agency. I believed then that there were some clues to indicate that he had done so and that he was a double agent working for Turkish interests.

Moyzisch was also inclined to think so. He suspected that a *Milli Emniyet* agent chased his car at night in Ankara. He had reason to think so. At a private party after the car chase, a guest from the Turkish Foreign Ministry commented about Moyzisch's careless night driving. So the Turkish officials knew or suspected that Moyzisch was involved in intelligence.

If Turkish officials knew what was going on, I surmised, they must have had a good picture of the Allied war strategy, besides having some laughs on the side—they were reading all the important documents about the conduct of the war and about the meetings of the Allied leaders and using the information to set a course for their foreign policy. The documents helped the Turks to protect their neutrality. The Turkish officials, including Prime Minister Şükrü Saracoğlu and Foreign Minister Numan Menemencioğlu, had learned from the papers that the Allies had given them code names. Some of these code names annoyed them.

Obviously, Allied intelligence did not have a lot of information about Turkish Prime Minister Şükrü Saracoğlu's wartime habits. If they had, I think they would have given him a more appropriate code name than the one they used. For Prime Minister Saracoğlu, the son of a saddler, was known as *Mucuk* ("Up yours"). He would meet his friends at the Anatolian Club in Ankara to talk about events mostly concerning the war. When a friend asked him a question he could answer, he would give a proper explanation. If the subject was too sensitive to disclose, or if he was strongly opposed to a proposal made by the Germans or the Allies to the Turkish government, he would tell his friend, "Look under the table." His right hand under the table would be in the shape of a *mucuk*, his thumb protruding between the index and middle fingers.

Some facts about Cicero that I found in *The History of MIT*, a book sponsored by the Turkish Intelligence Service MIT and published in Turkey in December 2001, were still a big surprise to me, even though I had had inklings of them.

In their book, the spy agency admitted that Elyesa Bazna had been a double agent during World War II for Turkey's counterintelligence. According to MIT, the information Bazna supplied was used to support Turkey's foreign policy during the war and to protect the country's neutrality. MIT also reports on its Web site, http://mit.gov.tr, that during World War II, their counterintelligence agents had scored successes repeatedly. Through their operations vital information had been collected. The agency adds that the information obtained was delivered to the Turkish government, playing "an effective role to keep the country out of World War II." According to the agency, Turkish counterintelligence during wartime was highly developed and extremely successful.

I believe that the agency may have passed vital information also to the Allies about German intelligence activities through the Turkish foreign minister. The agency states that Ilyas Bazna's spying was exemplary and highly detailed. The war years (1939–45) had been tough, however, for Turkish counterintelligence agents because both Istanbul and Ankara had been active centers of spying for the Allies as well as the Axis powers. Many hostile agents were arrested on charges of spying in Turkey.

There was additional astonishing information about Elyasa Bazna: he had done part of his compulsory military service at *Çankaya*, the presidential palace in Ankara, when Kemal Atatürk ruled the country. This information was enough to convince me that my earlier assumption about Bazna's connections to the Turkish Nationalists after World War I was correct. He had been sent to France to serve his prison sentence for stealing weapons and cars during the Allied occupation of Istanbul after the Ottoman Empire had collapsed. He had been a thief for the Nationalists and *Kuvayi Milliye* (National Forces), the vehicle for the fight for independence led by Kemal Atatürk. He had not lied to me when we had met for the first time on a staircase in Istanbul and he used the Turkish Security Agency as a threat.

In those years when I was chasing Cicero for some news, I was also a stringer for the *Daily Express* of London. The British were interested in Bazna's activities and I used to report them regularly. It was the *Daily Express* that printed on its second page the picture of Bazna on the staircase trying to cover his face. I have no idea if my reports about Cicero to the *Daily Express* attracted the attention of the editors at Reuters in London.

John Long, the Reuters correspondent in Ankara in 1955, had some serious problems with Turkish officials, who didn't like his reporting. The semiofficial Anatolian News Agency (AA) used to receive the world news from Reuters, so whatever John Long filed for London would be fed back to the AA and read by officials of the Menderes regime. Apparently, John Long's days in Turkey were numbered, and as he was leaving, he offered me the job, and I accepted. I would stay on as chief news editor of *Yeni Sabah*'s and on the side I would file my reports by cable day and night to

Reuters's headquarters in London. I was to cover all the important news developments all over Turkey, including the capital, Ankara. In return, I would receive a retainer and expenses from Reuters on top of what I was making at the newspaper.

This arrangement suited me fine, and I explained the situation to Safa Kılıçlıoğlu, my boss. I expected him to object to this second job while I was working for his newspaper. Surprisingly, he welcomed the idea and gave me his full approval. "Fine with me," the publisher said. "Do as you please."

Despite his shortcomings in other areas, his sharp tongue and explicit language, Kılıçlıoğlu was devilishly clever and cunning. He had sparkling black eyes that burned with intelligence. He knew that working for an international news agency was a highly competitive around-the-clock job with no existing deadline and no respite during breaking news. I would be on call twenty-four hours every day, including Saturdays and Sundays. Thus, he figured that this arrangement would be beneficial to the newspaper, as I would be more aggressive and alert in my duties.

Having received Kılıçlıoğlu's blessing to work a second job and use *Yeni Sabah*'s news resources in my reporting to London, my involvement with Reuters began. It was to lead me to a life of constant excitement and sometimes to dangerous adventures. My main and most aggressive rival in this endeavor was the Associated Press (AP), the big American news agency, which had well-staffed bureaus in Istanbul and Ankara. In addition, AP, like myself, had a pipeline to the news sources of a national daily, in their case, the rival newspaper *Milliyet*. Another competitor was Zeyyat Gören, who reported to United Press International (UPI). I thought I could handle Gören, but being able to compete with the Associated Press single-handedly was a major concern. The rest of my competition included European agencies: Agence France Presse (AFP) and the Deutsche Presse Agentur (DPA). Gustav Fumelli, who represented *AFP*, was very active and often surprised us by showing up unexpectedly during important events.

It was obvious that the competition would be stiff. I was due for a rough ride in gathering the news and a lot of running to the nearby central post office's cable center to send flashes—those urgent, breaking news reports.

It was a time of great excitement but fraught with danger, which led to incredible events that changed the destiny of a nation.

The Shah,
Winston Churchill,
and Jackie Kennedy

For a rich man even a rooster lays eggs.

Turkish proverb

*T*hanks to earlier assignments by *Yeni Sabah* to European and Middle Eastern countries, I had already gained some firsthand knowledge about world affairs. I went to Tehran when the nationalist Prime Minister Muhammed Mossadeq (Weeping Mosaddeq) forced Shah Muhammed Reza Pahlavi into a brief exile in August 1953. The trouble in Iran began when Mossadeq nationalized that country's British-controlled oil industry (the Anglo-Iranian Oil Company). The shah was by nature a creature of indecision, yet he had made an attempt to dismiss Dr. Mossadeq. This led to demonstrations in the streets by Mossadeq's followers and the shah's flight with Empress Soraya to Baghdad and then to Rome. Despite a Central Intelligence Agency campaign of bombings and planted articles in Tehran newspapers against Mossadeq, everything seemed lost.

Some Iranian journalists and army officers, all agents of the CIA, saved the shah's Peacock Throne. I saw them leading noisy crowds heading for the parliament. They were chanting pro-shah slogans. A royalist colonel named Nimetullah Nasiri in a tank helped them, and the tide suddenly turned against Mossadeq.

Soon after I watched the tanks of General Fazlollah Zahedi, backed by the United States and its CIA, take control of the streets of Tehran. This US engineered coup, code-named *TP-Ajax* and led by Kermit Roosevelt to maintain the West's control over Iranian oil, ousted Mossadeq and restored the tyrannical shah. It also paved the way for the Islamic revolution of 1979 and inspired the radical Islamist movement that led to fundamentalist rule of the ayatollahs.

The US policy of restoring the shah's regime by force over the Iranians in order to preserve the status quo ante would eventually lead to much resentment against America in Iran. It seemed that the United States, for the sake of the West's control of oil, did not wish any change in the status quo of the Middle East.

I had met Nadir Batmangilich, a general of Turkic origin, who was close to coup leader General Zahedi. His second name, Batmangilich, comes from the ancient Turkish words *batman*, a measure of weight, and *kılıç*, sword. With the help of this influential general, I met the shah and Empress Soraya at Mehrabad Airport upon their return to Iran after Mossadeq was overthrown.

One night during the state-imposed curfew, all foreign correspondents had gathered at the bar of Tehran's Park Hotel. Word came that a mass-circulated London newspaper had a banner headline announcing to the world "Mossadeq Hanged." It was a great scoop, if only it were true. The report was against the credo of journalism: get it first and get it right. The British correspondent who filed the story got it first but didn't get it right. He was also in the bar and looked pleased with his achievement. I knew that Mossadeq was still alive and in jail, in spite of this journalist's insistence that he had been hanged. The next day, it was curtains for him—the journalist was fired. I think he received a cable from the newspaper's editor saying something like, either Mossadeq hangs or you do.

Dr. Mossadeq, a small, frail, birdlike man with a bald head and long nose, was an amusing personality who usually dressed in pajamas and carpet slippers and was called *the Old Weeper* because he used to shed tears while defending his nationalist policies. Addressing parliament, he would often faint while tears rolled down his cheeks. He hated the British. By nature, he suspected evil designs not only from his opponents but also from others. He would study his opponents with beady eyes but trust no one, not even his closest aides. He remained in jail until 1956 and died in obscurity in 1967.

Tehran in 1953 was not a healthy place to be stationed because of the lack of sanitary conditions. We were extremely careful about what we ate; we knew the tap water too was unsafe. Just to be on the safe side, we would wash down a local beer or bottled mineral water.

There was also a lot of action in Cairo during those years. In July 1952, the Egyptian Society of Free Officers, a nationalist military group, had forced King Farouk I to abdicate. This coup had two major players: Major General Muhammed Naguib and Lieutenant Colonel Gamal Abdel Nasser. Naguib, commander-in-chief of the Society of Free Officers, became the first president and prime minister of the new Republic of Egypt. As is usually the case with coups d'etat, the playing field was too small for two big players. Nasser, vaguely implicating General Naguib in a 1954 assassination attempt against his life, placed Naguib under house arrest. Deposing Naguib freed Nasser of a major competitor for the position of prime minister and later president. Gamal Abdel Nasser used a complicated series of intrigues against Naguib and emerged as the leader of Egypt with the support of some army officers.

When the news of General Naguib's detention came through the wire services, Safa Kılıçlıoğlu, who was interested in affairs of the Arab countries, told me: "Fly to Cairo and interview General Naguib in his house. If you can't handle the job, don't bother to come back."

Some of the airlines flying to destinations in the Middle East during those years were not the best. On a rush assignment, we had to fly by whatever was available, including small, old, noisy, and rickety aircraft. Flying in one usually gave the passenger in a window seat the uncomfortable impression that the rivets on the wings were just about ready to pop from their sockets with each jolt of the plane. I took the first airliner to Cairo and, after a bumpy ride, drove straight to the house where General Naguib was under detention. The house was surrounded by armed soldiers who were not letting anybody in or out without a special permit.

During my travels in Arab countries, I had picked up a few native words and was able to introduce myself in Arabic. I waited near the house for an opportunity to sneak in but had no luck. Then I saw a group of young officers, obviously members of the society, who were supporters of General Naguib. They were walking toward the house, so I joined them. Quickly, I introduced myself in Arabic and told them about my special assignment. They were impressed that I had come all the way from Istanbul just to interview General Naguib. These officers took me right into Naguib's living room and to Naguib himself. I asked the general, who was wearing his sand-colored uniform, what was going on. He replied, "Just a storm in a teacup, nothing else."

But it wasn't. It was a huge storm that would eventually wipe out all his power, as Nasser was determined to take over and rule the country as dictator.

I asked General Naguib, "Was your resignation as president of Egypt earlier in February a result of a power struggle?"

"It had nothing to do with a power struggle," he answered. "We had disagreements and there were misconceptions about my own political beliefs. That's all. It will pass."

His dispute with Nasser was not that simple. It was basically a dispute about what type of government should rule Egypt. General Naguib wanted a quick return to constitutional government and a revival of the political parties. He was urging the Free Officers to allow the formation of a constitutional assembly to draft a new constitution. Naguib objected to the summary sentences that were being passed on former politicians by a revolutionary tribunal. The Egyptian Delegation, *Al-Wafd al-Misri*, known as the Wafd Party, had been the leading nationalist political party before the coup d'etat, and many of its members were under house arrest or in jail. Other Wafdists, fearing arrest, had gone underground. A multi-party system in Egypt was legalized by President Anwar al-Sadat twenty-four years later in 1978.

In February 1954, General Naguib resigned the presidency, but his supporters compelled him to stay on as nominal president. It is doubtful that he had anything to do with any assassination attempt on Nasser. In fact, the assassination attempt itself may only have been a ploy to get rid of Naguib. His house arrest was eased in 1960 and ended in 1970.

General Naguib's long detention, which brought an end to his role in Egyptian politics, drastically altered his country's relations with the West for years to come.

This assignment gave me another opportunity to compare the social and cultural conditions in Egypt with those in Turkey, which had gone through the Kemalist reforms. The difference between the two Muslim countries astonished me. The Turks, unlike the Egyptians, had adopted Western ways. Even the headlines of the Egyptian newspapers with Arabic letters seemed like incredible puzzles, and it was impossible for me to read them. Only educated people were wearing Western clothing. Others wore traditional Arab garb.

Another one of my unusual encounters in Cairo was with the Egyptian movie star Faten Hamama, an attractive woman of Turkish ancestry. I went to her home to interview her. There I intended to learn more about one of Egypt's really big stars. Unbeknownst to me, the truly interesting part of the interview was her husband, who was hardly known then. He was the handsome Egyptian actor Omar Sharif, who quietly sat next to his wife all through the interview. It was much later that he became world famous, acting in films like *Lawrence of Arabia* and *Dr. Zhivago*. Sharif and Faten Hamama were divorced in 1965, but Sharif still says that Hamama was the love of his life.

There were events I had problems reporting because of their obvious repercussions on Turkey's relations with other countries. One news story I wrote for *Yeni Sabah* caused me headaches because of the involvement of John Hyde, the information officer at the British Consulate in Istanbul. My problem developed because the story was about former British Prime Minister Sir Winston Churchill and his role in the disastrous Dardanelles campaign during World War I.

None of the involved parties—the British, the Australians, the New

Zealanders, the French, or the Turks—will ever be able to forget the battles on the Gallipoli Peninsula, a fifty-mile strip of land in the European part of Turkey between the Aegean Sea and the Dardanelles Strait and beyond that to the Sea of Marmara.

As a student in London, I used to go to Hyde Park Corner to listen to the speeches of would-be politicians and crackpots. One day I heard a speaker haranguing about the battles of Gallipoli. I had to interrupt his speech when he referred to my countrymen as dirty Turks. He was saying that in hand-to-hand fighting in the trenches with bayonets, the dirty Turkish soldiers used their foul-smelling socks to take the Tommies prisoner. It was an amusing story, but an absurd one at that.

The speaker's knowledge about the fighting in Gallipoli was limited at best, so I told him that the Dardanelles War had been unique in the history of warfare because over time a sort of camaraderie developed between the Allied soldiers and the Turks. There was even an exchange of food between the trenches. The Tommies would throw bully beef—canned corned beef—to the Turks and receive, in turn, fresh fruits. The Turks didn't like the bully beef, and they would shout: "No bully beef! Send biscuits." There were marksmanship competitions between the trenches and duels between individual soldiers. A bored Australian would stand up on an Allied rampart and call a Turkish soldier out for a duel or vice versa.

My verbal confrontation with John Hyde was also about Gallipoli. Sir Winston Churchill was a guest aboard the yacht *Christina* owned by Aristotle Onassis, the Greek shipping magnate. The yacht was then sailing through the Dardanelles, heading for Istanbul. The guests on board included Jacqueline Kennedy.

Aristotle Onassis had been born in Izmir in western Turkey. When he returned there aboard the *Christina*, he gave Jackie Kennedy a guided tour of his birthplace. He was a shrewd businessman, enhancing his social status and credibility by ingratiating himself with powerful statesmen and people of celebrity status. In order to gain the friendship of influential individuals, he showered them with lavish hospitality and gifts. During that cruise, he gave Jackie a diamond-and-ruby necklace.

All I reported was that Sir Winston Churchill, who as the British First Lord of the Admiralty had proposed the initial plan for the Allied Gallipoli landing in 1915, would now see the site of the battle with his own eyes. Churchill's plan had called for an Allied expedition of British, Australian, French, and New Zealand forces to occupy and defend the Dardanelles, and then to move on to Istanbul to knock the Turks out of World War I. The plan had failed but caused half a million casualties in hand-to-hand trench warfare. At the time Churchill was generally blamed for planning the operation that had ended with such disastrous results.

John Hyde made a fuss about my news report, claiming that my writing was insulting to the dignity of the great man. "All right," I said. "Why not tell this to the people who lost their loved ones in Gallipoli?"

Churchill by the end of the 1950s was old and suffering from various ailments that I learned about from security officials, but I refrained from writing about them.

I was an admirer of President John F. Kennedy. When I saw his wife, Jackie, visiting the St. Sophia Museum in Istanbul, in the company of Aristotle Onassis, a short man who could hardly be called attractive, I thought Kennedy had used bad judgment in letting his wife sail on the *Christina*. Onassis had the reputation of a being womanizer and was well known for his ways with the fairer sex.

One story I did not dare to write was about the former King Talal of Jordan, the late King Hussein's father. King Talal bin Abdullah had been treated in a Swiss clinic for schizophrenia before he became king. Because he had been found mentally unfit to rule, the Jordanian Parliament deposed Talal in 1952. His son Hussein was then only seventeen years old. Hussein's mother, Queen Zeyn, was involved in the affairs of state and was a powerful figure in the Jordanian royal palace.

The former king, who had studied at the British military college of Sandhurst, was brought to Istanbul and installed there to live at the Şifa Health Clinic on the Bosphorus. The policeman in charge of his security was a friendly source of news. One day he told me that Talal was not mad but just a very angry man. He was often heard shouting the name of a woman, someone very close to him, adding the Arabic insult *al-fahisha*, meaning whore. I learned the identity of the woman whom the ex-king was accusing of double-crossing him and a lot of details about the intrigues in the Jordanian palace. But I did not report them, fearing the rage of Prime Minister Adnan Menderes, who at the time was busy trying to improve relations with the Arab countries. Talal died in 1972.

As reporters, we would often see young King Hussein bin Talal in the Istanbul Hilton when he came to the city to visit his father. A friendly young man, who would later be known as the plucky little king, Hussein angered the Arab nationalists when he planned to join the anti-Soviet Baghdad Pact, an alliance among Iraq, Turkey, Pakistan, Iran, and Britain. Egyptian President Gamal Abdel Nasser branded Hussein a stooge of American imperialism. Because of nationalistic and pro-Soviet pressures, Hussein changed his mind about joining the pact and soon afterward, in 1956, fired John Glubb (Glubb Pasha), the British general who commanded Jordan's army.

King Hussein would go on to establish greater Jordanian independence from Britain after 1956, when he was just twenty-two years old. He died in 1999 after a lifelong struggle to keep his country safe in the volatile Middle East.

The Cyprus Crisis and the Turco-Greek Fracas

Forty wise men couldn't retrieve the stone a madman threw into a well.

Turkish proverb

yprus, the third-largest island in the Mediterranean after Sicily and Sardinia, is only forty miles from the coast of southern Turkey. The island was part of the Ottoman Empire for about three hundred years, between 1570 and 1878. This changed in 1878 when a victorious Russian army appeared in Yeşilköy, a suburb of Istanbul. As a condition for its support of the Ottoman Empire against the Russian invasion, Great Britain took over the administration of Cyprus under an agreement with the Sublime Porte (Ottoman government). However, the island still remained under Turkish sovereignty. In 1914, when the war with Turkey broke out, Cyprus was annexed into the British Commonwealth.

There are legends about Turkish warriors who fought to conquer the island in 1570–71. Namık Kemal (1840–88), the great patriotic poet of the Ottoman Empire who stood up against its despotic rule and corruption, was banished to a dungeon in Famagusta by the Ottoman sultan. One of Namık Kemal's poems about the darkest times of the Ottoman Empire cries out:

> It's not a rose that's on her back,
> It's a bloodstained shroud.
> Is it you, is it you, poor Motherland!

Cyprus's present population of about 800,000 is 80 percent ethnic Greek and 20 percent ethnic Turkish. Because of its eastern Mediterranean climate and beautiful panoramic views, the island is a favorite vacation spot for many Europeans.

Soon after World War II, conditions in Cyprus degenerated into a tumultuous fracas between Greece and Turkey when an old Greek movement for union with Greece, known as *Enosis*, started a cycle of violence. Orthodox Archbishop Mikhail Khristodolou Mouskos, among others, would play a major role in destroying the cordial relations between Greece and Turkey.

This good relationship had been established in the 1930s with the Ankara Treaty of Friendship signed by Greek Prime Minister Eleutherios Venizelos and Kemal Atatürk. Venizelos was the man who had ordered the disastrous invasion of Anatolia in 1919, yet he later understood the importance of good relations between Greece and Turkey. Two decades after the signing of this treaty, *Enosis* would destroy the trust between two nations.

The killing of Turkish Cypriots by Greek gunmen caused Ismet Inönü, then prime minister of Turkey's coalition government, to cancel this treaty on March 16, 1964. The cancellation directly affected the residency rights of about twelve thousand Greek citizens, mostly businesspeople, in Istanbul.

Before the Cyprus crisis, there had been one hundred thousand ethnic Greeks in Istanbul. Most of them left the country, fearing a war between Greece and Turkey. In 2003 only about two thousand, mostly old, ethnic Greeks were still living in Turkey as citizens. The one hundred thousand ethnic Turks remaining in northern Greece were not happy either. They had been treated badly by the government of Greece. For years Greek laws denied them the freedom of holding jobs or professions of their choice. The Greek authorities identified them as Muslims, not as ethnic Turks. Through the years, elected officials of the ethnic Turkish communities had been harassed.

The Cyprus crisis played such a destructive role between Turkey and Greece that numerous attempts to repair the damage were unsuccessful. They included meetings in the 1980s between Greek Prime Minister Andreas Papandreou and Turgut Özal, the Turkish leader. They were unable to overcome their differences not only on the subject of Cyprus but also on mineral and territorial rights in the Aegean Sea.

Enosis (union with Greece) was not a new movement and to be fair to Mikhail Khristodolou Mouskos, it did not originate with him. Soon after Great Britain took over the island's administration from the Turks on June 4, 1878, the Greek Cypriot leaders asked the British government to grant *Enosis*. This remained a dormant request for many years until 1931, when the Greeks again demanded *Enosis*. After World War II, there was active agitation on the island for a union with Greece, and the Greeks began smuggling arms into Cyprus.

Mikhail Khristodolou Mouskos was better known as Makarios III, who since 1950 had been archbishop and primate of the Cypriot Orthodox Church. Archbishop Makarios had clear links with the terrorist group *Ethniki Organosis Kypriakou Agonos* (The National Organization of the Cypriot Struggle, or EOKA). In the beginning, EOKA fought to end British rule by attacking British servicemen and establishments. Col. Georgios Grivas, an ex-officer of the Greek Army, was the leader of EOKA. The Turkish Cypriots lacked a resistance organization until 1957, when *Türk Mukavemet Teşkilatı* (the Turkish Resistance Organization) became active against EOKA terrorism. It was a small, poorly armed outfit organized by Dr. Fazıl Küçük and Rauf Denktaş, a public prosecutor under British rule.

In the beginning, not the government of Turkey but a journalist took on the cause of the Turkish Cypriots who were concerned about the *Enosis* movement. This man was Sedat Simavi, the founder of the newspaper *Hürriyet*, who created a national uproar over the island. Sedat

Simavi had established *Hürriyet* in May 1948, and one morning a banner headline pronounced "*Kıbrıs Bizimdir*" (Cyprus Is Ours).

Personal experience was also part of the publisher's motivation. Sedat Simavi's father, Hamdi, had died in 1907 in Khios, the island of *gum mastic*,* while he was that island's Ottoman governor. The Greek authorities later had destroyed the Turkish cemetery there, along with his father's grave, to build a road.

Sedat Simavi's Cyprus endeavors were not in sync with official Turkish policy at the time. This caused him serious problems with the regime of Adnan Menderes. His troubles began when Foreign Minister Fuat Köprülü made a crucial statement during a stopover at Athens's Hellenikon Airport. He said that Turkey had no problems regarding the island of Cyprus.

The Turkish government at the time had no set policy regarding Cyprus. It was understood from Köprülü's statement that the Turkish government had no objections to Greek plans in this issue. This policy soon changed, and the credit belongs to Sedat Simavi.

Hürriyet's publisher was furious. In a front-page article, Sedat Simavi accused the government of incompetence and ended up in criminal court on charges of insulting Foreign Minister Köprülü. He died at age fifty-seven, a sick man, while the trial was still ongoing.

In 1955, a tripartite Cyprus conference in London between the British, Turkish, and Greek foreign ministers failed to reach a solution to the crisis. The savage communal violence on the island increased during 1955 and 1956, causing an outcry in the Turkish press. I remember seeing every day front-page newspaper photographs of scores of murdered Turkish Cypriots, including women and children.

The worst rioting I covered in Istanbul was over Cyprus, and it took place in Beyoğlu's Istiklal Street, Istanbul's fashionable shopping district. This event has become known as the riots of September 6 and 7, 1955, and was caused by a news report. The report said Kemal Atatürk's birth-

---

* Gum mastic is collected in Khios from a wild shrub. It provides flavor for a Greek liqueur known as *mastikha* (rakı). It is also used to make a white jam and chewing gum.

place in Thessaloniki, Greece, had been bombed. The bombing report made front-page news with a banner headline in the *Istanbul Ekspres*, an evening newspaper. Its editor-in-chief was Gökşin Sipahioğlu, who, on receiving the bombing report, had stopped the presses and changed the front page. *Istanbul Ekspres* was a small newspaper with a daily circulation of about thirty thousand. Because of the bombing news, it sold three hundred thousand on September 6, 1955. The newspaper had exaggerated a report from a local news agency. The actual damage to the house was only a broken window.

A huge uproar followed and public emotions were inflamed. A protest demonstration in Istanbul turned violent and killed all remaining chances of a Turco-Greek rapprochement.

A nightmare ensued. I saw taxis dragging bales of cloth, refrigerators, furniture, and rugs through the street as looters and Communist agitators joined the melee, demolishing stores and businesses. A lot of Greek-, Jewish-, Armenian-, as well as Turkish-owned stores and businesses were looted and destroyed. Ankle-deep broken glass littered the sidewalks in front of stores that carried expensive merchandise. I saw policemen standing by, watching the looters and the destruction. With my journalist friends Necati Zincirkıran and Ilhan Turalı, I came upon some rioters trying to beat up the director of Istanbul's traffic police, Orhan Eyüpoğlu. We intervened and saved Eyüpoğlu, who later served as Turkey's interior minister. Before the night was over, martial law was announced, but it was too late—the damage had been done. The riots further strained the relationship between Greece and Turkey and caused shortages of imported goods.

The man in charge of martial law was General Nurettin Aknoz, better known as Aknoz Pasha, who arrived in Istanbul from Erzurum in eastern Anatolia, where he was the commander of the 3rd Army. Aknoz Pasha rarely smiled and treated journalists and newspapers with contempt for even small offenses against the rules of martial law. He ordered a curfew; suspended the publication of *Hürriyet*, among others, for fifteen days; and made a name for himself as *Kapattım Paşa*—"I closed down (newspapers)" Pasha.

I suspected that the KGB, the Soviet intelligence agency, had a hand in instigating the riots and aimed to destroy the easternmost flank of NATO. The KGB was well aware that any threat to Kemal Atatürk's birthplace in Thessaloniki would inflame the Turks. Another piece of evidence pointing to the Soviets was the presence of Marxist agitators among the demonstrators. Just before the demonstration, a young man on Taksim Square had climbed a ladder he had brought with him and made an inflammatory speech against the Greeks. "Next, they will demand Istanbul," he had said. "Let's teach them a lesson." Then, he disappeared into the crowd.

There was no proof that the riots were a Soviet ploy. However, forty-four years after these riots, I found a clue in the book *The Sword and the Shield, the Mitrokhin Archive and the Secret History of the KGB*. This book by Christopher Andrew, professor of modern and contemporary history at Cambridge University, and Vasili Mitrokhin is based on copies of classified documents from the KGB archives. Vasili Mitrokhin, who had worked for thirty years in the foreign intelligence archives of the KGB, had delivered these archives to the British Intelligence Service.

One of the documents discusses a political action proposed by the Athens Residency of the KGB in April 1969. The action aimed to cause moral and political damage to the southeast wing of NATO. This plot was an exact replay of what I had suspected during the Istanbul riots in 1955.

A special action plan proposed by the KGB's Athens Residency is disclosed in an operational letter. The date of the letter, cited as number 24, is April 14, 1969. It sets out a draft plan for carrying out a *Lily* (sabotage operation) called *Egg* against the target code-named *VAZA*.

VAZA is a two-storied house in Thessaloniki, Greece, the birthplace of Kemal Atatürk, near the Turkish consulate-general. The KGB agent playing the role of a Greek resident in Turkey, was dissatisfied with the situation of the Greek minority there. According to the plot, the KGB agent code-named *Gardener* was to place a "Bouquet," an explosive device, in the bushes near the house at night. The proposal states: "In order to increase the impact and achieve the desired results, the *Bouquet* must be wrapped in a newspaper published in Turkey for Greek citizens."

The KGB document shows how the Soviets exploited the tension between Greece and Turkey caused by the Cyprus crisis. It also proves how they did their best to inflame it in order to harm NATO.

In 1956 the British deported Archbishop Makarios to the Seychelle Islands (northeast of Madagascar in the Indian Ocean) but allowed him to return to Cyprus after a year. Dr. Fazıl Küçük, the Turkish Cypriot leader, asked for the partition of the island in 1957 to end the crisis.

In 1969, I had interviewed the head of the Greek Orthodox Archdiocese of North and South America, Archbishop Iakovos in New York City. The archbishop, who had been born on the Aegean island of Gökçeada (Imroz) in Turkey, had told me, "As Greeks and Turks, we ought to look squarely into each other's eyes." *Yeni Gazete*, a daily newspaper owned then by the *Hürriyet* holding company, printed the interview in full. The archbishop was known to have a negative attitude toward Turkey and the Turks in general. His feelings were even more inflamed later when, after the death of Patriarch Athenagoras, the Turkish government blocked his candidacy to become the patriarch in Istanbul.

The Turkish government presently has the authority to veto the candidacy of a person who is unacceptable to them. A candidate must be a native citizen to be elected by the synod of metropolitans. The Turkish government does not recognize the ecumenical* status of the Greek Orthodox Patriarchate and considers the patriarchate as serving the religious needs of Greeks in Turkey—only about three thousand souls, according to estimates in 2005. The patriarchate would like these rules to change and to reopen the patriarchal seminary on Heybeli Island. This seminary was closed in the 1960s by the government of Ismet İnönü because of the violence in Cyprus when Greek Cypriots brutally murdered Turks. Turkish authorities worry that, in the future, an ecumenical patriarchate in Fener by the Golden Horn may demand a status similar to the Vatican in Rome. The Turks know the patriarchate as Rum Patrikhanesi.

The status of this patriarchate outside Turkey is generally accepted as ecumenical, meaning worldwide, excluding some churches in Greece and

---

* The word *ecumenical* means universal and is derived from the Greek words *oikoumene* (the inhabited world) and oikos (house).

Russia. A small church, St. George in Fener, serves as the cathedral for the patriarch, presently Bartholomew I, whose original name is Dimitrios Archontonis. Bartholomew was born in 1940 on the Turkish island of Gökçeada and graduated from the patriarchal Seminary of Halki (Heybeli Island). I had sincerely hoped that Archbishop Iakovos might use the interview as an opportunity to help improve the relations between the two countries, but I was disappointed.

I met Archbishop Makarios, a bald, black-bearded man of swarthy complexion, in Athens once and wondered how a man of the cloth in the service of God could be so instrumental in creating such terror and bloodshed between people. The leader of the Turkish Cypriots, Dr. Fazıl Küçük, who loved Cyprus brandy, told me one day when EOKA bombs were exploding in Nicosia against British targets that "Makarios is destined to cause much trouble not only for the British, but also for all of us on this island. He should have been a politician, not a priest. The idea of *Enosis* will eventually lead to more bloodshed and the landing of Turkish troops in Cyprus." Dr. Küçük believed that the survival of the Turkish Cypriot community depended entirely on Turkey.

As the first president of independent Cyprus after the 1960 tripartite agreement of London, Makarios ignored the constitutional guarantees of the Turkish minority and the rights of Dr. Küçük as vice president. The island sank into violence three years after its independence from Britain. The power-sharing constitution, agreed upon during the London conference, collapsed and the Greek Cypriots assumed sole control of the Cyprus government. Bloodshed and terror against the Turkish Cypriots resumed. The bloody Christmas massacres of Turkish Cypriots in December 1963 brought Ismet Inönü, then the prime minister of weak coalition governments in Turkey, to the brink of military intervention. I kept sending cables to the editors of Reuters about the imminence of a military landing. Each time, the Americans stopped Inönü, sometimes with abrupt and discourteous language.

I don't believe the Turks ever forgot President Lyndon B. Johnson's strongly worded letter to Ismet Inönü, warning him in no uncertain terms. Johnson, in his letter dated June 5, 1964, told the Turkish premier not to use American weapons. If, he added, the Turkish invasion of the island provoked an intervention from the Soviet Union, NATO and the United States might not feel obligated to defend Turkey.

When President Johnson's letter was received, I remember that it caused a shock among the members of the cabinet because its tone was considered insulting. Student demonstrators hit the streets again, singing a new tune:

> Stuff Johnson in a sack,
> Swing the sack and swing him,
> And hit him against the wall.

Dr. Küçük's prophecy came true on July 20, 1974. The Turkish Army landed on the island and divided Cyprus by occupying the north. The event that triggered it was a coup d'etat on the island and an attempt to unify Cyprus with Greece. This happened despite the fact that Greece, along with Turkey and Britain, was a guarantor power that was supposed to ensure the independence of Cyprus under the tripartite London treaty. Five days earlier, on July 15, Nicos Sampson, who was well known as a former EOKA guerrilla, had staged a coup in Nicosia with the participation of the Cypriot National Guard led by Greek army officers. The coup had the backing of the junta of colonels in Greece. The independent republic's government was seized, and President Makarios was ousted.

Nicos Sampson, who later became a newspaper publisher, was known as the "eight-day president of Cyprus." Sampson had joined EOKA as a young man and fought against British colonial rule between 1955 and 1959. He was sentenced to death twice by the British because of his crimes but released from jail in 1960 under an amnesty when the island became independent. As a right-wing member of the Cyprus parliament, he was involved in clashes between ethnic Greeks and Turks in 1963. Due to crimes committed against the state, Sampson was sentenced to twenty years in jail in 1976, but he was allowed to seek medical treatment in Paris, where he then remained for eleven years. On his return to Cyprus in 1990, he was jailed again to serve the rest of his sentence and was given amnesty in 1993 due to his failing health.

Nicos Sampson, a well-known target of hate among the Turkish Cypriots, who considered him a ruthless murderer, died on May 9, 2001, in Nicosia of cancer at sixty-six. His wife, Vera Sampson, said: "He believed in Greece, he believed in the Parthenon, and he paid a high price for it."

At the time of the Turkish invasion of Cyprus in 1974, there was a coalition government in Turkey between Bülent Ecevit's left-of-center Republican People's Party and Necmettin Erbakan's pro-Islam National Salvation Party. Prime Minister Ecevit and his deputy Erbakan agreed to land troops in Cyprus but disagreed on how much of the island ought to be occupied. Erbakan was in favor of occupying the whole of Cyprus, not just the northern part. During the military intervention, nearly five hundred Turkish soldiers, about a thousand Turkish Cypriots, and three thousand Greek soldiers and Greek civilian Cypriots were killed. The intervention helped Greece to get rid of the junta of colonels in Athens.

The military intervention divided the island. The Turkish Republic of Northern Cyprus, recognized only by Turkey, remained dependent on a subsidy of over $400 million a year from the Turkish mainland. Rauf Denktaş, the president and an old hand of the tripartite Cyprus talks in London, often said that the division of Cyprus actually helped stop the internal violence.

There was a time when the Greek Cypriots had assumed full control of the government of independent Cyprus. We reporters had problems covering the events on the island. Archbishop Makarios simply refused to grant visas to journalists from the Turkish mainland. I was managing the Haber News Agency, an affiliate of *Hürriyet*, and tried to find a round-about way to get to the island to report the news. It was also a time when Greek officials were constantly harassing Metin Doğanalp, our staff cor-respondent in Athens.

I checked the hotels in Istanbul and found a likely substitute for our reporters, a young Dutch tourist. We financed his trip to Cyprus, instructing him where to go, whom to see, and what questions to ask. The Dutchman was successful, and our efforts to make an "instant" newsman out of him had worked. When he returned to Istanbul, we had the information and the news pictures we needed. *Hürriyet* then printed a series of articles by him titled *The Cyprus Report*. Seen through the eyes of an uninvolved third party, the Dutchman's articles conveyed a good picture of the conditions in Cyprus and established the fact that Turkish Cypriots on the island were treated as second-class citizens.

I remember my first brush with British intelligence in Cyprus at a time when EOKA was conducting acts of terrorism. In the 1950s, I used to stay at a small hotel located in what was then known as the Turkish part of Nicosia. Early in the mornings as the neighborhood roosters crowed, the bombs of EOKA aimed at British targets would explode, raising dark clouds in the sky. As the days progressed, EOKA terrorists would shoot people in the streets and vanish into the crowds.

Once, traveling at night by car in the Troodos Mountains, I was stopped by nervous British troops looking for weapons. My protests and presenting my press credentials were not much help. I was searched. The next day, I complained to a British information officer in Nicosia. He listened politely and invited me to dinner.

The dinner was in a private home, presumably a safe house and included three young English ladies, each one prettier than the next. The information officer and I were the only men present. It was obvious that I was being subjected to a seductive "honey trap" that was to be followed by recruitment to spy for them. I showed no interest, and that was the end of the dinner party.

Early in 2003, the age-old Cyprus crisis took an unexpected turn. The changes were a result of improvements in Turco-Greek relations, the membership of Cyprus in the European Union scheduled for 2004, and the election victory in Turkey of the Justice and Development Party with Islamic roots. Even *Hürriyet*'s old Cyprus policy was dead as a doornail, a victim of the times. Some *Hürriyet* columnists wanted a quick solution for the sake of membership in the European Union. Thousands of Turkish Cypriots, wishing to be part of the European Union regardless of the consequences, demonstrated against the nationalist policies of Rauf Denktaş, president of the Republic of Northern Cyprus. Denktaş wanted to maintain the status quo if a solution favorable to the Turkish Cypriots and

Turkey was not accepted by the Greeks. He considered the independence of northern Cyprus as a guarantee for the safety of the Turkish Cypriots. However, many Turkish Cypriots carried placards during demonstrations bearing sentences like "We are not Turks or Greeks, but Cypriots," and "Occupiers, get out." Denktaş blamed a left-wing group for instigating the demonstrations and said that he had been knifed in the back while the negotiations were still ongoing. Denktaş always defended a policy solution of equal sovereignty for both communities. The Greeks, however, considered the Turkish Cypriots to be a minority.

When the Justice and Development Party won the election in Turkey on November 3, 2002, its leader, Recep Tayyip Erdoğan, said that the time was at hand to get rid of the old Cyprus policies. The policy of previous Turkish governments had been based on the concept of "If there's no solution, no solution is a solution."

The Cyprus crisis was a big disappointment for the Turks. The Greek part of the island was booming economically while the northern part remained poor, depending on economic aid from Turkey. This yearly aid to the tune of over $400 million had become a burden for Turkey's troubled national budget. Several members of the media, including some *Hürriyet* columnists, often used the proverb *Ekmek elden, su gölden* for the Republic of Northern Cyprus. It means to get along without working while others provide bread to eat and a lake supplies the drinking water. For them, the status quo in Cyprus was bankrupt.

Surprisingly many Turks just wanted to wash their hands of the whole Cyprus mess by accepting a reunification plan presented by UN Secretary General Kofi Annan. The plan included the settlement of sixty thousand Greek Cypriots in Northern Cyprus and involved property exchanges. The UN-brokered peace talks collapsed because of disagreements between Turkish and Greek Cypriots. Still, for the first time since the partition, Denktaş opened the border to visits by members of both communities, and Erdoğan's Turkish government announced in January 2004 that it was ready to accept Kofi Annan's plan for the reunification of the island—with some changes. Peace talks resumed in February 2004. The Turkish government's great desire for membership at any cost in the

European Union was overwhelming. The Greek Cypriots rejected the Annan plan during a referendum held in April 2004, while the Turkish Cypriots voted yes. Cyprus remains divided.

The generals of the armed forces uneasily watched these developments. To them, abandoning Turkey's legitimate rights was tantamount to accepting Greece's domination in an area that begins in the northern Aegean Sea and ends in the eastern Mediterranean—a strategic stronghold for the Anatolian mainland.

Still, in the spring of 2003, Turco-Greek relations were in stark contrast to an event that had taken place one day in October 1997. Turkish jet fighters on that day buzzed Greek Defense Minister Akis Tsohatzopoulos's plane over the Aegean Sea. Tsohatzopoulos was heading to and returning from joint Greek–Greek Cypriot military exercises in Cyprus. Greece claimed that in one week Turkish fighter planes violated its ten-mile airspace zone on nearly two hundred occasions.

A year earlier, on October 8, 1996, Thanos Grivas, piloting a Greek Mirage 2000 jet fighter, had fired a Magic rocket at a Turkish F-16. The rocket had hit the Turkish warplane's engine; the pilot, Lieut. Col. Osman Çiçekli, had ejected; and Capt. Nail Erdoğan had crashed with the plane into the Aegean and died.

Three years later, in August 1999, an earthquake that killed over seventeen thousand people in northwestern Turkey acted as an inducement to reestablish a new kind of trust between Greece and Turkey. Greece provided swift and substantial help in the wake of the earthquake, which was warmly received by the Turks. When a second earthquake shook northern Athens, claiming 139 lives, the Turks, in turn, quickly sent aid to Greece. A third destructive tremor in northwestern Turkey that killed almost eight hundred people expanded further the earthquake diplomacy between the two countries.

A series of talks between the Turkish and Greek foreign ministers, Ismail Cem and George Papandreou, followed. In a speech to the UN General Assembly in New York on September 22, 1999, Papandreou said that the earthquakes had accelerated the process of cooperation between the two countries. Papandreou visited Ankara in January 2000 to sign agreements designed to build confidence between the two nations. It was the first official visit by a Greek foreign minister to Turkey in thirty-seven years. During a groundbreaking goodwill mission to Israel and Palestine together in April 2002, Papandreou and Cem met Israeli Prime Minister Ariel Sharon and Palestinian President Yasser Arafat. The purpose of their trip was to show the Israelis and the Palestinians that it is indeed possible to find ways to make peace. It served to demonstrate that even the Turks and the Greeks, sworn enemies for such a long time, could find ways to live as good neighbors.

History plays a crucial role in human relations. The roots of the hatred that drove a wedge between the Turks and Greeks are found in their histories, particularly the end of the Byzantine Empire. In 1453 the Ottomans captured Constantinople (or Konstantiniye), the present metropolis of Istanbul.

There is a long list of other reasons.

Almost four centuries of Ottoman occupation of Greece left Turkish cultural marks on Greek music, dance, and culinary influences, which the Greeks hate to admit. Biased history curricula in both nations' school books are numerous. They include the massacre of the Turkish population of Morea by Greeks during the nineteenth century; the hanging of Patriarch Gregory V on Easter Sunday in 1821 in Istanbul, on charges of aiding the Greek revolution against the Ottoman regime; the Greek War of Independence during 1821–29, the Greek invasion of Anatolia right after World War I, and the Turkish Independence War in 1919–22.

The existence of the Greek Orthodox Patriarchate in the Fener district on the Golden Horn felt like a sharp thorn in the heart of the Turk when the Cyprus crisis erupted. This despite the fact that the Ottoman government, after the conquest of Constantinople, recognized Gennadius II as the ethnarch—or ruler—of the Orthodox people living inside the borders of the Ottoman Empire. Fatih (Conqueror) Sultan Mehmet II had saved Gennadius the Scholar from slavery and made this theologian the patriarch with clerical and secular powers over his flock.

The Greek invasion of Anatolia in 1919, after the Ottoman Empire had collapsed, was a major cause of Turkish bitterness against the Greeks.

The turning of Saint Sophia (Hagia Sophia, Divine Wisdom, or Aya Sofya), the symbol of Orthodox Christianity, into a mosque after the conquest of Constantinople and the hanging of Patriarch Gregory V were more than enough fodder for Greek bitterness against the Turks. George Aggelopoulos had served many years as Patriarch Gregory V and is venerated as a saint by the Orthodox Church. The main gate of the patriarchal basilica where Gregory V was hanged in 1821 remains bricked up to this day as a gesture of protest.

In his time Kemal Atatürk did his best to establish good neighborly relations with Greece. He was concerned about the constant source of aggrievement, which the Saint Sophia mosque presented to Orthodox Greeks. It had been a church for nine hundred years and then a mosque for four hundred fifty years. This massive Byzantine cathedral, completed in 537 CE during the reign of Justinian I, had become a symbol for both Christianity and Islam, mixing the values of both religions. Atatürk found a nonreligious solution for this cathedral-mosque to win the goodwill of the Greeks—he made it a museum open to all. Now, sixty-five years after Atatürk's death, mischievous voices of Islamic fundamentalists can be heard demanding that the museum be opened again for prayers. It is hard to understand why they require the museum when Istanbul is chock full of great mosques. Such attempts by the Islamists can only inflame bitter feelings of the Greek Orthodox. The Islamists, too, would be upset if the extremist Greek Orthodox wanted this historic building opened for Orthodox prayers. It's much better to keep it as a neutral museum, where all are welcome.

During the 1990s, one more incident happened to disturb Turco-Greek relations. That was the Greek protection of Abdullah Öcalan, the leader of the outlawed Kurdistan Workers Party (PKK), and the support given by the Greek government to his separatist organization. Soon after leaving the protection of the Greek Embassy in Nairobi, Kenya, where he had fled from Syria via Athens, Öcalan was captured by Turkish security agents on February 15, 1999. He was carrying a Cypriot passport that identified him as Mavros Lazaros. According to the news reports, he told Turkish interrogators that Greek governments had supported the

PKK for years, providing it with weapons and training Kurdish guerrillas in camps on Greek soil.

The report caused a huge uproar in Turkey. Bülent Ecevit, the prime minister at the time, described Greece's support of the PKK as "an unseemly attitude that doesn't become an ally."

Consider the fact that through several centuries, the Turks and the Greeks have lived in peace together and intermarried. Those were the good times of the Ottoman Empire. The Greek aristocracy, the descendants of Byzantine families who lived in Fener at the Golden Horn near the Greek Orthodox Patriarchate, played a major role in commerce during the Ottoman Empire. These Greek aristocrats were called *phanaries*, from the Greek word *phanar*, meaning the lighthouse, and many of them had served as governors in the Balkans, appointed to represent the Ottoman regime. In Turkish history, other ethnic Greeks acted as dragomans, privileged translators for the Ottoman state and for foreign embassies at the Sublime Porte.

It is also a fact that many Greeks as well as Slavs held prestigious offices in the Ottoman Empire. The Ottoman sultans themselves were not of pure Turkish descent, having among others Greek mothers.

Sultan Beyazıd I, known as the Thunderbolt because he repeatedly and quickly smashed rebellions, had to endure the indignity of watching his Greek wife Despina being forced to serve naked at Tatar warrior Tamerlane's table. He had been defeated and taken prisoner on the plain of Çubuk near Ankara by Tamerlane's army in July 1402. Because of his arrogance, Timur the Lame placed the sultan in a cage like an animal. A year later, Beyazid I died in shame and sorrow by bashing his head on the bars of his cage. He was only forty-three when he died.

The greatest architect of the Ottoman Empire was a man of Greek origin, and his story is fascinating. In the year 1512, a young man named Joseph from the village of Ağırnaz, near Kayseri in central Anatolia, was drafted as *devşirme*, a tribute boy, into the Janissary forces. His parents were Greek Orthodox Christians, and his father worked as stonemason and carpenter in that village. Joseph had learned his father's trade and, after extensive training by the Ottoman regime, became a construction officer in the Ottoman army. He rose to the rank of chief of the artillery forces and built fortifications.

Joseph was promoted to the post of the royal architect of the empire during the regime of Süleyman the Magnificent. This man, who was close to Süleyman and his family, built the greatest mosques, bridges, and public buildings, many of them national treasures. His masterpieces are the Şehzade, Mihrimah, and Süleymaniye mosques in Istanbul and the Selimiye Mosque in Edirne (in western Turkey, near Greece and Bulgaria).

Another of his architectural marvels is a long stone bridge at Büyükçekmece near Istanbul, not too far from a steep climb of an old caravan route over the Hill Which Makes Camels Scream as they climb it. His name, Yusuf Abdullah, is carved in stone in Arabic letters on the bridge now used only by shepherds and their flocks of sheep.

This old Janissary died in 1588 at the age of ninety-nine and was buried in a tomb with a fountain that he had built for himself behind the Süleymaniye Mosque. Joseph had stayed loyal to his Greek family and to the people of Ağırnaz, whom he had helped throughout his life.

Joseph, or Yusuf, is known in Turkish history as Sinan Abdul-Mennan, or simply as Mimar Sinan, Sinan the Architect. He built seventy-nine mosques, fifty-five religious schools, thirty-four palaces, twelve caravanserais ("caravan palaces"), thirty-three public baths, and a number of bridges.

Turkish history abounds with slaves, several of them Greek, who became powerful and even served as grand viziers in the Ottoman empire. One colorful Greek personage, who reached a high position in the Ottoman Sultan's court, is known as Marko Pasha. He had the reputation of a solicitous listener to the people's grievances who never attempted to solve any of their problems.

There is a humorous saying, "Derdini Marko Paşaya anlat!" (Tell your troubles to Marko Pasha!) It literally means, complaining is useless, as nobody but Marko Pasha is willing to listen to your grievances. Markos Apostilides Pasha was the dean of the Military Medical School in Istanbul and Sultan Abdul Hamid II's chief physician. He had also served as the Ottoman Empire's minister of health and chairman of the Red Crescent Society. He was renowned for his patience while listening to complaints of his patients and students of the Military Medical School.

One day a cadet at the school complained to Marko Pasha about some problems that had developed in his class. Marko Pasha told him, "I understand son, I understand, but what are you saying?"

Marko Pasha's friendly attitude and willingness to listen to people's grievances won him many friends. He was a short and ugly man who had married a tall, stunning Greek beauty. The couple had thirteen children—ten died early, and only a son and two daughters survived. Marko Pasha is buried at Kuzguncuk Cemetery in Istanbul.

Ferai Tınç, a newspaper columnist, had found in Athens Marko Pasha's great-grandson George K. Papadopoulos and great-granddaughter Despina. George K. Papadopoulos said, "My great-grandfather just listened to everyone's problems, but never found a solution."

Marko Pasha was a pioneer not only in public relations but also in human intercommunication. I think this beloved figure of Turkish folklore left a clear legacy for the Turks as well as the Greeks: Be friendly. During a visit to Athens by Turkish Prime Minister Recep Tayyip Erdoğan and his wife, Emine, in May 2004, the Greek prime minister Costas Karamanlis and his wife, Natasha, welcomed them warmly. When the couples bid their farewells later, Prime Minister Karamanlis even managed to surprise Emine Erdoğan with a kiss on her left cheek. Emine Erdoğan, who wears a turban and is a devout Muslim, managed to gently repulse a second kiss that was meant for her right cheek.

The Greek media had a fantastic time over this event, while the Turkish media kept a mysterious silence. The reporters of both the official Turkish Radio and Television and the Anatolian Agency were present during the kissing episode. Both the TRT and AA were advised not to report it.

Marxists, Islamists, and Ottoman Nostalgia

One eats while another watches. All strife results from that.

Turkish proverb

*C*ommunism in Turkey is as old as the earliest Bolshevik movement in Russia. During Kemal Atatürk's reign, a small group of leftists stayed underground, as the Communist Party was banned in 1922. Under Ismet Inönü's dictatorial regime following the death of Atatürk, the Communists, for fear of punishment, were obliged to keep a low profile. Even during the democratic experiment of Adnan Menderes's Democratic Party regime beginning in 1950, undemocratic laws were suppressing the Marxist-Leninist movement.

The coup d'etat on May 27, 1960, that ousted the Menderes regime allowed the return of many leftists who had been living abroad. Others already employed as newspaper columnists adopted social justice as their slogan. Later, however, the military regimes targeted left-wing writers, detaining them in barracks and subjecting them to trials military courts.

I remember that the coup d'etat of May 27, 1960, presented the Soviet Union with an opportunity to help expand the leftist movement in the country. Some Soviet diplomats and consular officials, who were actually KGB agents, actively began recruiting local people and sending them to terrorist camps in Syria and Bulgaria for training. The result was a hard-core, ruthlessly militant Marxist movement that is still very much active.

Early in the 1950s, we had leftist reporters among us in Babıali, but they were few, not yet "out of the closet" for fear of going to jail despite their support of Kemalist ideals. When the Turkish submarine *Dumlupınar* collided with a Swedish freighter in the Dardanelles Strait on April 4, 1953, and sank, a lot of reporters from Babıali flocked into the town of Çanakkale. There was a crew of eighty-one officers and sailors trapped inside the submarine. They lived seventy-two hours at the bottom of the strait—ninety-two meters deep—knowing full well that they could not be saved. The technology to do so did not exist then.

The leftist novelist Yaşar Kemal was also there on assignment as a reporter from the left-of-center daily *Cumhuriyet*. Often I would tease him in the lobby of the hotel in Çanakkale, saying, "Hey, you, Commie," and my words would rightly irritate Yaşar Kemal. He is an Anatolian like me. He was a tall, young man then, of dark hair and complexion and only one good eye that gave him a fearsome look, which always reminded me that Yaşar Kemal's maternal ancestors were brigands.

Upset by my words, he would shout, *"Deyyus! Bir yakalarsam, gebertecem!"* (Cuckold! Once I catch you, I will kill you!) Not the grammatically correct speech, *gebert8eceğim*, but *gebertecem*, a figurative expression meaning I will kill. That was pure Anatolian talk.

Yaşar Kemal Göğçeli was married to Mathilda, a woman of Jewish descent who had worked as a translator for the Associated Press. Known as Tilda, she was the translator of Yaşar Kemal's novels into other languages. Her grandfather, Jack Mandil Pasha, had been Sultan Abdul Hamid II's chief physician. She was tried in 1972 in a military court for alleged leftist activities.

Yaşar Kemal would chase and grab me, then say: "Shut up, shut up! The cops will hear you! You will burn me!" He was right to be concerned, for in 1950 he had been arrested for alleged Communist propaganda but was acquitted.

Italy's Fascist dictator Benito Mussolini's penal code, adopted in Turkey in 1926, was like a solid barrier to the rules of democracy and free speech. Through the years, this penal code would destroy the lives of many intellectuals and writers.

In those years, especially when Ismet Inönü ruled the country as a dictator during World War II, Communists were hunted. The First Bureau of the Police Directorate kept and upgraded files of all known leftists. Anyone identified by the police as an *Azılı Komunist*, a dangerous, extreme Communist, found all doors closed to him or her. He couldn't get a job, and if by chance he did, the cops would immediately inform his employer: He is a notorious Communist, so why do you give him a job? Beware!

It was very difficult for a known Communist to hold onto a job or even to obtain a passport to leave the country. Through the years, conservative governments targeted leftist writers and their works. Copies of Reşad Enis's book *Toprak Kokusu* (*The Smell of the Soil*) were confiscated. Mahmut Makal, the author of *Bizim Köy* (*Our Village*) found himself in deep trouble with the regime. Leftist writers regularly became defendants facing serious charges in the criminal courts. Many were jailed.

The officials even forbade the distribution of some books written by foreign authors and translated into Turkish. These books included Jack London's *The Iron Heel*, a terrifying anticipation of a Fascist regime, and John Steinbeck's *In Dubious Battle*, an account of a strike by agricultural laborers encouraged by two Marxists.

These intolerable conditions forced several leftists to attempt some dangerous things. A good example is the fate of Sabahattin Ali, who with Aziz Nesin had published the humor magazine *Marko Paşa* and had been sentenced to jail terms for insulting other writers. Fed up with pressures on his writing and life, Sabahattin Ali attempted to escape and was murdered in 1948 near the Bulgarian-Turkish border. A severe blow to his head with a piece of firewood killed him. The writer's murderer remains a mystery, but it is generally believed that he was killed by the Turkish Intelligence Agency, known at the time as *Milli Emniyet,* the National Security Agency. His leftist friends believe that the guide he trusted to help him cross the border into Bulgaria was actually an intelligence agent.

Değirmen (*The Windmill*), *Kürk Mantolu Madonna* (*Madonna with a Fur Coat*), *İçimizdeki Şeytan* (*The Devil within Us*), and *The Ox-Cart and the Voice* are among Sabahattin Ali's writings.

Yaşar Kemal, too, could not stay out of trouble. Even at the age of seventy-three he ended up in court in Istanbul for writing a pro-Kurdish article printed in the German magazine *Der Spiegel*. He received a twenty-month prison sentence, which was not carried out. Yaşar Kemal, who is of half-Kurdish descent, wrote *Memet, My Hawk*; *They Burn the Thistles*; and *The Undying Grass*; among others.

During the coup d'etat in 1960, I was editor-in-chief of *Akşam*, a morning newspaper, the name of which paradoxically meant evening. We did have a leftist cell in the paper's editorial department led by the columnist Aziz Nesin. Other columnists, who described themselves as progressive and advocated changes in the country's social structure, included Çetin Altan and Müşerref Hekimoğlu. Injustices existed in Turkey then as they do now, and poverty was (and still is) a major problem. The gap between the haves and have-nots has even increased since then.

Aziz Nesin was called by Islamic fundamentalists *Şeytan Aziz* or Aziz, the Devil. He was nearly burned to death by angry religious bigots in July 1993 during a festival in Sivas, a central Anatolian city. This incident is known as the *Massacre of Sivas*. Islamic reactionaries set fire to a building where Aziz Nesin was holding a literary discussion honoring Pir Sultan Abdal, a sixteenth-century Alawite mystic poet who was born in Sivas. Pir Sultan Abdal lived during the reign of Süleyman the Magnificent and got involved in an Alawite rebellion. Deli (Mad) Hızır Pasha, the regional Ottoman governor, hanged him. Before he died, Pir Sultan Abdal wrote about that governor:

> Hey, you, Hızır Pasha, now move along,
> Your fate too is bound to be broken.
> You do rely so much on your Sultan,
> He, too, one day will be overthrown.

Pir Sultan Abdal's poems—written in the simple, spoken Turkish of his time—show traces of social and political protest.

Come, come, my yellow tamboura,*
Why do you moan and groan?

In one of his poems about *çiğdem*, the yellow crocus or saffron plant, Pir Sultan Abdal wrote:

I asked the yellow crocus,
Where do you stay in winter?
Oh, Dervish, what are you saying?
In the winter I stay underground.
I asked the yellow crocus,
What do you eat under the ground?
Oh, Dervish, what are you saying?
I survive on God's morsel of power.
I asked the yellow crocus,
Why is your face so pale?
Oh, Dervish, what are you saying?
I have the fear of God.
I asked the yellow crocus.
Have you a father and mother?
Oh, Dervish, what are you saying?
The earth is my mother and the rain is my father.

Pir Sultan Abdal also wrote, "Don't turn away when you see me,/My affection for you is forever." And:

I arrived in this false world,
And I am leaving,
I found no other place such as you, my heart.

One day before the fire, Aziz Nesin had given a public address with anti-Islamic overtones in Sivas that was printed by the local press. This caused an angry response from the Islamic reactionaries. They were already upset, as Aziz Nesin had earlier sponsored the publication in

---

* The tamboura is a musical instrument resembling a lute.

Aydınlık, a leftist weekly, of a translation of Salman Rushdie's novel *Satanic Verses*. About fifteen thousand Islamic reactionaries surrounded the Madımak Hotel in Sivas, where the festival was being held. They were shouting slogans like, "Damn secularity, we want the Shariah," and "Damn Aziz, the Devil." The police were unable to control the demonstrators. The reactionaries demanded the removal of the Poets' Monument located in front of the Cultural Center. The officials removed the monument and cancelled the festival.

Still not satisfied, the fundamentalists rioted. They captured the monument, dragged it through the streets, and destroyed it. In the evening, they burned a vehicle in front of the hotel, stoned the building, and finally firebombed it repeatedly. The hotel was engulfed in fire, and about one hundred people took refuge on the fourth floor. According to the Sivas police, thirty-seven people died in the burning hotel. Firemen saved Aziz Nesin along with ninety-two others from the fourth floor using a fire-engine ladder. Upon discovering his identity, the firemen got upset and kicked and insulted Aziz Nesin for provoking the tragic incident.

A Turkish court in May 2000 handed out death sentences to thirty-three people convicted of seeking to abolish the Kemalist reform laws by imposing an Islamic regime based on the Shariah and for that arson attack in Sivas.

Aziz Nesin was a great storyteller. During the suppressive regime of Ismet Inönü in 1946, he had co-published with Sabahattin Ali the humor magazine *Marko Paşa*. When the authorities closed it and jailed Sabahattin Ali for insulting other writers, they kept publishing the magazine under new names like *Dead Paşa* and *You Know Who Paşa* and *Ali Baba*.

Aziz Nesin's humorous stories include "Madman on the Roof," "Oh, We Donkeys," and "Green Honor Gas." He was often arrested for his writings in the 1940s and jailed, staying in prison at different occasions for a total of over five years. He had been an army officer and was discharged for left-wing extremism.

This highly talented satirist was a short, dark-complexioned man with angry eyes in a face that rarely smiled. In collaboration with the other leftists at the newspaper *Akşam*, he also tried to recruit me to the cause of

Marxism-Leninism. His writings contributed a lot to the division between the extreme right and the extreme left in the country.

It is now arguable that the leftist columnists, who were strict secularists, were unwittingly instrumental in the spread of Islamic fundamentalism. Their hope was the establishment of a Marxist-Leninist regime. The conservative Anatolians, however, rejected Communism outright because they did not want to live under a Godless regime. This presented an opportunity for the fundamentalists and the merchants of religion. In order to incite and infuriate people, they revived the Ottoman Empire's old reactionary slogan: *Din elden gidiyor*—We are losing our religion.

After the collapse of the Soviet Union, the disunity in the country continued between the *aydınlar*, or the enlightened (in other words, the secular leftists), and the *yobazlar*, or religious bigots. Before he died of natural causes, Aziz Nesin had sponsored the leftist newspaper *Aydınlık* (*Enlightenment*).

Aziz Nesin's idol was the Marxist poet Nazım Hikmet Ran, who also had served prison terms. Nazım Hikmet was a gifted poet who drifted between two worlds and encountered grief in both. Fresh out of a Turkish jail, he fled to the Soviet Union in 1951, when he was forty-eight years old.

In Moscow Nazım Hikmet complained that Soviet writers were unable to express their true feelings. His words angered the Soviet authorities. In a book titled *Eski Dostlar* (*Old Friends*), published in Istanbul in 2000, journalist Hıfzı Topuz reported that Nazım Hikmet received a threatening phone call from Alexei Adzhubei. Adzhubei, Nikita Khrushchev's son-in-law, who was *Pravda*'s leading writer, said: "Who are you to criticize us? You are someone seeking refuge in Russia." Adzhubei added that the next day he might be shot in the head while walking in the street. Adzhubei said: "Then you would disappear, so get your act together."

"You may kill me," Nazım Hikmet had answered, "but my name will survive. What about you, if you die tomorrow, what will you leave behind?"

This conversation, according to the sources of Hıfzı Topuz, had shocked Nazım Hikmet deeply. Angry and hurt, he began to tremble.

Those were difficult times for a poet who had devoted his entire life to the cause of Marxist-Leninist ideals and for the freedom of thought and free expression of ideas. Once he had written in a poem, "We will see happy, wonderful days, children."

Nazım Hikmet didn't see happy days.

He expected to find freedom and happiness as an exile in Moscow. Instead, he found utter disappointment and solace in the bottle. We used to hear stories about his nights with wine, women, and music in Budapest, Moscow, or somewhere else inside the Soviet Union and felt pity for the waste of this extraordinary talent.

According to Hıfzı Topuz, *Optimism*, written in Moscow on September 12, 1957, was one of his last poems:

> I write poems
> They don't get published
> But they will get published.
> I am waiting for a letter with good news
> Perhaps it will arrive the day I die
> But for sure it will come.

Nazım Hikmet was born in Salonica (Thessaloniki) in 1902, studied at Heybeli Island Naval Academy in Istanbul, and served as an officer in the Turkish Navy. He was discharged from the navy for poor health. Nazım Hikmet's poetry teacher Yahya Kemal Beyatlı was also the lover of Celile, Hikmet's mother. One day Nazım Hikmet slipped a note in his teacher's pocket that said: "You've entered this home as my teacher, but you may not enter it as my father."

That cooled off Beyatlı's love for Nazım Hikmet's mother.

A blond man with blue eyes, Nazım Hikmet as a young man went to study in Moscow. In 1924, upon returning to Turkey, he was arrested on charges of working for a Marxist magazine and later managed to escape to Russia. A general amnesty in 1928 during the Kemalist reforms allowed him to return to Turkey. He found himself under constant surveillance by the National Security Agency. Hikmet, jailed several times as a political prisoner, was arrested in 1938 once again on a trumped-up charge of inciting mutiny in the navy. He was sentenced to twenty-eight years in prison, served eighteen, and was released in 1950.

According to the poet, there were two attempts to kill him with staged car accidents in the streets of Istanbul. Then the authorities drafted him for military service near the Turkish-Russian frontier in eastern Anatolia. A military doctor gave him a certificate of perfect health while privately warning him that half an hour of standing in the sun was enough to kill him. In 1951, he escaped to Moscow once more. After that, the Democratic Party regime of Adnan Menderes stripped him of his Turkish citizenship.

Nazım Hikmet's second escape to Russia is mysterious.

During a stormy night, he took off in a tiny motorboat in the Bosphorus, trying to find a Soviet ship sailing to the Black Sea. He saw a Romanian cargo ship and shouted and waved his handkerchief. The ship didn't stop. While Hikmet ran circles around the Romanian ship, shouting his name, his little motor stalled. Finally, the Romanians hauled him aboard and called Bucharest for instructions.

"I was half dead when I staggered into the ship's officers' cabin," Nazım Hikmet told the French writer and feminist Simone de Beauvoir later. "There I saw a big photograph of myself with a caption: *Save Nazım Hikmet.*"

The poster had been created during his years in prison. He told Simone de Beauvoir that the irony of it was that at the time he was taken onto the ship, he had already been out of prison for a year.

Once in the Soviet Union, Nazım Hikmet obtained Polish citizenship because of his explanation that his blue eyes came from a Polish ancestor. In Moscow, Hikmet was given a house in the writers' colony of Peredelkino and died there in 1963 of a second heart attack, disillusioned with the Soviets and Marxism. He was buried in a Soviet cemetery and rehabilitated in Turkey almost a decade after the collapse of the Soviet Union. In November 2000, Turkish socialists sent a petition with half a million signatures to Prime Minister Bülent Ecevit, demanding posthumous restoration of the poet's citizenship.

Nazım Hikmet was an admirer of Chairman Mao Tse-Tung's Red China and expressed his progressive social attitude in poetical form. His writings in the 1930s revolutionized Turkish poetry by using the language of the people and free verse. Nazım Hikmet's poetry was brilliant because he had abandoned the courtly conventions and complex language of the old Ottoman literature. In a poem titled "Angina Pectoris," he states to his doctor that if half of his heart remained in a Turkish jail, the other half would be in China with the Red Chinese Army, flowing toward the Yellow River. His poetry books include *Letters to Taranta Babu, The Telegram That Arrived at Night, Human Landscapes*, and *New Poems*.

Nazım Hikmet had a dog named *Şeytan*. He wrote about his pet when the dog died in 1956:

> He was like a human being
> Most animals are like human beings
> So much like a good person.

The United Nations Educational, Scientific, and Cultural Organization (UNESCO) declared 2002 as the Year of Nazım Hikmet.

My friend Abdi Ipekçi's assassination may have had something to do with the strained relations between Greece and Turkey and Nazım Hikmet's disappointment with Marxism and the Soviet Union. Even when we were young Kemalist reporters, Abdi Ipekçi wanted to see relations improve between Greece and Turkey. Later, as the editor-in-chief of *Milliyet*, he was very active in promoting reconciliation between the two countries, and he did his best to restrain hotheaded Turkish politicians and journalists. This did not suit the Soviet intentions of weakening the NATO alliance by destroying the relationship between Greece and Turkey, two members in NATO's southeastern flank.

Abdi Ipekçi had done something else that angered the local leftists and the Soviets. Apart from the incident with Chobanov, the Bulgarian ambassador in the 1950s, Abdi Ipekçi had published in fall 1978 in *Milliyet* the memoirs of Zekeriya Sertel, a veteran left-wing writer. Sertel had been in exile in Russia with Nazım Hikmet and stated in his memoirs that the poet had been highly disappointed with Communism and the Soviet Union.

The memoirs shocked the Turkish leftists. The Soviets, too, were wrathful for they feared the loss of an idol.

The mystery of Abdi Ipekçi's killing still remains and the finger of accusation points not only to Sofia and Moscow but also to the political bosses and the criminal elements of the Turkish ultranationalists. Abdi Ipekçi had angered right-wing extremists and ultranationalists, some of them high government officials, by investigating their close relations and joint activities with criminal gangs. He wrote columns critical of the nationalists, particularly the members of the Nationalist Action Party.

The man who was jailed for Abdi Ipekçi's murder, Mehmet Ali Ağca, appears as a ghostly shadow in the murky wilderness of recent Turkish politics. He was identified as a right-wing terrorist, an *Ülkücü*, an Idealist. *Ülkücü* was another name for Gray Wolf, a follower of and street fighter for the late Colonel Alparslan Türkeş, founder of the Nationalist Action Party. Ağca, aided by mysterious sources in 1979, was able to escape from Kartal, a heavily guarded prison, where he was kept on charges of murdering Abdi Ipekçi. He is the terrorist who later shot and nearly killed Pope John Paul II in St. Peter's Square in Rome on May 13, 1981, the feast day of the Virgin of Fatima. Ağca, serving a life sentence, pleaded clemency from his prison cell in Italy in May 2000 as the pope made a pilgrimage to the shrine of the Virgin of Fatima in Portugal. John Paul II believes that the Virgin of Fatima saved his life in the attack.

Ağca, now forty-six, was pardoned and released from the Italian prison in June 2000. Once in Istanbul, he was taken to the maximum-security Kartal prison. He is being held in solitary confinement to serve out the ten-year sentence for Ipekçi's assassination.

Was Ağca, who now claims to be Jesus Christ, a madman, a Communist agent, or a gunman of the Turkish extreme right?

He is not telling his secrets. In the high-security jail, Ağca kept a tight mouth and did nothing to implicate his supporters, some of them powerful figures in Turkish politics. His secrets may include the connections between the state apparatus and criminal gangs, drug smugglers, and far-right and far-left gunmen.

A bigger mystery of the Ağca affair is the shooting of Pope John Paul II. The pope, Karol Wojtyla, a Pole, the first non-Italian pope in 456 years, was shot when Solidarity in Poland had been transformed into an organized political force. John Paul II had a strong appeal to the Polish people and other Christians inside the Soviet Union and as such had become a threat to Communism. The Polish leaders Stanislaw Kania and Woyciech Jaruzelski were under constant pressure from the Soviets to pursue decisive action against the Solidarity movement. They were threatened with Soviet military intervention. Thus it appears that the assassination of the pope could have been more useful to the Soviets than to the Turkish right-wing nationalist gangs or Islamic reactionaries.

Or was it?

The KGB would have been foolish not to realize that the killing of the spiritual leader of over one billion adherents of Roman Catholicism would point the finger of accusation at the Soviets. Would Moscow be able to disregard such a worldwide reaction against the Soviet Union by carrying out such an assassination? Not likely, even if we disregard the policies of the ultranationalists in Turkey at the time of the pope's shooting.

The ultranationalists were virulently anti-Soviet and anti-Marxist, seeking pan-Turanism, the unification of all Turkic peoples, the dream of Enver Pasha sixty years earlier. Among the nationalists there existed a determined lot that aimed to liberate all Turkic peoples living under the domination of the Soviets. A plot to assassinate the pope by rogue right-wing terrorists during a false flag operation would cause an immediate worldwide reaction against the Soviets.

Despite the trials in Rome and Istanbul, the accusations, and the finger pointing, the attempt to kill the pope is not an open-and-shut case. Like the murder of Abdi Ipekçi, it still remains a mysterious puzzle.

The pope's 2002 denial of a Communist Bulgarian conspiracy to kill him back in 1981 points a finger to a mixture of organized Turkish extremists. They include racist, ultranationalist, extreme rightist, leftist, pan-Turanist, and surprisingly even Maoist followers or members of Islamic brotherhoods who consider the legendary land of Turan and its legend *Ergenekon* the ultimate solution. Their shared aim of the ideal of *Kızıl Elma* (Red Apple), the founding of a United Turkish States also unites these strange bedfellows. Well represented inside the Turkish state, they claim that evil forces both inside and outside the country are at work to partition Turkey and destroy its nation.

I remember that the first major Communist infiltration of Turkey occurred during the mass expulsion of ethnic Turks from Bulgaria in 1951 by Todor Zhivkov's regime. Turkish-speaking agents of *Darzhavna Sigurnost* entered the country with the legitimate refugees and later became very active in labor unions and student organizations. A possibility exists that one of the primary objectives of this mass expulsion of ethnic Turks from Bulgaria was to infiltrate Turkey with Communist agents on a grand scale.

The attempt to spread the Soviet Union's influence had been a crucial move to change Turkey's destiny, and it did in an unexpected way. The Anatolian Turk, conservative in general, rejected Communism, as stated earlier. Communism found support among the intellectuals, labor union members, and high school and university students. The threat of Communism indirectly gave pro-Islam an opportunity and a reason for an unprecedented and unrestrained revival.

Within the Islamic movement, there already was a powerful nostalgia for the glorious times of the Ottoman Empire. The fundamentalists believed that the Ottoman Empire had a magnetic power to hold the world's Islam together with its temporal and spiritual leadership, the Caliphate.

The Turks, even throughout their secular republic's eighty-one-year history, felt proud of the military conquests of the Ottoman Empire. The stories, songs, and poems of the heroic times of their vanished empire were always part of the education of the Kemalist young.

The Islamists believe that what had made the Ottoman Empire great was the strength of its Islamic religion. According to the Islamic fundamentalists, Islam lost its influence in world affairs after the collapse of the Ottoman Empire, leader for centuries of the Islamic world.

Interestingly, Abdullah Gül, the Turkish foreign minister from the Justice and Development Party, which has Islamic roots, tried to clarify this point. In a statement to *Milliyet* on June 2, 2003, Gül blamed authoritarian rule for the Islamic world's problems. Gül said, "The reason Islamic countries are backward today is their regimes. It is not Islam." He added that the regimes that are closed and based on authority, such as monarchies and emirates, are the real obstacles for development.

Still, Islamic reactionaries consider a reformist leader like Kemal Atatürk an enemy because he had made the Turks stray from the world of Islam and from Ottoman and Islamic traditions. Atatürk and his Kemalism had westernized Turkey, an act viewed as a crime against the strict rules of the Holy Qur'an. Atatürk is an enemy because he abolished not only the Islamic state but also the Caliphate.

According to Islamic fundamentalists, Kemal Atatürk was the *deccal*, an antagonist, and the leader of malicious intriguers (the Kemalists) with bad morals. The word *deccal* is Arabic and represents an evil being who is supposed to appear before the end of the world to spread wickedness. The Islamic reactionary believes that a *deccal* can be conquered only through a powerful Islamic revival. This is especially true for the members of the Light sect, *Nurculuk*, founded by Said Nursi. According to the Light sect, the secular Turkish republic is a *kefere düzeni*, an order of the infidels. His disciples believe that Said Nursi was the *Bediuzzaman*, meaning the wonder of the age or the prophet of his time.

Said Nursi was born in the spring of 1877 in the village of Nurs in the province of Bitlis in eastern Anatolia. The son of Sufi Mirza, a small landowner of Kurdish origin, Said Nursi was educated in various *medreses*. Known also as "The Light Man," Nursi was influenced by the teachings of Sheik Abdul-Qadir al-Gailani (1078–1166), who, in the twelfth century, had founded the Qadiriyah sect in Baghdad. The Qadiriyah Brotherhood is the oldest Muslim mystic Sufi order and is widespread in Turkey and Central Asia. Sheik al-Gailani's concept of Sufism was an individual's struggle against selfishness, egotism, and worldliness. The Qadiriyah sect calls the individual to submit to God's will. This dervish order mingles the elements of Sufism with Islamic Orthodoxy. Sufism in general is a Muslim mystical philosophical and literary movement that stresses divine love, wisdom, and personal communion with God.

Said Nursi, despite his attachment to the teachings of al-Gailani, described Sufism as being inappropriate for the needs of the modern age.

Nursi, also known as Mullah Said, was a member of the Society of Muslim Unity that was involved with the Dervish Vahdeti revolt in 1909 against the reforms brought about by the CUP. He served in the Ottoman Army during World War I, fighting against the Russians on the eastern front. His legacy was a reactionary Islamic movement based on an Islamic union or pan-Islam.

Reactionary Islam's worldview is centered on a critical point. The Christian world—the United States and Europe—compared to the world of Islam, is now rich and far ahead in science, technology, and social development. Islam has remained backward and poor, the reactionaries claim, because of Western influences and a Christian conspiracy to keep it poor and underdeveloped. The West's decadence in the eyes of the Islamic fundamentalist is also a point against it.

Islam's retreat, however, from its glorious past is nothing new. Ziya Pasha, an Ottoman statesman and poet, reflected this truth 140 years ago with this poem:

> I traveled in the land of the unbeliever,
> And saw well-developed towns and mansions.
> I made a tour of the countries of Islam,
> And all I observed were places in ruin.

The Turks still live with the memories of their fallen empire. They yearn for the greatness of Süleyman the Magnificent, in whose reign the Ottoman Empire had reached its zenith.

The present nostalgia in Turkey for the greatness of the Ottoman Empire is also related to a refugee crisis. The collapse of the empire as a result of the Russian expansion in the Balkans, Crimea, Caucasus, and central Asia, and then World War I, created this refugee crisis. Waves of refugees arrived in great numbers from the Balkans, the Aegean islands, the Caucasus, and central Asia.

As a reporter in 1951, I met a group of Kazaks who arrived from Chinese Turkestan traveling from faraway Tibet and through India. I was impressed how clearly we could communicate.

The Chechens were often in the news in 1996 because of their fight for independence against the Russians. Among large groups of immigrant communities and their descendants, there exist about twenty-five thousans Chechens and a small Gagauz community in Turkey.

Nihal Atsız, my ultranationalist teacher in high school in Istanbul, used to talk often in class about the Gagauz Turks. The word *gagauz* is believed to originate from the Turkish words *kara* (black) and *Oghuz*. The Gagauz, about 180,000 souls in all, are mostly farmers and live in the Komrat area, south of Chisinau, the old Kishinev, in Moldava. That piece of land is part of Bessarabia and was acquired by Russia from the Ottoman Empire in 1812 in the Treaty of Bucharest. The Gagauz are Christian Orthodox and use Turkish surnames. They have been seeking independence for many years.

In 1906, the Gagauz proclaimed their autonomy, but their freedom lasted only two weeks when Czar Nicholas II sent in his police forces. Leonid I. Brezhnev, the Soviet leader, used to jail Gagauz leaders. Their dream to form a *Gagavuz Halkı Cumhuriyeti*, a Republic of Gagauz People, stayed alive for over a century. Now, they do have the Gagauz Autonomous Republic, and its prime minister is Mihail Kendigelen. Premier Kendigelen said during a visit to Turkey, "We consider you to be our sincere friend." His surname *kendigelen* means one who arrived alone or by himself.

The existence of these Turkic kinsmen is one of the important reasons of nostalgia for the greatness of the Ottoman Empire that helped to revive pan-Turanist and pan-Islamist movements. I recall that the idea of pan-Islamism brought about a fatal adventure to a daring but often nervous and angry politician.

Politics and an
Ottoman Princess

A bee knows which flower has nectar.
Turkish proverb

I was a close observer to how Adnan Menderes, the prime minister between 1950 and 1960, caused his own downfall along with that of the Democratic Party, his political organization. As a result of his policies, Menderes estranged the media and drew the irate attention of the military. At first, there was an appearance of great tolerance toward Islam when Menderes came to power. The purpose of this tolerance was to promote to the religious population the Democratic Party, which used the courtyards of mosques for political speeches. Menderes went so far as to state in his political campaign speeches that there was no limit to his religious tolerance. He even said, "If you so desire, you may even bring back the Caliphate."

This was a dangerous policy, anathema to the Kemalists and all others, like the Communists, who supported the secular reforms.

The Turkish Republic had abolished the caliphate on March 3,

1924, and renounced all claims related to this civil and religious title. Caliph is the title given to a successor of the Messenger of God—the Prophet Muhammed. All Ottoman sultans since Selim the Grim had been caliphs, successors to the Prophet Muhammed as temporal and spiritual heads of Islam.

The word *caliph* originates from the Arabic word *khalifah*, meaning successor. Yavuz Sultan Selim, known as Selim the Grim, had defeated the Mamluk army in Egypt in 1517 and captured the last caliph, a descendant of the Abbasid dynasty in Cairo. The Sharif of Mecca presented the keys to Mecca, Islam's holy city, to Selim the Grim, and the Ottoman sultan was then acknowledged as the new caliph. This title passed from one sultan to the next through centuries until 1924.

I remember that during the reform years, any proposal for the return of the caliphate or the sultanate was an act against the secular laws and cause enough to invite a jail term. Adnan Menderes's election rhetoric to attract votes for the Democrats gave the impression of a challenge against the secular establishment. His pro-Islam policies led to an eruption of religious movements in Anatolia and to a countrywide rash of mosque building when it was secular schools that were really needed.

Long before the Islamist Necmettin Erbakan appeared on the Turkish political scene with his idea of an Islamic NATO, Menderes had tried to win the Arab nations by promoting the American-sponsored Baghdad Pact. He failed because some of the Arab leaders, led by Gamal Abdel Nasser of Egypt, were friends and often allies of the Soviet Union. NATO member Turkey's leadership within a Baghdad Pact against the Soviets did not appeal to them.

Menderes, while encouraging a revival of Islam, was also involved with members of the Ottoman dynasty. In 1952, thirty years after the sultanate had been abolished and all the members of the Ottoman dynasty expelled, Menderes pardoned as a goodwill gesture its female members and allowed them to return. A general amnesty was approved in 1974.

One morning in the early 1950s, Kazas, the Armenian manager of the Park Hotel, whispered in my ear: "Hanzade is here!" His words shocked me. Hanzade's first name was Zehra, and *Hanzade* meant born to a khan, a ruler. She had been born at the Dolmabahçe Palace in Istanbul on September 12, 1923, just before the expulsion of all the Ottoman royalty. Her father, Ömer Faruk, was the son of Sultan Abdulmecid II and her mother, Rukiye Sabiha, was the daughter of Sultan Mehmet VI, better known as Vahdettin.

Following the defeat and collapse of the Ottoman Empire in World War I, the Nationalist movement considered Vahdettin, the last sultan, a traitor. After the nationalist victory in Anatolia, Vahdettin could not safely stay in Istanbul. One night the officers of the British occupation secretly took Vahdettin and his son Ertuğrul from the Yıldız Palace and hid them in a British army ambulance. The last sultan boarded the *HMS Malaya*, a British warship, on November 17, 1922, and fled to Malta. His final request from General Sir Charles Harrington, the British high commissioner in the Ottoman Empire, was pathetic: Would the general send to him his five wives left behind? When he died in San Remo, Italy, on May 15, 1926, the former sultan and caliph did not have the funds to pay his household expenses.

The Kemalists hated Vahdettin and did not want anything to do with the old Ottoman royalty. This made it perfectly clear to me at the time that the policy of allowing Vahdettin's granddaughter Zehra Hanzade back in Turkey was a bad omen for the regime of Adnan Menderes.

I called her suite for an interview. I had never met before a descendant of the Ottoman sultans. This Ottoman princess was a young, beautiful, smartly dressed woman. She was mesmerized with the spectacular view of the Bosphorus and the Marmara Sea from the terrace of her suite. Hanzade, who had left Istanbul for exile as a six-month-old baby, said, "I am so excited to see my birthplace." She was pleased to visit the city from where her ancestors, the members of the House of Osman, had ruled the far-reaching Ottoman Empire for centuries. Hanzade talked about her life. She had a young daughter named Nebile Sabiha Fazıla Ibrahim and a son named Ahmed Rıfat. Her husband, Mehmet Ali Ibrahim, was an Egyptian prince who was fond of sailing. Her husband's boat *Rakkase* (*Dancer*) was anchored in the Bosphorus.

Zehra Hanzade, who later became a Turkish citizen and took the surname of Osmanoğlu (Son of Ottoman), did not tell me that day the real purpose of her visit. It appeared that Menderes had decided to become a matchmaker between two dynasties: the Ottoman and the Faisal dynasty in Iraq. Later, when Iraq joined the American-sponsored Baghdad Pact, which featured Turkey as the principal player, we learned the truth. Menderes had been trying to foster a closer relationship with young King Faisal II of Iraq and the king's uncle, crown prince Abdul-ilah.

Iraq as an independent country had been (and still is) a difficult land to govern. Its population of Shi'ite Arabs in the south, Sunnite Arabs in the center, and Kurds and Turkmen in the north is not a unified nation. It is a country of tribes, clans, Islamic brotherhoods, and feudal chieftains. This was one reason for the Ottoman Empire's ruling Iraq as three different provinces called *vilayets*—Mosul, Baghdad, and Basra, each ruled by an Ottoman governor. I remember that Nuri as-Said, known as Nuri Pasha and the strongman of Iraq in the 1950s, talked with Adnan Menderes about this serious problem. Both officials were searching for a solution, and they found one in a young and very attractive girl.

Nuri Pasha, as the prime minister of Iraq, met Neslişah Sultan, a granddaughter of Sultan Abdulmecid II and sister of Hanzade in Istanbul in 1957. He told her that a marriage between King Faisal II and Fazıla, Hanzade's young daughter and great-granddaughter of the caliph, would unite the Iraqi population and help the king to rule.

Young King Faisal's ancestry had been intertwined with that of the Ottoman Empire before and during World War I. The British had enlisted Hussein ibn Ali, sharif and emir of Mecca who later became the king of the Hejaz. A sharif is believed to be a descendant of Prophet Muhammed through his daughter Fatima.

Hussein ibn Ali, playing both sides against each other, had obtained fifty thousand pounds in gold in the spring of 1916 from the Ottoman government to raise and equip forces against the British. Instead, he revolted in June of that year against the Ottoman regime with his sons Faisal and Abdullah. Britain spent £11 million to subsidize the sharif's revolt, hoping that a great Arab uprising against the Ottoman regime would follow.

That never happened—the Arab revolt was very limited.

Abdullah, Hussein's second son, who was educated in Istanbul and after the Revolution of the Young Turks in 1908, represented Mecca in the Ottoman parliament. A small Arab army commanded by Sharif Hussein's son Faisal, who was also a member of the Ottoman parliament, was formed in Hejaz with Arab officers who had defected from the Ottoman military forces. Among these former Ottoman army officers was Nuri as-Said, who had received his commission in 1909. During the first two years of World War I, Nuri Pasha fought against British forces and was captured by them. In 1916 he joined the Sharifian Arab forces and fought against the Turks. Other dissident Arabs serving in the Ottoman army in Mesopotamia included Major Abdul Aziz al-Masri, who had organized al-Ahd (the Covenant), a secret society against Ottoman rule. The British had captured Cafer Pasha al-Askeri, a prominent figure of *Teşkilatı Mahsusa*, the Ottoman intelligence in the Libyan desert. Cafer Pasha, Major al-Masri, and Nuri as-Said trained Arab troops to fight against the Turks. Sharif Hussein started the Arab revolt on June 5, 1916.

Faisal, the father of young King Faisal II, supported Lawrence of Arabia during World War I. He entered Damascus, the regional capital, with Lawrence on October 1, 1918. Following the collapse of the Ottoman Empire, he was rewarded by the British and installed as Faisal I, King of Iraq.

Sharif Hussein ibn Ali declared himself the caliph in 1924, but the Wahhabis, led by Abdul Aziz ibn Saud, forced him out, seizing the guardianship of the Muslim holy places Mecca and Medina and creating the Kingdom of Saudi Arabia. Sharif Hussein's second son, Emir Abdullah ibn al-Hussein, supported by the British, ruled Jordan until his assassination by the Muslim Brotherhood in Jerusalem in 1951.

The Arab revolt was, in fact, not as great or glorified as described in the book *Seven Pillars of Wisdom* by T. E. Lawrence. Only a few thousand Arab tribesmen enlisted to fight against the Turks. The result of the revolt was a disappointment for the Arabs. Their dreams of independence failed to materialize for many years to come. Instead, Britain and France ruled them.

Still, the political intrigues that had formed the map of the Middle East after World War I, creating artificial states like Syria, Jordan, Iraq, and Lebanon, would shape the catastrophic events in the region for a long time to come. In fact, when a British Arabist named Colonel Sir Mark Sykes and a former French consul-general in Beirut named Francois Georges-Picot signed their secret accord on May 9, 1916, to dismember the Ottoman Empire, they had no idea what kind of Pandora's box for the future they had opened.

The Sykes-Picot agreement envisaged a British protectorate in Iraq and a French protectorate in Syria. Palestine was to become a joint responsibility of Britain, France, and Russia, while the French ruled Lebanon and the British controlled Haifa and Acre.

The Sykes-Picot agreement eventually brought about Arab resentment against the West, Arab disunity, violent nationalism, and militant Islam. The majority of the Arabs did not want to be ruled by Christian nations. To them, a Turkish administration that would grant limited autonomy was preferable. The leaders of the Allies, especially British Prime Minister David Lloyd George, as well as the Ottoman authorities failed to understand this vital point of view. David Lloyd George was a declared enemy of the Turks who believed that the Ottoman Empire's policies had brought about czarist Russia's collapse.

Forty years after the Sykes-Picot agreement, Adnan Menderes and Nuri Pasha decided to arrange a royal marriage between King Faisal II and Hanzade's daughter Fazıla. Through this marriage, Menderes tried to advance the friendly ties with Iraq within the framework of the Baghdad Pact. Involving the government with members of the Ottoman royalty caused displeasure among the Kemalists, particularly those in the armed forces. The first time I wrote about Zehra Hanzade, my piece was cut down to not more than ten lines and was buried on an inside page of *Yeni Sabah*. This time the coverage of the young couple's engagement turned out to be a major news event, and the reason was obvious: a fairy-tale match between a young king and a beautiful princess.

In earlier years, I had covered events in Baghdad and met members of the young king's family and Nuri as-Said. Crown Prince Abdul-ilah,

King Faisal's uncle, was a notorious womanizer who lived in an opulent style reminiscent of *The One Thousand and One Nights*. He had ruled Iraq as regent until 1953 and was dominant in Iraqi affairs even under the rule of the young king and the government of Nuri Pasha.

One day in Baghdad, I met a Turkish woman. She was a young peroxide blonde, very pretty with an attractive figure, walking alone on a Baghdad street, dressed lightly for the summer heat, which had made the asphalt sidewalks soft and sticky. There were about twenty Iraqi men following her, twisting their black moustaches and staring at her derriere as she moved. It turned out that she was a bellydancer from Istanbul, performing at a Baghdad nightclub. She invited my colleague Ilhan Turalı and me to the nightclub and offered us drinks. Halfway through our visit, a messenger arrived and whispered some words in her ear. She told us, "Sorry, boys, I have to go. The great Lothario of Baghdad is requesting my services."

We had no idea who this "great Lothario" could be, but she explained that the messenger was from Crown Prince Abdul-ilah's palace. "He is the mighty lord around here, and he lives in opulence," she said and left.

Crown Prince Abdul-ilah was the real head of the Iraqi royal family that Zehra Hanzade's daughter Fazıla was marrying into.

Preparations went ahead for the marriage of the twenty-year-old, darkly handsome but short King Faisal II with Fazıla, who had a fair complexion. I remember that she had beautiful green-blue eyes and was almost the same height as the king himself. The young girl was born in Neuilly-sur-Seine in France in 1941. When the engagement was officially announced in September 1957, Fazıla, displaying a large diamond engagement ring, was introduced to the members of the press at an Istanbul *yalı*, a waterside residence on the Bosphorus. I could not miss noticing that the shy, young girl was pretending to be happy, as the marriage she was getting into was an arranged marriage of convenience.

This match was doomed from the start.

I had seen signs of discontent against the Iraqi royal family and the regime of Prime Minister Nuri as-Said during assignments in Baghdad. The crown prince, a tall man with dark eyes, wearing Savile Row suits, was not popular, nor was Nuri Pasha himself. Even during the coronation of King Faisal, Nuri Pasha's police had been arresting dissidents. There was no freedom of the press in Iraq, and Iraqi censorship was very strict, controlling all news reports.

Necati Zincirkıran, reporter for *Hürriyet* at the time, having arrived in Baghdad for King Faisal's coronation ahead of other journalists, had a scoop over us with pictures of arrested dissidents in chains. He had shipped the story and the pictures to Istanbul via a railroad messenger on the Baghdad Express, avoiding the Iraqi censor. These pictures were printed three days later on the front page of *Hürriyet*, angering Iraqi officials. During a garden party at the palace grounds, Husameddin Juma, then the interior minister in Nuri as-Said's cabinet, cornered Turalı and me and announced that he was planning to arrest Zincirkıran and jail him in a Baghdad dungeon. We told him this was a bad idea that would cause strained relations between the two countries.

Zincirkıran in his book *Hürriyet ve Simavi Imparatorluğu* ("*Hürriyet*" *and the Simavi Empire*), printed in Istanbul in 1994, describes what happened. He was detained by two policemen outside his Baghdad hotel and badly mistreated and accused of being a Communist agent! His passport, airline ticket, and money were confiscated. After some rough treatment, he was freed in the middle of the night when Turkish Ambassador Nedim V. Ilkin intervened.

I had a serious encounter myself with Crown Prince Abdul-ilah in Baghdad during the celebrations over the signing of the Baghdad Pact. Safa Kılıçlıoğlu, the publisher of *Yeni Sabah*, had been invited by Adnan Menderes to Baghdad for the ceremonies and had traveled there on Menderes's airplane. Menderes also brought to Baghdad a group of Turkish musicians and singers led by the famous singer Münir Nureddin to entertain the Iraqi leaders during the ceremonies. Şükran Özer, a beautiful young singer, was among them.

She was married to Tütüncü Ihsan (Ihsan the Tobacco Merchant), a man much older than herself and well known in Istanbul society for his crafty business deals, which usually involved the introduction of attractive women. During a party in Baghdad, Crown Prince Abdul-ilah noticed the stunning singer and immediately wanted an introduction. She politely refused his advances. He persisted and became obsessed with the idea of bedding the singer. Finally, when he became a nuisance and placed two Iraqi agents on her night and day, the Turkish officials became alarmed.

The singer was hysterical, fearing that she might be kidnapped and locked up in Baghdad for good. In desperation, Şükran Özer went to Menderes and begged him in tears to be flown back to Istanbul. Menderes was fearful of a scandal and much concerned about offending Crown Prince Abdul-ilah. His policies regarding the future of the Middle East and the Baghdad Pact were at stake. Unable to do anything officially, Menderes asked help from my boss. "Get this woman out of here quietly," he told Kılıçlıoğlu.

I ended up with the job of doing just that. Kılıçlıoğlu figured out a plan. By posing as her jealous lover, I was to get the singer out of Iraq without being observed by Abdul-ilah's two bodyguards. This was not an easy job, as the bodyguards had settled down in the hotel's lobby, frequently checking the floor where Turkish journalists and musicians stayed.

One night before I intended to get the singer out, I caused a row with the two agents, shouting at them to leave my girlfriend alone. During the row, Nuyan Yiğit, my journalist friend, and I noticed Münir Nureddin, the lead singer, peering out through his slightly opened door and then quietly withdrawing. He had no wish to get involved.

The next morning, there was an early flight to Beirut, which, at the time, was known as the Paris of the East. I told the singer to get up before dawn and leave her luggage in the room. She was to dress casually and take her handbag only. I called no one and made no reservations. I would also leave my luggage behind to be taken back to Istanbul by Nuyan Yiğit. Still, I had a problem. Şükran Özer didn't have the Lebanese visa that was required at the time—and no passport pictures for a visa.

Early the next morning, I checked the conditions. The agents were half-asleep in armchairs in the hotel's lobby. I rushed back to Şükran Özer's room and took her out of the hotel through a back service door. I remember walking with the woman in the streets of Baghdad until we found a street photographer. The man's picture of the singer did not do justice to her stunning beauty, but no matter; it did the job. We took a taxi and headed straight to the Lebanese consulate, got her visa, and flew out of Baghdad. The singer took the opportunity to buy new dresses in Beirut and to call her husband on the phone. Then she flew back to Istanbul. Later, I was to hear rumors that this was not the end of the story. Abdul-ilah doggedly pursued her with lavish gifts of jewelry. In any case, his life, like that of the young king and of Nuri as-Said, was to end during a violent revolution in Baghdad—which simply buried the Baghdad Pact and Menderes's dream of an Islamist union.

When King Faisal II and his uncle Abdul-ilah were expected in Istanbul, Adnan Menderes and other officials were busy making preparations at Istanbul's Yeşilköy airport to welcome the Iraqi guests. Then, shocking news was received of a leftist pan-Arab revolution in Baghdad. Brigadier General Abdul-Karim Kassem, the coup leader, and his accomplice, Abd as-Salam Arif, had captured Baghdad with their forces. It was a pro-Nasser and pro-Soviet coup d'etat aimed to destroy the Baghdad Pact.

Adnan Menderes—of medium height, with a moon face and neatly combed, straight black hair and black eyebrows—favored dark suits, white shirts, and a fitting tie. He was beside himself when he received the first news of the Baghdad uprising. I saw his face turn purple and his fists clench. Menderes knew that a leftist revolution in Baghdad, if successful, meant the demise of the Baghdad Pact and the end of his dreams of leadership in a highly volatile area. He wanted to invade Iraq with Turkish armed forces in order to save the young king and his kingdom, but his aides advised against such an adventure. At any rate, as more breaking news confirmed, it was too late to save the king and his kingdom. The Iraqi regime had been overthrown.

General Kassem had declared the downfall of the Iraqi monarchy and proclaimed Iraq a republic. The young king and the crown prince, along with other members of the royal house, were killed. Nuri Pasha had been murdered by a mob. Reports claimed that their bodies were dragged behind cars through the streets of Baghdad and body parts fed to stray dogs.

That day, July 14, 1958, signaled the end of matchmaking between two dynasties and of Menderes's plan to lead a major alliance. The left-wing regime in Iraq withdrew from the Baghdad Pact (later known as the Central Treaty Organization, or CENTO) a year later in 1959. This mutual security alliance between Turkey, Pakistan, Iran, Iraq, and Britain, with the United States as the associate member, was supposed to complete a security chain beside NATO in order to contain a dangerously assertive Soviet Union. The alliance became defunct after Iran and Pakistan withdrew in 1979.

The killing of King Faisal II caused much grief and bitter disappointment in Zehra Hanzade's family. Seven years after King Faisal's death, Fazıla married Hayri Ürgüplü, son of Suat Hayri Ürgüplü, a former prime minister and Turkish ambassador to London. She had two sons, divorced Hayri Ürgüplü in 1980 in Istanbul, and returned to France, a surprising conclusion to a modern fairy tale. Hanzade died on March 19, 1998, in Paris, France.

The coup d'etat in Iraq foreshadowed the fate of Adnan Menderes two years later, whose ending, similar to King Faisal's, was brutal. He played political games for a religious revival, which saw the reemergence of the *tarikats* (the Islamic brotherhoods) and played a vital role in his downfall.

Before going into that tragic event, however, it is important to look at the role of the Muslim brotherhoods and the leftist Kurdish uprising in recent Turkish history.

The Muslim Brotherhood
and Old Sufi Masters

A dog pissing on the wall of a mosque knows his end is near.

Turkish proverb

*A*t the roots of the present militant Islamic movement is the Muslim Brotherhood, or *Ikhwan al Muslimin*. This anti-Western, anticorruption movement, with violently fanatical Islamic tendencies, was founded by Hasan al-Banna in Egypt during the 1920s. In 1951, the Muslim Brotherhood assassinated King Abdullah of Jordan, grandfather of the late King Hussein, because he had agreed on a truce with Israel. The Muslim Brotherhood has a powerful presence in Arab countries and has infiltrated Turkey, the only Islamic country that has been able to achieve a secular state system. The founders of the militant *Hamas* (the Islamic Resistance Movement) are followers of the Muslim Brotherhood. The military wing of Hamas, the *Al-Qassem Brigades*, is responsible for many of the murderous attacks in Israel.

In Syria, the Muslim Brotherhood had a bad experience with the regime of Hafez al-Assad, whose family belongs to the Alawite sect, known in Turkey as *Alevi*. The Alawites, a minority sect of heterodox Shi'ite Muslims, are believers of the teachings of Muhammad ibn Nushayr an-Namiri, who lived over a thousand years ago in Basra. The Alawites are called *kızılbaş* (redheads) in Turkey because they wore red caps in the past. The majority of the Turks are Sunni Muslims.

The religious differences between the Alawite minority and the Sunnite majority in Syria, as well as between Iraq's Sunnites and Shi'ites, are divisive. The late Syrian President Hafez al-Assad, an Alawite, supported terrorism against other countries and allowed terrorists to live and train in Syrian territory, but he was ruthless against any local opposition from the Sunnite majority. He crushed two Sunni fundamentalist uprisings organized by the Muslim Brotherhood against his regime in the cities of Aleppo in 1980 and Hamah in 1982. Syrian troops brutally killed the leaders of the uprising and thousands of people in the Brotherhood, and the center of the city was leveled. The Muslim Brothers involved in this rebellion were also followers of Sheik Abdul Qadir al-Gailani, the founder of the *Qadiriyah* order of dervishes of the mystical Sufi branch of Islam.

Earlier Syrian members of the Muslim Brotherhood, who were established by Marwan Hadid as *At Tali'a al Muqatila* (the Fighting Vanguard), had assassinated several hundred members of the security forces and government officials. They had also killed about twenty Soviet advisers.

Throughout history, Sufism helped spread Islamic culture and its *tarikats* (religious brotherhoods and dervish orders). According to the mainstream Sufis, the observance of the Shariah is indispensable. For the solid entrenchment of Sufism in Anatolia, the literary influence, especially through mystical love poetry, of the ancient Sufi masters was crucial. Yunus Emre (1240–1321), a great Sufi poet and mystic, well versed in the mystical philosophy of Mevlana Jalaladdin Rumi, wrote deeply emotional poems devoted to the themes of divine love and human destiny.

He was an Anatolian humanist and poet who believed that all men were equal. Most of his major works are collected in *Yunus Emre Divanı* (*The Collection of Yunus Emre's Poems*). UNESCO announced the year 1991 as "The International Year of Yunus Emre" in commemoration of the 750th anniversary of his birth. Yunus Emre wrote:

Knowledge and science is to understand,
To know who you are.
If you don't know who you are,
What is the use of reading and learning?

And: "We don't bear a grudge against anyone/For us, the whole world is one and the same."

He described the Western expression "You can't take it with you": "You are the owner of these goods and properties,/Pray tell where is their first owner?"

Emre wrote about love: "We have loved, became lovers/We were loved, and we became beloved."

He talked about death:

Get ready for your time,
For there is a time for death,
And one day it will come.

Yunus Emre's mentor, Mevlana Jalaladdin Rumi, was born on September 30, 1207, in Balkh, Afghanistan. His family escaped the Mongol invaders and immigrated to Konya, in central Anatolia. There he became the sheik of a dervish community. Rumi was the greatest Sufi master and poet whose didactic epic *Mesneviye Manevi*, spiritual poems in rhymed couplets, widely influenced Muslim mystical literature. He wrote: "Come, whatever you are, come, come again."

Rumi's disciples organized a *tarikat* and called it the Mevlevi Order, which is now known as the Whirling Dervishes. The principal ritual of the Whirling Dervishes is their mystical dance to the tune of a reed flute called the *Ney*. A master reed flute player is known as *neyzen*, as in Neyzen Tevfik, who was the greatest Ney player of my childhood years.

In Rumi's poetry, there is this line: "Dance when you're perfectly free." He composed the *Rubaiyat*, a book of quatrains, in a state of ecstasy induced by the mournful tunes of a reed flute and the sound of running water in a mill. Rumi's poetry reflects his love for a wandering dervish named Shemseddin Tebrizi. Rumi said about him, "What I had thought before as God, I met today in a human being."

Rumi's mausoleum in Konya (the Green Dome), is now a museum. The early Sufis were humanists, not fundamentalists.

Seeking only spiritual development, universal harmony, and love for the individual, Sufi dervishes rejected greed, divorce, and polygamy. *Hırka*, a cloak made of harsh wool, was their symbolic possession. A dervish is a poor man—simple, contended, and humble.

Hacı Bektashi Veli, the founder of the *Bektashi* brotherhood seven hundred years ago in Anatolia, said: "Seek and find the truth." The truth for the Sufi was *Hakika*, or enlightenment, third of the three basic studies on the way of becoming a complete man. (The other two were the *Shariah* and *Tarika*, the Path). The Sufis even today remember how a misinterpretation of the word *truth* in Arabic led to the execution of a Sufi master named Carder of Hearts. His real name was Hussein ibn Mansur Hallach, a grandson of a Zoroastrian and son of a convert to Islam. Over a thousand years ago, Hallach said in Baghdad: "I am the Truth." His Arabic words *Ana al-haqq* were interpreted as "I am God," and Hallach was denounced as a heretic.

The Sufi dervish orders were abolished during the secular reform years in Turkey and remained closed until the Islamist revival.

Despite the secular reforms of my childhood, Sufism and their Islamic orders have again become highly visible in Turkey. The Muslim Brotherhood, along with other Islamic movements of Saudi Arabia and Iran, spread its reactionary ideologies in Turkey. Some of these Muslim brotherhoods have strange customs. Shafis, for instance, consider a dog an abominable creature, but according to the Maliki Brotherhood, the dog is a clean animal. Among the most liberal are the Melami and Bektashi brotherhoods, whose members are against reactionary Islam. The Melamis believe that the Islamist extremists have no right to pretend that they have a God-given right to enter paradise.

While on assignment in Baghdad in May of 1953, I met Kemal Deniz, a Turkish university student. Deniz proposed to Ilhan Turalı and me that he could introduce us to the leaders of the Muslim Brotherhood.

This offer intrigued us for two reasons—first, we wanted to find out the designs of the Muslim Brotherhood regarding Turkey, and second, there was the case of Ahmet Emin Yalman, the strictly secularist editor-in-chief of the newspaper *Vatan* (*Fatherland*), who had been shot six times on November 22, 1952, while visiting Malatya in eastern Turkey. A high school student, who later became a columnist with the Islamic newspaper *Vakit* in Istanbul, was charged with the assassination attempt. He was jailed for ten years. There were reports that the Muslim Brotherhood was behind the Yalman shooting, and we wanted to solve the mystery.

We accepted the offer, and Kemal Deniz introduced us to Mahmud as-Saffaf and Abdurrahman Hidir, the leaders of the Muslim Brotherhood in Baghdad. At the time, the Muslim Brotherhood was not allowed to operate in Turkey, and all its members there were forced to go underground.

Mahmud as-Saffaf and Abdurrahman Hidir had their own plans concerning ourselves. They wanted to impress us with their organization so that we would write a series of articles in the Turkish newspapers praising their activities. With this in mind, they offered to take us to Syria and Jordan by car, and we accepted.

Our contact with them did not go smoothly because, as Islamic fundamentalists, they lived by the strict rules of the Qur'an and expected us to do the same. The Muslim Brotherhood advocated a return to the Qur'an, demanded purity of the Islamic world, and totally rejected secularization. They considered the Turkish Kemalist and secularist traditions as the alienation of the Turks from Islam. Turkish secularity, according to them, was anathema, the Turkish republic a heretical state. They believed that any means to bring back the Turks into the Islamic fold would be considered legitimate. Because we were raised by and believed in secularist ideals, our problems with them appeared right at the beginning of the trip. Mentioning the shooting of Ahmet Emin Yalman, Mahmud as-Saffaf claimed that "the Turks were no longer Muslims," and, as if to prove the truth of his statement, he challenged us in the Syrian Desert to pray in the Islamic tradition.

This dangerous episode of our journey, about which we grew more and more uncertain, took place during our stop at a small, dirty rest house in the middle of the Syrian Desert. Shortly before a sandstorm had ruined our lunch, the leader proposed that I should lead the noon prayers.

Regardless of my secular upbringing, I was not totally ignorant of Islamic religious practices. It was impossible to grow up in rural Anatolia without exposure to Islam's daily practices. To act as imam, a prayer leader, however, was beyond my capabilities. Turalı found our situation highly amusing and to my horror, he cracked up. As we prepared for prayers, I whispered in his ear, "Do you want us to get killed right here?"

That stopped him cold. Our predicament had its humorous side, which I fully appreciated only after it was over. It reminded me of Nasreddin Hoca, the great satirist mullah of the Ottoman era, and his story about a dangerous crossing in the desert. Once Nasreddin Hoca encountered a tribe of bloodthirsty desert nomads. Later, as the Hoca told the story of his adventure, someone asked him, "What did you do, Mullah?" He answered, "I caused the nomads to run!" Questioned as to how he had managed to do that, the mullah replied, "I was forced to run, and the nomads ran after me."

For us, there was no place to run in the desert but to find a plausible excuse to decline the offer. I told Abdurrahman Hidir, "You are the leader in this journey, and the honor of leading us in prayer belongs to you." My refusal left a bad impression on our hosts and thus a strain developed in our relationship.

Since the rest house had no water, we couldn't wash our faces, hands, arms, and feet, as required before prayers. Our hosts explained that desert sand was clean and thus could replace water, a scarce commodity in the desert, for that ritual. Cleaning hands by rubbing sand on them is called *teyemmum* in Arabic. So that is what we did, then lined up behind Hidir, our host imam, and performed the ritual worship. We bowed, kneeled, and touched our foreheads to the warm sand while the silence of the desert was broken only by the imam's Arabic chant proclaiming the greatness of God. This prayer in the desert was an extraordinary experience, which I still vividly remember.

In Jerusalem, which was then under Jordanian rule, we met other members of the Muslim Brotherhood and were taken to the Dome of the

Rock as well as to most other Islamic shrines in that city. We wanted to visit other sites also, since Jerusalem is a holy city to all the great religions. This request did not sit well with our hosts, but we did as we pleased.

In Amman, we were introduced to the brother of a Muslim Brotherhood member, a Palestinian nationalist who had assassinated King Abdullah ibn Hussein, the founder of Jordan. The king and his fifteen-year-old grandson Hussein ibn Talal had been on the steps of Al-Aqsa mosque in Jerusalem when the assassin fired, killing Emir Abdullah. His grandson Hussein, who later became king of Jordan, escaped death when a shot bounced off a medal on his chest. The members of the Muslim Brotherhood were very proud of the deed because they considered Emir Abdullah's truce with Israel a betrayal of the Arab cause.

Finally, when we had enough of the Muslim Brothers' repeated exhortation of the rightfulness of their cause, for which they had committed outright murders, we resisted going along with their full schedule. Mahmud as-Saffaf and Abdurrahman Hidir were so upset that they displayed handguns to intimidate us. Soon after our return to Damascus, we left quietly for Beirut.

We had learned that the Muslim Brotherhood had certain designs concerning Turkey and the Turkish armed forces—once the Sword of Islam. Their aim was to generate favorable pro-Muslim Brotherhood articles in the Turkish press, which were to influence Turkish public opinion positively of the righteousness of their cause and ultimately open a window for the direct involvement of the Turkish army in the Arab-Israeli conflict.

The Muslim Brothers hoped that their diatribes had converted us to their cause and that we would support them in spreading their reactionary movement in Turkey, a secular state they viewed as a corrupting model for other Islamic countries. They were, of course, also totally opposed to Turkey's cordial relations with the state of Israel (established since 1948).

To their disappointment, neither of us wrote a single line in our newspapers about our travels with the leaders of the Muslim Brotherhood. We found a better way to handle this sensitive issue. Selim Ragıp Emeç, the publisher of *Son Posta* and Turalı's boss, was a member of parliament for the Democratic Party and close to Celal Bayar, the president of Turkey at the time. At his suggestion, we wrote a special report, and the publisher took it directly to the president, alerting him to the Muslim Brotherhood's designs.

We received word from President Bayar that there was no danger from the Muslim Brotherhood because Turkey's secularist traditions were firmly established. Not many people realized then that the Turkish secular state, its modern reforms, and Kemalism were viewed as enemies by the Arab and Iranian Islamic reactionaries, who were determined to infiltrate Turkey with their extremist ideas to help destroy the country's secular character at any cost. The extraordinary revival of the Islamic movement in Turkey proves that this reactionary infiltration has been accomplished. Still, Celal Bayar did use our report a few months later in a statement criticizing the Muslim Brotherhood's attempts to spread their fundamentalist ideas.

Over four decades later, a surprising political and military change was to occur in the relations between Turkey and Israel, which terribly angered both Arabs and Iranians. This was partly caused by the Syrian dictator Hafez al-Assad's support of the Marxist-Leninist Kurdish PKK insurgents in southeastern Anatolia. In February 1996, the Turkish government signed a five-year military cooperation agreement with Israel. This alarmed the Arab countries and Iran.

According to Turkish newspaper reports, when Israeli Prime Minister Ehud Barak visited Turkey in October 1999, the Iranian state-run radio condemned the visit and claimed that it "inflicted a wound on Turkey's Muslim people." The Iranian newspaper *Jomhuri Islami* (*Islamic Republic*) said that Turkey had established an "evil alliance" with Israel. Similar to the Arabs and Iranians, the Turkish Islamic fundamentalists view this agreement as a betrayal of the Islamic movement in Turkey. Still, the all-powerful, secularist military brass in Turkey enforces the agreement with determination.

Turkey's friendship and military agreement with Israel was extremely troubling for the Syrians. As a result, the Syrian strongman Hafez al-Assad, shortly before his death, tried to play high-stakes poker with the Turks in his behind-the-scenes role in the Kurdish revolt in southeastern Anatolia.

16

The Revolt of the PKK and Water

Water may sleep, the enemy doesn't.

Turkish proverb

*I*n Hafez al-Assad's Syria, people lived in fear of being over-heard slandering the regime. I remember that one day a clerk at the central post office in Damascus found the courage to whisper in my ear, "As a province of the Ottoman Empire, we had happier lives."

He was talking about the pervasive climate of suppression and the existing division between the Assad family's authoritarian rule through their Baath Party (the military-Alawite system) and the majority Sunni population. The question often asked before the death of Hafez al-Assad in June 2000 was whether this ruthless dictatorial system controlled by the Alawites could survive him. The Syrian strongman had groomed his son Bashar al-Assad as the next Syrian president with this in mind.

Hafez al-Assad was not a reformer, yet during his dictatorial rule, Syria needed reforms similar to the Kemalist reforms. Since Hafez al-Assad's death, nothing has changed. On March 8, 2004, police at the par-

liament building in Damascus ordered about twenty human rights protesters to disperse. Police tore their single banner that said, "Freedom for
Prisoners of Opinion and Conscience."

Ever since a series of coups d'etat by army colonels, beginning in the
1940s, Syria was known as the country of toppled governments. In 1958
the Baath Party in control agreed to Syria's unification with Gamal Abdel
Nasser's Egypt to become the United Arab Republic. Gamal Abdel
Nasser was the president of this pro-Soviet union, and the Egyptians
treated the Syrians, to their disappointment, as subordinates. In September 1961, another coup d'etat led by Syrian army officers established
Syria once again as an independent state.

There was a surprising event in Damascus to which I became a close
witness. The wily president of Syria, always aware of the danger of a
coup d'etat, had cleverly prepared himself for such an eventuality. He
rented the first floor of his home in Damascus to the Turkish Embassy
while using the top floor of the building as his own living quarters. Then
the inevitable did indeed happen. As he was informed of the coup d'etat
and expected army officers to arrive and arrest him at any moment, he
walked down a flight of stairs and asked for asylum.

Ismail Soysal was head of the Turkish mission in Damascus, and,
with his help, I met the fallen president but was unable to make him talk.
As the rioters threw stones on the embassy ground, the fallen president
agreed to be photographed and filmed for the television news. The photojournalist accompanying me was Rüçhan Arıkan, who had two unusual
nicknames, *Kova* meaning bucket and *Deve*, the camel. Arıkan also
worked for NBC on the side as a news cameraman. A large man, he was
able to run like a camel with the heavy TV camera on his shoulder as he
shot fast-moving riots. He was also extremely lucky, always getting away
unscathed from dangerous assignments.

After our exclusive meeting with the fallen president, we had difficulty finding a way to ship the film back to Turkey. Since the Damascus
airport was closed to all flights, I decided to take our news stories and pictures to Beirut by car, from where I would air-freight them to Istanbul.
Arıkan handed me the undeveloped still film for the newspaper *Hürriyet*

and the film intended for NBC News. I put them all into the pockets of my raincoat. Other foreign reporters, including the TV news cameramen, also unloaded their material on me to ship to their companies from Beirut. Because there were so many, including some intended for major American TV news broadcasting companies, I placed those in my suitcase.

At the Syrian-Lebanese border, a Syrian army captain refused to let me leave the country without searching the suitcase. He found the TV and still-film rolls and became hysterical, yelling, "*Al flum, al flum*," meaning, "The films, the films." Next, he detained me but couldn't figure out what to do with me. He called Damascus for instructions from a higher authority. Finally, after repeated phone calls and a great deal of shouting in Arabic, it was decided that I could go on my way to Lebanon sans the press material in my suitcase. I protested aloud with all the Arabic I knew, which wasn't much, saying that the captain had no right to confiscate the film. My Arabic sentence of introduction that usually opened doors did not work this time.

I left, feeling the bulging pockets of my raincoat, as the Syrian had forgotten to give me a body search. That was how NBC News and *Hürriyet*, the newspaper I worked for at the time, had the worldwide scoop.

Rüçhan Arıkan resembled Joe Camel of cigarette advertising fame. He was an addict of novelty stores. He brought home pure gold cutlery from Beirut and a miniature toilet bowl, from which he drank coffee. He went totally out of control when, upon returning to our office in Istanbul, he tried out a rubber cushion on unsuspecting reporters, which caused a rude noise when someone sat on it. The cushion became an important part of his repertoire of crude jokes.

The news of my detention at the Syrian-Lebanese border reached the members of the foreign press in Damascus, who were disappointed by the seizure of their film. In those days, these were the normal risks reporters had to face when shipping their material from trouble spots. We did not have satellite phones, which can send and receive signals from geostationary satellites, or computers, e-mail, and instant faxes. All these recent inventions have greatly altered the profession of journalism.

Syria had been a major troublemaker for the Turks until 1998 because of Syrian support of the Kurdish separatist movement in southeastern Anatolia. After 1984 this revolt began to turn from a minor insurgency with few supporters into a disastrous war. Like the Greek governments, Hafez al-Assad had provided arms, training, and shelter for the Kurdish guerrillas of the *Partiya Karkaren-e Kurdistan*, also known as Kurdistan Workers Party, or PKK.

The members of this terrorist organization regularly crossed over into Iraqi territory after their raids and murders in Turkey. Abdullah Öcalan, the leader of the PKK, lived in the safety of the Syrian capital of Damascus and from there directed a brutal guerrilla operation that culminated in assassinations, murders, and terrorism in Turkey. In the beginning, Öcalan was subsidized by the Soviet Union and later aided and supported by Greece, Armenia, Iran, and Syria. For many years, the PKK guerrillas were trained in the Syrian-controlled Bekaa Valley in Lebanon, from where they then infiltrated back into Turkey to raid villages and army posts and to terrorize people.

The primary reason for Hafez al-Assad's support of Marxist Kurdish guerrillas, whose aim was to establish a Kurdish state in southeastern Anatolia, was to control the sources of water for a greater Syria, which was Assad's other major goal.

The eastern Anatolian mountains are the source of tributaries of two major rivers, the Euphrates and Tigris, which flow through Syria. The Euphrates, 2,235 miles long, rises in northeastern Turkey, meanders through southeastern Anatolia, and then flows into Syria. It crosses the plains of Iraq before joining the Tigris River to form the Shatt-al-Arab waterway that empties into the Persian Gulf. The great civilizations of Mesopotamia were fostered by the Euphrates and Tigris rivers, in an area known in history as the Fertile Crescent.

In their Southeast Anatolia Project, the Turks have been constructing a series of dams to harness the power of both the Euphrates and the Tigris. Even in 2003, this was only half completed because of its enormous cost—$32 billion. The huge project includes twenty-two dams and nineteen hydroelectric plants and aims to make this poverty-stricken region fertile and economically viable. The majority of the population is ethnic

Kurds. This expense, along with the cost of fighting the Kurdish revolt, has wreaked havoc with Turkey's national budget and has been a major factor in the country's high inflation rate.

For years, Syria and Iraq have complained about Turkey's plans to divert the water, despite Turkish guarantees of a steady water flow downstream. In the 1980s and early 1990s, PKK guerrillas attacked sections of the project and murdered several engineers. It is believed that these attacks were done on Hafez al-Assad's behalf. Al-Assad's plans collapsed in the late 1990s, when the Turkish army gained the upper hand and contained the insurrection.

According to Turkish officials, 24,000 Kurdish separatists have been killed since the imposition of emergency rule in 1987 in eleven eastern and southeastern provinces. Other casualties included 5,061 Turkish soldiers and officers and almost five thousand civilians. Emergency rule has ended only recently.

Hafez al-Assad also tried to use the PKK to pressure the Turks to cancel their five-year military agreement with Israel because he felt threatened by the possibility of his army fighting a two-front war in the future. In October 1998, the Turkish government handed al-Assad an ultimatum to stop supporting Öcalan or else the Turks would come to Damascus and get him. At the same time, the Turks concentrated a large military force at the Syrian border and openly threatened to go to war. The tension eased only when Hafez al-Assad capitulated and signed an agreement, ending his support of the PKK. Unprotected by Syria, the Kurdish terrorists crossed the border into northern Iraq. An estimated five thousand PKK terrorists were based there in the winter of 2004.

It took three years to heal Turkish-Syrian relations, and both countries later signed security agreements on fighting cross-border criminal gangs and smuggling.

Öcalan, who liked to be called *Apo* (or uncle, in Kurdish), a great admirer of Ho Chi Minh, ended up in jail in Imralı Island prison in Turkey. He had caused much bloodshed and destruction. Bülent Ecevit, Turkey's deputy prime minister in July 1997, said that 370,000 people had fled the area of the Kurdish uprising. He added that 3,185 villages had been emptied. Kurdish terrorists had murdered dozens of teachers and caused two thousand schools to be closed.

During the armed conflict, the Turkish government employed about fifty thousand Kurdish villagers and tribesmen as village guards against the rebels, paying them a monthly stipend. In summer 2000, the government was trying to find new ways to keep these people employed, as the fighting had died down. Some of these village guards worked as night patrols against wild boars that damage crops. One village guard said, "We are now on watch against pigs."

Öcalan, the only inmate in the jail on İmralı Island, changed his political strategy in early 2002. In order to impress the member countries of the European Union, he tried to shed the PKK's terrorist image. He decided to metamorphose the PKK into a legitimate political party named the Kurdistan Freedom and Democracy Congress (KADEK) to campaign for greater Kurdish rights. His attempts bore no fruit, as KADEK was branded as a terrorist outfit.

The revolt, however, had hurt the Kurdish population severely by causing the Kurdish cultural rights to become a matter of fierce debate in the country. If there had been no separatist movement threatening the unity of the nation, I believe that official sensitivity to Kurdish cultural rights would not have taken on the proportions that it did.

There are between ten million and twelve million ethnic Kurds in Turkey, and the majority of them are law-abiding citizens. They desire the recognition of their human rights but do not wish for a separate state. One-fourth of the parliament members in 1997 were of Kurdish descent, including Hikmet Çetin, the speaker.

The official ban on the Kurdish language was lifted in April 1991. Still, as a result of the sensitivity of Turkish officials and the public about Kurdish terrorism and bloodshed, which continued for fifteen years, it has been impossible to express views and opinions on anything even remotely touching on Kurdish nationalism.

The final solution to the Kurdish problem is closely related to the developments in northern Iraq. This is because a no-fly zone, established before the destruction of Saddam Hussein's regime by the US forces, has allowed the formation of an autonomous, self-governing Kurdish region in northern Iraq. Masoud Barzani, the leader of the Kurdistan Democratic Party (KDP), and Jalal Talabani, the leader of the Patriotic Union of Kurdistan (PUK), agreed in September 2002 on a draft constitution for a regional autonomous Kurdistan with its own flag and parliament in a federation of Iraq. A regional parliament was assembled in Arbil later in October.

About twenty-five million Kurds live in Iraq, Turkey, Iran, and Syria. Turkey, like Iran and Syria, is concerned that a fully independent Kurdish state in northern Iraq may revive the separatist civil war. There is also concern about the welfare of the Turkmen population in northern Iraq, who used to live in the Mosul and Kirkuk areas. The Iraqi regimes had in the past displaced many of them in order to populate these oil-rich areas with Arabs.

Mosul was an important commercial center during the Ottoman Empire. The question of Mosul and Kirkuk was left to the League of Nations at the Lausanne Conference (1922–23), which in 1925 gave them to Iraq despite Turkey's protests. Mosul, ruled by the Turks between 1534 and 1918, had been the administrative center of the Ottoman Empire's province (*vilayet*) of Mosul. It lies on the right bank of the Tigris River, across from the ancient Assyrian city Nineveh. After the decision of the League of Nations, Mosul lost its commercial importance until the development of the oil fields nearby.

In the 1950s, while on an assignment in Baghdad, I traveled to Kirkuk in a helicopter. The party led by Prime Minister Nuri as-Said of Iraq included Prime Minister Adnan Menderes of Turkey. We met a number of ethnic Turks and Turkmen working at the oil fields. I remember that this visit was one of those occasions when Menderes used to regret deeply the collapse of the Ottoman Empire.

A Morning Newspaper Named "Evening" and the Last Days of Adnan Menderes

Man is his own devil.

Turkish proverb

*O*ne morning in 1959, during an editorial meeting, editor-in-chief Osman Karaca surprised us by saying that he had just resigned from *Yeni Sabah* and that he would move to another newspaper called *Akşam*. Would I like to go with him as chief news editor, he asked, and I accepted the offer even though this move was not an advancement. The Turks describe such a move as dismounting from a horse in order to ride a donkey. Together with a few other staff members from *Yeni Sabah*, I began working for *Akşam*, which, despite its name meaning "evening," was a struggling morning newspaper. Ilhan Turalı was the editor, Meryem Abigadol was the reporter on the Beyoğlu beat, and Burhan Tan was the chief photographer. Aziz Nesin, Müşerref Hekimoğlu, and Çetin Altan were the columnists.

Akşam was founded in 1918 and had four partners, each of whom had invested two hundred liras. This newspaper had covered the nationalist movement in Anatolia, the War of Independence, and the secular Kemalist revolution. It was a unique newspaper, for in its long history it had been printed in both Arabic and Latin scripts. After the Latin letters were adopted in 1928, the newspaper had to change from the Arabic to the Latin script.

Kazım Şinasi Dersan, the last remaining partner, had sold the newspaper in 1957 to Malik Yolaç, a ship owner and exporter of *helva*, a Turkish sweetmeat. At the time, the daily circulation of *Akşam* was only a few thousand compared with *Yeni Sabah*'s much bigger sales. Although it was once the leading newspaper, its circulation decreased after World War II, when its loyal readers had aged or died. The newspaper had not been able to adapt itself to the changing times to gain new readers. But it was the first Turkish daily to insert classified ads on its pages.

Contrary to *Yeni Sabah*'s bright new building, up-to-date printing press, and linotype machinery, *Akşam* was in an ancient building with a squeaking staircase located on Cemal Nadir Street, named after the famous caricaturist. Malik Yolaç was a Democratic Party member of parliament and greatly desired to own a newspaper for its prestige. *Hürriyet*, the leading daily, having imported a giant Mann printing press from Germany, had sold its older and smaller printing press, prone to breakdowns, to Yolaç. Thus, in the proper Turkish manner of describing our predicament, we were joining the caravan with a lame donkey.

Surprisingly, it was a happy move. Contrary to the constantly stressful atmosphere of *Yeni Sabah*, the daily broadsheet *Akşam* was a comfortable place to work, and Yolaç, a small man with gentle manners, was easy to get along with. To prove who was stronger, I used to wrestle with him at the editorial offices when things were slow, throw him down on the floor, and squeeze him so tight that his bones would make cracking noises. The publisher would take the punishment in good heart but still brag later that he had won. His newspaper ownership didn't last long though, and he sold *Akşam* to the Federation of Labor Unions after I left the paper. The federation couldn't make it profitable either, and the newspaper folded. It began publishing once more much later under different ownership. Malik Yolaç was elected later as a Justice Party member of parliament and in 1968 was the sports minister in Ismet Inönü's coalition cabinet.

My desk at *Akşam* was at the front of a small newsroom. We had total of six reporters covering the city. I began building up Anatolian coverage by finding new reporters and stringers in the countryside. We had bureaus in Ankara, the capital; in Izmir, in western Turkey; and in Adana, in southeastern Anatolia, and communicated with them via a single telex machine. The newspaper was receiving airline tickets from Pan Am, at the time the leading international airline, in return for advertising. This was a great help for the financially strapped *Akşam* to send reporters abroad when needed.

A short time after our move, Karaca decided to start a literary agency called ONK and left. Yolaç appointed me editor-in-chief, and we began competing aggressively with *Hürriyet*, *Yeni Sabah*, and *Milliyet* without the resources of these three dailies. I was thirty-four years old and still filing daily news reports to Reuters.

Meryem Abigadol, our reporter on the Beyoğlu beat, was a pretty brunette who spoke Turkish with a slightly twisted but pleasant accent. She also spoke English fluently and was a hard worker and well liked by everyone. Her parents were Jewish who had emigrated from Baghdad a long time ago. (She would later marry Ilhan Turalı, have two daughters, and die from a brain tumor at a young age.) Speaking with her often, I would see her as a symbol of integration in a country composed of different ethnic groups.

Another journalist of Jewish descent I knew from my days as a reporter was Sami Kohen, who distinguished himself in later years as editor and columnist of *Milliyet*. I had a difference of opinion with Sami Kohen during the United States's presidential election in 1968. I had covered Richard M. Nixon's election campaign closely, often joining the candidate's press entourage. Having seen the enthusiasm for Nixon among the voters, I had declared him the winner before the full vote count. Thus *Hürriyet* had an early scoop with a banner headline over the other Turkish dailies, including *Milliyet*. Sami Kohen was visiting United Nations headquarters in New York City then, and he criticized my reporting.

This dispute I had with him over journalistic ethics also caused me to wonder about relationships between people of different religions and ethnic backgrounds living in the same country. If ethnic and religious differences are serious reasons to cause tension between people, like the Greeks and the Turks, or the Turks and the Armenians, I surmised, then why not with others? Like the Turks and the Jews, or the Turks and the Poles, for instance.

The Jews during my youth in Istanbul, like other members of minorities, were mostly businessmen. They had prospered and lived peacefully with the Turks. The major reason for this relationship was simple. The Jews during the Ottoman Empire, even in its bad times, were citizens whose "umbilical cords," unlike the Greeks and Armenians, were not connected to an outside power. The Jews and the Turks had also no reason to fight over disputed land.

The Ottoman Empire had been a sanctuary for Jews escaping persecution from the fifteenth-century Spanish Inquisition. When they were expelled from Spain in 1492, Sultan Beyazıd II ordered his governors to receive the Spanish Jews kindly and help them to resettle. They were considered a gain for the Ottoman Empire because of their knowledge of the Western crafts and finance.

They came in hoards. Many became Muslims and formed influencial families in Ottoman and later in republic times. The fundamentalist Islamists identify them even now as *Sabetaycı* or *dönme*, meaning convert and renegade, respectively. According to a recent book titled *Efendi* by Soner Yalçın published in Istanbul, their descendants included Adnan Menderes's wife, Berin; Kemal Atatürk's foreign minister Tevfik Rüştü Aras; author and feminist Halide Edib Adıvar; and my journalist friend Abdi Ipekçi.

The Turks protected some Jews from Nazi Germany's genocide during World War II. Necdet Kent, a Turkish diplomat posted in Marseilles, France, between 1941 and 1944, saved many French Jews from Nazi concentration camps by giving them Turkish passports. Kent died at ninety-one in Istanbul on September 20, 2002.

There are now about twenty-seven thousand Jews in Turkey, and their weekly newspaper *Shalom* in Istanbul still publishes articles in *Ladino*, the Spanish of the Sephardic Jews.

I think Jerusalem, that most sacred city for the Jews, the Christians, and the Muslims, teaches us a lesson in history of the survival of a community with different ethnicities and religions. The people there had lived for centuries in peace under Ottoman rule. In our time, too, we have a clear example of the freedom of religion and the rights of ethnicity granted to the citizens of the Ottoman Empire. It is a Christian settlement well inland on the Asiatic side of the Bosphorus, which is locally known as the Polish Village, or Polonezköy. During my teenage years in Istanbul, we used to visit in family outings places like the Sweet Waters of Europe, the Bosphorus, Florya Beach, the Belgrade Woods, and the Princes Islands. That Polish village was also a place we visited, but not often enough because of the distance.

We used to go there especially at cherry-picking time. Polonezköy in the 1940s was like a replica of a village in Poland, with its characteristic houses, its church, and its well-kept fields. The villagers were farmers, pig herders, and, in the winter, boar hunters. During the summer months, they still rent rooms to tourists and run restaurants serving Polish dishes and Turkish specialties. Polonezköy supplies leading gourmet stores in Istanbul with butter, yogurt, jam, and pork and, during the hunting season, with boar and wild duck. In the well-kept cemetery, one can still see the graves of villagers who had risen to high government office during the Ottoman Empire.

The founder of this unique village was Jerzy Adam Czartoryski, a member of a well-known Polish family of Lithuanian origin. At the entrance of Polonezköy sits a church built in 1914 and dedicated to the memory of Prince Jerzy Adam. This Polish patriot had been the president of the revolutionary government of Poland after the insurrection of 1830. The Russians suppressed the revolt and forced Prince Jerzy Adam into exile in 1831. In search of a safe haven for his followers and soldiers, the prince eventually found sanctuary in Turkey and established the village. The present residents there are the descendants of Prince Jerzy Adam Czartoryski's followers and soldiers and some of their brides, who arrived later from Poland.

For more than 150 years, the people of the village have kept their Polish identity, their Catholic religion and traditions, and the Polish language. Only during the last few decades have they begun to be affected by the changing times. There were about 255 individuals left in this village in 1983, about 150 of them female, some young men having gone to Germany as guest workers. The village people are proud of Prince Jerzy Adam's role during the Crimean War, in which the prince was the commander of an Ottoman Kazak unit.

Michael Czajkowski was the man whom Prince Jerzy left in charge in the village, and he was destined to become an eminent official of the Ottoman Empire. This was not unusual in a colorblind country where throughout its history slaves of any race or color had reached the highest offices, including premierships. Michael Czajkowski himself, at a precarious time of Ottoman history, earned the title of pasha and was appointed *beylerbeyi*, or governor general, of Rumelia, the entire European territory ruled by the Ottoman regime. Michael Czajkowski is generally known as Mehmet Sadık Pasha.

☪

Our move to the newspaper *Akşam* had coincided with vitally important political developments. During the editorial meetings we began discussing our inklings of a possible coup d'etat, which if it happened would be the first in the young secular republic's history.

One morning Meryem Abigadol came into my room in *Akşam* and startled me with a question: "Is Adnan Menderes so blind as not to see the growing opposition against his regime?" Since Meryem had been filling in for me covering the news for Reuters when I was away from Istanbul, she had followed politics closely. And she was right. Menderes, an experienced politician, seemed unaware of the looming signs of danger against his government.

It was a time of growing Kemalist discontent against the pro-Islam and often undemocratic policies of Prime Minister Adnan Menderes. There was a yearning for social justice and widespread disillusionment with the democratic process because of corruption and injustices. The students, provoked by the wrathful opposition, the Republican People's Party, were demonstrating almost daily in the streets and campuses against the Menderes regime.

During the last years of his regime, Adnan Menderes clearly showed his displeasure with criticism. He often became angry and arrogant: "I could even get a log of firewood elected as a member of parliament." Once this statement was publicized in the media, it sparked outrage. I had seen the signs of this change on occasion, especially during one incident I witnessed in Damascus. Returning from a trip to the Arab countries on a DC3, Dakota, the workhorse of the time, Menderes aides faced a problem. The airplane had been overloaded with gifts and crates of dates. In order to lighten its load, a police chief assigned for the prime minister's security, among others, was left behind. As Nuyan Yi it, then reporting for *Cumhuriyet*, and I stood on the tarmac at the Damascus airport with that police chief, we saw tears in his eyes. I told him, "The prime minister may not be aware that you are being left here." The cop answered, "He knows. The dates were more important."

Menderes, a married man with children, was having an affair with the wife of a sectional chief of Istanbul's police department. She was rotund, even bigger in size than Menderes himself. One day in search of Menderes to ask his reaction to a political development, I went to her home in Istanbul. The mistress, seeing a reporter knocking at her door, was angry and chased me away, shouting obscenities.

Menderes was increasingly following a policy of excessive and unproductive investments, rewarding the strongholds of the Democratic Party while punishing the opposition. The prime minister and his regime became more and more authoritarian. The promulgation of antidemocratic laws concerning the freedom of the press and the right to assembly caused more tension. The opposition to the regime and the student demonstrations increased, while Menderes, as prime minister, for the first time in the history of the republic, surpassed the president in power and importance. Menderes printed more money in order to sustain the rate of economic growth.

As the supreme authority, Menderes had relaxed some of Kemal Atatürk's secularist policies. He permitted the opening of Qur'an schools and allowed the extension of religious instruction. The Arabic language was reinstated for prayer in mosques, and Qur'an readings began on the state-owned radio. There were no TV stations yet, and privately owned radio stations were not allowed.

The Republican People's Party, led by Ismet Inönü, accused Menderes of reversing the principles of secularism and of favoring conservative religious establishments for political gains. Menderes, in turn, launched reprisals against the opposition. He ordered the confiscation of Republican People's Party properties and closed the People's Houses. Up to that time, 222 People's Houses had been built, and two thousand branches in villages had been opened for the cultural advancement of the people. Their closing, especially of their libraries, was a great loss for the youth of the country.

The printing presses of *Ulus* (*Nation*), the organ of the Republican People's Party, were confiscated. Laws already passed in 1954 called for heavy fines for journalists, who damaged the "prestige of the state." This translated simply to intolerance of any criticism of officials of the ruling Democratic Party, particularly Menderes himself. Any journalist who dared to do so would face not only fines but also a stiff jail term.

The newspapers opposing the regime were deprived of income from government advertising. These official advertisements, called *Resmi Ilanlar*, such as announcements for bidding government tenders that were vital for the survival of newspapers, were used as a weapon to keep the press in line. If a newspaper criticized Menderes and his government, that newspaper would be deprived of official advertisements and the income from them.

Any criticism upset Menderes, and even the members of the Democratic Party were not immune to expulsion for finding fault in his policies. Irritated often by the leader of the Republican People's Party, Ismet Inönü, Menderes used to call this respected old politician a Doomsday Broker. Already in 1956, public meetings were restricted. The same year in October, it was made public that a group of young army officers, like

Orhan Kabibay and Ahmet Yıldız, had formed a junta "to save the country with or without bloodshed."

When the government formed a committee to investigate the affairs of the Republican People's Party and ordered the armed forces to prevent Ismet Inönü from campaigning in Kayseri, it became clear that the days of the Republican People's Party were numbered. As journalists, most of us believed that Menderes was getting ready to close down the opposition.

His actions brought the army directly into the political arena. In 1959, nine army officers were arrested and charged with conspiracy to overthrow the regime. The army's officer corps, like the university students, some of them strong supporters of the opposition Republican People's Party, had become restless.

These, then, were the signs of the coming upheaval and a personal tragedy for Adnan Menderes himself.

18

The Tragedy at Gatwick and the Fall of Adnan Menderes

Each night in every officers' club and army restaurant,
a few young officers save Turkey. Some even talk of revolution.

Ismet Inönü

In 1959, while the country was in turmoil, Adnan Menderes decided to attend the signing of the agreement for an independent Republic of Cyprus. This tripartite agreement would recognize constitutional guarantees for the Turkish minority in Cyprus and permanently divide offices based on ethnicity. The agreement to be signed in London called for Greek and Turkish communal chambers to deal separately with matters such as religion and education. Later, Archbishop Makarios would be elected president and Dr. Fazıl Küçük vice president of Cyprus. It was an arrangement that was doomed to fail because the Greeks had not given up on *Enosis*, the island's union with Greece.

I tried to get two seats on Menderes's airplane for the trip to London on February 17, 1959, and asked Malik Yolaç, the publisher of *Akşam*, to help me using his connections. I wanted to travel to London with Burhan Tan, *Akşam*'s chief photographer. Word came back that the space in *Sev*, the British-built Viscount turbo-prop airliner, was limited. A single seat only could be provided, and this would be for Burhan Tan. Menderes, like all politicians, was fond of being photographed. I decided to take a commercial airliner to London one day before the premier's departure.

Moments before I left the newspaper building on my way to the airport, I happened to meet Burhan Tan on the newspaper's creaking staircase. Burhan was climbing the stairs and upon seeing me, he stopped.

"Well, Köfte," I said, "see you tomorrow in London."

We used to call him *köfte*, or meatball, because he was fond of that Turkish specialty, especially the long ones loaded with spices and grilled on skewers like shish kebab.

"I surely hope so," he answered. "Who can say what destiny may bring. I have this terrible, depressing feeling in my gut as if something awful is about to happen. It is so strange. Even while covering the Korean War, I did not experience such a bad presentiment. It scares me."

"I hope it's nothing," I said, trying to cheer him up. "Just take care driving in Istanbul's crazy traffic."

Usually joyful, he didn't smile even at this. A tall, handsome young man, Burhan Tan had a beautiful French car, a Citroen, which he liked so much that he would not let anyone else drive it. This strange meeting was to be our last.

I still wonder if it were a play of destiny, which the Turks describe as *kader* or *kısmet*? However it may be defined, it turned out to be a premonition of approaching death. This encounter on a staircase is still vivid in my mind. I often wonder why I was spared because the prime minister chose the photographer instead of me to travel on that airplane.

Upon arrival in London, I met Necati Zincirkıran at the Strand Hotel, and we agreed to go to Heathrow Airport together the next day in order to meet Menderes's plane. Zincirkıran was reporting for *Hürriyet*, the big rival newspaper. By that time, the conversation I had with Burhan Tan on the staircase had slipped from my mind.

The next day at Heathrow, we were informed that the prime minister's airplane had been diverted to Gatwick Airport because of fog and that Menderes's party would arrive by train. Zincirkıran and I took a taxi to Victoria station, where we waited. There the news of the plane crash in the woods near Gatwick Airport reached us, and, in our shock and grief, I remembered Burhan Tan's words.

It was already evening at Victoria station, and it was essential that we would not let our shock delay us in our duty to report the news. We took over the waiting room of Her Majesty's Strand Post Office and set it up as our office, with full use of the post office's telephone and typewriter. Telephone communications between London and Istanbul were still at a primitive stage, and it was impossible to transmit long texts. We concentrated on cables. We worked there frantically, calling Gatwick Airport, the police precinct, and the hospitals. Between Zincirkıran and myself, we probably wrote a whole book in cables that night and the next few days.

Adnan Menderes had been in a starboard window seat in the tail section as the plane heading to Gatwick Airport flew over a pine forest. Two miles from the airport, the passengers experienced the plane beginning to hit treetops. The crash was sudden and with an awful, grinding noise as the fuselage dragged along the ground, then split into two sections. A fire started and spread quickly in the main part of the fuselage. The broken tail section had turned upside down, and Menderes's right foot had been caught in the floor. Rıfat Kadızade, a Democratic Party deputy, saw the prime minister hanging upside down and pulled him down. Menderes was dazed, covered with mud, and slightly injured in his face. Both of them climbed out quickly and saw the main fuselage on fire.

"Our friends are burning in there, and we are unable to help them," Menderes told Kadızade.

In their farmhouse nearby, Tony and Margaret Bailey heard a tremendous explosion. They quickly drove their car to the place of the disaster. The couple took Menderes, Kadızade, and Refik Fenmen, the prime minister's secretary, to their home. Mrs. Bailey had worked earlier as a nurse, and she helped the injured. The prime minister was later taken to the London Clinic.

Burhan Tan, with fourteen others, had been killed.

Our urgent reporting done, we had a London cabbie take us to the crash site. I have never seen anything comparable to this carnage. I saw body parts and pieces of clothing hanging on broken branches of trees. The trees were splintered as if they were matchsticks. The ground was full of pieces and bits of the wreckage, along with personal belongings of the passengers and the crew.

It was a nightmare that troubled me for days and nights to come.

The investigation later showed that the plane crash had been caused by pilot error. There was talk about an altimeter malfunction, showing the pilot a higher altitude than the airplane's true altitude as it approached the airport. Vague allegations about sabotage of the altimeter for the purpose of killing Menderes were never proven.

Adnan Menderes returned to Turkey to face severe opposition to his regime. Saved from one disaster by a miracle, he was to face the hangman's noose at Imralı, the prison island in the Marmara Sea.

There were many reasons for the fall of his regime. The armed forces, having gone through a period of modernization with US aid, had become disillusioned with the government. The army officers considered Menderes and the Democratic Party a threat to the secular Kemalist reforms. When student demonstrations against the regime intensified, military was declared on April 28, 1960. This brought the army officers face to face with the demonstrating students.

In the media world, we all knew that the hardliners of the opposition Republican People's Party had never forgotten their party's crushing defeat in the 1950 election. Soon after the election, they started a strong campaign against the Democrats that would last for ten years. Covering the events in the spring of 1960, I would regularly observe the members of the youth organizations of the Republican People's Party inciting student demonstrators. I had the clear impression at the time that the opposition was playing a crucial role in the overthrow of Menderes.

The signs of a coming coup d'etat became apparent. I saw tears in many army officers' eyes as they dispersed the demonstrators, who sang the song about the historical warrior hero Osman Pasha of the siege of Pleven. Two lines of the text, changed by the demonstrators, went straight to military officers' hearts: "Is this possible?/Could a brother shoot his own brother?"

Things began moving fast. On May 3, 1960, General Cemal Gürsel, commander of the land forces, demanded political reforms. Well liked by the officer corps, Gürsel resigned when Menderes refused his demand. Jailing of journalists became a daily event as more restrictions were imposed on news reports. In order to keep essential creative personnel from becoming jailbirds, we relied on a critical position at the paper, namely, that of a volunteer editor, who assumed full legal responsibility for the newspaper's contents. This editor, a sacrificial lamb so to speak, was willing to go to jail if convicted in a military court for printing articles not liked by the regime. And many newsmen ended up in jail and saved others from nerve-wracking trials in military courts.

My reporting to Reuters brought on a direct confrontation with Menderes himself. During a demonstration in Ankara on May 5, 1960, the university students booed him. The prime minister left his limousine, stepped toward the students, and asked, "What's it that you want?" Slipping on a curbstone, Menderes fell down, then stood up, demonstrators harassing him. The students shouted, "Resign!" Reports claimed that his shirt was torn. I filed the news to London as it happened, and the report from Reuters was fed back to the semiofficial Anatolian News Agency. Menderes was furious! He immediately sent word warning me to curb my reporting or else I, too, would end up in prison. I did not curb my reporting, and it turned out that there was not much time left for Menderes to imprison anyone else. While Menderes was visiting the air force base in Eskişehir, in western Anatolia, the officers insulted him by turning their backs. It was obvious that the time to overthrow his regime was at hand.

Most newspapers had been resisting the censorship imposed by martial law by leaving obvious blank spaces where censored news or articles would have appeared in print. There were so many blank columns in the newspapers each day that this too turned into a protest against the regime's restrictions on freedom of the press. Several newspapers were closed on charges of acts against the rules of martial law.

During my travels in Europe, in West Germany I had purchased something new and unique for those times—a tiny Japanese transistor radio made by Hitachi, smaller than my palm and running on a single battery. As the crisis rapidly escalated, I began carrying it in my pocket in order to listen to official statements or the martial law communiqués, whenever I was away from the radios at the office, at home, or in the car. I anticipated the news of or a sign of a coup d'etat at any moment.

One important news story was dropped in my lap by a totally unexpected source. Each night at home before sleep, I would listen to local and BBC news broadcasts and talk with the night editor about the latest developments. On the night of May 26, 1960, tired because of the day's activities, I went to bed earlier than usual.

Sometime after midnight, persistent ringing at the door awoke me from a deep sleep. I was not expecting anyone, but cables arrived from Reuters anytime during the night or day with instructions relating to news developments. Sometimes I would get a cable that said that my report on an important event had been so many minutes behind the opposition— usually the Associated Press—or that I had been so many minutes ahead. I was sure that I could not miss the breaking news of an important development because the night editor would call me as soon as the news of it hit his desk. So I thought that the postman was at the door with a routine cable from Reuters when I went to answer it.

This late-night visitor was my Uncle Ethem's son, Zeki Ergun, then an officer in the First Army, wearing his staff colonel's uniform. There was his jeep outside with a military driver, its motor running. I thought maybe he brought some bad news about the family.

"Hi," I said. "Is something wrong?"

"Plenty," he answered. "It took you long enough to wake up and come to the door."

"Too much work," I said.

"Listen, I don't have time to stay," the colonel said. "I have pressing business. Something very important is happening, and I'm sure it will interest you. The armed forces are in the process of overthrowing the Menderes regime. Here in town, we have taken the governor into custody. Menderes and all the high government officials are being arrested right now."

What a shock that was! This revolution just taking place would soon be known as the Colonels' Coup.

Although I had been expecting the coup for days, its news surprised me. As soon as the colonel left, I rushed to the phone and tried to place a call to London or the Reuters office in Athens, which had telex connections with London at the time. All telephone communications with the outside world had been cut, which is routine during a coup d'etat. I was in an excellent position for a major scoop, but I had no way of quickly transmitting my copy. Since airports would be closed, I was left with a single alternative. Hurriedly, I typed an urgent cable, a flash, and called the night editor at the newspaper, telling him to stop the press, get some staff together, and be prepared to change the news pages.

The night editor had no idea what was going on, so I told him, adding that he should secure a telex line to our bureau in Ankara with our single machine and hold it. I left home and drove directly to the central post office with the flash cable. There was unusual military activity in the streets and town squares.

I knew the clerk on night duty at the central post office, but he was not alone—a stern-looking army staff major had an automatic gun in his hands and inquisitively studied my face. The night clerk introduced me to this major by name, saying that I was a journalist and reported to Reuters in London.

"So he is a spy," the major said, staring at me.

The officer's words hit me like blows from a jackhammer. He was dead serious. I said nothing but wondered how a major, who had graduated from the military staff academy, could be so simple-minded, even if he appeared to be an ultranationalist.

I had learned through the years that journalists reporting from their native countries to foreign news organizations were always under suspicion of espionage. They could face severe danger, especially in times when governments were toppled. I had known a journalist in Baghdad, a citizen of Iraq, who had also reported to an international news service and got into big trouble because of it. This reporter had been very close to Prime Minister Nuri as-Said of Iraq and through this connection was able to repeatedly score important scoops. When Nuri as-Said and King Faisal II were overthrown and killed in 1958 during the leftist pan-Arab revolution, that journalist ended up in a dreadful Baghdad dungeon. When I met him later, he complained in tears that nobody had helped him during his time in jail, not even the news agency he had served so well for years.

The night clerk at the post office took my cable and said, "I will send it upstairs right away, but I doubt that it will be transmitted to London tonight. All connections have been cut."

There was nothing else I could do. In any case, early in the morning, Alparslan Türkeş, an army colonel, announced the coup d'etat to the nation on national radio, which then began broadcasting Turkish military music. Colonel Türkeş, a pan-Turanist and an ultranationalist, later on was to become *başbuğ*, leader of the extreme-right *Milliyetçi Hareket Partisi* (MHP), or Nationalist Action Party.

I left the post office to go directly to the newspaper's offices. Coups d'etat are dangerous because of the inherent suspense and the uncertainty that accompanies them. Adnan Menderes was visiting Eskişehir in western Turkey when he woke up at dawn and learned the shocking news. Accompanied by Hasan Polatkan, his finance minister, he at once tried to escape. A jetfighter spotted Menderes's convoy on the way to Kütahya. Upon arriving there, he was arrested and taken back to Eskişehir Air Force Base. President Celal Bayar was detained in Ankara, along with most of the leaders of the Democratic Party and the party's members of parliament. We heard reports about how some of them had done their best to avoid arrest by hiding under their beds at home. Four hundred prisoners were taken to Yassıada in Istanbul, where they were tried in a special tribunal. Yassıada is a small island with a naval base in the Marmara Sea, not far from our Robinson Crusoe's Sivri Island.

There were allegations that the Menderes regime had killed students and had made mincemeat of their bodies but these were lies. I inquired and checked the morgue located across the Sublime Porte but found no evidence supporting such allegations.

Celal Bayar, the former president, tried to commit suicide in his cell using his belt but was saved barely in time—blood was pouring from his ears. Menderes changed his strident tune during the trials and began addressing the judges with a lot of flattery, which didn't help his case and instead hurt his image. For eleven months, the *Yassıada Hour*, a broadcast on national radio, carried the tribunal's proceedings. Some charges brought against Menderes by the prosecutors were ridiculous, while others were very serious, such as having violated the constitution by ordering the police to fire on student demonstrators.

Menderes also tried to commit suicide with sleeping pills he had saved. His stomach was pumped at the hospital, and he was hanged at Imralı right afterward on September 17, 1961. Two members of his cabinet, Foreign Minister Fatin Rüştü Zorlu and Finance Minister Hasan Polatkan, had been executed a day earlier on the same prison island. Advanced age saved Bayar from execution. He died in 1987, when he was 103 years old.

The trials and hangings did not bring peace, as the Democratic Party and Menderes had been supported in every election by a solid four million votes. Later, these four million Democrats would play a crucial and somewhat disastrous role in Turkish political life through the emergence of several copycat parties.

The trials of Yassıada were brought about by a junta of thirty-eight officers formed under the leadership of General Cemal Gürsel, who would later become president. The junta was named *Milli Birlik Komitesi*, the Committee of National Unity, but there was no unity among its members. They bickered over matters of policy during meetings, often drawing guns on each other. For me, there was a respite from reporting the infighting of the junta members for a while.

Zeyyat Gören, who had left UPI in order to become press attaché at the Turkish Embassy in Washington, had arranged a scholarship for Turkish journalists with the late Eugene C. Pulliam, then the publisher of the *Indianapolis Star* and the *Indianapolis News*. During this first visit to America, I stayed in Indianapolis, Indiana, for a month, studying the American way of producing a newspaper at the *Indianapolis Star*. It was November 1960; presidential elections were taking place, and Democratic candidate John F. Kennedy defeated Republican Richard M. Nixon.

At the time, there was a dispute in Indianapolis about the historic courthouse. Most people wanted it demolished. I visited the courthouse and wondered why Americans wanted to destroy a historic building with a beautiful staircase. So I wrote an article suggesting that the courthouse ought to be kept for posterity, and the *Indianapolis Star* printed it. I doubt that anybody gave a hoot about it, due to the typical American love for anything new, bigger, and better.

The junta members were still bickering among themselves, surprisingly, even on the subject of the secularity of the state. I was shocked to learn upon my return that some junta members had spoken against the secularist principles of the Kemalist reforms. The senior members of the junta wished to bring democracy back as soon as possible, while others wanted to stay in power. Because of infighting, the Committee of National Unity was dissolved on November 13, 1960. When it was reformed, fourteen of its members, including Colonel Alparslan Türkeş, had been expelled and sent into exile in the form of diplomatic posts abroad. The junta brought about a liberal constitution that allowed labor unions and guaranteed rights such as freedom of the press. Yet the coup d'etat opened up a Pandora's box of politically charged problems.

My professional life, too, was about to change. *Hürriyet* had an opening for a chief news editor, and I applied for this position. This was the most challenging job in Babıali at the time. I already had experience in running a news service, and in addition I had developed, in time, a unique ability that I was sure could help me in my new job. That was *creative visualization*, or *creative imagination*, the ability to see unexpected and often exciting leads for other news by reading an existing news item.

Necati Zincirkıran had been appointed *Hürriyet*'s editor-in-chief and, together with a young crew of reporters and writers, we formed a team that put powerful emphasis on news.

Hürriyet in those days was an impartial newspaper fighting corruption and injustice and defending democracy and human rights. The members of its staff were loyal Kemalists. These were the principles of Sedat Simavi, the newspaper's founder who used to admonish *Hürriyet*'s writers to be impartial and not to be influenced by any government or any person. His famous words were, "Don't make your pen a slave. If necessary break it, but don't ever sell it."

I remember that this great newspaper was highly successful and much respected as long as the principles of its founder were fully observed.

One Newspaper and the Destiny of a Nation

"I have lived free since eternity and I live free."

M. A. Ersoy, poet of the Turkish national anthem

*I*n 1960, *Hürriyet* was a young newspaper that led a score of other national dailies in content and circulation. A progeny of the Kemalist reforms, it was the second newspaper by this same name, which means freedom. The patriotic playwright and "poet of liberty" Namık Kemal had been the first publisher of *Hürriyet* in 1857 in London, where he had fled from the Ottoman tyranny. In London, it was printed in the Arabic script. Kemal's writings would later influence the westernization of Turkish literature and the Young Turk Revolution of 1908.

When Sedat Simavi once again started *Hürriyet* in 1948 in Latin script, he boosted the circulation almost in one stroke by sending a team of reporters to the 1948 Olympic summer games in London. There, Turkish wrestlers won gold medals. Sedat Simavi, an experienced journalist, left the newspaper in the hands of his sons, Haldun and Erol, before his death five years after the founding of *Hürriyet*. Haldun, darkly handsome and taller than his younger brother, handled the edito-

231

rial direction of *Hürriyet*, while Erol was left in charge of administrative affairs.

The Simavi brothers were totally different in character, manners, and looks from each other. Erol, a playboy with a potbelly, was short and flamboyant. As habitué of the Istanbul bars, he reveled in the role of a womanizer. One of Erol's mistresses, a well-known singer, once claimed that he was trying to have sex with the whole world—despite the fact that his short height wasn't the only thing that short-changed him.

Years later, Erol, concerned about another coup d'etat and clashes between left- and right-wing groups, settled down in Switzerland. He sold *Hürriyet* in the mid-1990s to Aydın Doğan, a businessman and the owner of *Milliyet*.

Erol Simavi wanted to be known in Babıali, Istanbul's press district, as *Çapkın Patron*, or womanizing boss and dashing lothario. We never understood why he felt the need for such unflattering fame. His lack of grasp of journalism and his personal behavior was counterbalanced by his elder brother. Haldun Simavi was a disciplinarian who imposed order on the newspaper personnel. Haldun was interested with the technique of printing daily newspapers in color with web-offset rotation presses. He realized that this system was destined to drastically change the business of newspaper printing. In later years, he sold to Asil Nadir, the Turkish Cypriot tycoon of the Polly Peck business empire, for a fortune a colorful daily newspaper called *Günaydın* (*Good Morning*) that he had published. Then, he settled in London.

Nuyan Yiğit, correspondent of the Haber News Agency in London, was appointed *Günaydın*'s editor-in-chief. Yiğit told me much later, "We imported five new printing presses and installed a super fax system to print *Günaydın* simultaneously in different locations, including in distant provinces of eastern Anatolia. Circulation increased to one million a day. Later, the newspaper's demise was caused by Asil Nadir's attempt to bring in experts from England, who had no idea of Turkish journalism, and by the collapse of Polly Peck."

For Asil Nadir, who insisted on keeping the price of the newspaper low in order to achieve a large national circulation, *Günaydın* became a big financial drain. Necati Zincirkıran believes that the purchase of *Günaydın* played a role in the collapse of Polly Peck International.

Asil Nadir fled to northern Cyprus in 1993 after Britain's Serious Fraud Office laid sixty-six charges against him. Polly Peck, an international company business group specializing in everything from fruit to electronics, had collapsed in 1990 with huge debts.

When I started working for *Hürriyet* in 1960, I found that contrary to a scorching article I had earlier read in that newspaper, highly critical of the Simavi brothers, Haldun was respected as the publisher. He was not a writer but welcomed new and creative ideas. However, Haldun could not tolerate that scathing piece by the newspaper's own editor-in-chief, which claimed without naming names that the Simavi brothers were unfit to run a newspaper. Samih Tiryakioğlu, this editor-in-chief, was fired the next day. He was a friend of mine and had one big ambition, namely, to own a daily newspaper.

Often, even long before I joined its staff, I had considered *Hürriyet* to be the guiding beacon for the nation, playing a vital role in its destiny, for many reasons. *Hürriyet*, unlike a few opportunistic, fly-by-night newspapers, was incorruptible and served as the nation's watchdog against corruption. Since its founding in 1948, this newspaper had played a decisive role in guarding the republic's Kemalist traditions and the development of its budding democracy. *Hürriyet* was a strong advocate of secularism, democracy, freedom of the press, free speech, and human rights. Unfortunately, things later changed a great deal.

The new *Hürriyet* building in 1960 was next to the apartment building in Cağaloğlu, where my mother was still practicing dentistry. The street level housed the German-made Mann printing press, and on the second floor, Erol Simavi ran the administration and advertising departments. The editorial offices were on the third floor, and due to a battery of telex machines I had in my office, we had to cover the walls with velvet to absorb the noise. I used to spend most of my time there and didn't leave even for such things as haircuts. Instead, I had a barber come in and give me a haircut right next to the telexes so that I would be able to act quickly on breaking news.

The acrid smell of hot type used to seep into our offices from the composing room that was on the same floor (for fast access during news emergencies). In the composing room, a battery of linotypes, keyboard-operated typesetting machines, produced each line for the paper in the form of solid lead slugs. The slugs, in turn, were placed on a mock-up metal page from which matrices for the printing press were produced. Because of the molten lead, the composing room would feel like an oven in the summer since we did not have air-conditioning, causing complaints from the linotype operators.

Years later, all this changed with the introduction of web-offset rotation color printing presses that brought rich color to the black-and-white newspapers. The composing rooms and linotype machines became obsolete.

On the fourth floor, we had archives and photo labs. Top floor was the cafeteria that had a beautiful view of the Bosphorus. Most of the employees liked to pass time there, smoking and drinking their thick Turkish coffee from *fincans*, or demitasses, while enjoying the view.

During the hot summer days, the windows would be left open to let in the *meltem*, the refreshing gentle wind that blew in from the Bosphorus. One of the marvels of the world, the strait from our vantage point looked like a huge bright blue ribbon flowing between the steep hills, separating Europe from Asia.

The Bosphorus has an important place in Turkish literature. The poet Tevfik Fikret, who established the style of Western poetry in Turkey, lived there in a house he had named *Aşiyan*, or nest, now a museum.

H. E. Adıvar wrote, "In the dark blue night of the Bosphorus,/A fisherman's caique was gliding through."

The Bosphorus has fascinating hydrological features, such as its great depth of up to 394 feet in some places and its treacherous unusual currents. Its surface current, flowing from the Black Sea into the Sea of Marmara, is cold and can be hazardous for swimming. The deep, warm undersea current, flowing in the opposite direction from the Sea of Marmara and finally reaching the shores of the Crimea, brings a mild climate to that peninsula.

The *Hürriyet* building was on top of the hill, and the windows of its cafeteria provided a panoramic view of Istanbul's skyline fringed with domed mosques and spires of minarets. The busy Bosphorus was always full of ships, boats, and ferries plying the water back and forth between Europe and Asia. The whitewashed *Kız Kulesi*, or Leander Tower, lighthouse, rising on a tiny island near the shores of Üsküdar, sat in immovably in the middle of the hectic waterway.

One day Haldun Simavi shocked us all by removing the windows, building a straight wall, and shutting out that view to prevent loafing.

Haldun Simavi, contrary to his brother, Erol, had no objections to my association with Reuters, and I continued reporting to that international news agency. My primary job, however, was to read a dozen morning newspapers, news agency reports, and foreign newspapers to find new and exciting ideas for our readership. We began printing a weekly tabloid named *Little Hürriyet*, a house organ in which we would discuss our successes and failures. This little tabloid was sought after even by rival journalists.

The editorial meeting each morning was the heart and soul of *Hürriyet* and a decisive factor for the daily direction of the newspaper. Haldun Simavi insisted that the news be simplified in condensed form so that readers with limited education would be able to understand it. By pioneering the web-offset rotation color printing with *Günaydın* in 1969, he was trying to make a daily newspaper as smooth, colorful, and commercially attractive as a magazine. Haldun's earlier experiment with *Yeni Gazete*, a black-and-white morning broadsheet with extensive and serious news coverage, which struggled and folded, had proved to him that mass appeal meant mass circulation.

His biggest mistake was to sacrifice quality both in the editorial content and in a good number of journalists. The copycats of the color revolution followed. Eventually Babıali was deluded by technically advanced but editorially poor newspapers. In time scores of columnists were used to perform a reporter's job without having the experience of the reporter. Still, I believe that Haldun Simavi had visualized *Günaydın* in the format of *USA Today* a decade before *USA Today* hit the American newsstands.

Our news team was extremely aggressive, and this brought much sorrow along with repeated success. The tragic death of Burhan Tan at Gatwick had affected me emotionally, and I had realized early enough how precious but fragile life was. Yet we were in a terrific daily race with other newspapers to cover the news faster and better—in the heat of summer or the cold of winter.

Sometimes the winters in Turkish Thrace can be rough. One winter day, we received word that the Simplon Express, heading toward Istanbul, was snowbound. Two reporters, Yüksel Kasapbaşı and Abidin Behpur, accompanied by driver Yüksel Öztürk in a four-wheel drive vehicle, took off to make an attempt to reach the stranded passengers. We were not to see these young people alive again.

Inexperienced in survival techniques in conditions of deep snow and severe cold, they persisted in their attempt to reach the stranded train and got stuck in a snow bank on the road to Çatalca. Peasants from a nearby village came by and invited them to the village. The team preferred to stay with their vehicle. They used the gas to heat the vehicle and fell asleep. Rescue crews found their frozen bodies during the night.

The loss of these colleagues and friends was extremely difficult for all of us. Yet journalists are somewhat similar to policemen and firefighters in terms of danger, especially when covering armed conflicts. Since then scores of journalists have died in Turkey by assassination and outright murder, particularly during skirmishes between the rightist and leftist extremists, and later during the Kurdish uprising in southeastern Anatolia.

I traveled to Vienna in 1961 to cover the summit between American President John F. Kennedy and the Soviet leader Nikita Sergeyevich Khrushchev. Khrushchev was a boisterous, short, stubby man with a bald head, and he wore baggy trousers and shoes with thick rubber soles. When he arrived in Vienna by train and was welcomed by the Austrian Chancellor Bruno Kreisky, I sneaked in right behind them, trying to get an earful.

Tahsin Öztin at the time was the oldest and most traveled journalist on our team. Because he had interviewed scores of kings and queens and government leaders, I thought he should be the one to cover the Vienna summit. It was not to be.

Öztin was an amiable character. He had been sent to Mecca on several occasions on assignments to cover the Hajj, the annual Muslim pilgrimage to the holy places in Saudi Arabia. He used to talk about the overcrowding in Mecca, describing the Hajj with the Arabic word *mahsher*, which means the Last Judgment, a great crowd, or great confusion. He also used to describe the devil-stoning ritual by the pilgrims. During the Hajj, the pilgrims pelt pebbles at three pillars that represent *Shaytan al-Kabir,* meaning Great Satan in Arabic. "Wave after wave the pilgrims come in front of the gray stone pillars," Tahsin Öztin said. "Many people are killed in stampedes. Others die of old age or natural causes. It is believed that dying while performing the pilgrimage ensures entrance to the Muslim paradise. During the stoning ritual, each pilgrim throws seven small pebbles at the pillars and shouts insults in Arabic. Often, the pilgrims will take off their shoes or flip-flops too and throw them at the pillars representing the Great Satan."

Vienna by comparison was full of the joy and color of the late spring, where the fate of the world was being discussed. The press center for the Kennedy-Khrushchev meeting was located at the Hofburg, the old imperial palace and the favorite residence of the Habsburgs. Kennedy and Khrushchev were unable to agree on the German question, two months after the Bay of Pigs debacle of April 17, 1961. The agenda also involved fifteen intermediate-range US Jupiter nuclear missiles that were present in Turkey. They became a bargaining chip a year later, when, in October, the Americans discovered the existence of Soviet short- and intermediate-range missiles in Cuba. The removal of the Jupiter missiles from Turkey played an important role as a quid pro quo in solving the Cuban crisis.

The Balkan countries, in particular Bulgaria and Yugoslavia, were places I frequently visited to observe the conditions under strict Communist rule. In both countries lived many ethnic Turks who had settled there during the times of the Ottoman Empire. Since people were afraid to talk to foreigners, it was difficult to approach them. The police were always suspicious of foreign visitors, especially of anyone with a camera. Once in Skopje, then in Yugoslavia, now in Macedonia, a uniformed policeman kept sneaking around me, just because I was taking pictures of an old

Turkish woman. She was picking walnuts fallen from a tree in the court-yard of a mosque. Because of the policeman's presence, the woman had to explain in whispers and in pure Turkish the difficulties of life under the oppressive rule of the Serbs.

Once, in Yugoslavia, I had a mysterious experience. I had car trouble in Kragujevac, a town south of Belgrade. It was wintertime—plenty of snow coated the ground, and I was on my way to Belgrade. I felt restless and extremely anxious for no reason at all. As soon as the car was ready, I changed my travel plans and decided not to go to Belgrade. Instead, I turned around and headed right back to Istanbul. A feeling made me drive all through Yugoslavia, Bulgaria, and Turkish Thrace without stopping, except for border controls. I remember rabbits racing the headlights of my car at night while it snowed on the mountain roads of the Balkan coun-tryside. I arrived in Istanbul safely but exhausted.

A few hours later, the phone rang. It was the night editor calling to inform me of an airplane disaster. An airliner from a Middle Eastern country had collided over Ankara with a military plane. Burning bodies, airplane parts, and flaming jet fuel fell on people, who instantly turned into running torches. My file to Reuters was a big scoop, and it received considerable play in the world press.

20

The Folding of "Yeni Sabah"

If guilt were a bride, nobody would be willing to be the bridegroom.

Turkish proverb

efore handing power over to the civilians, the junta of 1960 took unusual measures to safeguard the rights of working journalists. New laws for such hitherto unheard of subjects, like the minimum wage and severance pay, were approved. Severance pay scared the newspaper publishers because of the law's long-term financial implications—it was retroactive to the year when the journalist was hired.

Previously, in the years since 1950, when the Democratic Party had come to power, journalists had had no job security, no labor union, or severance pay when fired. The Democrats decreed a new law that recognized the right for journalists to form a union. Still, the Democrats refused to give journalists the right to prove what they reported. In other words, if there were corruption in government and a journalist had proof of it, he was not allowed by law to write about it. If he did, he could be sentenced to a jail term. This was to change only after the coup d'etat of 1960.

The coup came at a busy time for Turkish national dailies because of the influx of Turkish guest workers to West Germany. Some newspapers, including *Hürriyet*, had started airfreighting editions to West Germany and other countries in Western Europe years before they actually started printing them there.

Safa Kılıçlıoğlu, my former boss, concerned about the financial liabilities of the coming severance pay laws, decided to close *Yeni Sabah*. There might have been other reasons for his decision to quit publishing *Yeni Sabah*, as competition for news in Babıali had turned into a vicious struggle. During an editorial meeting, Haldun Simavi told me to interview Kılıçlıoğlu and hear what he had to say. So I went to see my old boss in his penthouse, after going through the red-and-green-lights procedure at the door of his office.

Safa Kılıçlıoğlu was still exuding his old fiery attitude, yet the aggressiveness, with which he had played the game against *Hürriyet* so well for years, was no longer there. It was as if he had been in a race and, having lost it, didn't know what to do next. I asked him why he had decided to fold *Yeni Sabah*. He replied, "There is no cause left to defend." I thought that was a poor excuse for an answer, for there were plenty of challenges and causes to defend in a country where grinding poverty was widespread and social injustices in people's daily lives plain to see for anybody who would only care to look.

I wrote the news story starting with, "A daily newspaper died yesterday," and yet, I felt sad writing it.

I was to see my old boss in later years when I had achieved some fame, sunning on the fine sandy beach of Florya by the Marmara Sea, where he had built an arabesque palace. Being young and often pretentious, I would wave at him with an unspoken but obvious message: "See what I made of myself." My old boss, in turn, would wave back with his sly smile and the same old twinkle of mischief in his eyes. He didn't have to say it, but I could well guess what was in his mind: Don't be so proud of yourself! Did you forget how foolishly you missed that sensational photograph of Terry Moore?

The newspaper had been a source of great power for him while he

1. A recent photo of Muammer Kaylan.
(© *2004 Magrid Kaylan*)

2.
Necmettin Erbakan, the traditional Islamist who said, "Vote for us. If you do not vote for us, that means you belong to the potato party." *(The Turkish Embassy Office of the Press Counselor in Washington, DC)*

3.
Prime Minister Recep Tayyip Erdogan, leader of the Justice and Development Party. *(The Turkish Embassy Office of the Press Counselor in Washington, DC)*

4. Sublime Porte in Istanbul. (© *1999 Muammer Kaylan*)

5. Ahmet Necdet Sezer, the secularist president of Turkey.
(The Turkish Embassy Office of the Press Counselor in Washington, DC)

6.
Foreign Minister
Abdullah Gül of the
Justice and
Development
Party. *(The Turkish
Embassy Office of
the Press Counselor
in Washington, DC)*

7.
Veteran Turkish
politician Bülent
Ecevit. His name
has not been
involved in scan-
dals. *(The Turkish
Embassy Office of
the Press
Counselor in
Washington, DC)*

8.
Mesut Yilmaz, once the leader of the Motherland Party and prime minister. A picture of Kemal Atatürk is on the wall. *(The Turkish Embassy Office of the Press Counselor in Washington, DC)*

9. Tansu Çiller, Turkey's first woman prime minister. She said, "I am a creation of Atatürk," yet she formed a coalition with traditional Islamist Necmettin Erbakan.
(The Turkish Embassy Office of the Press Counselor in Washington, DC)

10. Süleyman Demirel, who, as the prime minister and later president, played an important role in the revival of the Islamic religion in Turkey. The picture on the wall shows Kemal Atatürk, the first president of the Turkish republic.
(The Turkish Embassy Office of the Press Counselor in Washington, DC)

11. The "band" of *Hürriyet*. Necati Zincirkiran *(first from left, playing the trumpet)* and Muammer Kaylan *(second from left, playing the accordion)*. The drummer is Kemal Biselman. None of the editors knew how to play musical instruments, and the picture was meant to be a joke.

12.
Muammer Kaylan
as chief news
editor of *Hürriyet*.

13.
The late Turgut
Özal, former
prime minister
and president of
Turkey who
brought about
economic
reforms. He was
a member of the
Nakshibendi
Brotherhood and
was known to
have the nick-
names "Dervish"
and "Tonton."
*(The Turkish
Embassy Office
of the Press
Counselor in
Washington, DC)*

14.
Kemal Atatürk
(right) with
Sabiha Gökçen,
his adopted
daughter, who
became the first
woman military
pilot. *(The Turkish
Embassy Office
of the Press
Counselor in
Washington, DC)*

15.
Kemal Atatürk,
wearing the
European hat and
speaking with a
child. The picture
was taken follow-
ing the hat
reform. He intro-
duced the
European hat to
the people in
1925 and abol-
ished the fez.
*(The Turkish
Embassy Office
of the Press
Counselor in
Washington, DC)*

16. Kemal Atatürk teaching Latin letters during the reform years.
(The Turkish Embassy Office of the Press Counselor in Washington, DC)

17. Kemal Atatürk in 1921 *(in the middle, front row)* with other leaders of the War of Independence wearing civilian suits and astrakhan hats. The man on his left with a moustache and wearing the light-colored military cloak is Marshal Fevzi Çakmak.
(The Turkish Embassy Office of the Press Counselor in Washington, DC)

18. Kemal Atatürk's mortal remains being removed to Anitkabir, his mausoleum in Ankra, after it was completed. The body had been kept in a museum in Ankara.
(The Turkish Embassy Office of the Press Counselor in Washington, DC)

19. Kemal Atatürk with his field marshal uniform, wearing the fez-shaped astrakhan hat. This photograph was taken shortly after the War of Independence and before the declaration of the Turkish republic.

(The Turkish Embassy Office of the Press Counselor in Washington, DC)

20. A section of the harem in the Old Seraglio in Istanbul, now a museum. Elaborate tile work and elegant old Turkish script are featured in the former residence of the wives and concubines of the Ottoman sultans. During the Ottoman Empire, this harem had about five hundred inhabitants at any one time.
(The Turkish Embassy Office of the Press Counselor in Washington, DC)

21.
Qur'an box made in 1505 by Ahmed bin Hasan for Sultan Beyazid II, now in the Turkish and Islamic Arts Museum. *(The Turkish Embassy Office of the Press Counselor in Washington, DC)*

22. Kemal Atatürk with schoolchildren. This picture was taken during the reform years, most likely in the 1930s.
(The Turkish Embassy Office of the Press Counselor in Washington, DC)

23. Kemal Atatürk *(left)* shaking hands with Ismet Inönü, who became president of Turkey following Atatürk's death in 1938.
(The Turkish Embassy Office of the Press Counselor in Washington, DC)

24. Mustafa Kemal Atatürk *(first from left)* on horseback in 1922 wearing an astrakhan hat shaped like a fez, saluting military units. This picture was taken shortly before the Great Offensive against the invading Greek forces.
(The Turkish Embassy Office of the Press Counselor in Washington, DC)

25. Prime Minister Adnan Menderes *(right, with sunglasses).* On his right is President Celal Bayar. This picture was taken in the early 1950s when their Democratic Party was in power. *(Courtesy of Necati Zincirkiran)*

26. Prime Minister Adnan Menderes's government was overthrown by the armed forces on May 27, 1960. After his trial, Menderes was hanged on September 17, 1961, on the prison island of Imrali in the Sea of Marmara. His hanging left a legacy of disunity in the Turkish nation. *(Courtesy of Necati Zincirkiran)*

27. Kemal Atatürk *(left)* with Rauf Orbay in 1919 during the Congress of Sivas. The year 1919 is the beginning of the Turks' struggle for independence following their defeat during World War II. Both men are wearing the fez.
(The Turkish Embassy Office of the Press Counselor in Washington, DC)

was running it, and without it, my old boss looked bored with life. In spite of his shortcomings, I had a grudging respect for the man. He had been a guiding light and an inflexible mentor for many young journalists, including myself, who had the opportunity to gain invaluable experience under his tough, unforgiving rules. Safa Kılıçlıoğlu was not a journalist but an extremely bright man, a businessman who understood the importance of competition in collecting news. I also remember him as a tight-fisted but ethical newspaper publisher who conformed to the accepted professional standards of journalism. Some journalists often tried to belittle Safa Kılıçlıoğlu by calling him *garson* (from the French word *garçon*), or waiter. Because he had done kitchen duty while in the army, the word *garson* stuck to him.

I think he was the heart and soul of the newspaper he had built. When Kılıçlıoğlu lost the ambition to make *Yeni Sabah* the number-one news-paper in the country because of the odds piled against him, he decided to fade away with his newspaper. True to his second name, Kılıçlıoğlu, he had been a real sword bearer in Turkey's developing media world.

Contrary to Safa Kılıçlıoğlu's decision to close shop, the Simavi brothers had figured out a better way to deal with the coming severance pay laws. They decided to organize a news agency affiliated with *Hür-riyet*, partly owned by the newspaper and partly by working journalists through the sale of stock. We called it *Haber Ajansı*, meaning the news agency. It was supposed to be an independent company, but due to *Hür-riyet*'s direct participation in the venture and its monopoly of the best news and photographs, this could not be realized.

I owned a house built with the help of the Union of Journalists at Esentepe, a residential compound for journalists. I sold it, investing all the proceeds in the agency's stock, thus becoming the major individual stockholder. Other staff members also bought shares in small quantities in the new company, and the fourth floor of the *Hürriyet* building became the agency's headquarters.

Everyone who worked to produce news and photographs and all the news bureaus were transferred to the new company. I was appointed general manager and editor-in-chief and began an aggressive campaign to open new bureaus in West Germany, London, Athens, and Moscow. West Germany became an important country for news coverage due to the presence of the large number of Turkish guest workers there. (By now, over two million Turks live in Germany, many of them second or third generation.)

One of my most memorable nights happened about this time. Staff Colonel Talat Aydemir, the commandant of the War Academy in Ankara, rebelled on February 22, 1962, and tried to overthrow Ismet Inönü's coalition government. It was an exciting time with a big surprise for us at *Hürriyet*.

A Rebel Staff Colonel and an Ex-Empress in a Precinct

A fox may have traveled far and wide but still ends up at the furrier's.

Turkish proverb

Colonel Talat Aydemir called his rebellion the "Offensive of the Savior Patriots." He persuaded other officers and the cadets of the War Academy in Ankara to join his revolt. The rebel forces surrounded the parliament and the army headquarters with tanks. They occupied the prime ministry and the building of Ankara Radio.

In those days, it was highly important to capture the national radio network in order to achieve a successful coup d'etat. TV networks did not exist then, and radio was the best and quickest way to spread and control the news of the coup.

The revolt was the result of the disappointment felt by some officers of the armed forces, a few representatives of the national press, and a number of disgruntled university professors. These people were unhappy about the outcome of the coup d'etat of May 27, 1960, which, they felt, had changed nothing. The old democrats, the cronies and supporters of

243

the fallen Menderes regime, were back in political life with new parties, which had totally adopted Menderes's old policies, including the exploitation of Islam for election gains.

Hürriyet and *Haber Ajansı* stood against the revolt at once. I stayed up all night, receiving constant information about this new coup. *Hürriyet*'s banner headline read "DEMOCRACY IN DANGER, REVOLT IN ANKARA," and when the newspaper reached the capital, it simply shocked and discouraged the rebel leaders.

Before the night was over, an unexpected and heavy blow hit us on our own heads. Only a few of us learned the shocking news that directly concerned our own world—Erol Simavi's involvement and support of Colonel Talat Aydemir's revolt.

We knew that there were newspaper publishers and journalists who supported Colonel Aydemir, including Falih Rıfkı Atay and Bedii Faik, then partners and well-known columnists of the morning broadsheet *Dünya* (*World*). In one of his editorials, Falih Rıfkı Atay had even praised Colonel Talat Aydemir. He wrote: "I have seen the gleam of Mustafa Kemal in Aydemir's eyes." Atay's view was that Colonel Aydemir could become an extraordinary leader for the country, perhaps a second Mustafa Kemal Atatürk.

I had met Colonel Aydemir a few times. He was of Circassian lineage, with average height, blond hair, and blue eyes, and had tried to give the impression that he resembled Kemal Atatürk in manners and looks. He had been one of the supporters of the Colonels' Coup of May 27, 1960, but was not a member of the junta. In 1962, he represented only one of several revolutionary groups inside the armed forces. Discipline in the armed forces had been ruined as a result of the coup of 1960. The junior officers were behaving as if they were generals, and the generals were trying to bring back some order to the chain of command.

Colonel Aydemir wanted to overthrow the civilian regime, close the political parties, and rule the country with an iron hand at the head of a junta of colonels. For that, he was expecting support from the main units of the armed forces, along with the media. When this support did not materialize, his revolt lost its punch.

The coup leader made a fatal mistake. One of his leading supporters, Fethi Gürcan, a major in the presidential guard, arrested Colonel Cihan Alpan, his commandant, while a meeting was in progress at the presidential residence at Çankaya in Ankara. Cemal Gürsel, the president; Ismet Inönü, the prime minister; and the top commanders of the armed forces were discussing measures on how to deal with the revolt. Major Gürcan called Colonel Aydemir at once and asked, "What are we supposed to do with these guys?" Colonel Aydemir told him, "Let them go. We have nothing to do with them." So the major, to his profound later regret, did not detain the leading government officials and the top commanding officers.

As the airforce jet fighters, loyal to the government, flew over the War Academy, Ismet Inönü then sent a message to Colonel Aydemir, granting full pardon for all involved in the revolt if they surrendered peacefully. That was the end of the revolt. Inönü, forcing Aydemir to retire from the army, kept his word and let him remain free.

Erol Simavi's involvement with the rebels was never made public at the time, and we kept this little secret to ourselves. We knew that Erol Simavi was very concerned about a new coup d'etat and wanted to assure his security in case a new coup took place. That and his concern of the growing Marxism and the spread of Islamic fundamentalism were to play a major role in his preference of companions in the Istanbul bars.

In his book *Hürriyet and the Simavi Empire*, Necati Zincirkıran describes the episode of Erol Simavi's involvement with Colonel Aydemir's revolt. It includes the reaction of Colonel Aydemir's supporters to *Hürriyet*'s crucial banner headline: "DEMOCRACY IN DANGER—REVOLT IN ANKARA." This early edition of the newspaper had already been widely distributed, including in the capital, Ankara. According to Zincirkiran,

> At 9.30 p.m. Hayri Alpar, one of the directors of the newspaper *Dünya*, came to our office. "You've made a mistake and placed yourself and this newspaper in danger," he told me. "You must change this banner headline." I was very angry and shouted at

him in front of everyone. "Who do you support? If you came here to tell me this, get out. As an ethical journalist, I will not take orders from civilian representatives of the rebels."

Hayri Alpar was a well-mannered man with a heart problem. Before he left, he leaned to my ear and said, "Erol Bey, too, is in this business." This admission petrified me with horror, and I began to tremble.

Colonel Aydemir would not give up his ambition for power. As a civilian, he tried once more to overthrow the coalition government on May 20, 1963, and again failed. This time eight people were killed in the fighting. Several cadets were expelled from the War Academy. Colonel Aydemir and Major Fethi Gürcan were executed.

Colonel Aydemir's adventures attracted still others who did their best in trying to topple the government. Many copycats started a chain reaction during the early 1960s. Revolutionary groups popped up all over the place, planning to overthrow the elected government. Members of a secret society within the armed forces, calling themselves the Young Kemalists, were arrested. Some of our colleagues began keeping records of these attempts to topple the government, counting and recounting the numbers.

☪

An event I well remember about the 1960s involved the former empress Soraya of Iran, Shah Muhammed Reza Pahlavi's ex-wife. She was the daughter of Halil Esfandiari Bahtiari, an aristocratic landowner in Iran. Soraya had become a former queen because she could not produce a male heir to the Peacock Throne. Her mother, Eva Karl, was German. Soraya settled in Paris, joined European high society, and ended up as a constant attraction in German magazines. This time she was in Istanbul accompanying the Austrian movie star Maximilian Schell, who was shooting a film there.

One morning I had a call from the *karakol*, the police precinct by the

Rumeli Hisarı, the big old fortress on the European side of the Bosphorus. I was told that photojournalist Özkan Şahin of Haber Agency had been involved in a brawl with Maximilian Schell while trying to shoot some pictures of Soraya. Schell, upset by this paparazzi-style intrusion, roughed up the photojournalist and tried to get the camera out of his hand. The photojournalist complained to the police, and all three of them ended up at the police station.

"I will be over there shortly," I said and hung up.

A similar incident had happened to me years earlier, so I was no stranger to this type of altercation. Movie star Jennifer Jones was a guest at a luxury hotel in St. Moritz in Switzerland, and I was hanging around in the hotel lobby to get a few shots of the actress. When she appeared, I raised my camera, but before I could get a shot, an angry David O. Selznick came straight after me. Selznick, the producer of *Gone with the Wind*, among other movies, was extremely possessive of Jennifer Jones, his wife. He tried to attack me by grabbing my arm so he could reach and take my camera. To my relief, Jennifer Jones rushed out to a waiting limo, and Selznick let go of me and hurried after the actress.

Our photo reporter's encounter with Maximilian Schell and Soraya had been worse. The photojournalist claimed that Schell had mistreated him. Özkan Şahin had managed to take some pictures of the former queen and Schell being driven in a police jeep. Schell was still fuming at the police station, a dilapidated wooden building on a hillside behind the fortress. The former queen, who had been given the title "Royal Princess" by the shah, was renowned for her beauty. She was sitting in an old, squeaky wooden chair. A policeman was typing up the deposition of the photo reporter, who wanted to sue the movie star for attacking him.

I didn't like the situation at all because Soraya had once been the empress in Iran, a neighboring country. She had officially visited Istanbul with the shah years earlier as Iran's queen. I felt that she didn't fit in a police station, even as a former empress, and thus I wanted to persuade the photojournalist to drop his charges. By then Schell noticed me standing in a corner and came after me with angry shouts. He accused me of duplicity and of planning the whole encounter.

I told him that he was wrong, as I had nothing to do with their fight, and that I had no wish to see more humiliation for Soraya by dragging the case through extensive police procedure and the courts. There is a popular rhyming verse about Turkish cops:

> Such events will occur,
> Turkish cops, they capture,
> Haul you to the station,
> And ruin your reputation.

I explained my views to the photojournalist, who reluctantly agreed to drop the charges. Schell, still angry, left the police station with Soraya. The news agency had a big scoop with pictures showing Soraya and Maximilian Schell riding in a police jeep. Princess Soraya, who aspired to a movie career as a young woman, died in October 2001 in Paris at the age of sixty-nine.

22

Reports from America

The heart is a glass palace and cannot be repaired if broken.

Turkish proverb

*H*aber News Agency in 1966 did not have a permanent corre-
spondent at the United Nations Headquarters in New York City.
The agency was also planning to increase its news coverage in the United
States. I was appointed to this position and left Turkey after resigning from
Reuters, ending almost twelve years of reporting to that international news
agency. Nuyan Yiğit became the Reuters reporter in Turkey.

In 1966, Staten Island was a peaceful place, compared with Manhattan, and traveling by ferry each day, back and forth, was relaxing and
afforded a dramatic view of the New York City harbor. The ferry cost a
nickel one way per person, and you could buy a hot dog on the ferry for
a quarter. When I arrived first on the island, I didn't have a car and used
to walk everywhere, which attracted curious stares from people passing
by in cars. At the time, Americans were occupied with the Vietnam War.

My wife, Magrid, had worked as a freelance reporter before, so we
teamed up to cover news developments. Since a car was an absolute

necessity, we bought a Ford Mustang for $2,000 that in time took us all over the country.

We had a desk in room 371 on the third floor of the United Nations building, which was also the office for other international reporters, including Necdet Berkand, who reported to another Istanbul daily called *Tercüman* (*Interpreter*). I knew Berkand well, as we had worked together at *Yeni Sabah* years earlier. He was not tall or handsome, yet he had *Şeytan tüyü*, Satan's hair, which is an Anatolian expression for a man's ability to attract girls. He knew how to charm women with sweet talk. I used to answer Berkand's phone when he was not in the office and, more often than not, would hear the voices of women asking to talk to him. Often we would have long lunches together on Berkand's expense account in the restaurant reserved for UN delegates.

Another regular reporter from Turkey was Mehmet Biber, a photo-journalist and an old hand from *Yeni Sabah* whose pictures appeared in *National Geographic* and *Time* among others.

I first visited the state of Maine when the people of the Casco Islands, off Portland, got together and invited members of the United Nations Correspondents Association for a visit. I had no idea then that later in my life I would be destined to spend years in that state, in virtual exile. My hosts on two occasions were Ted and Edith Yonan, who had a summer home on Little Diamond Island.

I knew Sinan Korle, then the chief of protocol at the United Nations who earlier had worked at the newspaper *Vatan* in Istanbul before coming to New York. We would talk in his office about the international delegates whom Korle met regularly along with the chiefs of states as part of his daily chores. Most of the time, I would refrain from using in my reports the usually juicy, sometimes explosive, tidbits I learned from Sinan Korle.

Seeing the workings of the United Nations up close, I found them highly disappointing and ineffectual in solving the world's problems and said so in my reports. The United Nations was a reflection of human nature in that its dealings were permeated with lies and self-interest, and the wheeling and dealing often was more to the benefit of the various del-egates than the countries they represented. On the other hand, the delegates might behave unscrupulously, twisting facts and truth in the interests of their own countries. The UN was unable to adequately respond to the problems facing the world. The absence of progress in the committees because of disagreements among the member countries and the monotonous debates in the General Assembly that led nowhere because of special interests were signs of the need for reforms.

Covering the news at the UN could become extremely boring at times because of the monotonous and lengthy debates. Thus I was attracted more to covering the events in America, which were much more exciting and interesting.

There was an ugly side and a good side to observing events in the United States. It was the time of the civil rights movement, Martin Luther King's Poor People's Campaign against the slum conditions in America, and later his assassination in Memphis, Tennessee. It was the time of the flower children and the rioting in the black ghettos of cities where whole blocks were torched, and it also was the time of Robert F. Kennedy's assassination. There was disunity in America because of the Vietnam War, and demonstrations against the war were daily news events.

"Get out of here, Whitey," an angry African American wearing a loose US Army issue field jacket and blue jeans warned me during the riots in Baltimore. "Or you'll get killed." I was taking pictures of the torched buildings while a cop in riot gear stood by. I was surprised to see the African Americans burning their own homes.

Once we covered the story of a young Turkish American from Queens, a Marine who was killed in Danang, Vietnam. In a Queens cemetery where he was buried, we saw the honor guard at the graveside firing volleys of shots over a number of caskets. It was a sad period for the American nation.

What we enjoyed most was traveling around the country in search of Turks who had immigrated to America and realized the American dream in a big way. We knew from experience with the Foreign Press Association in New York that other foreign correspondents were very interested in their own countrymen who had achieved success in the United States. In our case, there were a number of successful Turkish doctors, university professors, directors of companies, and businessmen. This became a regular part of our reporting because the stories gave hope and encouragement to the newspaper readers while informing them about life in America. In this way we, too, learned a lot about the American way of life.

One of these colorful people I met and interviewed in Birmingham, Alabama, was Muammer Öztekin, who was then the president of the Kent Corporation there, makers of supermarket checkout counters and shelves. Birmingham was also the place where for the first time I visited an American jail. Sheriff Melvin Bailey took me in and made me a deputy. Another interesting businessman I met was M. Turan Taner, then the board chairman of the Seismic Computing Corporation in Houston, Texas. Taner had studied engineering in Texas and founded the Seismic Computing Corporation, becoming wealthy in the process. He also enriched one of his professors by suggesting that he buy some of his company's stock. There were others, such as Ahmet and the late Nesuhi Ertegün of Atlantic Records, and many tailors who worked for Bond Clothes in Rochester, New York.

Louis J. Farrakhan, the present leader of the Nation of Islam, was a young imam of Muhammed Speaks on Northern Boulevard, Corona, New York. I interviewed him and was impressed with the Black Muslims' efforts to improve their lot. Farrakhan was not so well known in those years and also not as controversial.

Yet the most important and interesting event we covered in the 1960s had something to do with a monstrous rocket and the moon. This was a happening that had a powerful impact on our own lives.

23

The Moon Shot, an Old Soviet Spy, and Hi Jolly

She is as beautiful as the moon.

Turkish proverb

The most glorious moment in our times happened on July 20, 1969, with the landing of the *Apollo 11* module on the moon and a human voice from the moon declared, "The Eagle has landed." At that moment, we were at NASA's Johnson Control Center in Houston, Texas, with journalists from all over the world, watching the landing live on a big screen. When Neil Armstrong, 240,000 miles away in space, set his foot on the moon and said, "That's one small step for man, one giant leap for mankind," we all stood up in a large auditorium in the press center near mission control and applauded this incredible achievement.

The flight to the moon and landing there, without any doubt, was the greatest technological achievement of mankind. At that moment, I believe, the international journalists present forgot about their nationalistic, ethnic, or religious differences with others. There was this general feeling that not just the Americans but also that mankind had accomplished an impossible dream. It was a proud moment for all the peoples of the world.

The next morning, the big, bold headlines of newspapers were the same all over the world: *Men Walk on Moon.*

In anticipation of the moon landing, we had gone to Cape Canaveral in Florida ahead of time, taking pictures, describing everything we found interesting. The whole area, consisting of villages as Cocoa, Cocoa Beach, and Titusville, was all geared up for the coming moon shot, and wherever one looked, there was something about the *Apollo 11* mission. Our stories built up the momentum for the moon shot and the eventual landing on the moon.

In those years, there were no laptop computers. Most of us always carried Olivetti Lettera 32 typewriters with a zippered beige or blue case. Despite their smallness, these typewriters, compared with today's laptops, were heavy. I remember the constant typing, picture taking, and air-freighting of loads of material to *Hürriyet* from the John F. Kennedy Space Center in Florida and later from NASA's Johnson Control Center in Houston, Texas.

During a visit to the John F. Kennedy Space Center in Florida, twenty-seven years after the *Apollo 11* moon shot, I stood by the empty VIP stand and vivid memories returned. I remembered how excited we all had been when the giant Saturn rocket roared as it lifted off three miles ahead of us, carrying the crew of *Apollo 11* on their historic mission. This was a critical moment in the race to reach the moon. The blast of the rocket, spewing flames, shook the ground under me, and the shockwaves it created hit my body with a tremendous force, almost knocking me down. Having experienced strong earthquakes in Turkey before, I thought that the effect of the roar of the powerful kick of the rocket was not much different.

I recalled at this historic moment the wisdom of Nasreddin Hoca, the great humorist of the Ottoman era. Once asked, "What happens to the old moons when the new ones come up?" Nasreddin Hoca answered, "They make new stars out of the old moons by clipping them."

On another occasion, a friend asked Nasreddin Hoca, "Which is more valuable to man, the sun or the moon?" He replied "The moon, of course, because we need more light at night."

America shook the world by landing men on the moon. A grand accomplishment, the moon landing surpassed the worldwide impact of *Sputnik 1*, the first artificial satellite launched by the Soviets in October 1957. Later, we also covered *Apollo 12*, but by then the incredible worldwide interest had died down.

I regret to this day that we missed an interesting story while at Cape Canaveral, but this one had nothing to do with the moon shot. The US State Department had sent some Turkish officials to see the launch. A Turkish-English interpreter, an older man with a white moustache and gray hair, was escorting these officials. His name was Ismail Ege. After the day's work, we used to meet in the hotel with Ege, swim in the pool, and talk about politics in general. He was well informed about European history, especially that of Russia. Ege's Turkish was as good as mine, but he was not what he seemed to be, for he had kept his real identity secret from us.

In reality, he had been a colonel in Joseph Stalin's *Glavnoye Razvedy-vatelnoye Upravleniye* (GRU), the main intelligence directorate of the Soviet Army. Ismail Ege had been sent to Turkey years earlier by the Soviets as an intelligence agent.

I found out Ismail Ege's real identity only years later. One day in Bangor, Maine, I was going through a microfiche listing of books in print, and I saw a title by a man named Ismail Akhmedov, *In and Out of Stalin's GRU*. Always interested in books on the Soviet Union and on intelligence, I ordered a copy. When the book arrived, I had a shock. On the back of the book, there was a photograph of Ismail Ege with his actual name—Ismail Akhmedov.

A Bashkir Tatar, he had been born in Orsk, at the foothills of the Urals in Russia, and given the name of Ismail Guseynovich Akhmedov. After graduating from the Leningrad Military School, Akhmedov had been recruited by the GRU and at first sent to Berlin, Germany, disguised as a *Tass* correspondent with a false name, Georgy Petrovich Nikolayev. When the Nazis went to war against the Soviets, he was exchanged along with other Russians at the Bulgarian-Turkish border for Germans coming from the Soviet Union. This time, his spy cover was changed to a Soviet press attaché in Istanbul.

Sergey Aleksandrovich Vinogradov, the Soviet ambassador in Ankara who had connections with the NKVD, the precursor of the Soviet spy agency KGB, ordered Akhmedov to recruit Istanbul's leading newspaper owners and editorial writers. The targeted writers included Ahmet Emin Yalman of *Vatan*, Hüseyin Cahit Yalçın and Yunus Nadi of *Cumhuriyet,* and Falih Rıfkı Atay, who wrote editorials for *Ulus*, owned by the ruling Republican People's Party. He was told not to bother with Zekeriya Sertel of *Tan*, who, according to Vinogradov, was pro-Soviet.

Akhmedov states in his book that he was ordered to recruit the writers by bribery, by persuasion, or by clean or dirty methods. "Promise mountains of benefit for cooperation with us," Vinogradov told him. "Our party and government need control of an outstanding figure in the news world to mobilize Turkish public opinion in favor of the Soviet Union."

Being of Turkic origin, Akhmedov refused the order and was recalled to Moscow. Instead of returning to Moscow, where he expected to be killed, Akhmedov asked for political asylum in Turkey. He was protected by Ismet Inönü's regime during the war years and even lived in Isparta, my hometown, for a while. His book, which is, unfortunately, not widely known, is full of useful and interesting details about the Turkic peoples of central Asia and the Caucasus and the Soviet history of the 1920s.

The moon shot gave us also the opportunity to learn about a colorful individual who came to America from Turkey over a century ago.

In Houston, Texas, after covering the *Apollo 11* moon landing, we visited a nearby American Indian reservation in the east Texas forest. We found a small band of Alabami-Kushatta Indians living their simple lives, their women washing laundry by hand in tubs. Continuing westward, our trip took us to Arizona. There, by chance, we came across a roadside monument erected to a camel driver. Curious, we tried to learn more about this unusual individual. Some books we found at the library in Yuma about the man had limited information, and they placed the port of Izmir (Smyrna) mistakenly in Syria.

Born in Izmir, a busy port on the Aegean in Western Anatolia in 1829, this camel driver named Hacı Ali had immigrated to America as a young man, accompanying camels purchased for the United States Army. He took part in the US Army's experiment with the camels and accompanied the Beale Expedition of 1856 to Arizona. He remained in the Yuma area after the failure of the experiment. Since most settlers could not pronounce Hacı Ali correctly, the name became Americanized as Hi Jolly. He was also known as Philip Tedro.

When the Beale Expedition failed, Hi Jolly obtained some of the camels and started a freight service with them. Improvements in land and river transportation caught up with Hi Jolly and his camels. Twelve years later, he gave up the business of carrying freight through the Yuma Desert and turned his camels loose at Gila Bend. We were told in Yuma at the time that in 1925 there still had been some descendants of those camels freely roaming about the desert. Hi Jolly died in Quartzsite, Arizona, in 1902.

Our success in covering the *Apollo 11* moon shot that boosted the circulation of *Hürriyet* was to be the cause célèbre that would a year later affect our own lives. A telegram arrived from Erol Simavi, recalling me for consultations.

It was the spring of 1970. Our flight aboard a brand new Boeing 947 Pan Am jumbo jet was to be the beginning of an unusual adventure. The jet had mechanical problems in one engine over Newfoundland and turned around to John F. Kennedy International Airport in New York. We had a very bumpy flight back, with the whole plane rattling and all of the passengers holding on with white knuckles. After being housed at the Commodore Hotel on 42nd Street for the night by the airline, we changed to another flight the next day.

24

A Witch's Cauldron and Nest of Intrigues

Your friendship with the Devil lasts until you end up
swinging on the gallows.
Turkish proverb

The Divan Hotel, which overlooks Taksim Park in the Beyoğlu district, is one of Istanbul's luxury hotels. By 1970 it had become the center for *Hürriyet* publisher Erol Simavi's business deals. Since his elder brother, Haldun, had left *Hürriyet* a year earlier to publish his own daily newspaper, *Günaydın*, Erol began conducting newspaper business at the hotel bar.

Erol explained to me in the bar how the editorial offices of *Hürriyet* had become a cauldron of witches and a nest of intrigues.

"The conditions are out of control," he said. "Everyone, including the coffee boy, would like to be top editor. My brother is determined to destroy *Hürriyet*."

I was shocked.

"You must be joking," I said. "*Hürriyet* is your father's legacy. Why should your brother want to destroy it? Haldun Simavi knows how impor-

259

tant this newspaper is for the well-being of our country, for democracy, and for the protection of secular Kemalist reforms."

"It is true," he insisted. "Why do you think he left *Hürriyet?* Why is he publishing *Günaydın?*"

"Well," I said, rather undiplomatically, "Haldun Bey may have left *Hürriyet* because of your lifestyle and your involvement with revolutionary adventurers. Your appointment of Orhan Erkanlı, for instance . . . Erkanlı was a member of the junta that overthrew the regime of Adnan Menderes. Your appointment of him as the general manager of *Hürriyet* was a grave mistake. Erkanlı has a reputation as a revolutionary. His appointment gives the impression that the newspaper supports revolutionary adventurers. This appointment doesn't fit the principles of your father, *Hürriyet*'s founder."

Erol Simavi didn't like my answer. "You've been away and have no idea what has happened here," he retorted. "Our problem is the news agency, not my lifestyle or Erkanlı's appointment. Haber Agency has left us, but we still pay the highest rate for their services. What do we get in return? We get the basic, routine news coverage. The most interesting news stories and photos, including color pictures, are provided exclusively for *Günaydın.* Why don't we get the same service? The loss of the prime news coverage is killing us. It's hurting our circulation and the newspaper's bottom line. That's why you are here."

The news agency had become the object of a tug-of-war between the Simavi brothers. Besides, *Günaydın* was competing with its flashy color pages. Now *Hürriyet*, too, was planning to import web-offset rotation color printing presses. The newspaper's old Mann press, capable of printing only in black and white, was now obsolete.

Since I was still a partner and had enough shares in the news agency, my primary job, Erol told me, was to get control of that agency.

"We must have the agency back to survive," he said.

The yearly meeting of the agency's stockholders was due soon. My own stock, along with *Hürriyet*'s, was enough to take over. Soon we did that and moved the agency back to the *Hürriyet* building.

I wanted to return to New York. My boss told me that I must first do my best to boost the sagging circulation. I stayed, attending meetings with Orhan Erkanlı and the editors of the newspaper, where Scotch whiskey had replaced the regulation Turkish coffee.

Orhan Erkanlı had no idea how journalism functioned and tried to impose order with his military mentality. It didn't work, and the conditions deteriorated. According to Erkanlı, the newspaper employees behaved like spiteful old hags in a Turkish bath who spent their time gossiping. I was shocked when he persuaded the publisher to organize and promote commercial ventures by exploiting the newspaper's influence inside the state itself. These commercial ventures were unrelated to the function of the newspaper. I protested that journalists should not pursue the commercial interests of the newspaper's owner in the government ministries in Ankara.

Hürriyet, the powerful advocate of the Kemalist ideals of enlightenment and secularism and the nation's watchdog against corruption, was now lacking in inspiration. The legacy of Sedat Simavi, his principles that the newspaper had protected since 1948, was no longer considered important. I now firmly believe that this change of attitude in *Hürriyet*'s administration at that time was highly influential later in the degeneration and corruption of the Turkish state, the business world, and the media.

The internal situation in the country itself was outright perilous. The polarization between the political parties had taken a new direction. Bülent Ecevit, a young, ambitious left-wing journalist, highly influential in Kemal Atatürk's old reformist party, the Republican People's Party, caused this party to drift further to the left. Ecevit promptly faced Süleyman Demirel's right-wing Justice Party and Colonel Alparslan Türkeş's Nationalist Action Party. Türkeş, a hard-line nationalist, had begun training university students as urban guerrilla fighters. He called them *Ülkücüler*, the Idealists or the Gray Wolves. Türkeş was determined to fight Marxists with arms. His vision was that of Enver Pasha: pan-Turanism.

The division between the Communists, the nationalists, and fundamentalist Islam, had developed into a fight between left- and right-wing extremism. The bitter struggle for power between three political adventurers, Süleyman Demirel, Bülent Ecevit, and Colonel Alparslan Türkeş, would eventually cause social, moral, economic, and political upheaval in the country and bring Turkey to the threshold of a civil war. This struggle would also greatly undermine the principles of Kemalism.

Under the Justice Party government of Süleyman Demirel, corruption and nepotism had increased, causing the erosion of public faith in the honesty of politicians. There was a breakdown in the function of the state. Süleyman Demirel disregarded the Constitutional Court's order to proceed with a parliamentary investigation of the sources of his and his brother Şevket Demirel's wealth. The Justice Party in the 1960s had enrolled many members of the hardcore democrats, including Islamic reactionaries. Demirel, an engineer of dams, had worked for Adnan Menderes, who used to call him "my manager of water resources." Demirel was elected leader of Justice Party in 1964 after the death of Ragıp Gümüşpala, the party's founder.

In 1970, when a powerful Islamic reactionary movement was being revived, the left-wing Turkish Labor Party had been split into two factions. The party leaders were against a Soviet-style destabilization of the country. The militants in the party protested this policy and in 1969 organized the Federation of the Revolutionary Youth of Turkey, known in short as *Dev-Genç*. The radical murderers from the Marxist organization, called the Turkish People's Liberation Army, engaged in terrorism, kidnappings of foreign nationals, and assassinations.

Among the Marxist students, there were many admirers of the Chinese Communist leader Mao Tse-Tung. They planned a violent overthrow of the regime. I remember a street rhyme that people used as a joke as right- and left-wing extremists fought with guns on the university campuses or in the streets:

> We are not rightists,
> We are not leftists,
> We are football players.

Meanwhile, the pressure to keep me in Istanbul as editor-in-chief had increased. Finally, Erkanlı proposed to compensate me for my earlier losses of about $20,000 due to an odd situation in salary payment. Almost 95 percent of my income from *Hürriyet* in New York had been paid as expenses. This presented an opportunity for Erol Simavi, who scored a fait accompli by giving me an early severance pay that amounted to a low figure. When Erkanlı proposed to set this injustice right, I accepted the position. Nezih Demirkent had a terrific shock upon hearing my appointment during a meeting. Demirkent, with a broad, round face, regarded my presence in the newspaper an obstacle to his designs. He squeezed the whiskey glass in his right hand with such force that the glass shattered.

Orhan Erkanlı explained that in order to spare the company from having to pay taxes, my check had been drawn as a loan payment. I should have remembered what Ferhan Devekuşuoğlu, the last editor-in-chief, had told me about the car he had received upon his appointment. Erol Simavi, who had a reputation as an "Indian giver," tried to get it back once Ferhan was demoted.

I went to the bank and collected bundles of Turkish liras that occupied the front seat of the Anadol, a small, Turkish-built clunky car the newspaper had assigned for my personal use.

I had seen a new apartment building by the seaside at Yeşilyurt, a village near the city, and drove directly there and bought a small condo for the exact amount I had taken from the bank. The builder, in order to limit his own taxes, handed me a receipt for half the amount of what I paid him. This game of avoiding income taxes has now been perfected. According to a 2003 report by the Turkish Internal Revenue Service, businessmen, lawyers, and doctors are all needy and the industrialists, contractors, and owners of jewelry stores, starving. Almost 66 percent of the total Turkish income is not reported to the tax collectors, and nobody is in jail for cheating the internal revenue.

We moved into our new home.

My appointment did not stop the intrigues in the newspaper building. Two other conditions at the newspaper were disturbing: drinking hard liquor on the job and the heat in the composing room. The composing room crew complained incessantly. We never had air-conditioning in that building, but when Orhan Erkanlı installed a unit in his own office, the composing room crew almost rebelled, alarming the publisher. Erol Simavi was concerned about a walkout by the newspaper staff and used to say, "Let's not startle the mules carrying the porcelain demitasses."

I told Erkanlı privately in his office that what he had done was unfair to the composing room crew and suggested that air-conditioning should be installed there. Orhan Erkanlı had a short fuse. When upset, he behaved as if he were still a junta member. The service revolver came out from the desk drawer and hit the top of the desk. "I know how to stop their bellyaching!" he told me. I had the impression that the gun was also used to intimidate me because of my support for the composing room crew. Since he had a suspicious and uneasy mind, he may have wrongfully assumed that it was perhaps I who was trying to "startle the mules carrying the porcelain demitasses."

The threat of a Soviet-inspired civil war became a daily subject at our editorial meetings. The pro-Demirel articles, which Cüneyt Arcayürek, the newspaper's Ankara bureau chief, kept filing were another subject of grave concern. At times, I refused to print them, but the damage had already been done in the minds of the readers, who saw the newspaper as a mouthpiece of Süleyman Demirel's regime.

I had no personal feud with the prime minister but felt that as an influential daily, we had a duty to speak out. Other *Hürriyet* editors had the same idea: that it was our responsibility to draw attention to Demirel's encouragement of the Islamic movements and his evasive actions against the decisions of the Constitutional Court involving the corruption inquiries against him and his brother Şevket Demirel.

Haldun Simavi's newspaper, *Günaydın*, had already crossed swords with Demirel himself. This was about the death of Osman Nuri Tepe, the shoemaker for Nazmiye Demirel, the prime minister's wife. The shoemaker had died in a traffic accident in 1967, but his brother Ali Tepe, owner of the Ayko Hotel, in a notarized public statement alleged otherwise: "My brother was killed because he was a close friend of Nazmiye Demirel." No evidence supported Ali Tepe's claim, yet *Günaydın* reported it on November 15, 1969, in its Ankara edition without the knowledge and approval of the newspaper's headquarters in Istanbul. The report lacked proof and angered Demirel and his cronies. What happened next, however ,was an astonishing reaction by unknown people that was not only lawless but also bordered on outright terrorism.

Necdet Onur, the reporter who had written the news article, became an immediate target. Ibrahim Oral, the police chief in Ankara, questioned him. The reporter's car had been torched while parked in front of his home. Shots had been fired at *Günaydın's* regional printing plant in Ankara. There had been attempts to cripple *Günaydın's* distribution system. The packages containing the newspaper destined to the Anatolian distributors had been seized and burned by gangs.

"*Günaydın* printed a correction," Necati Zincirkıran, its editor-in-chief, wrote. "But even so, more threats were being received by the newspaper. This was a planned campaign." A British nanny named Brenda, taking care of *Günaydın* publisher Haldun Simavi's children in Istanbul, became a victim. She was accused of being a British spy and was deported.

Knowing what happened in the case of *Günaydın*, it was perhaps foolhardy of me to stand up against a prime minister and the supporters of his strong-arm regime, who burned newspapers and a reporter's car and used a newspaper building for target practice. I figured that a strongly worded, front-page editorial in *Hürriyet* could force Demirel to resign and make way for a new leadership able to deal with the dangerous situation in the country.

What a pipe dream that was!

The editorial had a tremendous impact, but it stirred up a wasps' nest. Demirel and his supporters were up in arms at once. What was spelled out in that front-page editorial then turned out to become raison d'être nine months later in March 1971. The senior military commanders, led by the chief of the general staff, General Memduh Tağmaç, forced Demirel to resign.

Hürriyet's editorial created a great opportunity for the Demirel supporters inside the newspaper building. They spread the allegation that I was an agent of the CIA. In order to alarm *Hürriyet's* publisher, some copies of the newspaper in Eskişehir, a town in western Turkey, were torched. I started to receive death threats.

Since the publication of the editorial, I had been noticing surveillance of my movements. My mail began arriving with apparent marks of tampering, the envelopes opened and resealed and packages delivered open. Each time my phone rang and I picked it up, I heard unusual clicking sounds. Someone was always listening. Strange men in dark suits began trailing me. Nezih Demirkent extended a helping hand to the official surveillance. He would appear in my neighborhood in Yeşilyurt to find out anything about my plans.

Demirkent's support of Demirel, especially after his own appointment later as editor-in-chief of *Hürriyet*, had been a financial boon for him. Once an employee living on fixed salary, Nezih Demirkent became wealthy even beyond his dreams. He became the owner of *Dünya*, a daily newspaper. Many journalists still wonder about the sources of his magical riches. Necati Doğru, a columnist for *Sabah*, questioned in a November 2000 article how much bank credit was extended to Nezih Demirkent and expressed his wonder about the sources of Demirkent's wealth.

Nezih Demirkent died of a massive heart attack in February 2001, while his aides were walking him to a car on the way to a hospital. The doctors said that it was a fatal mistake to let a man walk while he was having a heart attack.

In my own case, that editorial turned out to be a great lesson and experience in human psychology. The other editors, so eager and supportive before the printing of the editorial, were now frightened and washed their hands of the affair. Left alone to face the music, and defenseless against death threats, I kept wondering about a prime minister's and his government's grasp of the meaning of democracy, justice, and human rights.

The Turks and Human Rights

The rooster's ill-timed crow puts his head on the chopping block.

Turkish proverb

hroughout history Turkish governments have had a problem understanding democracy, freedom of the press, and human rights. In March 1998, human rights activists in Turkey criticized a provincial court's decision to sentence five police officers to seven-and-a-half-year jail terms for beating a journalist to death. They considered that sentence too light for the murder of Metin Göktepe, who had been detained during the funeral of two leftist activists in January 1996. Göktepe died of a brain hemorrhage and internal bleeding after he was beaten and kicked by the policemen.

According to Amnesty International, in Turkey in 1988 "thousands of people were imprisoned for political reasons. And the use of torture continued to be widespread and systematic."

Sema Pişkinsüt, the head of the Parliamentary Human Rights Commission, described in May 2000 how police had used wind-up telephones to electrocute suspects. This was done, she said, in cellars equipped with

267

an array of torture devices. According to her, the commission members' visits to the antiterrorism departments of police headquarters in Erzincan and Şanlıurfa, eastern Turkey, had confirmed the grim tales of torture from prison inmates and detainees.

A shocking six-volume report by the twenty-five-member commission included pictures of torture cells with exposed electrical wires. The walls of the torture cells were covered with black leather for sound-proofing. The photographs also showed wooden bars, called Palestinian Hooks, which were placed under prisoners' arms and used to suspend them in the air. Metal bars were being used to beat prisoners on their soles, similar to the infamous *falaka* (bastinado) of Ottoman times.

Sema Pişkinsüt was replaced as head of the parliament's human rights commission in October 2000 by a right-wing legislator from the Nationalist Action Party. Human rights watchers said she had been sacked because of her commission's report on police torture. In July 2001, Pişkinsüt herself was charged by the oligarchic state with "aiding criminals" after refusing to reveal the names of torture victims.

Torture, exile, and outright murder have always been used in Turkish history to control dissent. During the Ottoman Empire, the sultans were despots who suppressed dissent with harsh measures. A sultan was known as *Padishah* or *Cenab-ı Padishahi*, meaning His Sovereign Majesty, and believed to be the shadow of Allah in this world and the next. The *Padishah* was supposed to be the favorite of Allah on two horizons. This mentality allowed sultans to rule and punish at will. The favorite punishment for political dissent ranged between exile to remote provinces and execution. An old executioner's stone can still be seen outside the gates of the Old Seraglio in Istanbul, on which many citizens lost their heads without a chance of defending themselves in a court of law.

During Kemal Atatürk's regime, human rights could only go so far. One example was the attempt to form an opposition against his regime. In 1924, some of Atatürk's original companions in the War of Independence opposed his authoritarian regime. They resigned from the People's Party and organized another called Progressive Republican Party. Their names are well known: Rauf Orbay, Refet Bele, Dr. Adnan Adıvar, Kazım

Karabekir, and others. They were nationalists and, like Atatürk himself, modernizers. Less than a year later, in June 1925, the regime closed the opposition, accusing the party of having a program that encouraged Islamic reactionaries. The change came about with bloodshed. Ali Çetinkaya, known in Turkish history as Kel (Bald) Ali, became the most famous hanging judge of the regime through the infamous *Istiklal Mahkemeleri*, the Independence Tribunals. There had been a plot to assassinate Atatürk in Izmir. The opposition became the scapegoat and a purge followed, which was clearly seen as a manifestation of the struggle for absolute power.

The Grand National Assembly, Turkey's parliament dominated by the Republican People's Party, was the instrument of Atatürk's will. The members of parliament rubber-stamped all his decisions. The party had six rigid principles of Kemalism that were represented by six arrows in the party's red flag. They were republicanism, nationalism, populism, statism (state intervention in the economy, like the tobacco monopoly), secularism (*laiklik*), and reformism. These principles were accepted in the 1930s as vital as the constitution of the single-party state.

In 1953 Ismet Inönü changed the understanding of Kemalism in the Republican People's Party itself to *Atatürk Yolu*, the "Way of Atatürk." The party by then, under the onslaught of democracy and free elections, had lost its preeminence to the Democratic Party of Adnan Menderes. Still, Kemalism, the official state ideology of the 1930s, refused to change and remained dogmatic.

The Kemalist movement regarded organized religion as anachronistic and excluded religious organizations such as the *tarikats* from public life. Religion was considered a private matter between man and his God.

"The true guide in life is science," Atatürk had declared.

The members of the Grand National Assembly were selected from the best and the brightest of the country's elite, who were able to carry out incredible reforms from the top down in less than a decade. It is doubtful that such deep-rooted revolutionary reforms could have been carried out under the conditions that existed in those times while fully respecting human rights. Still, Turkey in the 1930s, under a single-party regime that brought about new laws to impose modernization, secularity, and discipline, was a fast-developing nation. It is a fact that in 1927, 85 percent of the population in Turkey was illiterate.

There is a period in the history of the Ottoman Empire called the *Tanzimat'ı Hayriye*, or *Tanzimat* in short. This Arabic word translates as the auspicious restructuring or reforms aimed to modernize the Ottoman Empire and to transform its neglected army into an effective fighting force. The *Tanzimat* era began during the reign of Abdul-Mecid I (1823–61), who as sultan issued a *ferman* on November 3, 1839, called *Gülhane Hattı-Şerifi*—the Noble Edict of the Rose Chamber, contained provisions regarding human rights. The *Tanzimat* safeguarded lives and property of all Ottoman subjects irrespective of race or creed and guaranteed each citizen's right to justice. It should be noted that the human rights, which the *Tanzimat* promised to grant, happened 624 years after the Magna Carta, the great charter of liberties that the English barons in 1215 at Runnymede had forced King John of England to accept.

Abdul-Mecid I, son of a Georgian woman named Bezmialem, was sixteen when he was proclaimed sultan and caliph. His mother, a former bath attendant, was a very bright woman who advised her son to appoint reformers to important government posts. These reformers included Mehmet Fuad Pasha and Mustafa Reşid, two of the architects of the *Tanzimat* reforms. Bezmialem had learned the importance of reforming the sick empire from her husband, Mahmut II.

I remember how the journalist Falih Rıfkı Atay once described that attempt to reform the Ottoman Empire: "The Tanzimat was a movement to save the Turks also from the hangman's noose or the confiscation of their properties and possessions and to utterly free them from servitude."

Long before Falih Rıfkı Atay, the Ottoman poet Eşref wrote about government oppression:

> Each official has his own style of cruelty,
> Seeing an official reminds one of a bandit.
> Oh, wretched citizen, why cry out in vain?
> For the cries of the oppressed in pain,
> Only sounds like music to the government.

It was this Ottoman mentality that the *Tanzimat* had tried to eradicate but failed. The era of the *Tanzimat*, however, started a movement for liberty and created a school of literature whose writers, the Young Ottomans, included Abdulhak Hamid and Tevfik Fikret. These writers helped to free Turkish poetry from Persian influences and to establish the style of Western poetry. Fikret's writings were against oppressive governments. In his book *Haluk'un Defteri* (*Haluk's Notebook*), which was dedicated to his son Haluk, Fikret expressed his hope that freedom and human rights would be achieved one day in his country.

To understand the accomplishments of the Kemalist reforms in an Islamic country, it is important to understand the history of the Ottoman Empire.

The newspaper arrived in the Ottoman Empire a century after the first English paper, the *Daily Courant*, was printed in London in 1702 and the first American paper, the *Boston News-letter*, in 1704. The *Gazette Française de Constantinople*, established in 1795 by the French Embassy in Istanbul, spread the message of the French Revolution.

Almost thirty years later, a business-sponsored newspaper was published in Izmir, followed in 1831 by the government-sponsored *Takvim-i Vekayi* (*Calendar of Events*) and in 1832 by the *Ottoman Monitor*. The *Egyptian Gazette* was another government-sponsored newspaper. In 1840, again with the support of the Ottoman regime, *Ceride-i Havadis* (*News Journal*), whose publisher was an Englishman named William Churchill, appeared in Istanbul. The newspapers were printed in Turkish language in Arabic letters written from right to the left.

Two influential newspapers, which were established in 1860 and 1862, had reform-minded editors and writers. These newspapers were named *Tercüman-ı Ahval* (*Interpreter of Events*) and *Tasvir-i Efkar* (*Picture of Opinions*). Both newspapers led a Western movement in Turkish literature and often criticized the Ottoman regime. Ibrahim Şinasi, the founder and editor of *Tasvir-i Efkar*, got into trouble in 1865 with the Ottoman regime and fled to Paris.

In 1857, eighteen years after the proclamation of the *Tanzimat*, Namık Kemal, the patriotic prose writer and poet, had to flee to London for expressing his views on freedom. Kemal returned to Turkey later but in

1873 was banished to and imprisoned in Famagusta in Cyprus for promoting patriotism and liberalism in his play *Motherland and Silistra*, which was about the 1854 siege of Silistra in Bulgaria. Kemal's social work *Rüya* (*Dream*) deals with human rights and freedom from oppression.

The French Revolution of 1789 and its Declaration of Human Rights had a clear influence for the creation of the Tanzimat. In fact, the French Revolution was the role model even in later years for Turkish intellectuals who wanted freedom of expression and respect for human rights. The students of the Military Medical College in Istanbul, for instance, had formed an organization called *Ittihad-ı Osmani* in 1889. It was this Ottoman Union, which changed its name to Union and Progress in 1895, that finally organized the Young Turk Revolution of 1908. The Young Turks, too, were very much under the influence of the French Revolution and its slogan "Liberty, Equality, and Fraternity."

Still, 130 years after the era of the *Tanzimat*, in 1970 the idea of democracy and the rights of writers to freely express their views without fear of punishment were not yet accepted in Turkey.

Despite the secular Turks' overwhelming desire to have a modern, Western-oriented country, they were still unable to get over the demagogic mentality and traditions left from a defunct empire. This includes the idea of the sacred state. Turgut Özal, leader of Motherland Party in 1983, understood this problem well. During the general election that year, he attacked the mentality of the sacred state: "The citizen does not exist for the state, the state exists for the citizen."

I was a citizen, and the regime in 1970 had become my enemy because I asked for the prime minister's resignation for disregarding the constitution. That constitution had no meaning for the oligarchic people who controlled the government. They considered themselves the law.

I placed my apartment for sale with a classified ad in *Hürriyet*. That was not very smart because it alerted the Demirel supporters inside the newspaper building. A conspiracy was arranged against me with the help of agents of Demirel's regime. There was only one bite: a seamstress named Makbule who had worked in America and whose husband was still employed in New Jersey. She was a relative of the manager of *Hür-*

riyet's cafeteria and needed the apartment for her retirement, so she told me. And she would pay in US dollars.

I am still holding the worthless check for $20,000 drawn on an American bank on which payment had been stopped. For such occasions, in this case, a check that bounced, the Turks have a fitting expression: "Geçmiş olsun! Drink a glass of cold water over it," meaning, "Forget it—You've been swindled; the money is gone for good." Usually, "Geçmiş olsun" is said to congratulate someone on recovery from an illness or escape from death or disaster. In this case, it means, "This too shall pass."

26

The Time
of the Vultures

Cooking pot, your bottom is black! Yours is blacker than mine.

Turkish proverb

What happened during the following years in Turkey is an eye-opening lesson in history. It is also an anguish for the true secular idealists of Kemalism, for Kemalism has become a victim in the hands of unscrupulous oligarchic leaders.

Let's start first with the above Turkish proverb. It is similar to the American version, the pot calling the kettle black. It is also a good illustration of the constant squabbling in Turkish politics, the business world, and the media because scoundrels and bandits have infiltrated these spheres. Several media moguls have been cooperating with corrupt politicians or often blackmailing them for material gains for years.

I remember that Refik Saydam, who was appointed prime minister by Ismet Inönü following the death of Atatürk, described the conditions of the Turkish state: "It is in disorder from A to Z." Saydam in his time could not even imagine the scope of the disorder that settled like a bogey on top of the same state in the 1990s.

Since the free elections of 1950, the oligarchy made a mockery of democracy and abused the Islamic religion to get elected. In later years, the oligarchy robbed the state's resources and its treasury. While relatives and supporters of the politicians became wealthy, critics were punished severely. A public yearning developed for a just leader marked by integrity, a second Kemal Atatürk. That leader never materialized.

In the early 1970s, signs appeared of a destructive triangle of corrupt politicians, businessmen with connections to criminal gangs, and crooked media moguls. The members of this den of thieves acquired much more power in later years and felt free to plunder the state's resources. They did their best for decades to protect the status quo in order to prolong without impunity the duration of the loot and plunder. Not only the state and private banks but also state institutions, factories, and land and forests owned by the Turkish treasury were all fair game.

The members of this triangle considered themselves special people, protected by power and influence, immune to punishment, untouchable, and with a privileged right to steal. They abused the laws and used the judicial system for their own protection. Everyone knows who these powerful thieves are, but no authority for years has had enough courage or support from the establishment to bring them to justice. The judicial system itself under the existing conditions of corruption has become sluggish and ineffective. Turkey is a country where wealthy thieves who steal millions of dollars go free while a poor and hungry man who steals a loaf of bread is punished.

The years of financial irregularities and plunder finally helped to bring about severe economic difficulties to the state itself. The tax revenues collected during the first six months of 2002 were not enough to service the yearly interest of the state's debt. The Turks ended up using this expression: *Devletin hazinesi tamtakır kurubakır*, meaning the state's treasury is absolutely empty, with only a few coppers remaining.

Recep Tayyip Erdoğan, the leader of the Justice and Development Party, with Islamic roots in power, told journalists in February 2003 that the country needed to pay about $73 billion that year to service the existing debt. This debt was being serviced with new loans. It was later officially announced that during the first seven months of 2003, the country had paid off $66.5 billion in debt and would pay another $40.4 billion until the end of the year with borrowed money.

Cemil Çicek, the minister of justice in Erdoğan's cabinet, in June 2003 said: "Turkey is being plundered, and the laws are powerless to prevent it. . . . Turkey is led into poverty before our own eyes, and the laws are unable to deal with it."

Corruption in the 1990s had gone out of control. An unblemished political party or government official was, as the Turks say, as rare as a phoenix. Bülent Ecevit, the leader of the Democratic Left Party and prime minister off and on, stood out for years as a unique individual just because his name has not been involved in scandals! In contrast, Necmettin Erbakan, the leader of *Milli Görüş*—the National View of the Islamic fundamentalist movement—and Tansu (Uçuran) Çiller, who claimed to be a secularist, cut a deal in 1996 allegedly to halt any investigation into how either of them became millionaires. Other deals made during a shocking parliamentary act of purification cleared the two former premiers, Tansu Çiller and Mesut Yılmaz, from any material imperfection. Çiller said, "*Aklandım*," meaning, "Parliament cleared my honor."

Fuzuli (1495–1566), the great Turkish poet who wrote *Şikayetname* (*Complaints*) during the reign of Süleyman the Magnificent, described bribery of the Ottoman times: "I said hello, and there was no response, for greeting someone was not considered a bribe."

General Kenan Evren, the leader of the 1980 coup d'etat, admitted years later that his military regime solved several problems but could not beat bribery, which has been the legacy of the Ottoman Empire.

The Ottoman poet Eşref wrote:

> For God's sake, no one should visit my grave,
> I will even reject my own brother, I swear by God,
> He should not come at all.
> Because my eyes are so terrified of the sons of Adam,
> I desire *no* prayers for my soul from anyone,
> Just let me be, and don't steal my gravestone.

The poet's gravestone was later stolen, perhaps for a joke.

Corruption and bribery had been a disease during the Ottoman Empire when grand viziers were presented with *sadaret kürkü*, the sable fur coat of the prime minister. *Ye kürküm ye*, meaning, "Eat, my fur coat, eat," is a well-remembered description of grand viziers who took bribes.

The poet Tevfik Fikret attracted the hostility of corrupt officials of the Ottoman government in 1912 with a poem titled *The Dining-Table of Plunder*:

> This delicious dinner, gentlemen,
> Waiting to be devoured,
> While trembling before your presence,
> It's the life of this suffering nation,
> It's the life of this dying nation.
> But why hesitate, just eat, gorge, and gobble,
> Eat, gentlemen, eat, to satisfy this appetite of yours,
> Stuff yourselves, until you gag and burst.

The occasion for this poem was the publication of the menu of a palace banquet. The menu included pea soup, cold turkey, fish fillet, flavored spinach roots, a chicken dish with walnuts, pie with almonds, stuffed cabbage in olive oil, rice pilaf, and fruitcake. It was a time when many people could not even find bread.

I think the present corruption in Turkey even beats that of the Ottomans. The looters fully adopted the old motto *Devletin malı deniz yemeyen domuz*, meaning, "The wealth of the state is as vast as the sea, and anyone who does not eat of it is a pig." The scoundrels often described by the people as the sons of pigs also robbed the assets of private banks.

Many officials made fortunes receiving kickbacks on government tenders, especially in construction and energy fields. The banks and factories owned by the state became cash cows for politicians, who behaved like medieval barons. The state institutions provided jobs for relatives and supporters of influential politicians.

According to research conducted by the office of the prime ministry, Turkey in 2000 was the number-one country in the world in official bribery. Three years earlier, Turkey had been number six. The opacity report of Pricewaterhouse Coopers, made public during the World Economic Forum in Davos, Switzerland, in January 2001, disclosed that Turkey was number four in the world for economic losses caused by corruption. China was number one, Russia number two, and Indonesia number three among thirty-five countries.

After President Turgut Özal's death in 1993, some of his associates ended up in courts on charges of corruption. There are allegations that former president Süleyman Demirel's brother Şevket Demirel, a businessman, became wealthy through influence peddling. Yahya Murat Demirel, Süleyman Demirel's nephew, former owner of Egebank, was jailed in October 2000 on charges relating to the bank's collapse. According to the office of Nuh Mete Yüksel, the prosecutor of the State Security Court (DGM) in Ankara, Yahya Murat Demirel was accused of transferring, with the help of his relatives, the assets of Egebank to offshore banks in northern Cyprus and the Virgin Islands. When Egebank's assets, including deposits, had vanished, the bank collapsed and went in receivership.

The bank's collapse is allegedly described as the work of an organized gang.

On June 28, 2002, the prosecutors demanded a record 4,727 years in jail for Yahya Murat Demirel, accusing him of multiple counts of fraud. Yahya Murat Demirel's wife and his thirty-six other associates were also charged with involvement in the conspiracy. After staying 711 days in jail, Yahya Murat Demirel was freed on September 13, 2002. The court decided that since others accused of similar bank frauds were released from prison, there was no need for him to stay in jail. He received a fine of about $138.

Yahya Murat Demirel, free pending several trials, produced exciting news for the media on New Year's Day of 2005. He boarded a commercial fishing boat in Istanbul on December 31 and arrived at the Bulgarian Black Sea port of Burgas just before midnight. He was accompanied by his US citizen wife, Ayşegül Esenler. Some members of the Bulgarian police, who were obviously not celebrating the new year, found them in the fishing boat. Yahya Murat Demirel was carrying two passports—one from Bulgaria and one from Belize. He also had a large amount of money on him in euros, dollars, and Turkish liras. The Bulgarian police said he offered a bribe of one hundred thousand euros in order to be freed. The bribe was refused, and the couple was sent back to Istanbul, where Yahya Murat was arrested and jailed in Kartal prison. His wife was freed. Yahya Murat said that he and his wife wanted to celebrate the new year in the fishing boat, but the boat somehow drifted into the Black Sea and ended up in Burgas unexpectedly.

On January 25, 2005, the *Dünden Bugüne Tercüman* newspaper reported that the Second Serious Crimes Court in Istanbul justified Yahya Murat Demirel's explanation about the fishing boat's drift to Burgas because of bad weather. The court ordered Demirel's release on this count. He remained in jail due to his pending trial in the Eighth Serious Crimes Court, also in Istanbul, on charges of banking irregularities.

These releases came after the crooked politicians, who are themselves behind the irregularities, changed the laws in order to protect the people who siphoned off the banks. Nineteen private banks were robbed of $55 billion in assets in addition to $21.9 billion stolen from several state banks. The great Turkish bank robbery totaled $77 billion, including $5 billion that vanished from the Uzan family–owned Imar Bank in the summer of 2003.

Legal authorities earlier had named the investigation of bank irregularities *Operation Whirlwind*. This whirlwind, however, often got stuck in a blind alley as the individuals involved in this institutionalized plunder have taken preventive measures to protect themselves. The robbers withdrew huge amounts of money from the banks by showing their low-wage employees, such as laborers and coffee servers, as the actual borrowers. The courts wasted their time by hearing the testimonies of these employees, who signed the loan documents but did not receive any loans!

The siphoned assets of Egebank when it went into receivership on December 31, 1999, was $1.2 billion and nobody, including the officials involved, could explain how the money disappeared.

Compared to the state's debt of an estimated $275 billion, the amount of the loss suffered by the banks was shocking news. How many years it took to accumulate these losses and why have remained a state secret. *The Financial Times* reported that powerful politicians were able to obtain credits from state banks.

During the investigation of the Egebank's collapse, public prosecutors questioned Yahya Murat Demirel's sister Neslihan Demirel, who had been a member of the bank's council. She defended her brother and said, "Since idols are always sacrificed, the system sacrificed us."

The father of Neslihan and her brother Yahya Murat Demirel is Şevket Demirel, the brother of Süleyman Demirel and a man of great wealth. Ali Şener, the brother-in-law of Süleyman Demirel, is allegedly involved in the illegal buying of Fatih Forest, owned by the treasury. Then there is the story of Süleyman Demirel's close friend Cavit Çağlar, a former member of parliament from Demirel's True Path Party (formed after the military in 1980 closed the Justice Party), who is a wealthy businessman. Cavit Çağlar was appointed a minister of state in 1991 in Süleyman Demirel's government. Charges against him include bank fraud in relation with the collapse of three banks: Interbank, Etibank, and Egebank. Turkish prosecutors allege among others that Çağlar obtained a $7.4 million loan from Egebank for commercial activity but pocketed the money with a group of conspirators. He allegedly failed to repay the funds. He was accused of alleged banking irregularities and losses of $1 billion.

Cavit Çağlar was arrested on a warrant from Istanbul's State Security Court and put in chains on April 17, 2001, in New York's John F. Kennedy International Airport. A New York court rejected Çağlar's release on a $5 million bail offer. He was extradited to Turkey, jailed in Istanbul's Kartal prison pending trial, and later released. His close friend Süleyman Demirel publicly expressed "deep sorrow" for Çağlar's arrest and jailing.

Süleyman Demirel considered the corruption props unfair. Speaking on May 11, 2002, at the University of Bahçeşehir, he declared that Yahya Murat Demirel, his brother's son, was jailed without a definition of his crime. The former president added that Cavit Çağlar "supported twenty thousand workers in his factories," and still he was chained and jailed. He added, "What has been done to Cavit Çağlar is cruelty."

According to columnist Fatih Altaylı of *Hürriyet*,

> Cavit [Çağlar] and Murat [Demirel] were jailed unjustly, so says Süleyman Demirel. They have been oppressed.
>
> The Demirel style of understanding the law is correct. In this understanding, close friends and relatives are above the law and they have immunity.
>
> A former prime minister, a former president is insulting Turkish courts for their judgments. Because these courts are asking for an accounting from his relatives and close friends.
>
> . . . Murat [Demirel] transferred the funds to non-existing companies, imaginary establishments, bankrupt firms.
>
> But according to his uncle, he is innocent.
>
> In a country managed for 40 years by this uncle, let's give thanks for our present condition.
>
> We could even lack this land to live on in a country managed by this mentality.

Hürriyet had earlier published a famous color photograph of the Demirel family, taken at a party on August 14, 1999. The picture showed Süleyman Demirel flanked by the children of Ali Şener, his brother-in-law; Nazmiye Demirel, his wife; and Cavit Çağlar, his close friend. Kamuran Çortuk, another friend of Demirel, who, the newspapers allege, hired a mobster to scare away a rival in the purchase of a bank, was also in the photograph.

In December 2004, the Third Serious Crimes Court in Bursa in western Turkey, sentenced former state minister Cavit Çağlar and four others, including his son, to three years and ten months each on charges of irregularities in the collapsed Interbank case. They also received heavy fines.

One of the biggest banking scandals in Turkey was about the alleged siphoning of the assets and depositors' accounts of Etibank, established in 1935 on Atatürk's order. Following the years of Kemalist reforms, this bank had played a vital role in the development of Turkish industry. The scandal shocked the whole country in October 2000 because it involved media mogul Dinç Bilgin, owner of *Sabah*, a daily newspaper. Bilgin, sixty-two, the head of Sabah Media Holding, was arrested in April 2001 and jailed on charges of siphoning off the assets of Etibank. He told authorities he couldn't say much because of the involvement of politics.

Bilgin was released from prison ten months later and transferred in October 2002 the publication rights of Sabah Publishing for fifteen years to *Merkez Grubu* (Central Group), a company established by Turgay Çiner. The transfer was officially approved because the state was to receive $10 million a year from the group's media outlets, such as *Sabah* and ATV television. Ali Atıf Bir, commenting in *Hürriyet* on January 23, 2005, said the group last year paid the state only $2 million. Once a state bank, Etibank was privatized in 1997, but the buyer could not pay the state. The bank was sold again in March 1998 to Dinç Bilgin's Sabah Media Holding and to Cavit Çağlar's Ipek Holding for $150 million. Bilgin later acquired a 50 percent share from his partner. When the Banking Supervisory Board, which administers a state fund for troubled banks, took the bank in receivership, the reasons were disclosed as "using the sources of the bank in the owner's favor and bad administration." The media has clearly played an important role in the bank irregularities.

Of eight business conglomerates involved in ownerships of newspapers, magazines, and TV and radio networks, seven are or were owners of banks. In February 2003, all media barons, with the exception of two, were prohibited to travel abroad due to their alleged involvement in banking irregularities.

Çukurova Holding—the owner of *Akşam* and *Güneş* newspapers, *Show TV*, Turkcell, Superonline, and Digiturk—allegedly owed in June 2002 $2.7 billion to Pamukbank and another $2.3 billion to Yapı Kredi Bank. Mehmet Emin Karamehmet, the holding's owner, a few years earlier was listed as the richest Turk and twenty-ninth richest man in the world by *Forbes* magazine. Çukurova Holding reached an agreement with the Banking Supervisory Board (BDDK) to pay back a total of $6.2 billion within fifteen years.

The legal troubles of the Uzan family members, who owned two newspapers, including *Star*; three *Star TV* channels; the mobile telephone network Telsim; and two banks were all over the newspapers in summer 2003, and Bahattin Uzan was arrested. In September warrants were issued for the arrest of Kemal Uzan, his son Hakan, and Hakan's uncle Yavuz Uzan for banking irregularities. Allegedly over $5 billion was stolen from the assets of the Imar Bank, which the Uzan family had controlled. In July 2003, the Banking Supervisory Board took over the control of the Imar Bank when the bank fell behind in payments to its 380,000 depositors.

During the investigations of the Uzan family members, a search of their company offices, homes, and yachts produced tapes allegedly used to blackmail people. The state ordered the confiscation of their properties, including the media outlets. Kemal Uzan, the patriarch of the family, had once been listed among the richest people in the world (number 371) by *Forbes* magazine. In February 2005, the police were still looking for him, his son Hakan, and Hakan's uncle Yavuz Uzan. They had left the country and disappeared.

Uzan family members also have legal problems in the United States. They were sued for $3 billion by the global mobile phone giants Motorola and Finland's Nokia on fraud accusations under US antiracketeering laws. Motorola and Nokia allege that members of the Uzan family had borrowed billions with no intention of paying back. The Uzans denied any wrongdoing and said Motorola and Nokia had supplied them shoddy goods. A New York court in July 2003 sentenced the Uzans to pay $4.2 billion to Motorola.

Forty-two-year-old Cem Uzan, who headed the Uzan-owned media outlets, has political ambitions. He formed a political party in 2002 and called it the *Genç Parti*, or Young Party. He lives in Istanbul.

Doğan Media Group emerged as the leading media organization with the ownership of the newspapers *Hürriyet*, *Milliyet*, *Radikal*, and *Posta*. In addition, this group owns other newspapers and magazines, including *Fanatik*, *Tempo*, and *Finansal Forum*. The publisher Aydın Doğan also owns a couple banks, the TV networks Kanal D and CNN Turk, Radyo

D, Radyo Frekans, and Hür FM broadcasting. Aydın Doğan has financial interests in the energy sector. Haber Ajansı, the news agency I founded and organized in the 1960s, is now called Doğan News Agency.

In fall 2003, Aydın Doğan had an ongoing media war with Mehmet Emin Karamehmet of Çukurova Holding, Dinç Bilgin's *Sabah* (Central) Group, and the Uzan family. His campaigns against them regarding their alleged banking irregularities generated attacks on his own business dealings. It was alleged that the due date of a state loan on his oil-related company, Iş-Doğan, had been extended by the state to five from three years.

In a statement on October 14, 2003, to Doğan News Agency, the publisher said that the attacks against him from the "Coalition of the media barons, who had siphoned off billions of dollars from the banks" were simply blackmail to shut him up. He said, "I will not be silenced. I did not siphon off money from banks, and I do not owe taxes to the state." Aydın Doğan added that parliament ought to investigate the plunder of the banks. He disclosed that the amount of money his group owed was $234 million, while it had $100 million in ready cash and $70 million worth of movable assets for immediate cash.

He was questioned during a crowded news conference a few days later about his purchase of DemirHalk Bank from the state for $84 million—where he already had an outstanding loan. He answered, "I did fine, they sold it, and I bought it." According to bank inspectors, the bank was sold cheaply.

Aydın Doğan said the Turkish media were being used for blackmail, forming a dreadful swamp, a cesspool. "I am doing my best not to be part of that filth," he said. "There are journalists-for-hire in Turkey."

Aydın Doğan's rivals accuse him of plans to monopolize the media by eliminating other newspaper and media sources that oppose his publishing and business empire. His rivals also blame Doğan's media group for supporting each new government during its term, including the Justice and Development Party with Islamist roots, which came to power on November 3, 2002.

The Islamic newspapers and broadcast companies, who are frequently called "The Hereafter Media" and who daily preach fire-and-brimstone religion, watched this media war with glee. The Islamic dailies include *Yeni Şafak*, owned by the Albayrak family, who allegedly received favored treatment for city contracts from Recep Tayyip Erdoğan, former Islamist mayor of Istanbul and later prime minister; *Milli Gazete* of the Islamist *Saadet* (Felicity) Party, which supports Necmettin Erbakan and his pro-Islam reactionary *Milli Görüş* (National View) policies; *Zaman*, the newspaper owned by Fethullah Gülen, the leader of the Light sect; *Vakit,* which used to be known as *Akit* but changed its name when slander suits against it mounted; and *Yeni Asya.*

Lütfü Livaneli, a columnist for *Sabah*, complained bitterly about the corruption in the country. He wrote: "The scoundrels are everywhere so that we ask ourselves: Is there a taintless organization left anywhere?" Livaneli added that the public is not spared corruption scandals for even a single day. "You can count if you want," he wrote right after the Etibank scandal. "The state apparatus, private enterprises, insurance companies, municipalities, legal, security, and health services are all involved. There is no place left free of dirt and degeneration. A great country has been transformed into a hell of crime."

Ilhan Selçuk of *Cumhuriyet* stated in his column "The Window" that the seeds of deep corruption were planted during the rule of Turgut Özal. Selçuk reminded his readers of Turgut Özal's words: "The constitution is not going to be hurt if for just once a hole is punctured in it." Then Selçuk accused Özal of establishing a TV network for his son by abusing state regulations. Writing about the "degenerated media," Selçuk added that usually a press boss would reward a columnist with tens of thousands of dollars for attacking the "deep state" and that then the "deep state" would transfer hundreds of millions of dollars to the press baron through the banks to shut him up. He added, "This deep relationship with the deep state destroyed the structure of the media, and the nature of the media became rotten."

Emin Çölaşan of *Hürriyet* blamed all the political parties for the spread of corruption in the country and for allowing their supporters to plunder the banks. Commenting on the bank scandals on November 8, 2000, Çölaşan wrote, "If you want to steal in Turkey, do it in a grand style. Nothing will happen to you. If you steal only a little, you will be caught and you will eat the quince." (*Ayvayı yemek*—to eat quince, meaning you will be done for, in this case, arrested and jailed.)

The same was also true during the Ottoman Empire's times of high corruption. The poetry of Ziya Pasha includes this couplet:

> The thief who steals millions is dignified and respected,
> The thief who steals a few pennies gets hard labor.

Çölaşan in his article added,

> And now Tansu [Çiller] emerges and accuses the present [Bülent Ecevit's coalition] government of the banking scandal.
> Is she less guilty than this government?
> Mesut [Yılmaz], who is involved in the Türkbank scandal himself, has joined the caravan of accusation!
> My God, we in Turkey are living in a dreadful black comedy.

Çölaşan commented that during the 1980s, when Istanbul Bank and Hisarbank collapsed, their owners and administrators were not punished: "Özer Çiller, who was the general manager of Istanbul Bank, used to grant credits after receiving a commission. As commission, he would pocket 15 percent of that credit himself. I have proof of this here with documentation. Then he became husband of the prime minister and managed Turkey."

Çölaşan also wrote, "Fine, what happened to the owners and managers of Marmarabank, Impeksbank, and TYT Bank, which were emptied of their assets during Tansu's [Çiller] term of office? In those banks, too, there were the princes of Turgut Özal. Trillions were siphoned off, and now these people go about in our midst like lions."

Interior minister Sadettin Tantan had a name for the corrupt political bosses and businessmen in October 2000. He called them *akbabalar*, or vultures. Addressing a conference on corruption in Istanbul Tantan said,

"The thieves and exploiters, who should be locked up, are able to wander among us as respected people." Tantan warned that corruption threatens Turkey's economic and political stability: "Unless we grasp that corruption is the main source of radical Islamism, dirty politics, and dysfunctional state and take steps to drain the swamp, we will spend our time swatting mosquitoes." Tantan's warning was ignored, resulting two years later in a crucial Islamist election victory.

As scandals rapidly followed one another, the Turks were furious and complained about the lack of ethics in the affairs of the state.

Dinç Bilgin's *Sabah* is known to have covered the allegations of corruption against Tansu Çiller, Turkey's first woman prime minister. Right after the seizure of Etibank, speaking at a youth organization meeting of her True Path Party, Çiller blamed the Banking Supervisory Board for acting late. That, she claimed, caused misery to "this poor nation." She said that Turkey was under unresolved circumstances and added, "It is high time to bring a stop to this putrefied system."

Çiller, speaking in another meeting of the True Path Party, said that Egebank was robbed in two days and that the banks were sold (by the state) to the Mafia. She added: "If we can't break up today's oligarchy, if we can't change the corruption, which is powered by capital and singular politics, then a social explosion in Turkey may become unavoidable."

Tansu Çiller herself, facing charges earlier for alleged corruption, claimed she had inherited her wealth from her mother.

This highly ambitious, blonde, and stylish woman was born in Istanbul in 1946 and studied at Robert College, presently known as Bosphorus University. She married Özer Uçuran, also a graduate of Robert College. The couple went to the United States for Tansu's PhD and had a son there. The word *uçuran* comes from the verb *uçurmak*, meaning to cause something to fly. Özer preferred to adopt his wife's surname, Çiller.

Back in Turkey, after a period of teaching economics at Bosphorus University, Tansu Çiller entered politics. Süleyman Demirel, the leader in 1990 of the True Path Party, became her mentor. The Çiller couple began accumulating real estate in Turkey and in the United States. She was elected Member of Parliament in 1991 and shared responsibility for the ministry of economy. Her careless economic figures and unusual requests surprised her party colleagues. Once she proposed to forego civil servants' salaries for a month as a budgetary measure.

Upon the death of President Turgut Özal in 1993, parliament elected Süleyman Demirel as Turkey's president. Tansu Çiller, with the support of Demirel, won the leadership of True Path Party and became Turkey's first woman prime minister. As prime minister, she made incredible blunders, such as asking journalists on one occasion, "Isn't Russia already a NATO member?" According to Ustun Reinart's article *"Ambition for All Seasons, Tansu Çiller,"* published in March 1999 in *Women's International Net Magazine*, she had a hard time remembering the names of foreign heads of state. Government planes flew in the brands of ice cream she liked and special ingredients for her meals.

According to Reinart, Tansu Çiller—who uses the perfume Beautiful by Estee Lauder—changed from a liberal to a nationalist and took a hard line against the Kurdish separatist movement. In 1994 political murders increased, and her wealth made headlines. The Islamists called her *Gavur Gelini*, or Bride of the Infidels.

She would soon change her image once again when there was no clear winner in the general elections of 1995. The *Refah Partisi* (Welfare Party) of the Islamist Necmettin Erbakan had received 21 percent of the votes, and the party began negotiating with Mesut Yılmaz of the Motherland Party to form a coalition government. Çiller, who once claimed, "I am the creation of Atatürk," accused Yılmaz of "pushing Turkey into darkness."

The Islamists, through an extensive investigation about Tansu Çiller's wealth, had thick files on her, including the mystery of missing money from a slush fund. When Çiller was prime minister between 1993 and 1996, the opposition charged that she and her husband, Özer, a businessman, allegedly enriched themselves through illicit use of government funds. Tansu Çiller claimed that she had inherited $1.1 million, including gold, from her mother, Muazzez, but her mother's neighbors claimed that she had been poor.

According to the *New York Times*, Özer Çiller bought properties in New Hampshire through GCD, an American company in which the Çiller family has a controlling interest. The properties included a Holiday Inn in Salem, Massachusetts, and the Granite State Business Center in Hooksett, New Hampshire. The Çiller family has included its American properties in a disclosure of wealth and, in addition, stated ownership of 424,965 shares in Marsan Marmara Holding, two yachts named *Denge* and *President*, and a farm in Kuşadası in western Turkey.

Tansu Çiller, in a clever move to protect her own interests, agreed to form a coalition government with the Islamists, whom she had earlier called the forces of darkness. The Welfare Party became her protector within their coalition; Erbakan and Çiller acted together to appease prominent members of the Islamic brotherhoods. They invited various sect leaders to *iftar*, the dinner parties to break the religious fast. Their cooperation was a boon for the advancement of the Islamic reactionary movement—and harmful to the principles of Kemalism.

Professor Kemal Kirişci, a political scientist at the Bosphorus University, said of Tansu Çiller: "She is probably the most Machiavellian politician Turkey has seen for a long time. She'll do anything for the sake of her goal. Part and parcel of her Machiavellianism is that while she has a lot of dirty linen herself, she knows of a lot of other politicians' dirty linen and does not hesitate to use it." Her nemesis was Mesut Yılmaz, a former prime minister and leader of the Motherland Party. On numerous occasions, they both suffered the indignity of parliamentary investigations into their alleged corruption. They also did their best to trip each other up when the occasion arose.

Tansu Çiller's reputation took a heavy blow when a government report in January 1998 implicated her in serious corruption. This so-called *Susurluk Report*, partially disclosed by Mesut Yılmaz, links Prime Minister Tansu Çiller's term (1993–96) to death squads, drug trafficking, botched secret operations abroad, and the extortion of money from the owners of gambling casinos.

Susurluk is a provincial town where, in November 1996, a car crash caused a huge scandal. A police chief, a right-wing hitman, who also worked as a secret government agent, and his girlfriend were killed, and a Kurdish politician survived. This car accident opened a window disclosing the close ties between organized crime, the killings of political dissidents, and the state apparatus itself. The report confirmed the earlier allegations that state-sponsored death squads killed Kurdish separatists, including journalists who supported the Kurdish revolt. The report added that the right-wing hit man named Abdullah Çatlı had played a leading role in a 1995 coup attempt in Azerbaijan to overthrow President Haydar Aliyev in order to open up a new route from Baku to the West to smuggle drugs.

On January 1, 1997, in a report about the Susurluk scandal, Kelly Couturier of the *Washington Post* wrote, "At the heart of the furor are the accusations that a network of criminal gangs has infiltrated Turkey's parliament, security forces and police apparatus. The gangs, in return for helping rid government officials of enemies, have been allowed to grow rich through extortion, gambling, money laundering and heroin trafficking, according to the accusations."

In a political horse trading in June 2000 between the partners of Prime Minister Bülent Ecevit's three-party coalition, parliament cleared both Mesut Yılmaz and Tansu Çiller on charges of corruption.

İlhan Selçuk wrote in *Cumhuriyet*: "There were mountains of corruption files on the backs of Mesut Yılmaz and Tansu Çiller. They sat down, bargained and Ecevit gave his approval. The corruption files about the two leaders in parliament's commissions were removed. An immoral bargaining was brought to life."

Meanwhile, without the knowledge of Energy Minister Cumhur Ersümer, a probe called Operation White Energy had been spearheaded in 2001 and was conducted not by the police but by gendarmerie (paramilitary police), some officials of the ministry of interior, and the general staff. Both the energy ministry and the interior ministry were then under the control of Mesut Yılmaz's Motherland Party of the three-party coalition that was led by Prime Minister Bülent Ecevit.

Ecevit, facing pressure to crack down on corruption, especially as a condition for a new IMF and World Bank loan, had to accept on April 28,

2001, Ersümer's resignation. Parliament on May 22, 2001, rejected a motion by the opposition Islamist Virtue Party demanding investigation into alleged corruption by Cumhur Ersümer. The votes were 259 to 167 when 430 deputies participated. There were allegations that the Nationalist Action Party cleared corruption charges against the former energy minister in order to save the coalition. Turkey's parliament continued to be the place to whitewash the irregularities inside the state itself.

There appeared a peculiarity of the Operation White Energy investigation. Sadettin Tantan, the interior minister, stated that he did not inform Mesut Yılmaz and Cumhur Ersümer of the ongoing investigation, which lasted three months. During the investigation, Energy Minister Ersümer's phones were tapped without his knowledge. The investigation included the awarding of the contract of the Blue Stream undersea pipeline project to carry overpriced Russian natural gas to Turkey.

The corruption scandals reminded many people of the stories of the humorist mullah of the Ottoman times:

One day, Nasreddin Hoca enters a vegetable garden intending to steal watermelons. A guard catches him. "Why did you enter this field?" he asks.

Nasreddin Hoca answers, "I didn't. The storm threw me here."

The guard replies, "Why do you have a watermelon in your hand?"

"I was trying to hold on to its root in order not to be thrown about by the storm. The watermelon was left in my hand."

"Fine. What do you say about the sack next to you? Who filled this sack with watermelons?"

Nasreddin Hoca by now has run out of plausible explanations. He answers: "Well, just now I was trying to figure out myself what to tell you about the sack."

C☾

Finally, the corruption scandals and Prime Minister Bülent Ecevit's impotence to deal with them caused an unprecedented row during a meeting of the National Security Council (MGK). During that meeting, on February

19, 2001, President Necdet Sezer accused Bülent Ecevit of ignorance and interference in legal affairs. Sezer complained about Ecevit's weakness to fight corruption. The meeting was attended by leading government officials and army generals.

An angry President Sezer stated that he would not allow the country to be plundered or let the corruption scandals be covered up. President Sezer then threw across the table a copy of the constitution toward Prime Minister Ecevit, which was flung back and forth as they argued about fighting corruption. Soon after, Hüsamettin Özkan, Ecevit's favorite deputy premier and adopted son, called President Sezer a *nankör kedi* (an ungrateful cat) who forgot who had made him president.

Finally Ecevit, badly shaken, stormed out of the meeting and, once outside, declared a "serious crisis," disclosing to the press the full details of the row. Ecevit's statement triggered a financial meltdown and Turkey's worst recession since 1945 that cost billions of dollars and severe unemployment. The fear of another clash in the government kept haunting the financial markets.

As a result of this incident, the Turkish lira lost 50 percent of its value overnight against the dollar. In addition, the one-and-a-half-year-old disinflation program of the International Monetary Fund collapsed. The average monthly income plunged, and the Turks found themselves poorer still. In October 2001, $1 was worth over 1.5 million Turkish liras. In October 2003, a family of four needed 1.6 billion Turkish liras (about $1,110) a month to survive. The lowest monthly salary for a government official was 517 million liras (about $369), while anyone earning 490 million liras (about $350) was close to starvation.

The workers were badly hurt. According to a statement of the Türk-Iş Labor Union in September 2003, a worker's minimum monthly wage was 306 million liras (about $218). After the federal, social security, and unemployment taxes were deducted, his net pay was reduced to 225,999,000 liras (about $161). The same worker had to work eight hours and forty-three minutes in order to buy a kilogram of ground meat and one hour and twenty minutes for a loaf of bread weighing one kilogram. According to official figures, the number of unemployed in December

2004 was 2,396,000. It is believed that the actual number is almost 9 million, as some people, especially unemployed women, stopped looking for jobs. The number of employed stood at 20,811,000, mostly in low-income jobs. The State Institute of Statistics stated in 2003 that 12.2 million people were each earning only $1 a day. Meanwhile, the *Guinness Book of World Records* named the Turkish lira the number-one worthless money among the currencies of 112 countries.

27 ★

Did You Say Corruption?
What Corruption?

They pilfered Hasan's flaky pastries.

Turkish proverb

ell-known writer H. R. Gürpınar once wrote, "Is that possible? Would we permit you to do it? There can be no plunder my dear fellow, no plunder."

Gürpinar could not even imagine the size of the future looting and plundering that shook the foundations of the secular republic. It has almost bankrupted the state.

For years, because of the lack of transparency in government dealings, the loans received from the International Monetary Fund and the Turkish treasury's own resources have been stolen or wasted. Zeki Ergezen, the new minister of development, said in parliament on June 6, 2003, that one-third of the country's budget had been wasted, while another one-third had gone to irregularities. "There have been such irregularities," he said. "Even the Devil himself couldn't have figured them out."

Justice Minister Cemil Çiçek said in a statement to *Hürriyet* in

August 2003, "The citizen is asking me why the thieves who robbed banks are not in jail. He is complaining that the big thieves are getting away, while a thief who steals a tape is punished."

According to Minister of State Ali Babacan, 30.6 percent of the income from taxes in 1990 was used to pay the interest for the national debt. Speaking in the Planning and Budgetary Commission of Parliament in March 2003, Babacan added that in 2002 this increased to 87 percent.

The waste includes unnecessary construction contracts, such as airports built in small towns or tunnels completed for nonexisting railroads, awarded to relatives and supporters of the old-guard politicians. Fourteen airports are useless. The airport in Isparta, convenient to use only for Süleyman Demirel when visiting his hometown, was the biggest money loser before it was closed. Another airport, built next to Islamist leader Necmettin Erbakan's summer villa in Edremit, in western Turkey, is a cow pasture. The Turks have a few fitting expressions for such exuberant prodigality, including, "He doesn't have buttermilk to drink, yet he goes to the bathroom riding a palanquin."

A parliamentary motion in July 2003 requested the formation of a commission to investigate the alleged corruption in the construction of the Yuvacık dam near Izmit, in western Turkey. The investigation request involved Tansu Çiller, the former premier, and eleven former ministers. The dam had been built while they were in office and cost the state $5.2 billion. It was alleged that the value of the construction was actually a mere $217 million. Tansu Çiller stated she had nothing to do with it. "I am shocked," she said.

The High Planning Council, fighting irregularities and waste, canceled in February 2003 all additional investments in 614 unfinished state projects. According to the council, there were 5,556 unfinished projects on which the state had already spent $130 billion. In order to complete these projects, an additional $355 billion was needed. Yet the state's investment budget for 2003 was only about $3 billion. The projects included roads, factories, schools, and hospitals. A regional school completed at Gümüşhane, in northeastern Anatolia, was not being used because the contractor had forgotten to build dormitories.

Mehmet Yıldırım, the chairman of Istanbul's Chamber of Commerce, on September 26, 1998, described how state tender is awarded: "You cannot receive tender from any state institution right now without paying a commission to gangs. This goes all the way to the cabinet members and highest state officials." Things got so bad that the IMF requested reforms in public tender before signing off on new money. Due to pressure from the IMF, the government formed a new board to oversee a revised system of state tender and procurement in April 2002.

The bill for the loot and plunder of the 1990s alone is believed to be billions, but the real figure remained a mystery. The severity of the condition of the country's finances reminded many intellectuals of the encroachments of the capitulations into the bankrupt and war-weary Ottoman state. I remember so well what Namık Kemal wrote during these dark times of the Ottoman Empire: "The enemy has pressed his dagger to her breast,/There is no one to save your luckless Motherland."

Tevfik Fikret gave a fitting answer to that during the bad times of the Ottoman Empire:

> Do not feign not to see the sunlight,
> When its brilliance is fading,
> It can't be extinguished for eternity,
> A new day has to follow the night.

Yet, about a century after Tevfik Fikret wrote this, that sunlight still evaded the Turkish people. There has been no satisfactory response to the question in people's minds: Why are the thieves who stole the country's wealth still free? Most Turkish observers agreed that the election victory of the Islamists on November 3, 2002, was an act of public desperation in search of that answer.

Over a year earlier, in February 2001, Kemal Derviş, a senior World Bank executive, was appointed minister of economy by Prime Minister Bülent Ecevit in hopes of saving the collapsed economy. Derviş obtained new loans, became a politician, joined the Republican People's Party, and was later elected a member of parliament.

For years, the economic policies of the government have been a vicious cycle: collect loans, spend the money, and go back for more loans. Interior minister Sadettin Tantan, sixty, fighting almost single-handedly the deep plunder of the state, the business world, the banking sector, and the media, had to face tremendous pressures from political bigwigs. The media bosses, who received billions of dollars during Turgut Özal's regime as credits and grants for their support, were against Tantan's corruption probes. The old-guard political party bosses and their media supporters started a smear campaign against Tantan, whom they saw as the spearhead of the anticorruption drive.

At first Tantan's Operation White Energy investigation was transferred from the paramilitary police (*gendarmerie*) to the police force. The excuse was that the country was fast turning into a police state. This move raised suspicions that Operation White Energy probes, especially of the alleged links of the irregularities with the Russian Mafia through a natural gas pipeline project, were being undermined. Then, on June 5, 2001, the bombshell came: Sadettin Tantan, the top anticorruption crusader, was forced out of his post by Mesut Yılmaz, leader of the Motherland Party and Prime Minister Ecevit's deputy. Tantan was appointed to the post of state minister in charge of customs, but the next day, he resigned from both his new post and the Motherland Party. Tantan had been in constant conflict with Mesut Yılmaz over his handling of the anticorruption operations. On occasion Tantan claimed that elements in the Motherland Party hampered his corruption investigations, especially the Operation White Energy probe.

Meanwhile, Prime Minister Bülent Ecevit seemed to be focused only on the survival of his coalition for which the corruption probes could be sacrificed. He ignored the calls for his resignation and said there was no alternative to his government. Ecevit, looking for new loans, asked for financial help from the leaders of the Group of Seven leading industrial countries. Western lenders wanted to see bold economic reforms before lending more money, having seen that earlier loans had been misused or stolen.

Hüsamettin Özkan, known as Ecevit's *manevi oğlu*, or adopted son, emerged for a while as a leading player in Turkish politics. As the country entered a highly critical period in its history, Hüsamettin Özkan appeared to be involved with the government's policy regarding the corruption probes. There were allegations that Özkan had unlimited influence in the prime ministry. Nazlı Ilıcak, then a columnist for the Islamist newspaper *Yeni Şafak*, promptly named him the Turkish Rasputin.

The army, the country's most trusted institution, announced measures to ease the financial and economic crisis. It postponed thirty-two spending projects worth $19.5 billion, including the replacement of its aging tank and helicopter inventory.

More bad news was in store. The Federation of Turkish Chambers of Commerce and Stock Exchanges (TOBB) issued a report in April 2001 called "The Economy of Extravagance." TOBB disclosed that in the years from 1990 to 2000, $195.2 billion had been stolen or wasted through shortsighted and politically motivated projects. These included $32.5 billion in banking losses, $95 billion of interest paid for loans, and $32.2 billion lost in irregularities on contracts awarded by the government. The report added that in those ten years, the government had changed ten times. The political bigwigs Süleyman Demirel, Turgut Özal, Mesut Yılmaz, Tansu Çiller, Necmettin Erbakan, and Bülent Ecevit led the governments during those ten years.

In summer 2002, there were indications that the seventy-nine-year-old secular Turkish republic had entered a critical and dangerous period in its history. There were powerful signs of insecurity and unhappiness in people's lives. A change in the country's political, social, cultural, and economic life seemed inevitable. The public calls against the degeneration of the state, of the political parties, and of business and the media and for sweeping reforms were becoming overwhelming.

It was as if a magic wand had awakened the Turkish population from a deep sleep and made it see the reality that they had been hoodwinked and deceived for a long time with lies of greatness and heroism, that they had been fooled with false promises by thieves and bandits. When the mythical balloon of the greatest and the most heroic nation on earth burst, Turks found out that they had been made fools. The ruling class had manipulated them with tall tales of heroism, frequent calls for national sacrifice, and the constant reminders of its greatness, while the Turks' own leaders were robbing them. Slogans such as "Turkey is the greatest country," or "A single Turk is worth the whole world," diverted their attention from reality. In fact, ordinary citizens now began to realize that their country had been left far behind by other developing nations.

Still, the increase of the media's criticism of the state surprised me. Necati Doğru commented in *Sabah* in March 2001, "We became a beggar country seeking a foreign loan, then after consuming this foreign loan, seeking another foreign loan and spending that one, too."

Doğru complained, "Once again they have discredited Turkey at the door of the United States of America for being a shameless, ill-mannered, cheeky beggar. . . . Nobody trusts their own country's money. They don't trust their country, their leaders, and their leaders' program."

Sema Pişkinsüt, former head of the Parliamentary Human Rights Commission, was blunt in describing Turkish affairs. Speaking during a meeting in April 2001 with the judges of the Appeals Court in Ankara, she stated that the Turkish police use torture. She added that the members of parliament were *avam*, uneducated common people, ignorant and provincial. According to Pişkinsüt, "It is impossible to pass laws with ignorant deputies. The road that leads to parliament is through feudalism, capital, and the party leaders."

Pişkinsüt, then a member of parliament from Ecevit's Democratic Left Party, said that no system exists that provides for the election of parliamentary representatives for the people and that election rules and laws governing the political parties must be changed: "My view is that the members of parliament are not the real representatives of the people." According to Pişkinsüt, democracy in Turkey is dysfunctional, and numerous corruption probes have lead nowhere, despite pressures from the IMF because of the immunity of the members of parliament.

I was not at all surprised when Pişkinsüt, a fifty-year-old doctor of medicine, soon found out that speaking the truth in Turkey can be unhealthy. During the fifth congress of Ecevit's Democratic Left Party on April 29, 2001, she was denied any platform as a delegate and a candidate for the party's chairmanship. Pişkinsüt was called a traitor and was mistreated and booed, and well-trained Ecevit loyalists wearing the party's traditional blue shirts beat her son Yüce, twenty-two, a university student.

Mehmet Özcan and Nazire Karakuş, two parliamentary deputies, resigned from the Democratic Left Party the next day. Mehmet Özcan, a member of parliament from Izmir, said at a press conference that the politicians involved in corruption were being protected. He also said that the prosecutors conducting corruption probes were being intimidated with investigations initiated against them. In September 2001, Sema Pişkinsüt (her surname means "well-cooked milk") left Ecevit's party, saying it had broken its promise to the people.

The party's leader and prime minister, seventy-seven-year-old Bülent Ecevit, with his trademark blue cap, black moustache, and black hair thanks to coloring, kept breaking new records with his blunders. Once, visiting a flooded region in southern Anatolia, he claimed that the disaster was an earthquake, unaware that it was, in fact, flooding.

This episode was shown live by Turkish TV networks.

The Islamists
and the Kemalists

Calling a man mad for forty days will drive him to madness.

Turkish proverb

üleyman Demirel, my nemesis, survived two coups d'etat and an assassination attempt when a deranged lone Islamist opened fire in May 1996, wounding two bystanders. During an earlier attack inside the prime ministry in 1975, Demirel received a beating. He served as prime minister of Turkey seven times and finally in 1993 became president. He remained president until 2000.

Demirel is well known by the nickname *Baba*, or father. As they say in Isparta, my Anatolian hometown, *hasbel kader*, or by the irony of fate, Demirel also hails from that town renowned for its handwoven rugs. He had been a shepherd boy in Islamköy (Islam Village), not far from the town, and had gone through the same republican educational system as I did as a child. Known as Süllü the Shepherd, he became an engineer and worked as a dam builder during the regime of Adnan Menderes. The Justice Party, the first political organization Demirel led, was the unofficial revival of Adnan Menderes's Democratic Party. During the general elections of 1965, five years after the military ousted Adnan Menderes, the Justice Party won 53 percent of the votes.

As soon as Demirel became prime minister he tried to release former Democratic Party members, who were still in jail. He made a deal with the military to the effect that in return for releasing the old democrats, the sentences of the jailed supporters of Colonel Talat Aydemir, who, on May 21, 1963, had rebelled for the second time against Ismet Inönü's coalition government, would be reduced. The democrats were released from jail on condition that they would not involve themselves in politics. There is an oddity in Turkish politics that may help to explain why Kemal Atatürk's dream of a strictly secular Turkey has now been irreparably damaged.

Before 1946, the government, led by the Republican People's Party, had allowed Islamic education in the state schools *if requested by the children's parents*. Ismet Inönü was then ruling the country as a dictator. When he opened the door to democracy, four prominent members of the Republican People's party—Celal Bayar, Adnan Menderes, Refik Koraltan, and Fuat Köprülü—left to form the Democratic Party on January, 7, 1946. The Democrats, soon after winning the general elections in 1950, announced that Islamic teaching would be provided for all students, *unless parents requested exemption*. The exemption clause was meaningless. No parent in an Anatolian town would dare ask for such an exemption from religious instruction for his or her child. Such a request would be enough to start talk that these parents must be infidels or atheists.

The reactionary Islamic organizations active underground in secrecy against the secular republic found a welcoming home in the Democratic Party. The Democrats increased the government funding for mosques and eased the secular laws that restricted religious movements and *tarikats*, the Sufi Islamic brotherhoods. Islamic orders suppressed during the secular reforms reemerged and later new Islamic sects were organized. Hizbullah, the Party of God, a terrorist outfit, is one of those. In 1951 the Democrats in power set up special secondary religious *Imam-hatip* (cleric) schools that mushroomed later when Süleyman Demirel was the prime minister. I strongly believe that these imam-cleric schools hurt Turkey's secular image and have done irreparable damage to the Kemalist ideals. Besides these schools, there are now nineteen newspapers, eleven periodicals, fifty-one radio, twenty television stations, twenty-five hundred associations, five hundred foundations, and over a thousand companies that fully support the Islamic revival.

It was a few years after the coup d'etat of 1960 that the Justice Party, emerging as a copycat of the outlawed Democratic Party, helped to change Turkey's destiny. The Justice Party developed itself as a base in which leaders of a determined Islamic reactionary movement and an ultranationalist group found fertile ground to spread their own policies.

One of the leading supporters of the Justice Party had been the fervent Islamist Necmettin Erbakan, a publicly declared enemy of the Kemalist reforms. Despite being a classmate of Süleyman Demirel at the Technical University of Istanbul, Erbakan received the cold shoulder from the Justice Party. Demirel saw him as a rival. Erbakan then formed in 1969 his own Islam-based *Milli Nizam Partisi*, or National Order Party. A leading member of this ultrareligious party was Turgut Özal, who belonged to the Nakshibendi Brotherhood. Other Justice Party members also left to form the *Milliyetçi Hareket Partisi*, or Nationalist Action Party, which played a disastrous role during the bloody struggles of the 1970s.

Looking back, I remember how as a young journalist in Istanbul I used to encounter antisecular, Islamic-oriented politicians who made the rounds in Babıali, the press district. One of these politicians was Necmettin Erbakan. He did not seem to be a politician with a future, for he was old-fashioned and not realistic about the world of Islam. His politics were based on reviving Islamic and Ottoman traditions. Erbakan, however, knew that there was a public yearning for the glorious era of the Ottoman Empire.

I think that the corruption and the public disillusionment with the secular political parties, the imam-cleric schools, and those oligarchic politicians in power also helped Necmettin Erbakan's pro-Islam movement. The fear of Communism, the lack of social justice, and the absence of serious efforts by the poorly led government to improve the educational standards and the lot of the peasants and have-nots also helped Islamic fundamentalism grow.

Support and heavy financing from Saudi Arabia, Libya, and Iran, played an important role in creating Turkey's return to political Islam. Years ago, it was common knowledge in Istanbul's press center that Saudi and Libyan money was used to fund certain pro-Islam political parties and newspapers. Saudi Arabia, in fact, played a significant role in the revival of Islam-bankrolled Erbakan's Welfare Party. Welfare used part of these funds to build mosques and religious schools and to support the poor to get votes. Still, Necmettin Erbakan and his three Islamic parties formed between 1969 and 1983 were the catalysts in polarizing the Turkish public into two directly opposing factions—the Islamic fundamentalists and the staunchly secularist followers of the Kemalist reforms and rigid ideology.

Necmettin Erbakan is known as the man who has established Islam in Turkish politics. The name *Necmettin* means the Star of Islam. He has strong emotional ties with the past—the Ottoman Empire. Erbakan—known as *hocaefendi*, or revered preacher—lets his disciples wash his feet during the ritual ablutions before prayer. His disciples also know him as the Champion of Islam, and some even believe that he is the Mahdi, an Islamist messiah who will bring about Islam's world domination. Erbakan has repeatedly assaulted the secular constitution and the Kemalist reforms.

It is also known that during his time as a politician, Necmettin Erbakan has acquired great wealth. According to his declaration of properties, this wealth includes 148 kilograms of gold bullion and a fortune in dollars.

Erbakan is the son of a *kadı*, an Islamic judge, who practiced during the last years of the Ottoman Empire. As a student at the Technical University of Istanbul, like his schoolmate Süleyman Demirel, Erbakan came under the pro-Islam influences of a professor. He denounced the Gulf War of 1991 as "Zionist aggression."

Despite the banning of his National Order Party right after the coup d'etat of 1971, Erbakan remained persistent in his Islamic agenda. He formed a second pro-Islam party, the *Milli Selamet Partisi*, or National Salvation Party, in 1973 and served as deputy prime minister in the coalition led by Bülent Ecevit, then the leader of the Republican People's Party. The coup d'etat of 1980, led by General Kenan Evren, the third in twenty years, dissolved the political parties in order to end social and political chaos. All the party leaders were arrested and banned from politics.

They soon returned when the military once more handed the power over to the civilians. Süleyman Demirel's Justice Party, outlawed like the other political organizations by the military, changed its name and platform to that of *Doğru Yol Partisi*, or True Path Party. Demirel promised the electorate a new start in human rights and a car and a house for every family. The promise was no better than pie-in-the-sky. When Demirel was elected prime minister in 1991, one of his more memorable promises was transparency in his government. According to this promise, the walls of police stations were to be made of glass.

One of Demirel's biggest political mistakes in his long political life was his support of Tansu Çiller, a member of the True Path Party, which she used as an engine to become Turkey's first woman prime minister in 1993. Demirel in his later years is known to have regretted his earlier support of Tansu Çiller.

Necmettin Erbakan in 1983 formed his third Islamist party the *Refah* (Welfare) Party, and his fundamentalist movement advanced throughout the country at the expense of the Kemalist reforms.

Soon, a new era, appropriately named the Özal Years, began. Turgut Özal, an economist and son of an imam who later became a bank manager, was ethnically part Kurdish. In the beginning he appeared as a fresh breeze on the Turkish political scene. Turgut Özal formed a new right-of-center party, the *Anavatan Partisi* (ANAP), or Motherland Party. Motherland won 45 percent of the votes during the election of 1983. Özal, known as "Uncle Tonton" for his charisma and friendly attitude, served as the prime minister from 1983 to 1989 and as president between 1989 and 1993. Özal's regime brought a Western-oriented free market and other economic reforms along with deep corruption in the state and the business world. Turgut Özal's regime was a mixture of liberalism, religious dogma, and corruption. He created a class of corrupt, ultrarich society,

whose male members are still known as Turgut Özal's princes. His economic measures increased poverty.

Özal called his political rival Süleyman Demirel *statukocu*, meaning
a politician who protects the status quo. Özal described Demirel once:
"He gets puffed up like a rooster, but goes around like a turkey."

Turgut Özal's worst legacy was to push an old Islamic brotherhood
into the political arena and into the state itself. His mother, Hafize, had
been under the influence of religious teachers called *hocas*. She was an
ardent follower of the sheik of an Islamic sect based in Istanbul's conservative Fatih district, where the mosque named for Fatih (Conqueror)
Sultan Mehmet is located. This was the Nakshibendi (Nakshibendiya)
Sufi Order, the most powerful and largest Islamic brotherhood in Turkey.
The leaders of the Nakshibendi lodge used the Motherland Party, as a
vehicle to advance their causes. The leading Nakshibendi members of the
Motherland Party along with Turgut Özal, the party's leader, included
Özal's brother Korkut and some of Özal's cabinet members.

In Turkish history, as mentioned earlier, Sheik Said, the Kurdish rebel
during Kemal Atatürk's regime; Said Nursi, the founder of the Light sect;
and Dervish Mehmet, who, in December 1930, beheaded the secularist
officer and teacher Kubilay had all belonged to the Nakshibendi sect.
Mehmet Zeki Kotku was the mentor of Turgut Özal, and some members
of his family and Necmettin Erbakan. Kotku, of Caucasian origin, was an
influencial leader of the Nakshibendi Brotherhood. He died in November
1980, and the movement continued to grow under Professor Mahmud
Esad Coşan, his son-in-law.

Muhammed Bahaüddin Nakshibendi, the founder and sheik of the
Nakshibendi Brotherhood, was born in 1318 and lived in Bokhara, in
present-day Uzbekistan, until his death in 1389. He was called *an-
Nakshiband*, the painter. This Arabic-Farsi name was given to him
because of the way he had prescribed *dikir*, the ritual Muslim prayer. He
had said that the repetition of *dikir* should leave upon the heart the
impression of Allah. His *mürits*, or disciples, became known as
Nakshibendiya, followers of the painter. The followers of this orthodox
fraternity of Sufis or Muslim mystics are found in central Asia, China,

India, Pakistan, Malaysia, as well as other Muslim countries. The members of the sect believe that the lineage of *an-Nakshiband* extends back to Abu Bakr, the first caliph.

A photograph of Turgut Özal is displayed in the Nakshibendi Museum in Bokhara. Özal had visited the grave of the sheik and the Center of Nakshibendi when he was in Uzbekistan.

As a result of the appearance of the Motherland Party in the political arena, several members of the Nakshibendi sect and other Islamic orders and feudal chieftains or their representatives were elected into parliament.

During Özal's Motherland Party rule, leading Nakshibendi members, such as Vehbi Dinçerler, the minister of education, have played important roles in the government by lending a helping hand to Necmettin Erbakan's own efforts to change the secular face of Turkey. The teaching of Arabic, the language of the Qur'an, was added to school curricula and also *namaz*, the daily prayers. In parliament itself, and inside several state universities, mosques were constructed. The number of mosques in the country increased to 72,000 while the number of schools—even today—remained at 52,650.

The followers of the Nakshibendi religious order led the movement against the teaching of Charles Darwin's theory of evolution in primary and secondary schools. They played a leading role in banning beer advertisements on national radio and TV.

Necmettin Erbakan, meanwhile, after founding in 1983 his third Islamic party, the Refah Party, expanded his party's countrywide grass roots organization. Erbakan said, "The Welfare Party will bring the order of justice. If this is to be realized with bloodshed or not will be decided by the population. . . . You must work for the Welfare Party. If you don't, it means that you are a follower of the potato religion [something absurd]."

This time the Islamists appeared to be a disciplined lot with a determination to take over the power. While Welfare was using every means to strengthen its grassroots organization as the best electoral machine in the country, the secularist parties, resembling squabbling tribes with their mediocre leaders, still behaved as disorganized entities. The leaders of these parties were opportunistic individuals who lacked ideas to reform the system. They used Kemalism as an absolute dogma while abusing the pro-Islam card. At times it was difficult to form an opinion about their loyalty to the secular reforms. These politicians didn't want any change in the status quo, as they had chosen politics as a vehicle to enrich themselves and their own family members and supporters. If some of the Kemalist ideals were to be sacrificed for their ambitions, then so be it, was their attitude.

Their weakness was Welfare's opportunity. Welfare embraced the have-nots, winning 327 mayoralties during the municipal elections of March 27, 1994. These included victories in such major cities as Istanbul and Ankara. Some Welfare Party mayors kept the towns clean and, thanks to funds from Saudi Arabia, supplied electricity and food to the people at greatly reduced prices. Members of the Welfare Party delivered sacks of rice, macaroni, and bulgur free of charge to the homes of poor people. They listened to the complaints of people, and, unlike Marko Pasha, they tried to find solutions to these complaints. Thus Welfare was able to claim four million members in 1996. The trend of the Islamists to distribute free food to poor people continued. In 2003 the government of the Justice and Development Party, organized by the moderate leaders of the Welfare Party, gave every student needed school books free of charge and distributed sacks of free coal to the poor.

Welfare could have gained even greater support in 1994 and later if its political platform had not been solely Islamic fundamentalist and anti-secularist. This is where the party's biggest mistake was made and eventually brought the full force of the army and secularist elite against this Islamist movement. A moderate faction of the Islamists learned from this experience and even denied their Islamist roots to win a crucial election on November 3, 2002.

If the primary base for the Welfare Party's strength was the mosque with a strong emphasis on public morality and Islamic and Ottoman traditions, its seemingly caring attitude toward poor people was another. Thus, Welfare was able to win 21.3 percent of the votes in the parliamentary elections of December 1995, winning 158 seats in the 550-

member parliament. Another power base for the party was the mush-rooming growth of the religious imam-hatip schools, in which about 8 percent of 3.8 million middle and high school students were enrolled in 1996. The imam-cleric schools were later able to survive as high schools after their middle school classes were abolished because of pressure from the military.

In February 1997, a video shown during a meeting of the National Security Council in Ankara shocked the military brass. On the tape, students of a Qur'an school lined up to spit on the bust of Atatürk, vowing to fight against his atheism and to create a state based on the Shariah.

Necmettin Erbakan, who dreamed of an Islamic NATO, an Islamic union like the European Union with an Islamic currency, formed a government in July 1996. He was able to come to power for eleven months as the first Islamic premier in the history of the secular republic, all because of a marriage of convenience. It was Tansu Çiller, the leader of the True Path Party, a declared secularist, who made it possible for Erbakan to become the prime minister on June 28, 1996—despite the irony that the Islamists branded her when she was Turkey's first woman premier in 1993 as *Gavur Gelini*, the Bride of the Infidels. She had earlier publicly promised, "No coalition with the Islamic fundamentalists." She had said the Welfare Party "would bury the country in darkness."

Her ambition for power and her concern about a file that the Welfare Party allegedly kept on her were much greater than the danger from the fundamentalists. Çiller had cooperated with Erbakan in June 1996 in overthrowing her own coalition partner Mesut Yılmaz of the Motherland Party. She was concerned that her rival Yılmaz might form a coalition with Erbakan's Welfare Party, and she would be left outside the government. So Çiller moved fast to beat her rival in his own game and agreed with the Islamists to form a coalition. Erbakan was prime minister in this new coalition of strange bedfellows and Çiller the deputy premier and foreign minister.

Erbakan immediately caused grave concerns among the generals and the Kemalists with his pro-Islamic policies and his travels to Iran and Libya. He wanted to repeal laws forbidding female civil servants and students at public universities to wear the turban or Muslim headscarf. He tried to infiltrate the officer corps of the armed forces with graduates of imam-cleric schools, which he planned expanding even further. Protected by his own security agents, Erbakan carried on a systematic recruitment of loyal Welfare supporters for government jobs.

Erbakan had failed to understand in the 1990s that the Ottoman Empire, often harsh to its citizens as it collapsed, had left bad memories among the populations of its former nations. He visited Libya and was met with undiplomatic rudeness by Colonel Muammar al-Quaddafi, the Libyan dictator, who publicly criticized the way the Turks handled the Kurdish revolt. This shocked Erbakan and his close aides, for it was the first unexpected setback in their dreams of a revival of Ottoman glory.

Erbakan and his supporters also failed to understand that contrary to their beliefs, what had made the Ottoman Empire great had not been the strength of its Islamic religion but the leadership of enlightened sultans and grand viziers; a disciplined, powerful army; and the early Ottomans' advanced knowledge of warfare. The empire was great when it was ruled by brilliant leaders such as Fatih (Conqueror) Sultan Mehmet, his grandson Selim the Grim, and Selim's son Süleyman the Magnificent. Selim the Grim, known as Yavuz (inflexible), a military genius, had been the greatest general of the Ottoman Empire.

The potentially harmful acts of Necmettin Erbakan during his term as Islamic prime minister were his contacts with the Tunisian opposition leader Rashid al-Gannushi and other Arab opposition figures. He supported Egypt's Islamist opposition, the Muslim Brotherhood, and cultivated the Palestinian Hamas and Lebanon's Hezbollah groups. He neglected Turkey's ties with the West and the new Turkic republics of the Caucasus and central Asia.

Prime Minister Erbakan would travel around the country, laying foundations of various establishments that were soon forgotten and never completed. His public speeches were empty promises. As an industrialized nation, he claimed, Turkey would soon produce one hundred thousand tanks and one hundred thousand artillery pieces each year.

Soon the generals reacted and began to pressure the Islamic government. According to Yalım Erez, a former minister from the True Path Party who was close to Çiller, the military handed an ultimatum on February 20, 1996, to Çiller and Yılmaz regarding the Islamist government's policies. Both politicians panicked. They were concerned about a coup d'etat, yet both still wanted to be the next prime minister.

About a week later, on February 28, the military forced the political leaders in Ankara to sign a decree prohibiting the activities of all Islamic orders and brotherhoods. This meeting of the National Security Council (MGK), dominated by the military, was crucial in the later fall of Erbakan's Islamic regime. The signatories of the decree included President Süleyman Demirel, Deputy Prime Minister Tansu Çiller, and Mesut Yılmaz.

Necmettin Erbakan's government collapsed on June 18, 1997. The Islamists claimed that the pressures from the generals caused a post-modern coup d'etat. The Islamic orders and brotherhoods, however, remained intact. A crisis followed when Çiller wanted to be the next prime minister and Yılmaz refused to serve under a woman. President Demirel in June 1997 had to ask Yılmaz to form a government.

The Constitutional Court closed the Welfare Party on January 16, 1998, on charges of "acts against the secular principles of the republic." The court banned Erbakan and six other Welfare politicians from politics for five years, which ended in February 2003. Before the court order, moderate Welfare members were already planning to remove Erbakan from the party leadership. They disapproved of Erbakan's old-fashioned ways of conducting political business and his unrealistic views of the Islamic world.

While Erbakan and other Welfare members were being charged with a range of offenses, including incitement to hatred, a number of Welfare members of parliament joined a new party called the *Fazilet Partisi* (Virtue Party) in February 1998. This new Islamist party was formed without consultation with Erbakan, yet he still ended up directing Virtue behind the scenes.

The Virtue Party that replaced Welfare was watched daily by the public prosecutors and was short lived. The Constitutional Court banned it in June 2001 on charges of acts against the secular state. Its closure caused the Islamic movement to split into two parties. The progressives formed the *Adalet ve Kalkınma Partisi* (Justice and Development Party) under the leadership of Recep Tayyip Erdoğan. Erbakan's supporters, the traditionalists, named their party *Saadet* (Felicity) Party. About half of the 103 parliamentary deputies of the Virtue Party chose to join Felicity, and the others joined Justice and Development.

The Felicity Party remained steadfastly loyal to Erbakan's deep-rooted movement of fundamentalist Islam called *Milli Görüş*, or National View. Erbakan was elected leader of Felicity with 960 votes out of a total of 968. During a feast called the Night of Felicity, put on for the party youth organizations, a film of events in the Middle East was shown. The party followers booed the image of President George W. Bush and loudly applauded al-Qaeda leader Osama bin Laden and Iraq's then dictator Saddam Hussein.

Recep Tayyip Erdoğan, leader of the Justice and Development Party, in a dramatic change of heart, stated that his party would not challenge the secular regime and would focus on social welfare programs. He rejected the Islamist label and stated that his party would now follow a course of conservative democracy. This change was crucial in Erdoğan's later election victory, yet his past as an avowed Islamist has kept haunting him.

The public prosecutors and secular columnists fumed in April 2002 against Erdoğan because of a speech he had delivered on May 22, 1992. Erdoğan, in a locally televised speech at the Black Sea town of Rize, had criticized the Turkish army's handling of the Kurdish revolt and praised the Taliban of Afghanistan. The uproar was caused when his speech was retelevised. The secular press alleged that Recep Tayyip Erdoğan as mayor of Istanbul had enriched himself. The chief public prosecutor in Ankara began an investigation in May 2002 against Erdoğan on allegations of corruption. Prime Minister Ecevit said to the members of his party that Erdoğan's party was the "heir of an era of darkness."

Recep Tayyip Erdoğan's troubles mounted. The *Official Gazette* reported on April 19, 2002, that the Constitutional Court had barred forty-eight-year-old Erdoğan from holding a seat in parliament. Despite Erdoğan's recent overtures to the army, pro-secular talk, and support for Turkey's European Union candidacy, the court's decision came as a blow to Erdoğan's hopes of becoming Turkey's next premier. The decision was made, the *Official Gazette* said, because of Erdoğan's ten-month prison sentence under article 312 of the penal code for using religion for political gains. This "decision" didn't work against Erdoğan's determination to become the next prime minister and the support he got from the pro-Islam voters.

Jailing of people for their political views, however, was easy for most of the Turkish governments, yet controlling the jails was not.

29

The Operation Jailhouse and Marxist Terrorism

If one eye is crying, the other eye can't be laughing.

Turkish proverb

*S*ince childhood, we all knew that the Turkish prisons were dreadful places to be locked up. Beatings of the inmates by the guards and torture and rape were known to be beyond the state's control. Things got even worst later. For ten years (until the beginning of 2001), Marxist terrorist organizations, gangsters, and scoundrels ran the Turkish prisons. Inmates used smuggled cell phones in the jails to coordinate hostage takings and riots outside and inside the prisons.

The inability of the state to control its prisons became apparent in December 2000. Bülent Ecevit's coalition government was forced to postpone a plan to move prisoners, who were living in large communal wards of old prisons, to newly built, modern type F jails with individual cells. Over two thousand inmates, supported by their relatives and friends outside the jails, refused to move. According to Hikmet Sami Türk, then the justice minister, 1,656 mostly militant Marxist prisoners, claiming that in smaller cells they would be subject to torture, had been on a hunger strike called the *Ölüm Orucu* (Death Fast) for almost two months.

Military troops stormed twenty prisons throughout the country on December 19, 2000, to force the Marxist inmates, some of them convicted PKK terrorists, to end their hunger strike. Their leftist supporters and relatives continued the protest outside with their own hunger strikes, and 107 convicts died of starvation.

During the raids, called Operation Return to Life, it was officially announced that thirty prisoners died. Two paramilitary officers were killed, and 131 other prisoners were injured. In one prison, inmates fired an AK-47 Kalashnikov assault weapon at the soldiers. The security officials used sledgehammers on the roof of one prison to enter the wards. In other prisons, the soldiers used bulldozers to break holes in the thick prison walls and were met with guns, gas bombs, and flame-throwers made of pipes attached to gas canisters. Soldiers reported that Marxist inmates were setting fire to their own comrades as a publicity ploy. In Istanbul's Bayrampaşa prison, the authorities captured one AK-47 Kalashnikov rifle, several pistols, knives, and ammunition. The inmates also used crossbows and arrows tipped with syringe needles. Following the operation, which lasted four days, Sadettin Tantan, the interior minister, said, "This operation cleaned up a disgrace in our state."

Earlier an amnesty approved by parliament had pardoned almost half of the common criminals of a total of seventy-five thousand prisoners but had ignored nonviolent political convicts. One notable exception was the Islamist ex-premier Necmettin Erbakan, who was saved from serving a one-year jail sentence for "provoking hatred." No quarter was given to Abdullah Öcalan, the jailed leader of the PKK. The amnesty was the result of political horse-trading between the governing parties and the Islamist opposition, but only 23 percent of the population supported it. The amnesty tried to ease prison overcrowding but brought more violence into the streets.

Prime Minister Bülent Ecevit declared that his conscience was clear regarding the amnesty. His wife, Rahşan Ecevit, had initiated the amnesty for prison inmates. She was not pleased with it: "This is not what I wanted. I wanted the boys who stole baklava to go free." She was blamed for the much-criticized prison amnesty that freed forty thousand convicts in two years.

As a result of the raids on the prisons, the radical leftist organs started a bombing campaign in revenge, killing and injuring innocent bystanders and policemen. Most of the radical leftist inmates belonged to the *Devrimci Halk Kurtuluş Partisi-Cephesi*, or Revolutionary People's Liberation Party-Front (DHKP-C), whose members assassinated a number of policemen, army generals, and other government officials. The DHKP-C, an urban guerrilla group, is the former Revolutionary Left (*Dev Sol*) organization formed in 1970 following the assembly of *Dev-Genç*, Revolutionary Youth. It changed its name to DHKP-C in 1994 and aims to subvert the constitutional order to establish a Marxist-Leninist regime.

Through the years, the DHKP-C has targeted military and diplomatic missions of the United States, committing fifty-three murders. The attacks of DHKP-C injured 193 other people; among others, they killed Andrew Blake, a British insurance agent, and Turkish businessman Özdemir Sabancı and bombed the US Consulate in Istanbul. Dursun Karataş, the leader of DHKP-C, known as the Left Hand of Darkness, directed terrorist operations in Turkey from his base in Netherlands. Karataş, an expert in disguise, has served a prison term and escaped from a Turkish jail.

The DHKP-C is the largest of Turkey's several far-left militant factions. The leaders of the DHKP-C used the large communal dormitories in Bayrampaşa jail in Istanbul as a center to direct terrorist operations throughout Turkey with cell phones, relying partly on financing from their supporters in Europe. The DHKP-C is active in England, the Netherlands, France, Belgium, Germany, Greece, and Syria and was allowed to operate freely in the Netherlands and Belgium to direct terrorist operations in Turkey.

According to the Turkish foreign ministry, a senior Dutch foreign ministry official and the mayor of Rotterdam received members of the DHKP-C and held a news conference with them. For years the Belgian government allowed this outlawed terror network to operate a center in

Brussels. Fehriye Erdal, a female member of the DHKP-C who was allegedly involved in the murder of businessman Özdemir Sabancı, openly lived in Belgium despite international arrest warrants against her.

Finally, the September 11th terror attacks in New York and Washington served as a wakeup call for the members of the European Union. The EU decided only in May 2002 that both the PKK and the DHKP-C are actually terrorist organizations and listed them as such.

In December 2000, the members of DHKP-C killed two policemen and injured twelve during a machinegun ambush in Istanbul. The shooting of the policemen caused four thousand members of the *Çevik Kuvvet*, or riot police, to demonstrate in Istanbul for the first time in the secular republic's history. The policemen raised their hands with guns and shouted, "*Kana kan intikam*" ("Blood for blood, revenge"), and religious slogans. They booed their commanders and called on the government of Bülent Ecevit to resign. The policemen protested that they were fighting terrorists armed with AK-47 Kalashnikov rifles with locally made Kırıkkale pistols. Their wages also were a subject of protest.

Such nightmares as the Times of Chaos, terrorism by Marxist-Leninist organs or militant Islam, and the Kurdish revolt haunt the conscience of the Turkish nation. The Times of Chaos brought about the third coup d'etat in the secular republic's history in 1980. Martial law courts then sent fifty militants, mostly young university students, to the gallows. The struggle between the far-left and extreme right still shows no sign of ending. On May 31, 2000, a state security court in Izmir, in western Turkey, sentenced six far-left militants to death. The court found them guilty of killing one soldier and severely wounding another while fighting security forces two years earlier in Denizli province. The militants were members of the DHKP-C. Although the sentence for the accused in Izmir was death by hanging, no one has actually been hanged in Turkey since 1984. The memory of the hanging of a high school senior still lingers hauntingly in the Turkish conscience.

His name was Erdal Eren, and he was the eighteen-year-old son of an elementary school teacher who had joined an outlawed left-wing militant group the Patriotic Revolutionary Youth. He was sentenced to death by a martial law court on charges of killing a soldier during a clash between leftist militants and security forces. The boy was hanged on December 13, 1980. Nihat Toktay, his lawyer, is still haunted by this hanging he had witnessed. "I was a young man then," he told the Associated Press. "My hair went gray overnight."

The terror of the militant Marxist-Leninists and the Kurdish separatist movement, along with the terror from the Islamic reactionaries, jointly create a nightmare for the Turkish nation. The neglect of continuing Atatürk's secularist reform movement by also reforming its ideals in accordance with the times played a crucial role in this nightmare. A national identity crisis developed, I believe, for one basic reason. A lot of Turks have never known or understood the history of the reform years of the 1920s and 1930s. A bitter controversy over a piece of cloth, the turban, proved that the ideals of these Kemalist reforms have not touched many people, nor were these reforms accepted by them.

30

A Crisis over the Turban and Islamist Terror

Our biggest sin is a veil covering our faces and a chador on our back.

The writer Aka Gündüz

The word *tesettür* is Arabic, and it means to conceal or to cover up. The religious understanding of this word has for centuries caused the enslavement of the Muslim woman. The harem is the ultimate objective of *tesettür*. The word *harem* comes from the Arabic *haram*, meaning forbidden or unlawful to male visitors. Harem represented the women's secluded quarters in a household. Male guests were received only in the *selamlık*, the place of salutations, or quarters reserved for men.

I remember a story about Mehmet Fuad Pasha (1815–69), who served as Ottoman minister of foreign affairs five times and twice as grand vizier relative to the sensitivity of this subject. He had studied in France and spoke excellent French.

One evening, Mehmet Fuad Pasha, who was one of the architects of the Tanzimat reforms, had invited the foreign ambassadors and their wives to a party in his Istanbul palace. The party was being held in the *selamlık* of the household while the ambassadors' wives visited the harem. One of the ambassadors, ignorant about the Turkish customs, expressed his desire to also visit the harem. Mehmet Fuad Pasha told him: "Mr. Ambassador, you are accredited to the Sublime Porte, not to my household."

When a Muslim woman accepts *tesettür* as a way of life, she conceals herself from the eyes of men other than her husband or close male relatives. She wears the shape-concealing *chador*, or long coat that covers the ankles even in the heat of summer, or the turban to hide her hair and her neck from the prying eyes of men. She never shakes hands with a male stranger because handshaking involves physical touch. Radical Islamists consider that women who show even a little of their hair, throats, legs, and body shape in public are morally unfit for matrimony. Such women are considered candidates for the hellfire in the next world.

Adopted from the Arabs and Iranians by the Ottomans as an Islamic tradition, the way of life promoted by *tesettür* was abolished by the reforms of Kemal Atatürk. It has returned with the revival of the Islamic movement as a challenge to the secularity of the Turkish state. I believe that the election victory on November 3, 2002, of the Justice and Development Party, with its Islamic roots, finally caused *tesettür* to take over the Turkish secular state. The turban became the untouchable symbol of the Islamists' *tesettür* movement. The Islamists believe that the fight for the turban is the fight for the survival of Islam. If the turban goes, so does the religion, they believe.

Prime Minister Mesut Yılmaz, bowing to pressures from the Islamic reactionaries, on March 2, 1998, backed off from an earlier decision to enforce a ban on the turban in public schools and universities. Thousands of university students protested the enforcement of the ban. Even some members of Yılmaz's Motherland Party supported the protesters. Following a cabinet meeting, Yılmaz backed off and announced that his decision was made as a sign of respect for customs and traditions. He said, "Girls will neither be forced to cover nor to uncover their heads."

The turban issue has become a damaging fundamental conflict in modern Turkish history. The issue flared up in April 1999, when Merve Kavakcı, a thirty-year-old Islamist Virtue Party member elected to parliament, decided to attend the oath-taking ceremony while wearing a turban. The National Security Council, then dominated by the military, had warned her not to do it, reasoning that the turban was contrary to the article on secularism contained in the oath, during which the deputies one by one pledge their allegiance to the "secular republic" and the "principles and reforms of Atatürk."

Hard-core secular Turkish leaders, especially the army generals, had been warning against full political freedom in the country for years. They were concerned that full political freedom would help the subversive doctrines of Islamic fundamentalists, Kurdish separatists, and militant Marxists.

Merve Kavakcı did indeed appear in parliament wearing a turban and wreaked havoc during the opening session on Sunday, May 2, 1999. She was greeted with cries of "Get out" from the members of Prime Minister Bülent Ecevit's Democratic Left Party, while the majority of the conservative deputies sat in awkward silence. The session was adjourned, and Kavakcı did not return later to participate in the oath-taking ceremony. Ecevit said, "This is the supreme foundation of the state. . . . It is not a place in which to challenge the state."

Thousands of Islamists clashed with the police in the central Anatolian town of Malatya when Vural Savaş, the chief prosecutor, sought to ban the Virtue Party. Over two hundred demonstrators ended up in court, facing a one-year jail sentence for breaking the law.

Malatya is a town whose people had changed their political loyalty repeatedly since the violent 1970s, when they had favored the Marxist-Leninist movement. When Turgut Özal, the late prime minister and president, implemented a program in the 1980s for economic reforms, lifted exchange controls, and supported increased rights for the Kurdish minority, the folks in Malatya shifted to the right. Besides, Turgut Özal, leader of the Motherland Party, was their native son born there in 1927. In 1995, the electorate in Malatya voted overwhelmingly for the Islamist Welfare Party. Four years later, the ballots in Malatya were filled with the votes for Nationalist Action, the party founded by the ultranationalist and pan-Turanist Colonel Alparslan Türkeş.

In June 1999, the young people of Malatya, including some women, became defenders of the turban. Right after Friday prayers at a mosque in town, they threw stones at the local policemen and fought them with sharpened sticks. They were angry with the dean of the local university, a retired army officer. He had earlier refused to allow female students wearing turbans to sit for their final exams.

Since my own days in elementary school early in the 1930s, while we sang the songs of the secular reforms, *başörtüsü*, or the ordinary women's headscarf ,was always present in our lives at home or in the streets of Anatolia. It never disappeared from the countryside or from the big cities, and women felt free to wear it anywhere. The wearing of the headscarf was never against the law. However, its use then was not meant to show support for an Islamic reactionary movement or as a reactionary statement against the secular government and its institutions. In addition, it didn't look like a turban. The turban the Islamic reactionaries adopted is a copy of the *hicab* of the Arab or Iranian women that covers the head, neck, and shoulders completely.

The Muslim headscarf crisis was deliberately started by Necmettin Erbakan and his hard-line Islamic supporters in the Virtue Party for the purpose of forcing the fundamentalist movement into the heart of the secular state, the schools and universities, and the offices of government and parliament. It is believed that only about seven thousand of over six hundred thousand female university students are turban wearers. It seemed as if the Turks, forgetting about their more serious problems, were needlessly fighting over a piece of cloth.

The last straw came when the newspapers reported that Merve Kavakcı had described her work in pro-Islamic conferences abroad as jihad, or holy war, and that she was a citizen of the United States. Because she had acquired US citizenship without prior permission from the Turkish government, as required by law, she was stripped of her Turkish citizenship. That was the end of her membership in parliament.

Prime Minister Bülent Ecevit, speaking about the case, accused Iran of promoting radical Islam in Turkey as well as backing Kurdish rebels. Vural Savaş, the chief public prosecutor, charged that the Virtue Party was trying to overthrow the country's secular constitution and replace it with

Shariah. Shortly before the Virtue Party was closed, Vural Savaş said, "Like blood-sucking vampires, they are exploiting religion." The prosecutor added that Virtue was not only the continuation of the Welfare Party. It was, he said, the continuation of all three of Erbakan's Islamic parties banned since 1971. The prosecutor described Virtue as "a malignant tumor that has metastasized." Vural Savaş likened the leaders of the Islamic party to vampires roaming the countryside and gorging on political ignorance. Despite the top appeals court's recommendation that the arch secularist Vural Savaş should stay on as chief public prosecutor, President Necdet Sezer replaced him on December 18, 2000, with Sabih Kanadoğlu.

The revival of the Islamic reactionary movement has dramatically changed the public appearance, even in the cities, where secularity had long been established. A new breed of scoundrels sprang up, all claiming to be the *Mahdi*, or Muslim messiah. These false messiahs proclaimed to have special powers to deliver the faithful. Some of them immigrated to European countries like Germany in order to abuse the religious feelings of Turkish guest workers there in outrageous get-rich-quick schemes.

The turban controversy kept on raising its covered head in Turkish affairs. In June 2000, a Turkish court sentenced a university student to six months in prison for wearing the turban to her exams. The sentence was commuted to a $3 fine. A student in January 2000 stabbed Professor Zekeriya Beyaz, the theology dean of Marmara University, near Istanbul, for his defense of the turban ban. The student, Halil Civan, later received a jail sentence of over eleven years.

A statement by Mesut Yılmaz while prime minister during the first Muslim headscarves conflict in 1998 signalled his political ambitions. Yılmaz was hoping to attract moderate Islamists into his conservative Motherland Party. His policies failed, and the turban controversy soon reached the highest offices of the Turkish state as a protest against the secular Kemalist reforms.

The involvement of the Islamic religion in politics and the affairs of the state are contrary to the principles set by Kemal Atatürk. In the 1920s, Atatürk ordered women to discard their *çarşaf*, or chador and not to wear a veil and the men to give up their fezzes. Ah, the fezzes, those Islamic symbols! So many men were sentenced to hang by special courts set up by the regime. Indeed, some did end up on the gallows for refusing to abandon their fezzes and for armed resistance to the reforms. Others were jailed for two to ten years. There were riots in Anatolian towns against the new dress code when mobs defiantly wearing fezzes killed secularists and unfurled the green flag of Islam, chanting slogans against the "infidel officials," the "heathens," and the "Godless regime."

The *Irtica*, Islamic reaction, and the *mürteci*, Islamic reactionary, considered the secular reforms of my childhood as the works of the *gavur* or *kafir*, or non-Muslim infidel. The Islamic reactionary also considered the *şapka*, or rimmed European hat, which had replaced the fez, a characteristic of the infidel. If he wore it, then he would also become an infidel. To the Islamic reactionary, writing Turkish in the Latin alphabet instead of the Arabic script of the Qur'an also appeared to be the work of the infidel.

All of these reactions were not for the sake of religion, for religion had been free during the Ottoman Empire and remained free after the establishment of the secular republic. The mosques never closed, and nobody prohibited Muslim ritual worship, or *oruç*, the religious fast. The strict rules were not against religious belief or the practice of religion but against the reimposition of a government based on the Canon Law.

The Islamic religion and the rules of the Shariah were used throughout Turkish history for political games, often causing violence. The danger from radical Islam, however, alarmed even the old-guard political leaders in recent years, who had abused Islam themselves in the past (and still do so to win votes). Süleyman Demirel, whose Justice and True Path parties had encouraged the Islamic religion in the past, warned of dangers from radical Islamists infiltrating the judiciary, police, civil service, and even the army. He was president of the country when he issued this warning. Such warnings came too late, for the Islamists had already turned the corner. In other words, the thief who stole the horse had long passed Üsküdar (a district on the shores of the Bosphorus) in the Turkish equivalent of trying to close the barn door after the horse had gone. The old-guard politicians, the oligarchic leaders of the tired old elite, were right to be alarmed.

Enver Çoban, prosecutor of the State Security Court in Istanbul, demanded on August 2, 1999, long-term jail sentences for nine Islamists accused of having links with the armed wing of IBDA-C, the Great Islamic Eastern Raiders Front. This Islamic terror organization, like Hizbullah (the Party of God) and *Islami Hareket* (Islamic Action), aims to replace secularism with the Shariah and is responsible for a number of bomb attacks.

On October 21, 1999, Ahmet Taner Kışlalı, a sixty-year-old prominent academic and columnist for *Cumhuriyet*, died of injuries from a bomb placed under the hood of his car. He was a former minister of culture. Kışlalı was targeted by radical Islamic militants for his attacks on political Islam and his pro-secular articles in *Cumhuriyet*. During his funeral, the armed forces, well represented at the ceremony, were praised and applauded. The politicians were targets of hostile slogans and were called members of the political mafia. The killing of Kışlalı angered the officers of the armed forces, who, a week later, during the seventy-sixth anniversary of the republic's founding, were present in force at the ceremonies at the Atatürk mausoleum in Ankara. The explosion of a pipe bomb near the administration building of the Marmara University near Istanbul the same day renewed fears that the radical Islamists were getting still bolder. The Great Islamic Eastern Raiders-Front (IBDA-C) claimed responsibility for the bombing.

The danger from the terror of religious fundamentalism is universal, as we have witnessed with the Taliban of Afghanistan and Osama bin Laden's al-Qaeda network. In 1998, the Turkish authorities thwarted an Islamic reactionary plot to crash a plane loaded with explosives into Kemal Atatürk's mausoleum in Ankara. The bombing was to take place during the seventy-fifth anniversary of the republic, when thousands of people paid their respects at the mausoleum. Three years later, on September 11, 2001, hijackers in Osama bin Laden's al-Qaeda terrorist organization used the same tactic with airliners to attack the World Trade Center and the Pentagon.

The man who plotted the bomb attack at the mausoleum in 1998 was Metin Kaplan, the leader of the militant Caliphate State (*Kalifatstaat*) group based in Cologne, Germany. The Caliphate State, as its name shows, aims to overthrow of Turkey's secular government to form a state based on Islam. Kaplan later served a jail term in Germany for incitement to kill a rival cleric and in 2004 deported to Turkey. The German government banned Caliphate State in 2001 in an effort to stop its extremist activities. The Federal Constitutional Court in Karlsruhe ruled in October 2003 that the militant Caliphate State was a threat to democracy. According to the German investigators, some members of the Caliphate State traveled from Germany to Afghanistan in 1996 and 1997 to meet with the supporters of Osama bin Laden. It is highly possible that during these visits, crashing a plane laden with bombs to Atatürk's mausoleum or into high-rise buildings may have been discussed within the al-Qaeda organization.

The European countries' attitude toward the activities of suspected terrorists before and even after September 11 is a shameful lesson in history. Let's consider the case of the Caliphate State, which was active in Germany despite repeated warnings and calls from the Turkish authorities for Metin Kaplan's extradition to Turkey on charges of serious crimes committed in that country.

Metin Kaplan is the son of Cemaleddin Kaplan, who supported Islamist Necmettin Erbakan's fundamentalist *Milli Görüş* (National View) politics. Cemaleddin was known as the Voice of Darkness because of his fiery sermons against the United States and Western values. After the coup d'etat in 1980, he moved to Germany and was accepted there as a political refugee. His and his son's eleven-hundred-member Islamist Caliphate State organization collected donations from the Turkish guest workers. When his father died in 1995, Metin Kaplan took over.

Metin lacked his father's powerful preaching prowess, yet he adopted his father's name, the Voice of Darkness, and added a new one—the Caliph of Cologne. He had grandiose dreams of world domination by Islam, and he agitated his disciples against Western society and in his sermons praised the September 11 attack. Still, convoluted German laws protected him. He was even paid 170,000 euros by the German government as social assistance. Now the German government wants this money back. When he was extradited to Istanbul in a private jet leased by the

German authorities for his security, he was taken to court. There, appearing without his usual turban, Metin Kaplan refused to stand up in court, complaining about his weak knees. He was promptly sent to prison pending trial on charges of crimes committed earlier, including the planned attack on Atatürk's mausoleum.

In a democracy, wearing a turban is considered to be a matter of personal choice. In Turkey the turban is used as a form of protest by a reactionary movement, supported for years by Saudi Arabia and Iran. As the Islamic movement grew, it has left impressive marks even on those politicians who claim to be secularists and Kemalists.

Kemal Atatürk's left-of-center reformist Republican People's Party has strayed even from its historic mission. This party, now with aging membership, follows a strange political dogma of nationalism and leftism mixed with a trend toward pro-Islam. Deniz Baykal, the party's leader said in a statement to *Milliyet* before the November 3, 2002, election, "I also want votes from the people who wear turbans." During a trip earlier to the town of Kırıkkale, Baykal visited the shrine of a holy man named Hasandede and prayed. He then declared that Turkey is a bewildered country because it has lost its compass and bearings. Others now consider the Republican People's Party as an ineffective opposition that lacks the determination to protect the secular reforms.

I remember that years ago Ismet Inönü, as the leader of the Republican People's Party, was urged by his aides to say something about God or just mention the word *Allah* in his speeches. The Republicans in opposition were struggling against Adnan Menderes's Democratic Party, which used Islamic religion for political support. Inönü's response was *Allahaısmarladık*, which is the Turkish word for Godspeed—meaning "goodbye." This is the problem in Turkey, where democratic values and human rights directly clash with religious freedom, when this religious freedom is under ruthless abuse and exploitation by the merchants of Islam.

In June 1999, the media in Turkey showed videos alleged to have originated from sixty-two-year-old Fethullah Gülen, the leader of *Nur*, the Light sect. Fethullah Gülen was allegedly urging his followers on these tapes to infiltrate the government and the armed forces and to wait for the opportune moment to take over. His sect controls an international network of businesses, a newspaper, a TV station, and scores of religious schools in Turkey, the Balkans, and central Asia, where classes are in English and Turkish. In Kazakstan, Gülen's Nur sect runs several high schools and one university. In a statement published in *Zaman*, the Istanbul newspaper he controls, Gülen denied the charges that he was planning to overthrow the secularist state.

Still, in order to reduce the influence of the Nur sect in Central Asia, Turkish president Necdet Sezer discussed with the leaders of Kazakstan and Uzbekistan the possibility of Turkey opening Anatolian high and technical schools in those countries.

Mainstream politicians and secular political parties have been courting Gülen's Nur sect for years for election gains. This was despite the warnings from the secularists and the generals that duplicitous radical Islamic movements are planning an Iranian-style Islamic revolution to destroy the secularist principles. The preacher is known to have close ties with leading political parties and politicians. Bülent Ecevit, has praised him for funding schools. Tansu Çiller, Mesut Yılmaz, Bülent Ecevit and Turgut Özal all received Gülen during their terms as prime ministers.

Fethullah Gülen was born in 1941, three years after Kemal Atatürk's death, in Korucuk a village in Erzurum province in eastern Anatolia. His father, Ramiz, was the imam of the village of Alvar, and Ramiz taught his son Arabic. Gülen, by the age of ten, had memorized the Qur'an and thus had become *hafız* or *hafez*. He left the regular elementary school after two and half years and attended a *medrese*, a religious school. At the age of fourteen, Gülen began giving *vaaz*, or sermons, in village mosques. His Arabic name *Fethullah* means conqueror for Allah. In 1971 the preacher got into trouble with the military regime and was arrested and jailed.

According to his Web site, http://m-fgulen.org, based in Perrineville, New Jersey, Gülen has been living in the United States since 1999 to receive medical care for his diabetes and heart problems. After an investigation into his organizations and companies, the State Security Court in Ankara tried Gülen in absentia in October 2000. An arrest warrant was issued in Turkey on charges of trying to overthrow the secular regime and to replace it with one ruled by the Shariah. Again, in January 19, 2003, Hamza Keleş, the prosecutor of the State Security Court in Ankara, asked for a jail sentence between five to ten years for Gülen. An amnesty helped to postpone the trial for five years on condition that Gülen does not violate any laws during the duration.

The pashas are Gülen's powerful enemies. General Hilmi Özkök, while he was the commander of the land forces, warned that the slightest concession to political Islam would return the country to the "darkness of the Middle Ages." General Hüseyin Kıvrıkoğlu, while he was the chief of general staff, said that thousands of militant Islamists were working to destroy the secular state: "They have infiltrated everything," and he added that eleven of the forty-six officers recently purged from the military were Gülen's followers.

Nuh Mete Yüksel, the prosecutor of the State Security Court in Ankara, said that Fethullah Gülen infiltrated his supporters into the ranks of the police and the ministry of education: "Gülen's aim is to establish a theocratic Islamic dictatorship and to put the Islamic orders in a position to take over the state." He said that the preacher's public statements were a tactic to cover his true goal.

This prosecutor was soon in trouble. In the fall of 2002, Nuh Mete Yüksel was involved in a sex scandal described by some observers as a "honey trap." Several videos showing the prosecutor having sex with a woman were distributed, and Yüksel was removed from his position. The prosecutor claimed he was a victim of a conspiracy aiming to ruin his reputation.

Three years earlier, on Sunday, October 17, 1999, the radical Islamists exploded a small bomb inside the Istanbul bookstore of the Department of Religious Affairs, which they fervently oppose. The outlawed urban guerrilla group Great Islamic Eastern Raiders-Front (IBDA-C) claimed responsibility. Members of the group left a sign saying, "Oh, Allah, the avenger, 7.4 was not enough." The sign referred to the August 17, 1999, earthquake in northwestern Turkey, which had killed over seventeen thousand people. The earthquake's strength was a powerful 7.4 on the Richter scale. According to the terrorist group, the earthquake was a divine punishment for the military. They claimed that the military leaders had drawn up a plan at the Gölcük naval base to topple the Islamic government of Necmettin Erbakan on June 18, 1997. The base was devastated during the earthquake, and hundreds of officers and sailors were killed.

The bombing of the bookstore happened a week after public prosecutors began investigating Mehmet Kutlular, a leader of the Light sect. (The sect's name, *Nur*, is derived from Said Nursi, the founder's name, which means shining light or sparkling brightness. Followers of this sect are known as *Nurcu*.) In a mosque in Ankara, Kutlular allegedly said that the earthquake was a divine retribution for the clampdown on the Islamic movement. Kutlular, the owner of the *Yeni Asya* (*New Asia*) newspaper, published in Istanbul, claimed that the generals had met at Gölcük naval base before issuing orders to start their campaign to topple Necmettin Erbakan's Islamist government. Kutlular was charged with "provoking hatred among the people."

During a mosque meeting to commemorate the thirty-ninth anniversary of the death of the sect's founder, Said Nursi, booklets with the title "Holy Warning: Earthquake" were distributed. On May 10, 2000, Kutlular was convicted by the State Security Court in Ankara for inciting religious hatred and sentenced to two years and one day in prison. When Kutlular was jailed, *Yeni Asya* declared, "Thought Is Now Jailed." During a second trial in Ankara, on April 10, 2002, Kutlular was acquitted due to recent changes in article 312 of the Turkish Penal Code.

Despite the clampdown on Islamic brotherhoods during the secular reform years, most of them survived after Turkey became a republic in 1923. They remained underground until pro-Islam politics caused a religious revival and the Islamic sects reemerged with a vengeance. A newer Islamic order that was founded much later caused a terrible shock to secular Turks. Its name was Hizbullah, the Party of Allah, and it left a violent and bloody mark on Turkey's recent history.

31

The Party of God, the Party of Terror

He owes only one debt to Allah, his life.

Turkish proverb

In October 1999, ninety-two radical Islamic guerrillas were arrested at Diyarbakır, in southeastern Anatolia. The armed militants belonged to Hizbullah (Hezbollah in Arabic, meaning the Party of God), a Kurdish radical Islamic guerrilla organization. Hizbullah is blamed for violent murders, kidnappings, and bomb attacks. Hizbullah aimed to establish an Iranian-style state in Turkey based on the Shariah.

Hizbullah abducted ten Kurdish businessmen in Istanbul and tortured and killed all of them after cleaning out their bank accounts. In January 2000, security forces found the victims' decomposing bodies buried in the garden of a house in Istanbul. The terrorists had planted onions to disguise the smell of decay. Some of the bodies had broken bones, and a masonry nail had been driven into one victim's head. During a shootout between the Hizbullah guerrillas and security forces, Hüseyin Velioğlu, the group's leader, who had recently arrived in Istanbul from Iran, was killed and two guerrillas were captured.

In Ankara three more bodies were found, while three men and two women terrorists were captured with explosives. Six bodies were found buried near Tarsus on the Mediterranean coast and twelve more in Konya, central Anatolia. The Islamic militants had used Konya as their interrogation center for the kidnap victims. It is believed that Hizbullah kidnapped hundreds of people, tortured all, and buried some of them alive. In a crackdown on Hizbullah, more than one thousand people were arrested. Thirteen of them were charged for the murders of 156 people. There are allegations that the Turkish security forces used and supported the Hizbullah for a time during the Kurdish uprising in order to kill the rebels.

One of the victims of this Islamic terror group was Konca Kuris, a Muslim feminist. The mother of five children, Konca Kuris had joined a religious sect as a young woman but quit when the sect's leaders ordered her to wash their laundry. She traveled to Iran with a Hizbullah delegation, where she was confronted with the Islamic regime's treatment of women. Hizbullah, too, supported the Iranian brand of Islam that was hostile to women.

In her writings and lectures, Konca Kuris asserted that male religious figures over the centuries had distorted the essence of the Qur'an in depriving women of their rights. She challenged the view of the religious orthodoxy that women ought to cover their hair and neck with a turban and attend schools for girls only. Kuris urged that public prayers should not be offered in Arabic but in Turkish.

In July 1998, she was kidnapped in front of her home in Mersin on the eastern Mediterranean coast. In January 2000, her burned and disfigured remains were exhumed in Konya, 220 miles northwest of Mersin. Police found a video showing how she had been tortured. Kuris was thirty-eight years old when she was murdered.

More surprise was in store when police arrested a suspected militant who was employed as a computer analyst at the prime ministry. The man had access to all transportation logistics of the prime minister and other senior civil servants.

The office of Prime Minister Bülent Ecevit stated in July 2000 that

118 teachers, sixty-nine Muslim preachers, and 201 judges, doctors, and engineers were under arrest in connection with the murders committed by Hizbullah. They were still on the state payroll. The statement added that light disciplinary punishment let them continue their work and thus weakened the government's efforts to fight radical Islam.

Five policemen were killed and six were wounded in two shootouts with the Hizbullah guerrillas in the eastern city of Van in February 2000. Five Islamic militants were shot dead. Officials said that the militants hurled grenades at the police and opened fire with automatic rifles. According to Sadettin Tantan, the interior minister at the time, the policemen were killed because they hesitated when the guerrillas used women and children as shields.

In November 2000, when security forces raided a Hizbullah depot in Cizre, southeast Anatolia, they were shocked to find a large amount of advanced weaponry. There were antitank rockets and mines and AK-47 Kalashnikov rifles.

Discoveries of corpses of people Hizbullah had murdered continued for several years. Mehmet Salih Kolge, a senior commander of the terrorist group and known as the Butcher of Hizbullah, was captured in April 2002 in Diyarbakır. He confessed that he had personally murdered twelve people and that the Islamist radicals had killed many more. The security forces excavated a roadside near Gaziantep and recovered three bodies.

Strangely, one victim of the Islamic terrorists was a sixty-three-year-old Muslim cleric in the eastern city of Van. He was killed for refusing the Hizbullah's demand to hand over the keys to his mosque.

Hizbullah is a specter of Turkey's recent history that has returned to haunt the conscience of the state. This monstrosity was allegedly created by the state in the 1980s and the 1990s as an anti-Communist force to fight the Marxist terrorists of the Kurdistan Workers Party. The Hizbullah violence caused angry responses from the commentators who reminded the state of the old saying: "You reap what you have sown." After dozens of bodies were dug up, Güngör Mengi wrote in *Sabah* that the state now is "in a position of being the target of the Frankenstein monster it has created."

"The state does not commit murders or order murders to be carried out," President Süleyman Demirel claimed. "There may be forces belonging to the state that act illegitimately, but in that case, they are committing a crime."

The discovery of gruesomely tortured bodies of Hizbullah victims and a crackdown on this religious terror group caused a scandal involving the government itself. Newspapers have charged that Prime Minister Tansu Çiller in the mid-1990s authorized officials in southeastern Anatolia to hand out weapons to terror groups that opposed the Kurdish revolt. The issue was a cache of missing weapons, including 443 automatic rifles, 115 rocket-propelled bombs, and 1,450 hand grenades sent by the government to the governor of Batman province in eastern Anatolia. According to the newspapers, many of those weapons were given to the Hizbullah.

In May 2000, Justice Minister Hikmet Sami Turk said that a shoot-out earlier in the year with Islamic terrorists had aided the police in solving the murder of investigative journalist Uğur Mumcu. Mumcu, a lead-writer for *Cumhuriyet*, had a reputation for attacking the influence of the Islamic fundamentalists and their close links with the political establishment. Mumcu also made enemies by exposing links between Mafia gangs, state officials, and politicians. The militants involved in Mumcu's murder were members of secret Islamic terror organizations called *Tevhidi-selam* (Arabic words that mean Greetings for Unification) and the Jerusalem Warriors, which is linked to Hizbullah. They had confessed to receiving support from Iranian sources.

I knew Uğur Mumcu during the 1960s, when he was an investigative reporter for *Cumhuriyet*. He was young, handsome, and a dedicated leftist then, highly serious about his work.

Milliyet reported in May 2000 that three Islamic militants confessed to the police that they had supplied two Iranians with C4 explosives. The suspects claimed that the Iranians planted the bomb under Uğur Mumcu's car. In September 2000, the investigation led to the arrest of a suspect named Rüştü Aytufan, who confessed that he had planted the bomb that killed Journalist Ahmet Taner Kışlalı. In January 2002, a court in Istanbul sentenced Necdet Yüksel and Rüştü Aytufan to life in prison. Eight other defendants were sentenced to jail terms for the murder of Mumcu and other prominent secular writers and intellectuals, including Kışlalı, Çetin Emeç, Muammer Aksoy, and Bahriye Uçok. The Jerusalem Warriors, who are connected to the Revolutionary Guards of Iran, were named for their involvement in more assassinations. These include the killings of the Israeli diplomat Ehud Sadan and Sergeant Victor Marwick of the United States.

The killing of the secularist intellectuals continued. On December 18, 2002, Dr. Necip Hablemitoğlu, forty-eight, a history teacher at Ankara University, was shot twice in the head as he left his car near his home. A close friend of the former state security prosecutor Nuh Mete Yüksel, the historian was an outspoken critic of radical Islam. Dr. Hablemitoğlu had taught classes on the secular reforms of Kemal Atatürk and had researched the activities of the Islamic brotherhoods, including Hizbullah.

In Istanbul the police announced on November 1, 1999, the arrest of fourteen members of the Great Eastern Raiders' Front (IBDA-C). They were charged with committing several bomb attacks in the city. The same terrorist outfit bombed the Istanbul offices of the Kemalist Thought Association on November 18, 1999, causing material damage. The assailants defaced the pictures of Kemal Atatürk with knives, spray-painted the walls with the name of their Islamic group, and planted the explosive before they left. Despite the fight against the Islamic guerrillas, the militants from the IBDA-C were able to explode four bombs in Istanbul in February 2000. One of the bombs was placed in the Atatürk Museum, a house where the secular hero once had lived.

One of the most shocking murders took place on January 24, 2001, in Diyarbakır, when Islamic terrorists killed Gaffar Okan, the city's police chief, and five policemen. Okan had received death threats earlier from Hizbullah. In March 2001, a special operation team in Diyarbakır killed Hasan Sarıağaç, an alleged Hizbullah gunman. Sarıağaç was believed to be one of twenty-six gunmen involved in Gaffar Okan's assassination. In order to carry out the operation, the killers kept their guns out of sight in their baggy trousers favored by peasants. They approached the police chief and his security, pulled the guns out, and began firing.

Iranian involvement in the killings of prominent secular Turks appears repeatedly in investigations. Prime Minister Bülent Ecevit accused Iran on May 17, 2000, of aiding armed Kurdish separatists and radical Islamist groups in Turkey: "It is well known that Iran seeks to export its revolution, and Turkey does not want to be a target."

The violence of the militant Islamic movements shocked the majority of the Turkish population, who dreamed to become a member of the European Union. In December 1999, the European Union, formed by Christian nations, finally invited Turkey as its first Muslim candidate for membership. The offer of this candidacy came with conditions. Drastic reforms had to be made in human rights issues as required by the Copenhagen criteria, which defines when a candidate is politically and economically ready to become a member. The Copenhagen criteria stipulate that a candidate country must have an open democratic political system before the start of accession talks. The Turks were later given the date of December 2004 for a progress review that could set a date for accession talks. Forty years earlier, in 1963, the European Union, as a six-member economic community, had invited Turkey to be a member by signing an agreement in Ankara.

The European Commission in Brussels, Belgium, recommended in November 2004 the start of EU membership talks with Turkey. The decision to recommend to EU leaders to start accession negotiations with mainly Muslim Turkey was taken with a very wide consensus among the commissioners, EU Enlargement Commissioner Guenter Verheugen told Reuters. There were stiff conditions to start the accession talks, including the continuation of sweeping democratic and human rights reforms, with no backtracking, the EU clearly informed the Turks. It was understood that the accession talks would last ten to fifteen years, during which time Turkey's progress in carrying out reforms would be watched. The commission warned that any serious and persistent failure to respect democracy and human rights would halt membership negotiations. It was expected that the entry talks could start in 2005. It was also obvious that

the EU officials, despite public opposition to Turkish membership, particularly in France and Germany, were concerned about the clash between
Christian and Islamic civilizations. Officials hoped that the membership
of Muslim Turkey would help ease the situation. A secular Turkey has a
vital mission not only in this very important and urgent subject but also
in fighting and preventing Islamic terror. The news that some EU members, particularly France, may hold referenda on Turkey's membership on
a future date irritated the Turks.

The tough rules, however, angered many nationalist and Kemalist
Turks who accused the EU with interfering in the country's internal
affairs and promoting the separation of the Kurdish minority. Some well-
known writers, including Emin Çölaşan of *Hürriyet*, insisted that the EU
officials' treatment of Turkey was humiliating and not accorded to other
candidate countries. The fundamentalist Islamist media were also in a terrific uproar, claiming that the Christians were buying land and properties
and opening churches all over the country. Some claimed Christian missionaries had invaded the country, distributing free Bibles everywhere
and converting Muslim Turks to Christianity by offering them large
amounts of money.

Rahşan Ecevit, wife of former prime minister Bülent Ecevit, joined
the commotion in January 2005 and in a written statement declared, "We
are losing our religion." She accused the government of allowing widespread missionary activities in the country for the sake of EU membership.

When I read her statement in the newspapers, I jumped up from my
chair and shouted, "Fesüphanallah!"—an expression of frustration of true
believers everywhere that means "Good God alive!" or "God help us!"
The secularist couple, later appearing on the TV program *Gündem
(Agenda)*, criticized Premier Recep Tayyip Erdoğan for officially opening
"The Garden of Religions" in Antalya, where a church, a synagogue, and
a mosque where built next to each other. Bülent Ecevit, speaking in the
TV program, asked, "Was this necessary?"

Turkish membership may affect EU countries whose populations are
growing older. About half of Turkey's more than seventy million people
are young, and EU countries where the birthrates are low will, in the

future, need younger workers. In addition, the EU needs the powerful Turkish armed forces for security. This army, because of its experience of a fifteen-year fight against Kurdish insurgents, knows how to fight terrorism. Turkish membership is an extraordinary move for the EU—it will bring the borders of the EU to such countries as Georgia, Armenia, Azerbaijan, Iraq, Iran, and Syria and will open a bridge for EU countries to the Far East. The membership of Turkey will no doubt affect Turkey's neighbors in a constructive way, particularly in politics, culture, and commerce.

Democracy with
Strings Attached

Eat the grapes but don't ask whose vineyard they came from.

Turkish proverb

he understanding of real democracy has never been established
in Turkey's squabbling, turbulent, and fragmented society.
Turkish democracy has always been a manipulated democracy. It is a
democracy in which political party bosses—who call themselves democrats and masquerade as Kemalists, secularists, or Islamists—who preach
fire and brimstone and repeatedly abuse and violate internationally
accepted norms of decency. It is a democracy where some members of the
media, parliament, and political leadership do their best to present disgrace and hypocrisy as virtues.

It is a special brand of democracy, a democracy "Made in Turkey" in
which flattery, favoritism, and bribery work hand in hand. Ilhan Selçuk of
Cumhuriyet explained his own views on Turkish democracy on September 16, 2000. About the prohibitions decreed during the Ottoman era,
Ilhan Selçuk wrote, "Suddenly it occurred to me how far we have
advanced." The writer quoted examples from Reşad Ekrem Koçu's

research in *The Prohibitions during the Ottoman History*, including laws prohibiting slave markets to sell concubines to non-Muslims; other laws banning the smoking of tobacco products and drinking coffee; riding in a carriage or on a horse; women sailing in a caique with men; women entering a shop in Eyup (the Istanbul district at the Golden Horn with religious distinction) where *kaymak*, a sweetened clotted cream, is sold; immodestly dressed women going about; travel to Istanbul by unmarried manservant; talking about the state in public places; gypsies riding horses and keeping mares; Albanians becoming bath attendants; ringing bells in churches; and singing, playing music, and telling stories in coffeehouses. And, to top them all, the law prohibiting non-Muslims to wear wooden clogs in a Turkish bath! It is an old custom to wear wooden clogs with high heels in a Turkish bath.

Selçuk added, "It is easy to understand our times when we look at *The Prohibitions During the Ottoman History*. Are we not the grandchildren of those, who prohibited non-Muslims to wear wooden clogs in a Turkish bath, we, who entered democracy from the back door instead of the front? What were we supposed to do?"

For the majority of the Turkish people, it is not easy to understand the meaning of American-style democracy. Turks have for centuries lived under the state's oppression and rules imposed by the traditions of Islam. And then there is the Ottoman legacy of a calcified bureaucracy.

This bureaucracy is the massive wall that confronts an ordinary citizen while conducting business with the state organs. Officials of the state apparatus, generally appointed through connections to a political party boss rather than for merit, treat ordinary citizens with disrespect and suspicion, even when a citizen's appeal has merit. It is a challenge for anyone to deal with bureaucrats if a citizen has no money for a bribe or is not a member of the elite class with influence. In legal affairs, a mentality opposite to Western or American ways prevails—guilty as charged until proven innocent, not innocent until proven guilty.

Burak Bekdil, a columnist for the English-language *Turkish Daily News*, was found guilty on May 17, 2002, for writing that ordinary Turks can have little hope for a fair trial. Bekdil was sentenced to one year and eight months in jail for writing "An ordinary Turk would probably have a one-in-a-million chance of a fair trial if he is foolish enough to trust the Turkish courts and judges." The court suspended the prison term, but Bekdil faces prison if he is convicted of a similar crime within the next five years.

Eraslan Özkaya, chief justice of the Supreme Court of Appeals, said in October 2003 that in Turkey independence of the judicial system does not exist. He added that the government settled down on top of the justice system, and this must be corrected.

The unfair treatment of the have-nots by the state because of their low position in life is undemocratic and one of the reasons of disunity, unrest, and the growth of the Islamic fundamentalist movement. But is it then possible for a radical Islamic regime to establish democracy in Turkey?

The failure of the traditionalist Islamist Necmettin Erbakan is a clear example of the handicaps stacked against such a democracy in a secular state. Islam aspires to handle religious, judicial, and political issues. The Muslim clerics impose the rules of the Shariah, ignoring basic human rights. In Islam, there is no separation of church and state. Therefore, in an Islamic state, such as Iran or the Kingdom of Saudi Arabia, a clear separation of the state and religion does not exist. In a state based on the Shariah, the Qur'an is the constitution.

The separation between the state and the church is one of the principles of an American-style democracy that accepts human rights and basic freedoms as birthright. In America immigrants learn early the meaning of being free and the First Amendment of the Constitution of the United States, which declares, "Congress shall make no law respecting an establishment of religion, or prohibiting the free exercise thereof; or abridging the freedom of speech, or of the press; or the right of the people peaceably to assemble, and to petition the Government for a redress of grievances."

In contrast, I have translated the 159th article of the Turkish republic's penal code that was in force in 2001: "Those who publicly insult and deride the moral character of Turkey, its republic, the Grand National Assembly, the government, the ministries, the state's military, and police forces are punished with imprisonment between one and six years."

Article 160 of the same code stated: "The investigation to be initiated over the matters expressed in the first paragraph of the 159th article is dependent on permission from the Ministry of Justice." In other words, all citizens were not equal under the law until the penal code was recently changed. Some of the citizens were subject to punishment if the ministry of justice so wished; others were not.

The Turkish political party leaders, the high officials, and the members of the elite need to adopt the idea that the laws are to be respected and equally applied to all, including themselves and the members of their families. A state that lacks transparency and does not treat its citizens equally in justice is not a democratic state.

Turkish people in fall 2002 did not consider their politicians, their governments, their parliament, and the media credible. If Turkey is ever to develop a Western-style democratic society, this public trust has to be established.

It is hard for an outsider to understand why high-ranking army officers in Turkey have been involved in the country's political affairs to fine-tune democracy. Reasons include the ineffectiveness of civilian governments in dealing with the pressing social and economic problems, the looting and plunder of the country's resources, the blatant abuse of secularist reforms by the Islamists, and the danger from the Kurdish separatists, the Marxists, and the Islamic reactionaries. The generals are highly protective of the country's unity and its secular Kemalist reforms. They consider most of the politicians to be incompetent, corrupt, and opportunistic individuals lacking visionary leadership.

According to the generals, "the struggle against Islamic reaction" is the most vital challenge facing the nation, and the government must crack down on religious extremism. When Mesut Yılmaz backed off from enforcing the dress code during the Muslim headscarf crisis, the generals were upset because they consider the turban a symbol representing Islamic ideology. During a meeting of the National Security Council (MGK) in March 1998, the generals asserted that the Islamists had even infiltrated the agencies assigned to combat religious fundamentalism.

The military interventions in 1960, 1971, and 1980 were meant to be preventive measures against corruption to stop bloodshed and to protect the oneness of the nation and the Kemalist reforms. The generals imposed new rules and regulations and even changed the constitution to protect the secular republic. However, the pashas failed each time because the civilian regimes that took over continued their harmful policies. The military interventions, on the other hand, did not help democracy either. In fact, they delayed social, economic, and democratic reforms and were ineffective in stopping reactionary movements.

Mesut Yılmaz, as the deputy prime minister in December 2000, stated that the role of the Turkish army is bound to change eventually as the country approaches membership of the European Union: "The duty the army has assumed in the recent past regarding the struggle against terrorism and fundamentalism proves that this change will not take place very soon."

The word *horde* comes from the Turkish *ordu*, meaning "army." The Turkish army is a beloved and privileged institution. Most people fed up with extremism and governments diseased with corruption look up to the armed forces and see a guardian institution of their security. General Hüseyin Kıvrıkoğlu, who was then chief of general staff, told *Cumhuriyet* in January 2000 that the clampdown on political Islam will continue for a thousand years if need be. He described corruption as a great a peril to the country as terrorism.

Turkey's annual defense budget of $9 billion was until 2003 four times the amount spent on education. The threat from the Soviet Union, the Kurdish separatist revolt, and the disputes with Greece were the major reasons for high military spending. There are 298 generals and fifteen full rank army, navy, and air force commanders. They command an army of 639,000 active troops, the second biggest in NATO, which plays a balancing role between the Christianity and Islam in a strategic area between Europe and Asia.

33

Legacy of an Empire

*A camel won't become a hacı
even if it enters the Kaaba in Mecca.*
Turkish proverb

find the history of the Turkic peoples, their move from central Asia to the West, and their adoption of a religion not compatible with their early lifestyles fascinating, for the early Turkish women of central Asia were not covered head to toe. They wrestled with men in public, practiced archery, and rode horses as well as men did.

Over a thousand years ago, the Turks were not Muslims. It is known that the Turkic tribes in Siberia and central Asia practiced Shamanism since ancient times. The word *shaman* originates in the language of the Tungus or Tunguz, a tribe of wandering hunters and fishermen of Siberia. The seminomadic Tungus are from a lineage of the Ural-Altai family group, and their language is related to Turkish. A shaman or medicine man, a religious leader believed to be possessed with ancestral spirits, was looked upon as the protector of the tribe who could foretell the future.

When the Turkic tribes began to expand throughout the Asian steppes in the sixth century, they kept their Shamanistic rituals. In their early history, however, the Turks were exposed to a variety of religions other than Islam, including Christianity, Judaism, and Buddhism. These Turks of the steppes of Asia played a vital role in the spread of Manichaeism. The khagan or *hakan*, ruler of the Uighur Turks in the eighth century, was converted to the Manichaean faith and founded a state based on this dualistic religious movement. Founded in the third century in Persia by Mani, the Apostle of Light, Manichaeism was known as the Religion of Light. Mani, who called himself a prophet, was born in Babylonia with one short and twisted leg and claimed that he was divinely inspired about the meaning and purpose of the world. The Manichaean faith survived in East Turkestan until the Mongol invasion. The Mongol conquerors later carried Mani's teachings into China. Still later, Manichaeism was considered a Christian heresy.

For the Turkish warrior in central Asia, the West was his horizon and he raced to it on horseback. The horse of the central Asiatic steppes, noted for its speed and stamina, was his vehicle; the bow and arrow and the sword were his weapons. The Turk, a born rider, had through time bonded himself to his horse and the horse to his rider. As the Turkish tribes moved to the West from central Asia, their women were never veiled. In the tenth century, influenced by the Abbasid caliphs of Baghdad, the Turks converted to Islam, and their traditions began to change as they adopted the customs and traditions of the Arabs.

There are still Turkic peoples with religions other than Islam, as, for instance, the Gagauz, who are Christian Orthodox, and the Khazars. The Khazars ruled in southern Russia, and the Caucasus and were overwhelmed between 969–1030 by the Russians and Byzantines. Their king and nobility had adopted Judaism in 740 CE. Judaism is also the religion of Turkic Karaim, or Karay of Poland, and southern Lithuania.

The Seljuk Turks, who ruled a great empire, changed their religion three times in two centuries, finally converting to the Sunnite form if Islam. It was in 1071 that Alparslan, the Seljuk leader, defeated a Byzantine army at Manzikert and captured Romanus IV Diogenes, the emperor of Byzantium. This opened the way for Turkmen tribes to migrate to Anatolia and to leave there a strong legacy of Islam.

The mentality of fundamentalist Islam, however, played highly destructive roles during the Ottoman Empire. The Ottoman Empire's official ideology was Islam, and, in time, Islam turned out to be an obstacle to innovation. The Islamic state and its restrictive Canon Law were among the important reasons the Ottoman Empire missed historic opportunities in science and exploration. Once in their early history, the Ottomans, compared with the Europeans, had been far advanced in economy, social development, law, and the arts and sciences. They were superior in administration, military arms, planning, and strategy. All this changed when inertia and corruption settled over the empire's administration, and the Ottomans earned the title the "Sick Man of Europe."

The rules developed by hard-line Islam, and the misleading interpretations of the verses of the Qur'an by ignorant mullahs, caused the state to neglect reforms. Reforms, often against the interests of the religious *ulema* (the doctors of Muslim theology and the interpreters of the Shariah), were needed for the people's cultural enlightenment and economic advancement. Ignorance and absolute submissive behavior expected from the citizen, known as the *kul* of Allah and in addition, *kul* of the Sultan, played critical roles in a collapsing Ottoman Empire.

The word *kul* literally meant "slave." From that, *kapıkulu* emerged, meaning "Slave at the Gate." The slaves, who served the sultan for life—including those who reached the highest offices in the sultan's court, such as grand viziers or prime ministers—were known as Slaves at the Gate.

It is a historical fact that the Ottoman Empire during its years of glory was liberal and gentle with the nations under its vassalage. It was an empire where throughout the centuries slaves became masters. Slaves who were born Christian and who later embraced Islam, or sons of these slaves, played a crucial role both in the empire's rise to greatness and later in its fall. Time and again, a brilliant slave would appear as a great administrator to halt the decline of the sick empire. The Ottomans did not exploit the lands they conquered. They collected reasonable taxes instead.

As an advanced and gentle empire, it incorporated thirty-six different nations (*millets*), which were free to conduct their own religious affairs. Many languages were spoken in the empire. Minority subjects, such as Greeks, Armenians, and Jews, were professionals and conducted all trade and business.

Because of religious restrictions, however, generations of young girls, even the most gifted, were locked in harems, uneducated and cheated of their calling. There are few female representatives in the arts and sciences of the long Ottoman history.

The boys of the elite grew up with a fixed tradition—to become a pasha or to be employed for life by the state as army officers or officials of the government in order to earn a living with salaries drawn from the state's treasury. This trend continued for Turkish boys even after the republic was established in 1923. Only during the last fifty years did Turks enter the business world on an impressive scale.

Many Ottoman high officials were Slavs, Arabs, Greeks, Bulgars, Armenians, and Circassians. The empire's elite corps of soldiers, the Janissaries (*Yeni Çeri*, new troops), organized in the fourteenth century and once highly respected for their military prowess, were *devşirme*, Christian tribute boys from the Balkan provinces. They, too, played a vital role during the decline of the empire by frequently engineering palace coups and refusing European-style reforms. The *devşirme* in general kept the Ottoman princes uneducated and through intrigues controlled the sultans. Born Christian, most of them later became Islamic bigots and learned to kill in the name of religion. Sultan Murad IV abolished the system of the *devşirme* in the seventeenth century. For a period in its history, the "Sultanate of the Harem Women" and *Ağalar*, the commanding officers of the Janissaries, ruled the Ottoman Empire.

These then were the causes for the years of decline, which soon followed the reign of Süleyman the Magnificent. Progress had come to an end even during the last years of that enlightened sultan. The influence of the Islamic fanatics increased while the empire declined, and they were successful in introducing a dark era of coarse fundamentalism. The fundamentalists considered innovation heresy and forbade it. The Muslim leaders used the fear of Allah to gain public respect. The judges took bribes and sentenced the innocent and freed the guilty. Grand viziers often sold high government positions to the highest bidders and pocketed the money. Other officials in important positions followed in their footsteps. There was a time when appointments to official positions could not be granted without substantial bribes.

The gentle state disappeared; the advanced arts and sciences retreated and were forgotten. When distinguished craftsmen died, their knowledge and know-how died with them. The Islamic religion and pan-Islamism played a wider role in the affairs of the Ottoman state. In time the *fatwa*— a religious ruling, or the opinion on a matter of the Shariah given by the Grand Mufti, the Sheyhulislam, the Sheik of Islam, the minister responsible for the religious affairs—replaced common sense. Grand muftis, together with pressure from the rebellious Janissaries, were able to depose reformist sultans. Throughout the Ottoman history, there were enlightened sheyhulislams, but they were far and in between. Elmalılı Hamdi, the Grand Mufti in 1909, for instance, claimed that the nation's sovereignty "is superior to the caliphate."

In the nineteenth century, the caliphate finally became the myth to hold the empire together. During his rule, between 1879 and 1909, Sultan Abdul-Hamid II, as the caliph, used Islamic religion and its threat of jihad in order to stop the disintegration of the empire and to protect his throne. While he used the threat of jihad against foreign powers, he manipulated the support of the Islamic sects to rally the Muslim population in the empire to his rule.

The secular education of my childhood rejected Abdul-Hamid II as a despot who had a hand in the destruction of the Ottoman Empire. I am shocked to see that the present Islamic reactionary movement in Turkey considers Abdul-Hamid Khan, as they call him, a patriot, a wise and just ruler who had been a victim of the Young Turks. The Islamists also blame the Young Turks for the demise of the Ottoman Empire, ignoring other reasons that brought about the long decline.

Neglect of exploration and lack of knowledge of potential developments such exploration would bring about played a crucial role in the decline of the Ottoman Empire. For a long time, the imperial expansion of Western nations to distant and yet undiscovered places of the world did not impress the Ottomans. This expansion, ushered in by the voyages of such navigators as Christopher Columbus for Spain, Vasco da Gama and Fernando Magellan for Portugal, and Francis Drake for England, was outside the sphere of influence of the Ottomans and did not concern them until it was too late.

The discoveries of Vasco da Gama at the end of the fifteenth century brought far-reaching consequences for the Ottoman Empire, for the Portuguese navigator had sailed around Africa into the backyard of the Ottoman Empire, the Indian Ocean. This discovery opened a new sea route to Asia for the Europeans, which reduced the importance of the Ottoman Empire's trade routes to India and the Far East for spices and other goods and turned the eastern Mediterranean into a backwater. The ocean voyages were the way of the future, but the Ottomans barely understood their importance.

The emerging powers of Europe were poised to control the rest of the world, while the Ottoman upper class remained isolated from events that changed the world. Even if they had realized the dangers from the European explorations, the Ottomans lacked an ocean-going fleet. The Europeans were building big, heavy, and well-armed carracks and galleons for their long ocean voyages and wars, while the Ottoman navy remained a Mediterranean fleet with smaller galleys.

The discovery of the New World by Christopher Columbus (1492–1502), the son of a weaver and born in Genoa, Italy, opened the way for European exploration, exploitation, and colonization. With the discovery of the sea routes to the West and to the Far East in the fifteenth and sixteenth centuries, the European powers—among them the British, the Spanish, and the Portuguese—had great advantages over the Ottomans. The European expansion into south Asia and the Far East was instrumental later for Russia's expansion as a counterforce into the Balkans, the landmass north of the Black Sea that includes the Crimea and the Caucasus and north and central Asia. That expansion was accomplished at the Ottomans' expense.

Finally, the inflation brought about by the vast amounts of Mexican silver bullion and Peruvian gold of the newly discovered Americas played a destructive economic role for the Ottomans. The bad economy brought about by inflation and the lack of progress and social development led the way to deeper corruption. The resistance of the Ottoman ruling class to change increased because this class benefited financially from anarchy.

During Christopher Columbus's discoveries of the New World the ruler of the Ottoman Empire was Sultan Beyazıd II who reigned between 1481 and 1512. He was the son of Fatih Sultan Mehmet, the Conqueror of Constantinople, but he lacked his father's pro-European orientation. Fatih had paid favorable attention to the Renaissance, despite its initiation of humanism by secular men. As a young prince in Manisa, Fatih had received lessons in Western history from Italian teachers. In fact, Fatih's conquest of Constantinople was a boost for the Renaissance because many scholars fled to Italy after the fall of the Byzantine Empire. That was a great loss for the Ottomans.

One of the Conqueror's terrible mistakes was his proclamation of the fratricidal law to prevent power struggles between the princes. In order to secure the ruling of the empire by one man at a time, many princes and brothers and cousins of the next sultan were executed. Often a brilliant young man with excellent leadership qualities was strangled to make way for an idiot. This sultan also abolished established old traditions, such as breaking bread with the troops and attending state councils. Fatih Sultan Mehmet's son Beyazıd II was a pious Muslim, and as such he removed the paintings made by Italian painters of his father from the palace.

Beyazıd II was also very stubborn, superstitious, and melancholic. Known as *Beyazıd Adli*, Beyazıd the Just, he was highly influenced by the *ulema*. He strictly observed the precepts of the Qur'an and the Shariah and ignored the consequences that the explorations were about to cause. His and his advisers' view was that the Christians of Europe had nothing to offer in science and knowledge to Islam's glorious Ottoman Empire.

In fact, the Ottoman ruling class and conservative *ulema* belittled the Christians and their innovations, their achievements in the arts and sciences and their explorations. The view of these doctors of the Muslim theology for a long time was that the Ottoman Empire was the greatest, and

Islam was more powerful and much more advanced than the Christian states. The realization that this belief was no longer based on reality hit the Ottomans only when wars were lost and the national treasury of the disintegrating empire was left absolutely empty.

For centuries information about such important developments as reforms in the European countries reached the Ottoman rulers through renegades and intermediaries. The intermediaries were *dragomans*, mostly Greek-born interpreters known in the Greek language as *dragomanos*. The *dragoman* is a distorted version of the Turkish-Arabic word *tercüman*, meaning the translator. The Ottoman sultans considered the system of *dragomans* as a satisfactory way to deal with foreign powers, and thus there was no need to open embassies in major European capitals.

At the time of the European discoveries, Beyazıd II was busy spending much of the state revenues on building mosques, religious schools, and hospitals. Still, this sultan concentrated in general on consolidating Ottoman rule in the Balkans, Anatolia, and the eastern Mediterranean and was successful against the Safavid dynasty of Persia.

The Ottoman Empire skipped a great part of the role that the Renaissance played in European civilization in the fourteenth, fifteenth, and sixteenth centuries. The discovery and exploration of the oceans and the new continents, and the decline of the European feudal system brought the development of a new understanding of wisdom and humanistic spirit for the Europeans. The great progress in Western art followed, with such masters as Leonardo da Vinci, Michelangelo, Raphael, and scores of others. The humanists and scholars like Desiderius Erasmus (1469–1536), Galileo Galilei (1564–1642) and Voltaire (1694–1778) created powerful bases for the European enlightenment. While the Renaissance considered man as the center of the universe and as such able to embrace all knowledge, the Ottomans fiercely resisted change and innovation. The empire finally fell behind during the advent of the modern nation-state in the sixteenth century and missed the Enlightenment and the Industrial Revolution of the eighteenth and nineteenth centuries.

A system of capitulations granted to European powers earlier, designed to undermine the authority of the Ottoman government inside the empire's borders, degenerated in the seventeenth and eighteenth centuries. These capitulations began during the reign of Süleyman the Magnificent, who had granted diplomatic immunity to the European merchants living in the empire, who could not be put on trial in Ottoman courts for crimes committed anywhere in the empire. The consuls of the foreign powers acted as judges, ruling for or against these merchants according to the laws of their own countries. France received similar concessions in 1569 regarding the offenses of French missionaries and traders. In 1740 the Christian *millets*, too, as Ottoman citizens gained the same rights. By then Ottoman sovereignty had already been damaged beyond repair.

Attempts to modernize the empire were unsuccessful because of ignorance and religious bigotry. As the civil, military, and diplomatic decline of the Sublime Porte continued, bribery and intrigues in the center of Ottoman power (the harem) led to garroting with the fatal silken cord of sultans, most of them driveling idiots, and grand viziers, a few of whom were brilliant administrators.

The best example of the "sultanate of the harem women" intrigues inside the harem and the influences of foreign-born female slaves in the Ottoman state—is the case of Roxelana. She is known as *Hürrem Sultan*, the "Laughing One" who played a crucial role in the decline of the Ottoman Empire. In fact, Hürrem Sultan was instrumental in changing the destiny of the Ottomans.

The daughter of a Russian Orthodox priest a stunningly beautiful twelve-year-old with red-gold hair and sapphire eyes, she was captured by Tatar raiders on the banks of the Don. Hafize, the wife of Selim the Grim and mother of Süleyman the Magnificent, was not a slave but an enlightened Ottoman lady. She had earlier presented her son with two young concubines, who bore him children. Having been informed about the extraordinary beauty of the Russian slave girl, Hafize purchased her at the Crimean slave market in Kaffa. After training and grooming her for a few years, Hafize presented the young girl to her son Süleyman the Magnificent.

Süleyman was captivated by the slave girl's charm. She was a story-teller with high spirits and soon became the sultan's favorite concubine. Once she bore him children, Roxelana persuaded Süleyman the Magnificent to marry her and became the first woman to marry a ruler of the Ottoman Empire. She remained the love of Süleyman's life until his death.

Süleyman the Magnificent (1494–1566)—the most distinguished Ottoman ruler in whose time the empire reached the highest achievements of Ottoman civilization in the fields of architecture, literature, and law—had a weak spot for Roxelana. That weakness brought disaster. Roxelana's first target was Ibrahim Pasha, the *kapıkulu*, a Greek-born Slave at the Gate. Ibrahim played the violin well and often entertained the sultan with his music. Süleyman the Magnificent had purchased this Greek as a young slave from a widow while he was the governor of the province of Manisa. They became close friends.

Ibrahim, born in Parga, Greece, in 1493, had distinguished himself as an able administrator, politician, and military commander. He reestablished Ottoman authority in Egypt during a military expedition in 1524 and introduced administrative and fiscal reforms there. He was commander-in-chief during the Danubian campaigns and the sultan's official negotiator with the Holy Roman emperor Charles V on the question of Hungary. Through his efforts, most of Hungary became a tributary of the Ottoman regime. This grand vizier occupied Tabriz in August 1534, following a war against the Safavids of Persia. He also captured Baghdad.

Süleyman had elevated his Greek slave's authority almost equal to his own by giving him extraordinary powers. This power finally went to the slave's head, and he began seeing himself as ruler, signing official documents as Sultan Ibrahim—a grave mistake. His second mistake, however, was fatal. Ibrahim opposed Roxelana's influence on Süleyman the Magnificent, and Roxelana took her revenge. After a dinner party on March 15, 1536, mute executioners strangled Ibrahim on orders from Süleyman the Magnificent. He was forty-three years old when he died.

Roxelana's son-in-law Rüstem Pasha, a lesser man, replaced him as the grand vizier. Rüstem Pasha had married Mihrimah (Beautiful as the Moon) Sultan, daughter of Süleyman the Magnificent and Roxelana.

Rüstem and his brother Sinan Pasha were sons of a Croatian peasant. Once pig herders in Croatia, the brothers had not been drafted as *devşirme*, or tribute boys. They were actually captured in war and thus enslaved as *pencik** youths. The boys were educated in *Enderun*, the palace school, and Sinan later became lord high admiral.

Rüstem Pasha, a penny pincher but a good administrator, was mean-spirited and greedy. Known as the Abominable Rüstem, he served as grand vizier for fifteen years, and when he died in 1561 of dropsy, he left a fabulous fortune. His wife, Mihrimah, became the richest widow in the world.

Rüstem Pasha also left a legacy for the Ottoman Empire of widespread bribery and deep corruption. According to *The Panaroma of the Ottoman History* by Reşad Ekrem Koçu, the fortune he left included one thousand farms, 467 water mills, 2,900 horses, thirty-three highly valuable diamonds, 1,160 mules, and five hundred golden saddles encrusted with diamonds. Rüstem Pasha had acquired this treasure, estimated to be worth fifty million gold coins, through corruption and the intrigues of Roxelana, his mother-in-law.

The special treatment accorded to Roxelana drew the ire of Gülbahar (Spring Rose), Süleyman's senior consort, whose son Mustafa was the crown prince. As the fratricidal law was still in force, Gülbahar was worried about her son. If her son could not become the next ruler of the empire, he would be strangled. Grand Vizier Ibrahim believed before he was killed that Mustafa had leadership qualities. Still, neither Gülbahar nor Ibrahim could match to Roxelana's intrigues. Roxelana, also concerned about the fratricidal law, wanted one of her sons to be the next ruler. As a result of her influence on Süleyman the Magnificent, Gülbahar was finally banished with her son to a far corner of the empire, and the crown prince became regional governor.

During a Persian campaign, Rüstem Pasha, on instructions from Roxelana, falsely reported to the sultan that Mustafa, well liked by the Janissaries, was plotting a coup to overthrow him. Süleyman, despite his old age, moved fast, overtook the army, and invited his son to his tent. Seven

---

* The word *pencik* means a title deed to a slave.

mute executioners waiting there tried to strangle the crown prince, who was a bright, handsome man. The prince resisted his executioners.

"Help me, Father! For God's sake, help me," Mustafa pleaded while Süleyman the Magnificent, resting on a divan behind a silken curtain, watched his son fight for his life. The sultan asked Zal Mahmud, a graduate of the palace school, a champion wrestler, and sword-bearer of the sultan, to finish the job. Zal Mahmud, also a page in the sultan's court, was a powerful young man. He grabbed the crown prince with a wrestler's hold, threw him on the floor, and strangled him with his bare hands. Hürrem Sultan always richly rewarded loyal service to her cause. In later years, Zal Mahmud, the crown prince's executioner and now a pasha, was elevated to the exalted position of *damat*, a bridegroom of the House of Osman. Hürrem married him to her granddaughter Shah Sultana, the daughter of Selim the Sot.

Prince Mustafa had one son named Mehmet and two daughters. Mehmet could not be left alive because of the fratricidal law, so he too was killed on orders from his grandfather Süleyman. Roxelana had three living sons. The hunchbacked and pigeon-breasted Cihangir, meaning Conqueror of the World, was the youngest, at age twenty-two. Cihangir was very fond of Crown Prince Mustafa, and when he heard how Mustafa was murdered, he died of shock and grief.

Hürrem's second son, Beyazıd, plotted a coup against his father, failed, and was forgiven thanks to his mother's intervention. He plotted a second time and failed again. This time he escaped to Persia with his four sons, where his father's executioners tracked them down and killed them.

Hürrem's older son, Selim the Sot (also known as Selim the Fair), was fat with a red-gold beard and blue eyes. When Süleyman died on September 6, 1566, Selim the Sot, the sole heir left to the throne, became sultan at age forty-two and ruled the Ottoman Empire until his death in 1574.

Selim did not have the courage to be a warrior and never led the Janissaries into battle. One of his grave mistakes was to allow freeborn Muslims to enlist as Janissaries, totally changing the structure of the Ottoman standing army. The discipline in the standing army as a result was ruined when some Janissaries acted as businessmen and others were allowed to marry, thus abolishing the earlier rules of celibacy. The degeneration of the Janissaries into drunk, corrupt, and unruly troops started early in Selim the Sot's reign. This sultan, however, was lucky because one of the best administrators of the Ottoman Empire, Sokollu Mehmet Pasha, remained his grand vizier through the years.

Sokollu was the statesman who kept the death of Süleyman the Magnificent a secret from the Janissaries for forty-six days. Süleyman had died of a heart attack while besieging the fortress of Szigetvar in Hungary. Sokollu, fearful that the Janissaries would revolt if they knew the Sultan had died, had Süleyman's body gutted and embalmed in great secrecy. While the victory was being won in Szigetvar, the dead sultan was dressed in his fine garments. The imperial turban with plumes and jewels was placed on his head. His face was painted, and his body in the imperial tent was kept upright with invisible supports on a golden throne. Now and then, Sokollu visited the imperial tent and reported to the dead Sultan in a loud voice about the developments in the battle. The proceedings behind the silken curtains seemed normal to the Janissaries and their commanding *ağas*. After the victory, the sultan's body was carried in a litter for four days to Belgrade, where Selim the Sot was waiting having been informed about the death of his father. When the army pitched camp near Belgrade, it was finally announced that Süleyman the Magnificent had died and his son Selim II had become the ruler.

During the reign of Selim the Sot, Sokollu, a Serbian Slave at the Gate, was the actual ruler of the Ottoman Empire. He, too, was a bridegroom of the House of Osman. At fifty-nine, already married with children, Sokollu had caught the eye of Esmahan Cevher Sultan, the young daughter of Selim the Sot and granddaughter of Süleyman the Magnificent and Hürrem Sultan. Named Cevher, meaning Jewel, she was only seventeen and demanded Sokollu become her husband.

Selim the Sot loved Cypriot wine and wanted to capture Cyprus. Sokollu as his grand vizier objected and said the invasion of the Venetian island would unite the European Christian enemies against the empire. Selim the Sot's wife, Safiye Sultan, was a Venetian slave who did not want a war between her native land and the Ottoman Empire. There was another influential woman in Selim the Sot's harem, and she did not support the plans to attack Cyprus. Also a Venetian slave named Cecilia, she would go into Ottoman history as Nurbanu Sultan, the mother of Murat III. Banker Joseph Nasi, a Spanish Jew, however, who had become a close drinking buddy to Selim the Sot, persuaded the sultan to invade the island for its wine.

Sokollu's prediction came true. The capture of Cyprus, following a fatwa obtained from the Grand Mufti Ebüsuud, caused the formation of a holy league against the Ottomans. Spain, Venice, the Knights of Malta, and several Italian states led by the papacy formed a fleet under Don Juan of Austria, a bastard son of Charles V. The result was that *sıngın* we discussed earlier, the rout of the Ottoman navy at Lepanto on October 7, 1571. Eight years later, on October 12, 1579, an assassin killed Sokollu with a dagger on the grounds of the Old Seraglio. It is believed that this killing was the result of a power struggle inside the harem.

A new era began. Hard religious dogma, along with the intrigues in harem politics, became a handicap for the empire's survival, despite the leadership of a few enlightened sultans and grand viziers who saw the need for reform. The decline might have been even faster if a *devşirme* recruiter had not spotted a bright young boy in Albania. This Albanian tribute boy, born in Rojnik in 1575, was brought to the Old Seraglio; educated at *Enderun*, the palace school; and became a page. He is known in Turkish history as Köprülü*. Mehmet Pasha, the founder of the Köprülü dynasty, an illustrious family of grand viziers who served the empire for many years with skill and wisdom.

Köprülü Mehmet Pasha was a highly capable administrator who served as governor-general of several provinces. He became a grand vizier in 1656 in old age serving under boy Sultan Mehmet IV, the Hunter, until his death in 1661. Köprülü's appointment as grand vizier was timely. The Venetians had blocked the Dardanelles Strait, bringing shipping to Istanbul to a standstill, including the all-important grain shipments. The Janissary and Sipahi (cavalry) forces had revolted over pay. Power was exercised by a faction of the women in the harem of the Old Seraglio, led by Valide Sultan Turhan, the boy sultan's mother.

---

* From the town of Köprü, which means bridge.

Mehmet IV was a six-year-old boy when he succeeded his father Mad Sultan Ibrahim in 1648. The boy sultan's grandmother Kösem was allied in harem politics and intrigues with Turhan Sultan. Kösem, by now old, was strangled in 1651 by a mob in her apartment when the empire was in social and financial crisis. Grand Vizier Tarhuncu (tarragon salesman) Ahmet Pasha had sought in vain to suppress revolts in Istanbul and Anatolia while he tried to bring some order to the empire's finances. Tarhuncu was the first Ottoman administrator who attempted to organize a budget system for the empire. The women of the harem, led by Turhan Sultan, were angry about his financial reforms. In 1653 they invited him to the palace for talks. Tarhuncu was met by the chief black eunuch at the imperial household and was ordered to hand over the seal of the Grand Vizierate. Before he realized what was going on, the Grand Vizier was grabbed by palace bodyguards and strangled on the spot.

Turhan Sultan, however, had the foresight to appoint Köprülü Mehmet Pasha grand vizier after Tarhuncu's murder and a series of failures by other grand viziers. Köprülü restored authority, suppressed insurgents and rivals, reorganized the army, and defeated the Venetian fleet at the Dardanelles on July 19, 1657. When he died in 1661, his two sons, Köprülü Fazıl Ahmet Pasha and Köprülü Fazıl Mustafa Pasha, became grand viziers, consecutively. They were as skillful as their father. The Köprülü family reestablished the prestige of the Ottomans, securing such territories as Crete and Polish Ukraine, consolidating the Balkan provinces and reforming the Janissary and Sipahi forces.

Disaster struck soon after Köprülü Fazıl Ahmet Pasha's death in 1676 and after Merzifonlu Kara Mustafa Pasha* had been appointed grand vizier. Merzifonlu Kara Mustafa was not a brilliant man and lacked his predecessor's abilities in administration and military strategy. A brother-in-law of the Köprülüs, he had led failed campaigns against Poland and Russia. Sultan Mehmet IV, by then forty-one years old, had devoted his time to hunting. He was not interested in affairs of state. Still, when Merzifonlu offered a grandiose scheme to conquer the Holy Roman Empire under Habsburg Emperor Leopold I, the Hunter initially opposed it but

---

* Black Mustafa Pasha from the town of Merzifon.

later agreed. Imre Thököly, the leader of the Hungarian Calvinists, had persuaded Merzifonlu to attack Vienna, the Habsburg capital. When an Ottoman army of 150,000 supported by the Hungarians appeared at the outskirts of Vienna, Leopold I fled the city.

The siege lasted about two months, until a combined Austrian-Polish army of eighty thousand commanded by John III Sobieski and Charles of Lorraine concentrated on the nearby hills. This army descended from the hills upon the Turkish camp on September 12, 1683. The battle continued for fifteen hours, and the invaders were driven from their trenches. Thousands of them were slaughtered. Merzifonlu escaped, leaving his luxurious tent and a great booty that included sacks of coffee. This led to the establishment of Vienna's renowned coffeehouses.

Because of the severe consequences, which came to light later, the siege of Vienna was the most critical defeat of the Ottoman Empire. It ruined Turkish prestige in Europe. The defeat at Vienna was also a factor in changing the Ottomans' attitude on religious tolerance. For the first time in their history, the Ottomans realized that the military power of Europe's Christian world was a threat to their own survival. This led to intolerance toward the Christian nations in the empire.

For his failure, Merzifonlu was executed in Belgrade on Christmas Day in 1683.

"Am I to die?" he asked his executioners.

"Yes," they answered. The order had come from *Hünkar*, the sultan himself, and nothing could change it. So it is written on one's forehead, death is unavoidable, they told him.

"As Allah pleases," he said and was strangled.

An old severed head claimed to be that of Merzifonlu Kara Mustafa Pasha is kept in a box in the basement of the Historical Museum of the City of Vienna.

I remember how Falih Rıfkı Atay, an Ottoman army officer and later a journalist in Istanbul, described almost three hundred years later the impact of the Ottoman failure in Vienna: "The Ottoman Empire began losing its European possessions with the failure at Vienna in 1683." The crushing defeat at the gates of Vienna was actually the end of the Ottoman

Empire's domination in Eastern Europe and the beginning of the collapse of the administrative system the Köprülü family had erected.

As children during the reform years, we learned in secular schools that the Ottoman Empire reached its glory under extraordinary leadership. The empire during its glory days was ruled with equal justice for the Turks, the leading *millet*, as well as all other ethnic nations. The early Ottoman rulers were warriors who commanded armies and led them to wars and lived among the people. The wars they won brought acquisitions of land and population, increasing the empire's power and the wealth of its treasury.

After Süleyman the Magnificent, his son Selim the Sot preferred the comforts of the harem. The empire's decline accelerated when Mad Sultan Ibrahim strewed his beard with pearls and jewels and Sultan Mustafa hurled coins into the sea, believing that the fish would spend the money. The recommendations of the royal astrologers, wizards, and soothsayers as well as the religious *ulema*, or the Grand Mufti, the Sheyhulislam, affected the decisions of the sultans even in such matters as the declaration of war.

Tulipmania swept the Ottoman royalty during the reign of Sultan Ahmet III in a flight from the grim reality that the empire, often defeated in wars, now was also becoming ungovernable. Ottoman leaders entertained an illusion of a fairyland in tulip gardens ablaze with flickering candelabras carried by giant sea turtles. The tulip was the emblem of the Ottoman dynasty, and Ahmet III's rule, between 1703 and 1730, is known in Turkish history as the *Lale Devri*, the Era of the Tulip. The maxim of the Tulip Era for the Ottoman Empire's elite society was "forget about tomorrow, just enjoy today."

"Let us laugh, let us play, let us enjoy the delights of the world," Ahmet Nedim, the court poet, declared. Grand palaces were built while the population languished in poverty.

Administering the Ottoman Empire effectively often proved to be an impossible task because of its immense size. Poor or nonexistent leadership brought with it more corruption, injustices, overtaxing, intrigues in the Old Seraglio's harem, and limits imposed by ignorant religious leaders on scientific research and exploration. A series of defeats in wars, a surge of nationalism, and independence movements within the nations instigated by the agents of Russia, Revolutionary France, and Austria and Islamic-based revolts against all attempts to reform also helped further the empire's demise. The Serbs revolted in 1804 and the Greeks in 1821. Yet one important event earlier in history helped to seal the fate of the Ottomans.

Sultan Ahmet III, the ruler during the tulip era, was forced into war with Peter the Great's Russia in 1710 because of Charles XII of Sweden. Charles XII had become a refugee at the Ottoman Court after suffering a catastrophic defeat at Poltava during the Great Northern War (1700 to 1721), after which Russia replaced Sweden as a major power in the Baltic Sea. Ahmet III was a puppet ruler, controlled by the unruly Janissaries, who forced the sultan to accept their choice of a grand vizier. A Turkish army of two hundred thousand troops encircled thirty-eight thousand Russians commanded by Czar Peter the Great between the River Pruth and a marsh in present-day Romania. The Russian army, along with Peter the Great, was trapped.

Grand Vizier Baltacı (Sapper) Mehmet Pasha was the commander of the Turkish army in Pruth. The unruly Janissaries earlier had imposed on the sultan the appointment of Baltacı as grand vizier. He was not an able statesman or an outstanding military commander. On July 21, 1711, Baltacı received a bribe of 230,000 rubles from Czar Peter the Great, for which the grand vizier let him escape the encirclement by his forces. The only Russian sacrifice was the retrocession of the territory of Azov. A great opportunity to break Russian power was lost.

Since Peter the Great's escape in Pruth, the Turks have been joking that Catherine, Czar Peter's mistress (later empress as Catherine I), had paid a secret nocturnal visit to the Turkish commander's tent to secure the freedom of Peter and his army. It is wrongly believed that thanks to a voluptuous sexual encounter with Baltacı Mehmet Pasha, Catherine was able to change the course of history. Born as Marta Skowronska, a Lithuanian peasant woman, she became Peter the Great's second wife in 1712 and took the Russian name Yekaterina Alekseyevna.

Things in the Ottoman Empire degenerated so badly that even a *tellak*, a fundamentalist bath attendant named Patrona Halil, was able to lead a rebellious mob on September 28, 1730. Patrona demanded Grand Vizier Ibrahim's head, and Sultan Ahmet III obliged, even though Ibrahim was his son-in-law. The grand vizier was strangled. On October 1, Ahmet III was forced to abdicate.

Soon after, Sultan Mahmud I, who ruled between 1730 and 1754, lured Patrona Halil, an Albanian-born former Janissary, into the Old Seraglio to receive Patrona Halil's advice on important affairs of the state. Promptly upon his arrival at the palace, Patrona Halil was killed, and order was restored. Mahmud I was advised by General Claude-Alexandre, Comte de Bonneval, a French convert to Islam known as Humbaracı (Bombardier) Ahmet Pasha.

Ahmet III, the former sultan, deposed by the bath attendant, lived six more years as a captive, confined in the *kafes*, the cage, in the inner sanctum of the Old Seraglio's harem. The fratricidal law, advocating the killing of princes to avoid rivalry for the throne, had been abolished in 1603. The cage had replaced it. The locked-up princes lived for years with barren concubines in that unreal world. If they were ever called to rule, they were by that time feebleminded or mad.

Selim III (1761–1808), the first reformist ruler influenced by the French Revolution, tried to Westernize the country by introducing a series of new regulations called the *Nizam-ı Cedid*. This New Order included forming a new army with modern weapons. Selim III adopted a cabinet system for the government, started a postal service, and introduced European dress and compulsory primary education. The Janissaries, who by then had degenerated into a privileged social menace, saw in these reforms, which were being established with French and German help, the end of their privileged position and mutinied. Selim III, fearing for his life, abolished the reforms. Still, he was deposed in 1807 and killed a year later.

The next reformist sultan, Selim's cousin Mahmud II, made secret and elaborate preparations before he moved against the Janissaries. His reforms helped to consolidate the Ottoman Empire despite rebellions in Greece and Serbia, defeats in the wars against Russia, and loss of territories.

Some historians believe that it was a young French girl who had inspired this first serious reform movement in the Ottoman Empire. She was Aimee Dubucq de Rivery from Martinique, and her cousin was Josephine Bonaparte, the French empress. Aimee, according to legend, was captured at sea by Barbary corsairs while en route home from a convent in France. This thirteen-year-old girl was presented as a gift to Sultan Abdul-Hamid I. She became a concubine in the Sultan's harem and was given the name Nakşidil, the Decorated Heart.

When Aimee Dubucq de Rivery bore a male offspring (Mahmud II), she became the sultan's wife and later *Valide Sultan*, the powerful queen mother, during her son's rule. Aimee's strong influence on her husband, her husband's nephew Selim III, and her son Mahmud II in favor of reforms caused the introduction into the Ottoman state of instructors from France and Germany. These included French military officers, some of whom were artillery instructors.

The end of the Janissaries came in June 1826, when they revolted once more by overturning their soup cauldrons* on hearing about the formation of new, westernized troops. This rebellion is known as *Vakayi Hayriye*, the Great Auspicious Event. Sultan Mahmud II declared war on the Janissaries, and when they refused to surrender, the barracks of an army of 140,000 were demolished with cannon fire. Thousands of them were killed, and any prisoner taken was executed.

Despite this reform movement and the destruction of the Janissaries the downward trend could not be stopped and the Ottoman Empire became known as the Sick Man of Europe. This epitaphial term was the creation of Czar Nicholas I of Russia in 1853, who was convinced that no reforms could stop the decay of the Ottoman Empire. Therefore, Nicholas I reasoned, it was about time to partition the disintegrating empire. The expressions "Sick Man of Europe" or the "Eastern Question" basically referred to the destruction of the Ottoman Empire.

I remember an interesting story about Mehmet Fuad Pasha (1815–69), a distinguished Ottoman politician. During a meeting in

---

* *Kazan Kaldırmak*, overturning their soup cauldrons or kettles was the Janissaries' traditional sign of mutiny.

Europe, the diplomats discussed the strongest power on earth. England, Russia, Austria, and France were named. Fuad Pasha did not agree. "Gentlemen, you are all wrong," he said. "The Ottoman Empire is the strongest power in the world."

When asked why, he answered, "For centuries, you from the outside and we from the inside did our best to destroy it and still it stands."

It is surprising that such a sick empire lasted so long and that its end came late as a result of its staggering defeat during World War I.

It took 275 years for movable-type printing to arrive in the Ottoman Empire after Johannes Gutenberg invented it in Mainz, Germany, in the 1450s. This system of printing was used all over Europe without major changes until the twentieth century. Gutenberg himself printed a book in 1454 called *Tuerkenkalender* in relation to the fall of Constantinople in 1453. In it he warned the Germans of a Turkish invasion.

A Hungarian convert who took the name Ibrahim Müteferrika was the first man to print books in Istanbul in 1727. The scribes, who considered movable-type printing a danger to their livelihood and were intolerant Islamic bigots, opposed him. The Ottoman government was forced to close Müteferrika's press several times, even though he had become a distinguished Ottoman diplomat.

I also remember a story from my school days about Mehmet Rüştü Pasha, known as the Translator. He was one of the last Ottoman grand viziers. During a private meeting, this grand vizier complained about the poor functioning of the state. A friend said, "Pasha, you've held high positions in that state. How come you did nothing to reform it?"

Mehmet Rüştü Pasha's answer was marked by a remarkable reflection of the truth:

> When we reach high office, we see a sailing ship far away at sea. The ship's rudder is out of order, its sails in tatters, and its masts all broken. We row as hard as we can to reach the ship quickly in order to save it. When we enter the ship, we observe that a joyful party is in progress. The people present are imbibing rakı and wine, playing music, singing and dancing.

We tell them, "Look here, the ship is a wreck. What are you doing?" They tell us, "Hey, stop complaining. Come join us. This is the way things are done, and we have no intention to change it." They press a glass of rakı in our hands and we, too, join the merry-go-round, squandering the money on pleasure.

Kuricalı Koçu Mustafa Bey, better known as Koçu Bey, an ethnic Albanian, was an early observer of the Ottoman decline. Koçu Bey, an Ottoman minister and reformer, in his brilliant *Risale-i Koçu Bey* (*The Treatise of Koçu Bey*) in 1630 warned the Ottoman state of the causes of its decline. Among these causes, he stated, was the empire's falling away from its traditions. The sultans no longer led their armies into wars or shared their meals with the troops. The *devşirme* principles for the Janissary forces had been corrupted. Anyone could apply and get accepted as a Janissary and use his position for personal advancement. The rulers had withdrawn from direct contact with their people; the grand viziers were usually weak, incompetent, and corrupt individuals and therefore powerless. The political factions had increased disunity, irresponsibility, and injustice in the empire, Koçu Bey warned: "the world can continue with irreligion, but not with injustice." His warning fell on deaf ears. Over a century later, the vast territories of a sick Ottoman Empire had become an attractive target for an expanding power in the north of the Black Sea.

This was czarist Russia.

34

The Turks and the Great Game II

Two circus performers can't dance on the same rope.

Turkish proverb

During the nineteenth century, Russia expanded its territory through the conquests of large slices of land from a weak Ottoman Empire. Czarist Russia then emerged as the principal opponent of British expansion. The attractive prize for both the British and the Russians was central Asia, including Turkestan and Afghanistan. Because the political and military play for this prize was like a game on a chessboard, the British politicians and military brass called it the Great Game.

The Russians called it *Bolshaya Igra* and considered India their own ultimate prize. The British were obsessed with the idea of defeating the Russian designs in central Asia, primarily to protect India from a Russian invasion. Queen Victoria described the British policy as "a question of Russian or British supremacy in the world." The traditional British policy was to use the Ottoman Empire against Russia's ambitious plans in the Balkans, Caucasus, and central Asia.

The Ottoman Empire during the great game of the nineteenth century was in no condition to play any significant role in central Asia. The Turks then were unable to protect their own interests, let alone render help to the Turkic peoples of central Asia or the Caucasus against the Russian onslaught. Czarist Russia played the game well against the British and gobbled up huge territories.

The game of today—or the Great Game II—is about the control, security, and marketing of the oil resources of the Middle East, Caucasus, and central Asia and fighting a common enemy—terrorism. This new game aims to spread democracy and human rights, including the emancipation of women, in this vast region and develop the economy. This time many nations are involved under the leadership of Americans, who gave it a new name—The Greater Middle East Reform Initiative. This project covers a huge area from the Arab nations of northwest Africa to Pakistan.

We are beginning to see the results of this new Western policy in Afghanistan, in Iraq, in Cyprus, and perhaps in Chechnya. The Chechens, fighting for their freedom for 170 years, have suffered greatly by an international diplomacy focused on terrorism. Chechnya is a good example of how a struggle for independence can suffer when religious militancy and terrorism are involved. Wahhabism, the puritanical Islamic movement supported by Saudi Arabian and Persian Gulf sources, has for some years made inroads in the Caucasus and central Asia. The result was a fatal blow to Chechnya's independence movement.

The Chechen and Arab terrorists of Jordanian Muslim warlord Khattab have damaged the legitimacy of the Chechens' cause by conducting cross-border raids and kidnappings. The anarchy that gripped Chechnya in the 1990s turned the country into a land of lawlessness and banditry. Under President Aslan Mashkadov, the institutions of statehood, specifically the courts and law, enforcement became ineffective.

A new and brutal Russian invasion followed, and Chechnya became a wasteland, despite the fact that most Chechens reject Islamic radicalism. Masked members of the Russian military units, acting like marauding criminal gangs known as *Zachistki*, engaged in extortion. The gangs of *Zachistki* rampaged through Chechen towns and villages, raping women and torturing and killing people.

This was not the Chechens' first struggle to gain freedom. I recall the stories I was told during my childhood years in Anatolia about Sheik Shamil's twenty-five-year fight for freedom. A leader of Dagestan and Chechnya, Shamil had established an independent state in 1834. In April 1859, the Russians stormed Shamil's fortress in Vedeno, and he escaped to Mount Gunib. Six months later, he had to surrender and died in exile.

The Caucasus, where two hundred different languages are spoken, is a critical area. It's part of a dangerous and volatile triangle of the Caspian Sea region, the Middle East, and the Balkans. It's known that al-Qaeda terrorists from Afghanistan have infiltrated Georgia's Pankisi Gorge, which borders Chechnya. About 150 special operations forces from the United States in May 2002 began training Georgia's tiny and underfunded army in antiterrorism tactics. This is part of Washington's worldwide campaign against terrorism, but it's also part of a conflict of interest between Russia and the United States. Frictions, therefore, were unavoidable. The Russian military forces, still based in Georgia, started jamming the radio frequencies used by American-built helicopters during the training of the Georgian recruits.

The Russians support Armenia, a landlocked country with a population of about 2.5 million. The hatred caused by wars and the land dispute over Nagorno-Karabagh between Armenia and Azerbaijan are obstacles to the Armenians' shaking off their reliance on Russia. The Russians have transferred $2 billion worth of arms to Armenia in order to counteract the US-Turkish plans for the southern Caucasus. In February 2001, Turkey offered to help Azerbaijan and Armenia resolve their dispute over Nagorno-Karabagh.

The war to eliminate the Taliban in Afghanistan and the al-Qaeda terrorist network, plus the toppling of Saddam Hussein's regime in Iraq, has altered the interests of the game players. Both Russia and America seem determined to have a permanent presence in the Caspian Sea region. US Troops have been deployed in Uzbekistan, Kyrgyzstan, and Georgia. The American troops in Uzbekistan are based at the former Russian base called Karshi Hanabad. Russia and Kyrgyzstan signed a security pact to base a squadron of twenty aircraft and up to one thousand Russian troops in Kyrgyzstan as part of a new rapid-reaction force. The Russian base at Kan airport is forty miles from Manas airport, where American troops are based. A collective Security Treaty Organization joins Russia, Kyrgyzstan, Kazakstan, and Tajikistan.

The Greater Middle East Reform Initiative has gained importance as a result of the realities of post–September 11. The fear of a rogue state or a terror organization able to produce or obtain weapons of mass destruction, including nuclear, is the most serious concern. The project, therefore, is based on securing interests linked not only with oil wealth but also with stability and how to prepare against common security threats. That is one of the reasons why NATO and Russia did their best to bury the cold war mentality by reaching a historic agreement in May 2002 in Reykjavik, Iceland. Still serious differences remain between the United States and the Russian Federation over Iran, which wants to play its own game in the region by acquiring nuclear weapons, and by spreading the Iranian brand of Islamic revolution.

Turkey is destined to be a key player in the Greater Middle East Reform Initiative because of its strategic location and the Turks' ethnic and linguistic connections with the countries of the Caucasus and central Asia. Turkey as a secular, democratic, law-and-order state is also a model state for Arab countries. The question is how a Turkish model will develop to impress the region in the future. Will it be a model country with a secular state loyal to Atatürk's reforms, or will it be a country with a state that identifies itself with the Canon Law of Islam? The success of the Greater Middle East Reform project, however, will depend on a just solution of the Palestine problem and on the consequences of the brutal resistance to the American occupation in Iraq. These events and others like them in the future will only increase the importance of the Turkish role in the region.

Turkey nevertheless is a bridge between Europe and Asia, between the worlds of Islam and Christianity. It is also a bridge to the West from the oil and natural gas fields of the Caspian Sea region, including that of the vast onshore Tengiz oil field of Kazakstan. The Caspian Sea region's oil resources are estimated to be 200 billion barrels of mostly untapped oil reserves, worth an estimated $5 trillion. In addition, BP Amoco's bellwether *Shah Deniz* in Azerbaijan is a huge natural gas field.

Several international oil companies are involved in a drilling venture at Kazakhstan's Kashagan oil field, four thousand meters below the shallow seabed of the Caspian Sea. Kashagan is three times the size of the Tengiz field that is believed to be one of the world's ten biggest oil deposits.

The existence of these natural resources started a race in the 1990s to build the pipelines to carry them to the world markets. Two pipelines crossing Russian and Georgian territories to carry crude oil from Tengiz to the Black Sea were favored because of the short distance. This involves huge tankers carrying the oil from the Black Sea ports through the Turkish Straits, the Bosphorus, and the Dardanelles. Turkish officials consider the increase in tanker traffic through this route unacceptable because of the danger of ecological and environmental disasters. The yearly tanker traffic through the Straits stood at fifty-five hundred in 2002.

One major pipeline now under construction will run from Baku in Azerbaijan to the Turkish port of Ceyhan in the eastern Mediterranean. It was preferred by Ankara and Washington despite its higher cost but opposed by the Russians. The Russians, in concert with the Iranians, consider the Caspian Sea region as a Russian-Iranian sphere of influence. This policy led Russia to sign a new military agreement with Iran. The American presence in the Caucasus and central Asia and Turkey's crucial role in the region still remain a nightmare for the Russian military.

A prospect exists for NATO member Turkey to establish military bases in Azerbaijan territory. Murtuz Aleskerov, the speaker of the Azeri parliament, said on February 8, 2002, that Azerbaijan might allow Turkey to have military bases in the country. He also stated that Azerbaijan might pass on information to Turkey from the Soviet-built Gabala radar station, which is a key element in Russia's missile attack early-warning system because it is capable of tracking rockets in real-time, in the southern and southeastern regions of the world.

Turkey, as an emerging market with a dynamic, resilient, and adaptable private sector, has an increasing need for energy. Russia and Iran supply natural gas to Turkey, but there has been a controversy over *Mavi*

Akım, or Blue Stream, a new undersea pipeline through the Black Sea. This pipeline, activated in January 2003, is expected to pump up to 16 billion cubic meters of gas a year to Turkey from Russia. Blue Stream, the deepest undersea pipeline, was constructed by the Russian gas company Gazprom and Italy's ENI despite objections from the United States and the Nationalist Action Party in Turkey. US and Turkish nationalist policy was that Turkey ought to buy gas directly from the Turkic countries in the Caucasus and central Asia, including the natural gas-rich Turkmenistan. Blue Stream, costing $3.5 billion, was also seen as a competitor to the Baku-Ceyhan pipeline.

The Blue Stream pipeline was a favored project of Mesut Yılmaz, the former leader of the Motherland Party. Yılmaz allegedly held talks with the Gazprom officials of the Russian Federation in Moscow, even though he did not represent the Turkish government. Cumhur Ersümer, a member of the Motherland Party and minister of energy, was also present during the Moscow negotiations on September 20, 1999, that involved Victor Chernomyrdin, the chairman of Gazprom.

The Operation White Energy probe in Turkey included an investigation about the Blue Stream project. It caused a war of nerves between Mesut Yılmaz, the deputy prime minister, and Sadettin Tantan, the interior minister from Yılmaz's own Motherland Party.

What surprised the critics of Mesut Yılmaz's policies was an odd confrontation on October 16, 1999, in Ashgabat between Saparmurat Turkmenbashi, the president of Turkmenistan, and Cumhur Ersümer, the Turkish minister of energy. The subject was the project of the Blue Stream pipeline. President Turkmenbashi of natural gas–rich Turkmenistan, speaking in front of journalists, told Ersümer: "We will supply you with cheap natural gas. Why are you buying more expensive Russian gas? Why did you go to Russia? Where is your solidarity?"

President Turkmenbashi's meaning was clear enough—the Russians were buying the natural gas cheaply from Turkmenistan and selling it at a much higher price to the Turks. The high cost of natural gas imported to Turkey through the Blue Stream pipeline is still a controversy there.

The Greater Middle East Reform Initiative is widely criticized in the

Arab world. An important reason is that secularity, democracy, and human rights, including the women's emancipation, are not accepted by most Arab states governed by the shariah and ruled by kings, sheiks, or presidents whose sons inherit such titles. Most countries also do not want other nations to dictate what's good for them. Others see the purpose of the Greater Middle East Reform Initiative as a plan by the United States, Britain, and Israel to control the people and resources of the region.

Milli Gazete, the newspaper of the Islamist Felicity Party, claimed on March 2, 2004, that the aim of the Greater Middle East Reform Initiative is to destroy Islam. In its lead news article, the newspaper reported, "The United States with this project plans to seize the resources of twenty-two Islamic countries."

Other obstacles to the Greater Middle East Reform Initiative include the distrust of pro-Islam for the Western powers, particularly the United States. The insecurity in Iraq and Palestine and the lack of a just solution for the people of Palestine also are serious concerns in the Islamic world. Unless a just solution is found to the Israeli-Palestine conflict and a serious attempt is made to improve the economy and reduce poverty in the countries involved, the Great Middle East Initiative will meet serious opposition.

I think Turkish foreign minister Abdullah Gül was more precise regarding the basic aims of of the Greater Middle East Reform Initiative. Gül, without mentioning the project itself, expressed his views in a February 2004 interview. He said that the Arab states should press domestic reforms to prevent foreign intervention on the grounds of reform. "If we don't take the reins and prefer to cover up and ignore [the problems of the Islamic World] then others will try to solve them their way and interfere in our affairs." He added, "And this interference will take place in the wrong way because they don't understand our sensitivities, habits, and cultures and our social structure."

35

A Return Journey

> *The thief who steals the minaret prepares its hiding place.*
>
> Turkish proverb

It was after twenty-nine years of self-imposed exile that I returned to Istanbul in the summer of 1999 when a powerful earthquake had just devastated northwestern Turkey. On the way to the city from Atatürk International Airport, I saw a cemetery. The mortal remains of Adnan Menderes and his foreign and finance ministers had been removed from the island of Imralı and interned in a mausoleum. Their burial ground was near Turgut Özal's, the man who had brought about the expansion of the Turkish economy, had spread deep corruption, and had infiltrated the Nakshibendi brotherhood into the state itself.

I was not surprised to learn that this mausoleum had been the result of a political power play to win the support of the old democrats of Adnan Menderes. Turgut Özal, in a cunning move to seize a political advantage over Süleyman Demirel, his leading rival, had built the mausoleum. He moved the mortal remains of Menderes and his two ministers to this site from Imralı Island, where they had been hanged.

Having seen their grave sites, I remembered Fatin Rüştü Zorlu, that tall, elegant gentleman, who, fluent in several languages, had been Menderes's foreign minister. I could never understand why and for what terrible crimes Zorlu had been hanged. In contrast, there was somewhat of a legal case against Adnan Menderes. He was accused during the trials of Yassıada of violating the constitution, encouraging Islamic movements, embezzling state funds, ruining the economy, repressing the legal opposition, and extravagance. Still, compared with the corruption scandals in Turkish governments that followed his regime, Menderes and his finance minister, Hasan Polatkan, look like a couple of amateurs.

The execution of Menderes and his two ministers was a grave mistake because it left a political legacy. The old democrats who were called *mahutlar*, or the notorious bunch, following the coup d'etat of May 27, 1960, never forgot this political legacy and never ceased to feel resentment about the trials of Yassıada.

I remember that Menderes used to say, "*Hafıza-i beşer, nisyan ile maluldür*," which is a Turkish proverb containing both Turkish and Arabic words. It means, "Human memory is prone to forgetfulness." Menderes was wrong, for his name remained very much alive in Turkish minds. The political legacy he left never disappeared. It is still kept alive today by the copycats of his Democratic Party.

Ayhan Aydan, an eighty-year-old former opera singer who had a long relationship with Menderes, says she could not forget Adnan Menderes, even after so many years. She believes hanging Menderes was a grave mistake. I think the worst legacy of the coup d'etat of May 27, 1960, and the execution of Menderes was the disruption of the democratical process and disunity in the nation that brought about decades of uncertainty in Turkish political life.

The description of the notorious bunch, therefore, caught up with the politicians who followed in Menderes's footsteps. Because of widespread corruption in Bülent Ecevit's coalition, the political parties, and the media, the private sector and aid groups feared in September 1999 that the international aid for earthquake victims would be stolen.

Enis Berberoğlu, a columnist for *Hürriyet*, wrote, "Will the earthquake aid be used to feed contractors close to the government, to build new houses for the members of parliament, and to purchase official cars for the pashas?" Berberoğlu added that there was a "crisis of faith" in the government. The aid for the earthquake victims was almost $200 million then and still growing. The business and civil aid groups wanted to see an independent monitor in charge of this aid money in order to prevent its plunder by the officials.

I met a young top executive of a mass circulated daily newspaper. He told me, "If you had been successful in getting rid of Süleyman Demirel in 1970, Turkey today would be a happy and prosperous country. Right now we are not prosperous, and our people are not happy." I told him that my biggest surprise after twenty-nine years of absence was the daily assaults I observed against the secular state and Atatürk's reforms. Since my arrival in Istanbul, I had been experiencing time travel. This was no longer the progressive, secularist, and enlightened culture I had known. A swelling population, alienated from the reforms of my childhood, had turned the Turkish clock right back one hundred years to the times of a collapsing Ottoman Empire.

The handling of the earthquake disaster clearly showed the impotence of the Turkish government. The officials, including Süleyman Demirel, then the country's president, admitted that they had not been informed of the earthquake, even four hours after it struck, destroying a huge industrial area and an important naval base. After learning what happened, they could not react quickly to help people trapped under the rubble. Thousands of people, including children, died needlessly. Erkan Mumcu, the minister of tourism, said that the government's response to the disaster was "a declaration of bankruptcy for the Turkish political, economic and administrative system."

Yet no official showed any sign of regret by handing over his or her resignation. Osman Durmuş, the health minister, a member of the Nationalist Action Party, declared that the earthquake victims had no need for medical aid from the United States. He said that portable toilets were not needed in the earthquake zones because the mosques there had toilets. The health minister added that the Turks should not accept blood donated by Greeks. *Sabah* in an editorial promptly told him to shut up and go away.

A second major earthquake in November 1999 hit Düzce, in north-western Anatolia, killing hundreds of people. Many were injured and left homeless. The seismologists generally agree that Istanbul might be due for a big tremor. An active North Anatolian fault line runs south of the city beneath the Marmara Sea. Big earthquakes have struck Istanbul roughly every one hundred years, in 1766 and 1894. Because of dishonest construction companies and bribery, buildings, including schools, have become death traps during strong tremors.

Turkey has become a country of severe contrasts. I saw economic improvements, accomplished by young and daring entrepreneurs and businessmen. The country has become the European Union's tenth-biggest trading partner and Russia's second. In 1997, Turkey exported $37 billion worth of goods and imported goods worth $41 billion. The income from tourism in 1997 was $8.89 billion, which later increased when Turkey attracted 13 million tourists a year. Because of the high inflation rate, people were not willing to hold on to their local money. Money exchanges, protected by heavily armed security guards have mushroomed everywhere.

Istanbul is a metropolis with a number of highways and two great suspension bridges over the Bosphorus. In the streets, you could see the polarization of the people between secularism and Islamic fundamentalism in their talk and manners and the way they dressed. The Islamic style of dressing, exactly as in the Ottoman era, has mushroomed as if Turkey had never experienced secular reforms. The Turkey I had known has disappeared; some of the reforms I had gone through as a boy have vanished. The secularity of the state was constantly under aggression by the specter of the Ottoman times and by Islamic radicals.

The legacy of Kemal Atatürk has been so dogmatized and is such a victim of neglect that millions are no longer touched by it. Kemalism has been unable to adjust itself to the changing times. It has been caught culturally unprepared against a powerful revival of Islam, and its message of enlightenment has not been applied in time to energize an exploding population. The most vital characteristic of Kemalism during the reform years was to mobilize the Turks to change by forcing them to accept Western ways. Now I observed that there existed a movement among the Kemalists themselves to transform Kemalist ideology into an inflexible conservative ideology against the West. These inheritors of the Kemalist ideology, not so familiar with the reform years and misguided about the real meaning of Kemalism, were turning it into a hard, unyielding doctrine against itself.

I went to Çamlıca, the beautiful hill that overlooks the Bosphorus on the Asiatic side. There I saw a *mescit* (a small mosque), food stalls, and coffee shops. In one stand, built with marble, a cook was busy roasting *döner kebab*. The view of the Bosphorus and the European parts of Istanbul from the top of the hill was still breathtaking, and that *meltem* blowing from the strait, refreshing. Young couples were sitting on park benches nearby. In the summer heat, a lot of girls and women were wearing long Islamic-style coats that reached their ankles, concealing their figures. They had turbans that left only their faces in view. Others wore the black chador that covered their bodies and faces, allowing them only to peep at the world with one visible eye. On the beaches, the Western idea of flaunting physical beauty was unacceptable to devout Islamic women, who wore full-body swimsuits that covered their heads, arms, and legs. The Islamic swimsuit fits loosely to hide the outlines of the female body. Still, other women wore blue jeans, skirts, blouses, and Western-style swimsuits. Astonishingly, even the fez was back. I saw men wearing the tasseled red fez and *sarık*, or turban. Arabic, the language of the Qur'an, had replaced Turkish in prayers.

The highest authorities in the state itself were pursuing plans to destroy Kemal Atatürk's personality, his secular reforms, and the secular republic he created in 1923, diligently and persistently. When I read stories in the newspapers about the daily activities of members of the Ottoman dynasty, I remembered the Colonel, my childhood mentor. The Colonel never wanted to see the members of *hanedan* back in the country. Now they were all back and being acclaimed by the media with such titles as sultans, sultanas, and *hanım* (lady) sultans for the younger generation.

Some newspapers, TV stations, radios, and magazines were the products of the growth of radical Islam, and were owned by religious reactionaries and followed their antisecular policies.

I was confronted with a steep moral decline. Pro-Islam-oriented financial organizations mushroomed in Anatolian towns. They promised to pay their investors *helal* (legitimate) profits in their nonexistent factories instead of interest, which is unacceptable to devout Muslims. In this way, thousands of Turkish guest workers in European countries were swindled out of their savings. Hundreds of millions in dollars evaporated, and the culprits masqueraded in Turkish cities as respectable men.

Among my biggest surprises was the power exercised in the state itself by members of the religious brotherhoods. The grounds of the Süleymaniye Mosque, where the mausoleums of Süleyman the Magnificent and his wife, Roxelana, are located, had become a magnet for the family of Turgut Özal, the late president. Because several sheiks of the Nakshibendi Brotherhood, including Mehmet Zahit Kotku, are buried there, the members of Turgut Özal's family, Nakshibendis themselves, also wish to be buried there after their deaths. Turgut Özal, while in power, was able to bury his mother, Hafize, there by a special government decree. Turgut Özal's brother Yusuf Bozkurt Özal was also interred in January 2001 in that burial ground.

Professor Mahmud Esad Coşan, sixty-three, had replaced his father-in-law, Mehmet Zahit Kotku upon his death in 1980 as sheik of the Nakshibendi Brotherhood. Professor Coşan went to Australia after the generals forced out Necmettin Erbakan's Islamic regime. He and his son-in-law Yücel Uyarel were killed in a traffic accident on February 6, 2001, near Sydney. Sheik Coşan helped to organize Turgut Özal's Motherland Party, and, as head of the Kotku Foundation of Australia, he opened new dervish convents there.

According to law, 677 Islamic sects and brotherhoods are illegal in Turkey. Under pressure from the military, the politicians in the National Security Council in Ankara also had signed a decree prohibiting the activities of all Islamic orders and brotherhoods on February 28, 1996. This decree caused the fall of Necmettin Erbakan's Islamic government on

June 18, 1997. Yet, apart from the Özal family, several well-known politicians are members of the Dervish Convent of Iskenderpaşa in Istanbul, the centerpiece of the activities of the Nakshibendi Brotherhood. Hypocricy has never been so widespread in Turkish politics since the founding of the republic in 1923.

To see secularist politicians use Islam for election gains was, to me, shocking. Bülent Ecevit, the prime minister at the time, decided to allow Sheik Coşan and his son-in-law Uyarel to be buried on the grounds of the Süleymaniye Mosque. President Necdet Sezer vetoed the government's decree, stating that burial there was against the constitution and cemetery rules. The Nakshibendi Brotherhood had to settle for the next-best burial place—the old cemetery on a hill that overlooks the Mosque of Eyup Sultan at the Golden Horn.

"As a family, we all belong to the Nakshibendi Brotherhood," Turgut Özal's brother Korkut Özal declared, adding that Coşan was their sheik. He said Sheik Coşan had been a teacher to his brother Turgut Özal, the former president, and that the government's decision about the burial had been right. Korkut Özal, like his elder brother, Turgut, was a member of Necmettin Erbakan's Islamist National Salvation Party in 1973. He was elected Member of Parliament in the 1973 and 1977 elections and had served as interior minister and minister of agriculture.

During the controversy over the burial site, Ilhan Selçuk commented in *Cumhuriyet*: "Is it possible to have a democracy with sheiks and their disciples? . . . Democracy is not a regime of dervish disciples. It is an order of secular citizens." The writer argued that a sheik is the leader of an Islamic order or brotherhood:

> A disciple is obligated to deliver his personality to his sheik's wishes.
>
> Has Turgut Özal conducted the affairs of the prime ministry as a disciple of the sheik of the Nakshibendi?
>
> Has he gone up to Çankaya [the official residence of the president in Ankara] with this identity?
>
> Was Turgut Özal a disciple of his sheik or president of Turkey's secular state?"

Upon reading this article, I remembered what Kemal Atatürk had told us during the reform years—that the Turkish Republic cannot be a country of sheiks, dervishes, and disciples and that the real sect is the order of civilization. The powerful revival of Islam and its brotherhoods, with their influential sheiks, dervishes, and disciples, was, to me, undeniable proof that Kemalism in its eighty-two-year history had failed to wipe out religious bigotry and ignorance.

I went to visit the old jailhouse that was going to be my residence in 1960 if Adnan Menderes had remained in power. The Sultanahmet Prison near the Hippodrome, Istanbul's center of tourism, had been sold. It had been one of the notorious prisons where Menderes had jailed scores of journalists. The new owners had transformed it into a luxury hotel. There was a smartly uniformed doorman at its door instead of armed prison guards.

Some of the old trams that were removed when I was a teenager were back. I rode one on Istiklal Street, once a highly fashionable avenue and popular shopping area, and the conductor did not bother me about a ticket. The ride was free for senior citizens.

Istiklal Street, which had been the center of disastrous riots over the Cyprus crisis in 1955, had also changed. A lot of people were walking up and down the long avenue, but they were not shoppers. Few people carried bags. The merchants complained about the lack of business and said that the new, fancy shopping malls have taken away well-heeled shoppers. Ah, I said, the American way of shopping has arrived.

One of the supermalls is called Akmerkez, or White Center, and to enter it I had to go through a security check. Security has become a big industry following the extreme right- and left-wing clashes during the Times of Chaos, the Kurdish revolt and that of the militant Marxists and militant Islamic radicals. Akmerkez is a huge marble-and-glass showcase of escalators and glitzy stores, selling European and American as well as Turkish brand name merchandise.

I observed that the Russians had indeed finally realized their goal and invaded Turkey, including even remote parts of eastern Anatolia. After the collapse of the Soviet Union, a huge suitcase trade started between

Turkey and Russia and the former republics of the Soviet Union. Market-places mushroomed all around the country to satisfy the Russian demand for Western goods. This lasted only until China, with its low prices and free airplane tickets for the traders, began taking over the Russian suit-case trade. The once-booming markets in the suitcase trade in Turkey col-lapsed. A merchant told me, "We are now hunting flies."*

There was another terrific invasion, which brought thousands of pros-titutes. It has been nicknamed the "Invasion of the Natashas." Hoards of young Natashas arrived in the country from the former Soviet bloc coun-tries to conduct their sex trade. The officials soon received complaints from local residents that Natashas were wrecking homes and ruining fam-ilies. Many restaurants and hotels were raided, and Natashas were arrested and deported, but the deportations could not stop the invasion. Thousands more still arrive each year after discovering that the sex trade in Turkey is a lucrative business. The invasion of the Natashas was fol-lowed by a huge tourist invasion from the Russian Federation.

Journalism nowadays has become a highly profitable profession for some. Checkbook journalism was rampant. Not many reporters and writers remember the words of Sedat Simavi: "Don't make your pen a slave. If necessary break it, but don't ever sell it." Some columnists have even been labeled traitors to the nation. I was surprised to read articles in *Cumhuriyet* written by Cüneyt Arcayürek, once a great admirer and sup-porter of Süleyman Demirel, criticizing Demirel on his lack of grasp of events and on his friendship with people whose fortunes were known to be tainted.

Arcayürek in his book *Etekli Demokrasi* (*The Democracy of Flat-tery*), published in February 2001, describes his experiences with former President Süleyman Demirel. Once, he wrote, while visiting the Isparta region with President Demirel, he encountered a local citizen. Arcayürek was having lunch by the shores of Lake Eğridir with journalist Fatih Çekirge when the man approached and told them an unusual story. He alleged that Şevket Demirel, the president's brother, had sold publicly

---

* The expression *sinek avlamak*, "to hunt flies," describes a severe lack of customers.

owned poplar trees by the roadside between Eğridir and Isparta. The man also alleged that the president's brother had plundered public lands.

Oh, I thought, *is that really you, Cüneyt?*

Süleyman Demirel was quick to respond to Cüneyt Arcayürek's allegations in *Sabah*, without mentioning the poplar trees and allegations of plunder of public lands in Isparta. Demirel called Arcayürek, his former press adviser, a knave because he was disclosing information he had learned as a government official.

Years of experience with terrorism had left its mark on the media. The laws meant to fight terrorism, specifically terrorism carried out by the Kurdistan Workers Party, outlawed statements that are judged to be favoring separatism. The courts had authority at the time to close political parties, and people could not speak their minds freely on such subjects as Kurdish separatism. More than 130 academics, journalists, and writers were jailed in recent years by special state security courts on charges of expressing opinions deemed harmful to the unity of the state. Because of pressure from human rights activists, a number of them had been released. Since 1992, twenty-five journalists who, with their writings or actions, may have supported the cause of the Kurdish rebels have died under mysterious circumstances. A parliamentary report said that there were 908 cases of murder between 1975 and 1994 still unsolved, including those of many journalists killed for their writings.

Parliament approved in the summer of 2002 the required human rights legislation to meet the Copenhagen criteria for the membership in the European Union. More sweeping human rights reforms were also passed on June 19, 2003, extending the right to broadcast in Kurdish to private radio and television stations. An antiterror law was dropped. It had earlier authorized prison sentences up to three years for speaking out in favor of Kurdish separatism.

An official move for human rights actually began with Necdet Sezer when he was the president of the Constitutional Court, the highest judicial body in the country. Sezer made an historic appeal for human rights to the newly elected members of parliament. Speaking on April 26, 1999, during the ceremonies commemorating the thirty-seventh anniversary of the Constitutional Court, Judge Sezer urged the members of parliament to repeal a series of laws and constitutional provisions that include article 312 of the penal code.

"Change the laws that restrict the freedom of expression," he stated and called for lifting the ban on teaching the Kurdish language. He said that the ban violated international agreements. The constitution of 1982 forbids "thoughts or opinions that run counter to Turkish national interests," Judge Sezer said, and Turkey should change its constitution and laws that limit the freedom of the press, labor unions, and political parties to harmonize itself with universal standards.

One year later, on May 5, 2000, fifty-eight-year-old Judge Sezer was elected president of Turkey when Süleyman Demirel's term ended. President Sezer said in his first news conference that in Turkey, "An understanding of democracy has not developed in social and political life, and a tradition of democracy has not been created."

Babıali, the press district of Istanbul, has changed a great deal since 1970, and not always for the better. Few newspapers remain there. The rest, controlled by press barons and powerful business conglomerates, have left the district to build huge new centers, allegedly with billions of dollars siphoned off from the banks they had once owned. The media, the watchdog against corruption and for human rights, was itself mired in an endless cycle of degeneration. As a result, newspaper circulation suffered. In a country with a population of over seventy million, the total sale of daily newspapers is 4.35 million. The daily circulation of *Posta* in January 2004 was 527,163; *Hürriyet*, 474,004; the Islamist newspaper *Zaman*, 394,062; *Sabah*, 386,833; *Milliyet*, 294,174; *Takvim*, 263,585; and *Akşam* 209,181. Most newspaper columnists, including the ones I knew once as defenders of social justice, were writing absolutely nothing about the plunders and swindles of some media bosses, fearing loss of their jobs.

Sadettin Tantan, the outspoken interior minister, in March 2001, before his ouster, said that the media has collapsed inside its own revolving wheel of self-interest. During an NTV program called *The Subjects of the Agenda,* Tantan added that the most important problem in Turkey's agenda was the media's suppression of facts on politics and bureaucracy.

Older members of the media complained that journalism had died, despite impressive technical advancements. They also complained that a lot of unqualified people, including girlfriends and mistresses of media bosses and editors, had become columnists. According to the old-timers, the understanding of the news has also changed, and gossip was being passed along as news. Some newspapers and TV channels owned by construction barons were being used to blackmail state officials who dared to stand against their owners' interests in state tenders.

I remembered how *Hürriyet's* circulation, even with rough competition in newsgathering, had climbed to almost one million copies daily in the 1960s. The country's population then was about thirty-five million. Almost thirty-five years later, and with a population of seventy million, there exists no national newspaper in Istanbul now with a daily circulation of one million or more.

The neglect of secular education played a major part in low newspaper readership, but there are other important factors. After the banking scandals involving the media moguls, there was an increase of public distrust toward the media; TV networks in color appeared with live news coverage and entertainment, attracting the masses with limited income and little education; the media itself ignored the training and development of the reporter and replaced him with scores of inexperienced, selfserving columnists. Coupon giveaways of every kind, including pots and pans, substituted for intelligent newsgathering.

Istanbul had lost a colorful character when my old boss Safa Kılıçlıoğlu died. His son sold *Yeni Sabah's* rights to *Sabah*. Several of my friends, including Tahsin Öztin, have passed away; others have retired.

On May 23, 1997, before Necmettin Erbakan was forced to resign as Islamist prime minister, the *Washington Post* printed an article by Nora Boustany under the headline "Diplomatic Dispatches—Working to Turkish Media's Discredit." Its subject was Melih Gökçek, the mayor of Ankara from the Welfare Party, who was sent to Washington by Erbakan "to discredit the Turkish media" for what Gökçek described as "their relentless bashing of the Welfare Party." Nora Boustany reported that the mayor was being ferried around Washington, DC by energetic image consultants and lobbyists with cellular phones. That article reminded me of Marko Pasha, the colorful figure of the Ottoman times renowned for his patience in listening to people's complaints. The Islamists, I thought, would have done much better if they had complained their grievances to Marko Pasha without bothering to travel to Washington.

I did complain to Marko Pasha about my own problems with Süleyman Demirel and the great lothario of Istanbul bars of times past. Marko Pasha promised years ago that he would take care of these complaints at once. It took him thirty years to defy Turkey's aged political elite and inflict a humiliating blow on Süleyman Demirel. In April 2000, parliament rejected Prime Minister Bülent Ecevit's proposal of a constitutional amendment allowing Demirel a second term in office as the country's president. Ecevit's attempt was once again an old-guard political gimmick not to change the status quo and not to rock the boat of the establishment. According to an opinion poll, 70 to 75 percent of the Turks had opposed a second term for Demirel, believing that he had been responsible in the past for the country's political instability.

Soli Özel, a university professor and newspaper columnist, said, "The real meaning [of the rejection of a second term for Demirel] is that our political system is starting to mature."

Since the reform years, the Turkish republic had lost over six decades to continue its remarkable secular and cultural advancement. No serious attempts were made by the state to improve the education and living standard of the peasants and have-nots, the majority of the population. As a result, there are still two Turkish realities in this new millenium—an urban Turkey of modern cities and towns populated with a minority of the educated, rich elite, and millions of dirt-poor, uneducated migrants from the Anatolian provinces in search of jobs. The other reality is a rural Turkey populated with older peasant folks and subsistence farmers living a simple life in still underdeveloped towns and forty thousand villages. Most of these villages are isolated for weeks and months every winter by heavy snow.

Over one million school-age children do not attend school because they have to work for low wages in factories and shops to help support their poor families. Most of the thirty thousand village schools do not have classes beyond the fifth grade. Most schools do not have computers and the average class size is sixty-four pupils.

The majority of Turks are not book readers. The average print run of a book is way under ten thousand copies, and a book that sells ten thousand copies is considered a best-seller. Since the People's Houses (*Halkevi*) and their libraries were closed during the Menderes regime, there has been an effort to rebuild a system of public libraries. There are now, 1437 public libraries. The number of people using the libraries has been falling.

Because of the economic crisis of 2001, the per capita gross domestic product (GDP) in early 2003 was $2,580, an amount equal to what it was in the 1980s. According to official figures, the economic crisis caused a severe retreat in the country's gross domestic product—it was reduced from the precrisis figure of $201.5 billion to $144.3 billion. The official literacy rate is 82 percent. Seven million people, the majority of them young girls and women, are illiterate. Only forty-four in one thousand people are newspaper buyers. For every one thousand there, are 171 TV sets and 141 radios.

In comparison, the World Almanac of 2000 shows that the per capita GDP in the United States is $30,200 and in Greece, $13,000. In every one thousand people in the United States and Greece, 238 and 135 buy daily newspapers, respectively. Again, for every one thousand people, there are 776 TV sets and 2,172 radios in the United States and 442 TV sets and 402 radios in Greece. The literacy rate in Greece is 95 percent. However, every three out of ten TV sets and a lot of appliances in European homes are Turkish made, and the country has 16 million cell phones.

One morning in Istanbul, I was standing across from the main gate of Gülhane Park and the nearby Sublime Porte. I remembered that this was the place where 160 years earlier the Imperial Edict of Gülhane had been proclaimed. It was called Tanzimat, and it was supposed to safeguard the lives and property of all Ottoman subjects, irrespective of race or creed, and to guarantee every citizen's right to justice. Tanzimat represented human rights and the Sublime Porte, the power of the Ottoman Empire of the years long gone. Since *Tanzimat*, every Ottoman and republican-era government has trampled on the human rights of its citizens.

Istanbul, that famed city, once a graceful capital of the Ottomans, with a history both cursed and magnificent, was still the queen of international intrigues and high-society gossip. Many members of this high society made fortunes through corruption and are now living a second Era of Tulipmania in a sumptuous environment. They are oblivious of or do not care about the threats involving the secular republic and the wellbeing of the country.

These nouveau riche, who are known as the looters and plunderers of the state and the banks, live in multi-million-dollar *yalıs* on the shores of the Bosphorus. Their nickname is *yalı gangs*, and their maxim, as it was during the original Era of Tulipmania, is to enjoy life today.

I looked around for *Hürriyet*'s former owner, the dashing lothario, in the bars of Istanbul's luxury hotels, but he was nowhere to be found. He has left, preferring to stay in Geneva, Switzerland, away from the scorching society gossip of Istanbul. He stayed away for eleven years and returned to Turkey in April 2004, an old man with a white beard and in great pain. He had back problems and was operated on by a Swiss doctor, which left him a cripple in unbearable pain. A second operation in Istanbul restored his health, or so he told a *Hürriyet* reporter, and that news surprisingly became the banner headline of the newspaper on April 8, 2004. That was not the end of the story. The *Hürriyet* editors and writers were upset when he told a reporter from the rival newspaper *Sabah* that *Sabah* during the last eleven years had become a better newspaper than *Hürriyet*.

Another gossip that was swirling through the city like the south wind *lodos* was about a famous songwriter. The songwriter became involved in a scandal not realizing that kiss-and-tell in homosexual affairs could be deadly in Turkey. According to society gossip, the homosexual partner of the songwriter was a well-known man about town. The songwriter, proud of what he had done to this *beyefendi*, or most honorable gentleman, foolishly spread the word and thus became a victim of revenge. One day he was kidnapped by three criminal gang members and sodomized by them.

While he was being sodomized, pictures were taken and were shown around the city to everyone who knew the songwriter. His reputation as a macho man was in shambles.

Among my other surprises about life in Istanbul was the story of Matild Manokyan (Manookian), a member of the Armenian minority. She had followed in the footsteps of Benli Belkis and had become Turkey's best-known madam. Manokyan's thirty-two brothels in Istanbul made her the city's top taxpayer in the 1990s. A seamstress before being a famous madam, Manokyan had used the profits from her brothels wisely in investments in a real-estate empire. She was known as the *Girl from Pera*, owned numerous apartment buildings and shopping malls, and drove around Istanbul in a Rolls-Royce. The Islamic reactionaries were furious when the government declared Matild Manokyan as Istanbul's top tax-payer for five years and honored her in official ceremonies. It is still not known who was behind a bomb attack against her in 1995 after she donated thirty-six thousand dollars to a hospital in Istanbul. The blast injured Manokyan and killed her driver and bodyguard. Matild Manokyan died in her sleep at the age of eighty-four in February 2001 and left her fortune to her son and brother.

There was another big surprise for me—the allegation that Turgut Özal, the former president, had been a victim of a mysterious conspiracy while still in office. Özal had been a phenomenon in Turkish politics, and a lot of Turks, despite the widespread corruption of his times (1986–93) and his support of Islamic movements still remember him as a visionary leader.

Was Turgut Özal Murdered?

> *Don't tell your secret to your friend,*
> *or he will tell your secret to his friend.*
>
> Turkish proverb

*I*n the spring of 2002, the Özal family came out with a bombshell and claimed that Turgut Özal, their family's patriarch and former president, had been poisoned, the victim of a conspiracy.

Ahmet Özal—the son of the former president, a member of parliament at the time from Malatya province—asked for an investigation regarding his father's untimely death. Speaking about an earlier assassination attempt against his father, Ahmet Özal questioned why an autopsy had not been performed to determine the cause of the president's death.

He added in his statement, "My father's blood was kept at Hacettepe Hospital [in Ankara] for five years. I learned that from a TV program and requested its return to my family in 1998. The next day, the blood vanished. I was told that the nurses had discarded my father's blood by mistake."

Turgut Özal, known as Dervish because of his membership in the

Nakshibendi Brotherhood, had died on April 17, 1993, at the age of sixty-six of a massive heart attack. He was also known as Tonton and the Fat Man. He had an enormous appetite and loved to eat anything he could get his hands on. In 1987 he had heart bypass surgery in Houston, Texas, and treatments there for heart and prostate problems.

Turgut Özal's secularist wife, Semra, the daughter of a ship welder, told the newspaper *Sabah* that on the morning of his death, her husband looked healthy, didn't have breakfast, and hadn't exercised. She added that her husband collapsed while walking to the breakfast room at Çankaya, the presidential residence in Ankara. Semra Özal bent down to check and noticed that her husband's heart had stopped. She stressed her own view that there should have been an autopsy to find out why the president had died: "You know there are time-release injections that work like ticking bombs." She had saved hair samples of her husband and believed that these should have been sent by the state or by parliament to the United States to determine the cause of death.

In his column in *Hürriyet*, Emin Çölaşan ridiculed the claims of the Özal family. "All right," he wrote, "who killed him and why?" Çölaşan revealed an interesting conversation he had in 1993 with Hüsamettin Cindoruk, then the speaker of parliament and son of Çölaşan's aunt:

> We were talking about President Özal. Cindoruk leaned to my ear and said, "He [Özal] is on the way out. "He will die soon."
>
> I was surprised and couldn't believe it. I said, "He can't be on the way out, brother. He will bury us all."
>
> Cindoruk persisted. "Baba [Süleyman Demirel] is the source of this news. This is a state secret. You keep it to yourself and keep your mouth shut. He [Özal] won't survive through the coming summer months. Baba's information is sound. If he says that he must know something."
>
> A short while later, Özal died on April 17. Baba [Demirel] was getting ready to become president, and on April 24, he invited some journalists for lunch. I told him [Demirel] what I knew and asked, "Did you really know that Özal was going to die?"

Demirel told Çölaşan that the government is also responsible for the health of the president: "Two months ago, we received information from a source that his [Özal's] health was not good. When I heard this, I asked him how he was feeling. He said he felt good. I couldn't tell him anything else. Our information was not related to his heart but to his prostate."

Süleyman Demirel had resigned as prime minister in May 1993, after he was elected president of Turkey during a parliamentary vote. That was a few weeks after the death of President Turgut Özal.

Milliyet's columnist Doğan Heper wrote on April 22, 2004, that there were still claims regarding Özal's death. Heper added that Özal's family insisted the president had been murdered. In his column titled "Not," Heper wrote: "For years no serious investigations have been conducted about Özal's death." According to Doğan Heper, Özal wanted to create a powerful Turkey, spread between China and the Adriatic Sea, and for this purpose he traveled in central Asia and the Balkans. He wrote that claims persisted that Özal was murdered by people who did not wish to see a powerful Turkey.

Halil Şıvgın, who was the minister of health at the time, also expressed his belief that Özal had been murdered. In a statement to *Yeni Şafak* on May 6, 2002, Şıvgın pointed out some irregularities he had learned on the morning of Özal's collapse. According to Şıvgın, two doctors were supposed to be on duty at the presidential residence, but no doctor was on hand on April 17, 1993, when Özal collapsed. Şıvgın added that there were problems in the ambulance and indecision about the choice of hospital.

"Nobody believed me that day," Şıvgın said. "But now more people believe me."

There are more mysterious circumstances about President Özal's death. Since Turkish government officials, including Prime Minister Demirel, knew that President Özal was soon going to die, why was this vital information kept a secret from him and his close family members? Was this secrecy detrimental to the medical care he should have been receiving for his heart condition?

Turgut Özal was born in Malatya in 1927, and he studied electrical engineering at Istanbul's Technical University, where he met Süleyman Demirel. They would later become political rivals. Özal worked as an economist for the World Bank between 1971 and 1973. He was an adviser in 1979 to Süleyman Demirel's government. When the military overthrew Demirel in 1980 for the second time, the coup leaders asked Özal to stay on as deputy prime minister to implement a program for economic reforms, including the lifting of exchange controls.

The coup leaders had no idea that Turgut Özal was an Islamist. General Kenan Evren, the leader of the coup d'etat, wrote in his memoirs: "If I had known that Özal was a member of that Islamic sect [Nakshibendi Brotherhood], I wouldn't have let him run for office." As the founder and leader of the right-of-center Motherland Party, and later as prime minister and the president, Özal did his best to undermine the secular state.

An incident regarding Turgut Özal is telling about his role in the revival of the Islamic brotherhoods. It happened during the funeral in Ankara of journalist Uğur Mumcu when Özal was the president. A huge crowd was shouting slogans of outrage against Özal for his support of the Islamists who were blamed for Mumcu's murder. "Damn the fat man," the funeral attendants shouted, "the enemy of secularism."

Özal admired America and was a devout Muslim in his public life but a liberal in his private life. He said, "I am not secularist, the state is."

He would regularly attend Friday prayers in a mosque and toast with a glass filled with water instead of champagne during official ceremonies. In his private life, brandy was one of his favorite drinks, accompanied by lots of chocolate.

The constituency of the Motherland Party, the right-of-center party Özal had founded with the backing of the Nakshibendi Brotherhood, lay in Anatolia's dominant political and religious conservatism. The Motherland Party won a big victory in the 1983 election. According to his brother Korkut, Özal believed that this election victory was Allah's work and not his own. If Turgut Özal was murdered as his family claims, was this killing a result of a power struggle at the top of the Turkish state? Or could there be yet another reason?

Özal was short, only five-foot-three (one meter, sixty centimeters) but heavy, with a weight of 308.6 pounds (140 kilos). All his friends knew that he was a voracious eater at the dinner table. Turgut Özal died soon after returning from an important trip to the emerging Turkic states in central Asia. On his return to Ankara, he had complained at the airport that he was tired. Özal's visit to central Asia was about two years after the collapse of the Soviet Union. In Bukhara, Uzbekistan, he had visited the tomb of Muhammed Bahaüddin Nakshibendi, the founder of the Nakshibendi Brotherhood.

When the Soviet Union collapsed in the late 1991 and several Turkic republics in central Asia and Caucasus moved rapidly to gain independence, Turkey quickly recognized the emerging states and opened embassies in each one. Turgut Özal believed that Turkey was poised to play an important role as a vital bridge to the West by cooperating with these emerging states. Turgut Özal's view was that Turkey could become a transportation route to the West for the oil and natural gas resources of the Caspian Sea region. He understood that his country could play a stabilizing role in that strategically vital area because of Turkey's linguistic, cultural, historic, and ethnic ties with the peoples of these emerging Turkic states.

Özal used to say that the twenty-first century would become the Turkish century. Most Turks still remember Enver Pasha's dream of pan-Turanism, the unification of all Turkic peoples. In October 1992, Özal had organized a Turkic summit aiming to form a Turkic commonwealth that would include cultural links, joint banks, and free-trade zones. He said, "We are from the same root, we are a large family. . . . We must integrate." It is interesting to note that after Turgut Özal died in 1993, some of the Turkish leaders that followed him neglected the emerging Turkic states in central Asia.

Özal's free-market doctrines were successful in Turkey despite their contradiction with the state's dominance of business and media, a tradition of Kemalism. He lifted the quotas on imports, organized a banking system, and established laws on foreign investments but could not control inflation and growing unemployment. He also behaved like an autocrat.

Turgut Özal's policies on central Asia and Caucasus concerned the

Russians and Iranians. Russia, still active in the Great Game II, wanted to protect Russian influence in the former Soviet republics. Iranian ambitions and economic targets were centered on spreading their ayatollahs' reactionary Islam in the region.

Some of the conspiracy theories speculate that Özal might have been given a high-potency time-release poison while overindulging himself on the delicacies of central Asia. There had been two attempts to assassinate him years earlier. Was he then a victim of the Great Game II or a conspiracy inside the Turkish state? Was his death due in fact to his heart problems? We may never know.

We do know, however, that Turgut Özal left a legacy of Islamic brotherhoods, corruption deep in the state and the media and business world, as well as remarkable economic reforms. It was a powerful legacy that changed the destiny of the nation.

The governments that followed him, including secularist Bülent Ecevit's incompetent coalition, were complete failures and could not improve the economic course set by Özal. In fact, after Özal, wide-scale corruption, along with a powerful Islamic revival, had settled over the secular republic as an indestructible bogey.

37

A Confused Premier and Tansu Çiller's Ducks

> *"My ducks have disappeared."*
>
> Tansu Çiller

remember Bülent Ecevit as a man of contradictions, a kind of an idealist struggling between Kemalism, globalism, hard-line nationalism, leftism, and anti-imperialism. He described himself as a democratic socialist, and as prime minister in the 1970s, he rejected the European Union's offer for Turkey's candidacy for membership. As an admirer of Vladimir Ilyich Lenin, at the time Ecevit was anti-American and anti-European and regarded the Europeans and the Americans as colonialists. His big mistake, when he had the chance forty years ago, was not to define a new strategy for the continuation of Kemal Atatürk's secular reforms.

Ecevit was born on May 28, 1925, in Istanbul, the son of a professor of medicine. He graduated from Robert College in Istanbul. When I was a student in England between 1946 and 1950, he was employed as an embassy official in London. Upon returning to Turkey in 1950, he worked for the newspaper *Halkçı* (*Populist*) in Ankara and later for *Ulus* (*Nation*), the official organ of the Republican People's Party. *Ulus* was then considered a stepping stone for the sons of leading party members. Ecevit's father was by then a member of parliament. Ecevit himself was elected Member of Parliament in 1957 and two years later became a member of the party council. As labor minister in Ismet Inönü's three coalition governments between 1961 and 1965, he was the man who, for the first time in Turkish history, brought about the right for labor unions to strike.

When we were young journalists, I knew Ecevit as a left-wing idealist who was not happy with Turkey's social and political systems and wanted them changed. He also wanted the national policy changed to a left-of-center, pro-Soviet, anti-West, anti-American agenda. Ecevit wanted political and social reforms to improve the living standard of workers and peasants, who made up the majority of the population. He wanted a fairer distribution of land. Ecevit's literary works include a Turkish translation of Rabindranath Tagore's song poems *Gitanjali*.

Much more than in journalism he was interested in politics. Known in his early political life as *Karaoğlan*, or dark young boy, Ecevit's trademark later in his life was a blue kepi and clipped black moustache. Despite his soft-spoken manner and his modest lifestyle, Ecevit was an autocratic member of old-guard politics. Ecevit was also a rare individual in Turkish politics—he was honest. Still, I believe that his yo-yo policies helped to bring about disunity, unrest, more corruption, and extreme poverty for the nation.

This was a man who, as a young and ambitious left-wing politician and secretary general of the party, caused Republican People's Party to drift further to the left, promptly facing Süleyman Demirel's right-wing Justice Party. This and his conflict with Colonel Alparslan Türkeş's Nationalist Action Party were moves that would instigate the bloodshed of the right-left struggles of the late 1970s. While he was prime minister in 1978–79, twenty Turks died every day in the streets in clashes between the armed militias of the extreme left and extreme right.

Ecevit had in 1972 ousted Ismet Inönü, the aging leader of the Republican People's Party. He had considered Inönü out of touch with the fast-changing times. Three decades later, Ecevit, five times prime minister of

Turkey, found himself on the other side of the equation with increasing cries for change and demand for his resignation.

Ecevit became chairman of the Republican People's Party in 1972 and prime minister in 1974. He opposed the Islamists and championed the secular state. Yet his decision in 1974 to form a coalition of Kemal Atatürk's strictly secular Republican People's Party with Necmettin Erbakan's Islamist National Salvation Party was a disaster for the secular republic. With this coalition, Ecevit handed the Islamists the best opportunity for political legitimacy. This was a crucial move for the spread of Islamic fundamentalism. While he was prime minister of this coalition of strange bedfellows, the Cyprus crisis flared and Turkey invaded the island.

Ecevit requested a vote of confidence in parliament in September 1974 and failed. The tenuous power of government passed to the Justice Party, and Süleyman Demirel, the father of the old-guard politicians, became prime minister. The struggle between Demirel, Ecevit, and ultranationalists for power, along with the bloodshed in the streets, increased. Finally, the military intervened in 1980 with a coup d'etat for the third time in the secular republic's history. Ecevit, like Demirel, was imprisoned by the military and banned from politics for ten years.

Bülent Ecevit's blunders are legendary.

Ecevit left the Republican People's Party and with his wife, Rahşan, formed his family party—the Democratic Left in 1985. This led to a coalition, and in December 1998 he formed a caretaker government. He began reversing his anti-Western stance and tried to obtain membership in the European Union after resisting it for over twenty-five years.

In 1999, Ecevit was the prime minister of a three-party coalition government that brought disasters to the Turkish economy. His statement to the press right after the "ungrateful cat" incident of February 19, 2001, is exemplary in political shortsightedness. Following his fight with President Necdet Sezer over corruption he had disclosed details of it to journalists, causing the worst economic meltdown and unemployment in the history of the republic since 1945. Ecevit did not realize at the time that President Sezer's criticism was aimed at Mesut Yılmaz and Hüsamettin

Özkan. Özkan, who was Ecevit's adopted son, accused President Sezer as being an ungrateful cat during that fateful meeting, and this was seen later as a skillful political manipulation.

Most people in Turkey were wondering in spring 2002 about the uncertain future of the country in view of Prime Minister Ecevit's problems with his memory and health. Economy Minister Kemal Derviş, a nonparty technocrat, suggested that there should be an election and called for a clear poll date. Foreign Trade Minister Tunca Toskay, Ecevit's coalition partner the Nationalist Action Party, said that Derviş as an unelected figure should hold his peace.

At any rate, the three parties in Bülent Ecevit's hamstrung coalition government had faced dismal ratings in opinion polls in the summer of 2002, and calls for an early election increased. Ecevit, due to his health problems, complained about the difficulty of climbing "each individual step" of the staircase leading to the prime ministry. He was admitted to Başkent hospital in May 2002 for treatment for the second time in a fortnight. Ecevit, the doctors stated, was suffering from thrombophlebitis in his left leg and also had a fractured rib. There were reports that he had been suffering from Parkinson's disease for five years. This he denied during a short press conference: "Look, my hands are not shaking."

Among the malcontented with Ecevit's lame-duck policies was Hüsamettin Özkan, his adopted son. In the summer of 2002, Ecevit's wife, Rahşan, was blamed for controlling her husband and limiting visits by his associates and doctors. "She is the gatekeeper," said Ilter Turan, a professor of political science at Istanbul's Bilgi University, during an interview with the Associated Press. "She wields influence by manipulating access to the prime minister."

Bülent Ecevit had been growing frail in recent years, often appearing dazed and forgetful in public appearances. His voice was shaky and slurred and his movements slow. Ecevit's talks during diplomatic receptions in early 2002 became the subject of jokes. On one occasion, Ecevit called his official guest, the prime minister of the interim government of Afghanistan, Hamid Karzai, the general manager of Afghanistan. Tony

Blair, the British prime minister, ended up being called the British foreign secretary. Upon returning from an official visit to the United States, Ecevit made a statement about his talks in Israel. His worst faux pas was about Israel's military offensive into Palestine in April 2002. Ecevit dropped a bomb when he described Israel's military move as genocide against the people of Palestine. He was reading a written statement. This caused alarm, and the international news agencies, suspecting a shift in Turkey's foreign policy against its ally Israel, flashed the statement all over the world.

In deep political trouble in June 2002, Ecevit told his party deputies that a general election was "on the horizon." He was often out of breath during the address and repeatedly confused similar words. One hour later, Ecevit told newspaper reporters that an early election was not being considered: "An election before April 2004 is out of the question."

Public calls for Ecevit's resignation increased, and some newspaper columnists even begged him to resign for the good of the country. The leader of the Nationalist Action Party, the major coalition partner, Devlet Bahçeli, to his later regret, called for an early election to be held in November 2002. The confusion continued while the members of the monopolized media threw their support to Hüsamettin Özkan as the next premier. To their credit, Bülent Ecevit and wife Rahşan saw the political game and took measures to clip the wings of their adopted son. Ecevit declared, "The Democratic Left is our own party."

According to press reports, Professor Ilter Turan said, "At a time when leadership is imperative, the prime minister is physically not capable of providing leadership."

"We're all confused. The market is a yo-yo," said Emin Öztürk, economist at Bender securities.

The tension in Ecevit's coalition government increased. Erkan Mumcu, the outspoken deputy chairman and chairman of the political affairs of the Motherland Party, the junior partner of the coalition, stated in May 2002 that impotent people were leading Turkey. He complained that a group of leaders without vision, who are "incapable to see and understand today, let alone tomorrow," had condemned the country by their own lack of vision and depth. Mumcu added that what had been learned from Turgut Özal, a visionary leader, was all but forgotten. Mumcu described Motherland as a party that appeared to be a business company involved in irregularities. He criticized Mesut Yılmaz, the party chairman, for lacking leadership qualities. Mumcu was removed at once from his position as the party's deputy chairman. Mesut Yılmaz appointed him party chairman for parliamentary relations. Four months later, Mumcu resigned from the Motherland Party and joined the Justice and Development Party.

An ambiguous absurdity continued to dominate Turkish politics. Former Prime Minister Tansu Çiller, now in opposition, saw prospects in the confusion. In a statement in April 2002 to *Hürriyet* she said that people were hungry because of the economic crisis caused by Ecevit's coalition government. Çiller, according to her statement, had been keeping eleven ducks in a small pool at her villa in Ankara's Bilkent district. The villa was under police protection twenty-four hours a day. Still the ducks had disappeared. Çiller said, "They told me that hungry martens and stray dogs grabbed the ducks and escaped. They took my ducks one by one and ate them. That's what I was told. The people are hungry. Even the animals can't find food, so they, too, are hungry."

Her husband, Özer, claimed to be a descendant of Zembilli Ali, a sixteenth-century Grand Mufti, or *Sheyhulislam*, the minister in the Ottoman Empire responsible for all matters connected with the Shariah. Özer Çiller told *Hürriyet* columnist Murat Bardakçı that his other ancestors were Mevlana Jalaladdin Rumi and Abu Bakr, the first caliph and successor to Prophet Muhammed. It was obvious that Özer's target was to attract the Islamist votes for Tansu Çiller's True Path Party in case the election was held.

A mounting rebellion in July 2002 inside Ecevit's party provided new horizons for Tansu Çiller. She declared that if her party won the election, she would improve the economic and political situation. Targeting women voters, Tansu Çiller promised each housewife an income from social security if she had paid her taxes for fifteen years. If the housewives were unable to pay such taxes, then the state would pay the taxes for them, she promised.

Courting American support ,Tansu Çiller stated, "I want to be premier during an American military action against Iraq because I have experience in dealing with terrorism."

Bekir Coşkun of *Hürriyet* wrote, "If Çiller comes to power, she intends to bring financial amnesty. That's what she said. In other words, the people who swindled the state will be pardoned."

The rebellion inside Ecevit's family party soon caused the loss of its preeminence in parliament. It almost brought about the collapse of Ecevit's coalition government, and Ecevit could no longer avoid the prospect of an early election. At first, Hüsamettin Özkan, the ambitious deputy prime minister who actually ran the prime ministry, allegedly plotted Ecevit's downfall. A man from Kayseri (the pastrami town), he was considered to be responsible for the collapse of the economy and the alleged protector of tainted officials and media cartels. His detractors often used a phrase attributed to folks from Kayseri: he would even paint his donkey to sell it.

Some in the media, trying to keep the old status quo, supported Özkan as the new hope, along with Mesut Yılmaz and Tansu Çiller. Ecevit, realizing what was afoot, asked his adopted son to resign from the party, and Özkan was obliged to do so. Foreign Minister Ismail Cem and fifty-seven other members of parliament from Ecevit's Democratic Left, including several ministers also resigned. In October 2002 only 58 deputies remained in Ecevits' family party and the coalition lost its majority in parliament.

Bülent Ecevit then used a scare tactic to prevent an early election. He said that Recep Tayyip Erdoğan's Justice and Development Party, with Islamic roots, and the Kurdish HADEP would make great strides at the polls if elections were held before 2004. "The regime will be in danger after the election," he added.

Ismail Cem, supported by Hüsamettin Özkan and Kemal Derviş, the economy minister and steward of a multibillion dollar IMF-backed crisis plan, organized a new party—Cem called it *Yeni Türkiye Partisi*, or New Turkey Party. Cem said that his party would work to achieve Turkey's full EU membership.

Kemal Derviş soon saw opportunity somewhere else. His attempts to unite the left-of-center against the growing popularity of Erdoğan's Justice and Development Party sparked angry calls from Bülent Ecevit. Ecevit asked him to stay loyal to the government or quit, hinting that Derviş played opposition to the government while remaining a member of the cabinet. Derviş resigned from Ecevit's cabinet and promptly joined the Republican People's Party. According to Derviş, "Turkey has accumulated huge problems, and these problems must be overcome." He was later elected Member of Parliament.

An odd situation developed when parliament voted to hold an early election on November 3, 2002. The vote for an early election was 449 to sixty-two. The coalition partners, fearing a defeat, soon tried to reverse the decision. That brought a stiff reaction from the army. General Hüseyin Kıvrıkoğlu, the outgoing chief of general staff, warned of possible chaos if the election were postponed. General Aytaç Yalman, the new commander of the land forces, complained that a collapse of morality had taken hold of Turkish society.

Such confusion and indecision in the secular government was a sign of more problems on the horizon. Ecevit, who had lost the battle, refused to bow out. By September 2002, his coalition government had become an inefficient and incompetent entity. Ecevit admitted, "The situation is confused."

That confusion, the collapse of the economy, and widespread poverty presented a great opportunity for the Islamists to grab the power.

A Victory
for the Islamists

For a mad man, every day is a holiday.
Turkish proverb

*I*n the spring of 2002, I was surprised to observe once again how much the Turkish nation has changed since the death of Kemal Atatürk. Recep Tayyip Erdoğan, the leader of the Justice and Development Party with strong Islamist roots, was on a campaign tour in rural Anatolia, where his speeches drew large crowds. His party consistently led opinion polls, daily gaining more strength at the expense of the right-of-center parties and the Felicity Party, which supported Necmettin Erbakan, the traditional Islamist.

Despite the legal proceedings against him for acts against the secular constitution and alleged corruption while he was the mayor of Istanbul, Erdoğan was getting ready to win the election. He believed that the old policies of Adnan Menderes and Turgut Özal had great appeal for the majority of the people. In his campaigns, he appeared to the electorate, particularly the Anatolian peasants and have-nots, as a friend of the destitute and poor. He promised a transparent government and a series of legal changes to expand freedom of religion and expression that most people understood to include the lifting of the turban ban.

"We won't be inheriting a Turkey that's full of roses," declared a confident Erdoğan.

Having seen the fate of previous Islamist parties, Erdoğan, in a dramatic change of policy, parted ways with his old mentor Necmettin Erbakan and Erbakan's reactionary *Milli Görüş*, the National View policies. Erdoğan, despite his leading roles earlier in the Islamist Welfare and Virtue parties, presented his new party as conservative democratic and rejected the Islamist label. If elected to power, he claimed, the regime of a Justice and Development Party would be a "democratic, secular, social state of law and order." A party statement said, "Secularism is a basic tenet for the peace of society."

During an interview with *The Times* of London, Erdoğan denied that he had ever chosen the label of an Islamist in his political career. This prompted a response from Emin Çölaşan, who wrote in *Hürriyet*, "Who spoke the following words: Thank God I am a believer in the Shariah—I am the Imam of Istanbul—For us democracy is not a goal but a means."

Recep Tayyip Erdoğan, forty-four, unlike Süleyman Demirel, Necmettin Erbakan, or Turgut Özal, belongs to a generation that has not participated directly in the reforms of the 1920s and 1930s. The son of a poor sea captain, he hails from Istanbul's tough Kasımpaşa district at the Golden Horn and is a graduate of an imam-cleric school. He sold day-old bread rolls and postcards as a boy to pay for his education. He once called the ballet "vulgar."

As a strong contender for the leadership of the Islamic movement, Erdoğan read the following poem on December 6, 1997, in the town of Siirt, eastern Anatolia:

> The mosques are our barracks,
> The domes are our helmets,
> The minarets are our swords,
> The faithful are our army.

According to the prosecutors, this poem, written years earlier by Cevat Örnek under much different circumstances, was an incitement for jihad, an Islamic holy war. The prosecutors claimed the reading of the poem was also an incitement against the secularist army. They filed charges against Erdoğan in Diyarbakır, southeast Anatolia, on February 13, 1998, for using religion to incite hatred in order to establish an evil order. A state security court in Diyarbakır on April 21, 1998, sentenced him to ten months in prison. The Supreme Court upheld the sentence, and Erdoğan had to resign as mayor of Istanbul. After the sentencing, five thousand Islamists demonstrated outside Istanbul's town hall, calling for the resignation of the government. Erdoğan was jailed on March 26, 1999, at Pınarhisar prison and freed four months later.

In 1993 Erdoğan was the local leader of the Islamist Welfare Party in Istanbul and fearlessly defended Welfare's pro-Islam policies. Once he declared that democracy was a tool to be used for advancing to a desired system of government: "The republican era accepted Kemalism as a religion, dictating it by force to the masses of people, denying the existence of all other religions. . . . There is no place for Kemalism or any other official ideology in Turkey's future. For us Muslims the principles of Islam define everything."

Often in trouble with the public prosecutors for Islamist sedition, Erdoğan stated, "You can't stop a movement; this is not possible."

The Supreme Court on September 16, 2002, upheld a lower court ruling banning him from running as a candidate in an election because of his earlier conviction for Islamist sedition. The High Electoral Board on September 20, 2002, ruled against Erdoğan and banned him from participating in the November 3, 2002 election. Erdoğan's wealth became controversial. Because he had not been a rich man in 1994, when he was elected as the mayor of Istanbul, allegations emerged about the sources of his later wealth. Other allegations of conflict of interest existed, such as accepting scholarships from a businessman for his three children. The scholarship was awarded for their education in the United States. Erdoğan, the bête noire of the establishment, said that his two daughters were obliged to study in America because they wore Islamic headscarves.

Shortly before the election, old-guard politicians, facing defeat, tried once again to recall parliament to postpone the election and change election laws. President Necdet Sezer issued an ultimatum: "I will dissolve parliament if the elections scheduled for November 3, 2002, are postponed." And once again, the voters were bombarded with lies and false promises of jobs, no taxes, land and a home for every family and other pie-in-the-sky. The majority of the population, stricken with poverty, waited to get revenge from those who created the looters' economy.

Recep Tayyip Erdoğan, in his final broadcast before the election, said, "Turn on the lights, let Turkey be enlightened, let the unemployed find jobs, and let there be an end to poverty." The symbol of his Justice and Development Party is a shining electric light bulb.

Pakize Suda, a columnist for *Hürriyet,* found humor for the women in the election. If, she informed her readers, the Justice and Development Party with Islamic roots wins the election, the price of a chador, or *çarşaf,* will go up because of high demand. She noted cheerfully that because the wearing of chador would be the only dress code, women's problems would be solved. Besides, she wrote, there would be no more "What am I going to wear today" or "that other woman is more attractive than I." Better still, the women wouldn't have to worry about exposing their bulging midriffs, Suda explained.

Bernard Lewis, the eminent authority on Middle Eastern history, in his book *What Went Wrong?* discussed Atatürk's view on the emancipation of women. Lewis quoted Kemal Atatürk's words: "We shall not catch up with the modern world if we modernize only half the population."

Professor Lewis added: "This was a surprising line of argument in the early twenties, and came from an unlikely source, an Ottoman pasha and general, but also founder of Turkey."

On November 3, 2002, the day of the election, Kemalism and the secular reforms of my childhood years suffered a humiliating defeat in Turkey's 172,143 polling stations. The winners, despite their denials of having an Islamist agenda, were aiming to undermine Kemal Atatürk's secular reforms.

On that day, 34.29 percent of the 31,528,000 valid votes brought an end to Bülent Ecevit's lame, incompetent, and scandal-ridden coalition government. The election ended a fifteen-year era of coalition governments, and the secular republic entered a new and critical period of its life. The election brought about not only a complete overhaul to the country's political landscape but also much concern about the future with a democratic Islam or, as the Islamists preferred, a conservative democratic regime.

The winner was the Justice and Development Party (AKP). It received 10,779,489 votes, entering the 550-seat parliament with 363 members. The peculiarity of the Turkish election laws granted the Justice and Development Party a clear mandate with only 34.29 percent of the total votes. It was an unprecedented outcome and presented the party with the power to change even the secular constitution. The Republican People's Party won only 6,099,083 votes (19.39 percent), winning 178 seats. The Kemalists voted for the Republican People's Party, often dragging their feet, in order to block an Islamist victory. It didn't work.

The rest of the political parties, especially the right-of-center and the ultranationalists, could not draw even the threshold of 10 percent of the national vote to enter parliament and were eliminated. The votes spread among those parties were about 45 percent of the total and were discarded, regardless of the results in individual constituencies. As a peculiarity of the Turkish election laws, nine independents received fewer votes but were elected. Tansu Çiller and Mesut Yılmaz, badly beaten, had to resign from the leadership of their parties.

The new policies adopted by Recep Tayyip Erdoğan, such as the emphasis on social welfare, brought him success. The Islamists thrived on the anger about poverty, graft, and unemployment. A beaming Erdoğan said, "As Atatürk once stated, the sovereignty unconditionally belongs to the people."

After his party's victory, Erdoğan failed to appear at two court hearings in Ankara to face charges of illegal earnings that called for a prison term. Diarrhea was his excuse not to appear for the second hearing. The secular media found that excuse amusing when Erdoğan attended a dinner meeting with the ambassadors of the European Union countries later the same day.

He appeared in court on November 28, 2002, and said that the source of his wealth was the gifts of gold coins received at his son Burak's wedding. Erdoğan told the judge that the gold coins weighed thirty kilograms, and he sold them for 262 billion Turkish liras (about $158,000). The court acquitted Erdoğan in January 2003 due to lack of evidence regarding the source of his wealth. A court in Istanbul also cleared him of charges that he had interfered with commercial contracts when he was the mayor of the city. The prosecutor said he had insufficient evidence.

The election victory of the Justice and Development Party changed everything. It increased the tension between the Islamists and their opposition, the pashas and the loyal Kemalists. All of a sudden, the flatterers, locally known as *dalkavuklar* in the media, discovered great virtues in the personality of Recep Tayyip Erdoğan. The media bosses who siphoned off the banks and others who expect fat government contracts for their non-media companies or to obtain new credits began extolling the new regime.

The generals, clearly unhappy, watched the results of this election coup, wondering how to deal with the growing fundamentalist movement. General Hilmi Özkök, chief of the general staff, said that the armed forces would protect the state against fundamentalist Islam. President Necdet Sezer, on the anniversary of the death of Kemal Atatürk, said the country's secular principles are to be defended: "I want to stress that the struggle against movements that attempt to overthrow the democratic and secular republic will be determinedly maintained."

The outgoing Prime Minister Bülent Ecevit warned: "Turkey faces a serious problem with the election victory of the Justice and Development Party." Ecevit added that Erdoğan, barred from membership in parliament, was to appoint a prime minister and cabinet members. "Someone who is not the prime minister will run the cabinet. Turkey will be administered by a shadow prime minister and government," he said.

That prime minister happened to be Abdullah Gül, a strong advocate of Turkey's European ambitions. One-fourth of Gül's cabinet members were former members of Motherland, and the others were from Necmettin Erbakan's Welfare Party. The wives of fourteen ministers of Gül's twenty-five-member cabinet were turban-wearers, including Fatma

Seyma Akdağ, the wife of Recep Akdağ, the minister of health. Surprisingly, a photograph of Professor Akdağ's mother, Sevdiye, taken fifty years earlier, shows her without a turban.

Abdullah Gül, fifty-two, an economist, is a former professor of the University of Sakarya. He also worked for the Islamic Development Bank in Jidda, Saudi Arabia. Gül was elected to parliament in 1991 from the Islamist Welfare Party and in 1996 served as state minister in Necmettin Erbakan's pro-Islamic regime. He was elected into parliament again in 1999 from the Virtue Party and led a reformist movement in that party against Erbakan's traditionalists. As one of the founders of the Justice and Development Party, he was elected to parliament from Kayseri on November 3, 2002. Gül's father, Ahmet Hamdi, was a candidate from Erbakan's National Salvation Party in 1973 but failed to get elected. Gül's wife, Hayrünissa, like Erdoğan's wife, Emine, wears a turban.

The official *iftar*, the evening feast to break the fast of Ramadan, a favorite of the former Islamist Prime Minister Necmettin Erbakan and his deputy Tansu Çiller, returned with a grand show. Abdulkadir Aksu, the interior minister in Gül's cabinet, broke the fast in Ankara's Hilton Hotel with the leading members of parliament and some businessmen. After the feast, the minister led his companions to the Hilton's lobby for *namaz*, or ritual worship. When Prime Minister Abdullah Gül and most of his cabinet members prayed together on November 22, 2002, at the mosque located in the parliament building, *Milliyet* ran the banner headline: *Kabine Cuma Namazında*—"The Cabinet at Friday Prayers." It was also known that some of Gül's cabinet members spoke out publicly in the past against Kemal Atatürk and his reforms. Others had been involved in irregularities in government tender and were tax evaders.

Thus the contradictions and the clash of ideals between the Islamists and the secularists began early and continued with stubborn persistence. Because of the inexperience of the Justice and Development Party in politics and administration, one blunder followed another. One big surprise was Gül's appointment of Ramazan Toprak as chairman of the National Defense Commission of Parliament. Toprak, as a judge in the army with the rank of major, had been discharged in 1997 on allegations of being an

Islamic reactionary. As chairman of the commission, he was to face the military, but he decided to resign.

During a meeting of the Supreme Military Council, a decree was signed to expel seven noncommissioned officers from the armed forces. The charges were Islamist sympathies. The army brass had been complaining about oddities in some of the military units that affected discipline. For instance, a private who was actually the sheik of an Islamic brotherhood was serving under a sergeant who was one of his disciples. The sheik in this situation could outrank his disciple, the sergeant, according to the military. Prime Minister Gül and Vecdi Gönül, the minister of defense, had signed the decree entering reservations—that the rulings of the Supreme Military Council should depend on legal procedures. The chief of general staff, General Hilmi Özkök, said that the Islamic reactionaries could interpret the prime minister's reservation as an encouragement.

The worst foreign policy blunder of Abdullah Gül's regime was its April 2003 refusal to allow into the country 62,000 US troops in order to open up a northern front against Iraq's dictator Saddam Hussein. Gül's government believed that the United States would not attack Iraq without Turkish support. Based on this wrong assumption, parliament on March 1, 2003, rejected a motion to allow the deployment of US ground troops in Turkey. The majority of Turks were against the war, and the media had totally failed to bring out the vital importance of Turkish participation. Only a few writers, including Ertuğrul Özkök of *Hürriyet* who were aware of the facts of *real-politik*, supported the US request and were unfairly called American lackeys.

This historic blunder of Gül's government and parliament reminded me at the time of the poetry of Mehmet Akif Ersoy, the poet of the Turkish national anthem. Ersoy's patriotism is legendary: "Fear not," he said in 1920, "the red flag waving in these dawns will not fade before the flames of the last hearth of my nation are extinguished." Ersoy wrote about historic blunders:

> It's said that history repeats itself,
> If a lesson had been drawn from history,
> Could history repeat itself?

Gül's blunder about Iraq strained Turkish-American relations and damaged half of a century of strategic partnership. The cooperation of the organizations supporting pro-Islam and leftist and pro-Kurdish separatist movements played a vital role in this rejection. It was a terrible policy decision that harmed Turkish interests in northern Iraq, a strategically important area.

The detention by US troops from the 173rd Airborne of a team of a Turkish special forces in Suleymaniyah in northern Iraq on July 4, 2003, outraged the Turks and deepened public mistrust of the Americans. The earlier policy of the United States regarding Turkish concerns about northern Iraq had to be revised and resulted in close cooperation between the US and Kurdish factions. Turkey was left on the sideline.

The official admission of this gross political lack of foresight came on November 4, 2003, from Osman Faruk Logolu, the Turkish ambassador in Washington. He said Turkish officials now recognize they missed an opportunity to help shape postwar Iraq. Ambassador Logolu added that Turkey would have been in a more effective and influential position in Iraq by allowing the deployment of the US troops through the country.

An outspoken critic of Turkey's policy on Iraq was Paul Wolfowitz, the US deputy defense secretary. Wolfowitz told CNN-Turk that he was particularly disappointed with the Turkish military for not playing a strong leadership role. He urged the Turks to follow Washington's line in relations with Iran and Syria at a time when both Erdoğan and Gül were seeking close relations with these countries.

Gül stayed on as prime minister until Erdoğan was elected Member of Parliament during the by-election of March 9, 2003, in the province of Siirt. Erdoğan, as the prime minister, appointed Gül deputy premier and foreign minister.

Only seven months after the blunder of March 1, 2003, the same parliament, realizing the importance of cooperation with the United States, voted overwhelmingly (358 votes to 183) to send Turkish troops to Iraq. By then, it was too late for the deployment of Turkish forces. There was strong opposition in Iraq by many factions, including the Iraqi Kurds, who did not want to see Turkey playing a leadership role in the Middle

East. And the Erdoğan government decided not to send any troops to Iraq. General Hilmi Özkök, chief of the general staff, said on November 9, 2003, that the government's decision not to send troops to Iraq left the country without a say in the future political makeup of its neighbor.

The pressure by the Islamists on the secular state increased. Bülent Arınç, the newly elected speaker of parliament, became a crusader for the acceptance of the turban in official ceremonies: "The turban is our honor." Arınç then took his turban-wearing wife, Münevver, to the airport to see President Necdet Sezer off to the NATO summit meeting in Prague. His behavior was interpreted as a challenge to the secularity of the state.

The traditional Islamist Necmettin Erbakan was the mentor of Bülent Arınç, who was a leading member of Erbakan's National Salvation Party and served as a member of parliament from Erbakan's Welfare Party. He said, "Our ways parted with Erbakan Hoca when we established the Justice and Development Party."

President Sezer soon came out slugging. He said that wearing the turban in an individual's private life is a matter of freedom of choice, but wearing the turban in government offices would threaten the country's secularism: "Allowing the turban in areas of the government sector is impossible because it's unconstitutional."

His warnings were met with deaf ears. Fresh from an election victory, the leaders of the Justice and Development Party were determined to show a fearless and daring spirit in advancing their Islamist agenda.

One of the greatest landmarks of the Kemalist reforms is the Grand National Assembly, Turkey's parliament. Shortly before its eighty-third anniversary, on April 23, 2003, Bülent Arınç announced that he and his turban-wearing wife, Münevver, would host the customary reception in parliament. President Sezer, the generals, and the leaders of the opposition Republican People's Party boycotted the reception, the first in the republic's history. Mrs. Arınç, too, stayed away. Erdoğan declared, "Anyone who wants to attend the reception can do so, anyone who doesn't want to, shouldn't."

In his editorial titled "Destroy the Walls Inside Your Heads," Mehmet Y. Yılmaz, *Milliyet*'s editor-in-chief, wrote:

Turkey has to overcome this problem and reality must be faced to find a solution. Whether you like it or not, there are in our country millions of women wearing the turban. Again, whether you like or not, there are millions of other women who don't want to cover their heads. What's important is that nobody has the right to dictate his or her understanding of life to others. If we do not destroy these walls inside our heads, we will lose the twenty-first century like we did eighteenth, nineteenth and twentieth centuries.

Hasan Cemal, commenting about the turban crisis in *Milliyet*, wrote, "What a pitiful sight for this land. It is a mistake to play the tom-tom drums of crisis at the top of the state. This is wrong."

The Islamic headscarves (or turban) crisis revived itself repeatedly between the secular Kemalists and the devout Muslim officials of the Justice and Development Party. For his official National Day reception on October 29, 2003, the eightieth anniversary of the founding of the secular republic, President Sezer refused to invite turban-wearing wives of the parliamentarians. The members of the opposition Republican People's Party were invited with their wives, who do not wear turbans. Prime Minister Erdoğan, clearly pragmatic, said that he and his cabinet members would attend the reception, but he would not take his turban-wearing wife, Emine, along. The parliamentarians of the Justice and Development Party boycotted the reception, and a few returned their invitations to President Sezer.

President Sezer said that the Turkish Republic is a secular and social law-and-order state: "This is a state reception not my own personal invitation. The rules of the Turkish Republic are recorded in the constitution." His decision was permanent and would not change, President Sezer continued.

A lawyer named Hatice Hasdemir appeared wearing a turban in the 4th Criminal Appeal Court hearing in Ankara in November 2003, and she was ordered by Judge Fadıl Inan to get out, remove the turban, and enter the courtroom without it. She told the judge that she was the suspect of alleged irregularities between the company she represented and the office of the mayor. "No matter," Judge Inan told her. "Leave the courtroom." She waited outside the courtroom until the hearing ended. This confrontation upset the parliamentarians of the Justice and Development Party, who described Judge Inan's behavior as peevish. Eraslan Özkaya, the Chief Justice of the Supreme Court of Appeals, however, said Judge Inan's ruling was right.

The country remained persistently and irrevocably divided between the Kemalists, who remained loyal to Atatürk's secularist legacy, and the members of a ruling party determined to force Islam's doctrinaire values into the secular heart of the republic. The majority of the parliamentarians of the Justice and Development Party, about three hundred of them, are married to women who observe the rules of *tesettür* and wear the turban.

As a result of the ambitions of the Justice and Development Party, a parliamentary committee had voted on June 25, 2003, to increase the number of Islamic clerics and preachers employed by the Department of Religious Affairs by fifteen thousand. This department already employs about 64,750 staff members and preachers to run 72,000 mosques across the country and others located abroad.

Foreign Minister Abdullah Gül issued a circular to the Turkish embassies in April 2003, requesting them to "show an interest" in the Islamist-oriented movements in the countries in which they served. This circular was interpreted as the government's support of organizations such as *Milli Görüş*, the National View, which has a reactionary Islamic agenda. The National View, based on the Shariah, was started by Necmettin Erbakan and is well represented in the European countries. The National View (*Islamische Gemeinschaft*) has 26,500 members in Germany. Otto Schily, the federal German interior minister, in a report about protecting the federal constitution said that the National View aimed for a lifestyle dependent on the Shariah.

Necmettin Erbakan and his Felicity Party and some members— including a number of leaders—of the Justice and Development Party are loyal to the principles of the National View.

In the summer of 2003, the Justice and Development Party continued adjusting its policy in accordance with the developing situation while denying its reactionary objectives. This policy is named *takiyye*, meaning "a hidden agenda." The party used the style of the Janissaries' swaying walk to advance: two steps forward, one step back. Behind the party's adoption of the "bright future" slogan tried earlier by Menderes, Demirel, and Özal, there is the determination to protect and advance the pro-Islam movement. One example is the party's campaign in summer 2003 to retire civil servants at the age of sixty-one instead of sixty-five in order to replace them with trusted Islamists. The Constitutional Court ruled against that project. In December 2003, the government also abandoned plans to ease restrictions on Qur'an courses, including those on the premises of state's educational institutions. The secular establishment opposed the plan, accusing Erdoğan's regime of trying to undermine the country's constitutional separation of politics and religion.

Party leaders followed the reaction of the secular military to their Islamist policies closely. When the pashas saw the need to react in order to protect the state's secularity, the party leaders paid attention and postponed their Islamist plans.

The word *takiyye* means "to hide one's purpose," to give a wrong impression in order to mislead one's opponent, even to lie about one's real objectives and to behave hypocritically. Speaking on the subject of parliament and democracy during a September 2003 meeting at the Foundation of Turkish Democracy, Bülent Arınç reportedly said: "If you do not have the freedom to express yourself, you are obligated to behave hypocritically, to tell lies, to hide your objectives with takiyye in order not to slip and fall while on the way to power."

This report made big headlines in the newspapers. Arınç, however, issued a clarification a few days later: "I am not someone who follows a policy of takiyye," he stated "I didn't say we have used takiyye and we are carrying on with takiyye. I said if you open the way for freedoms, nobody would be obliged to use takiyye."

Orhan Sür, a member of parliament from the opposition Republican People's Party, said in response: "This is no surprise to us. The politicians of our party and those in parliament know what the aim of the Justice and Development Party really is. Arınç has disclosed their real face. That's how they came to power."

Türker Alkan, a columnist of *Radikal* newspaper, labeled Hüseyin Çelik, the minister of education of the Justice and Development Party, as someone connected with an Islamic brotherhood. Alkan wrote on October 3, 2003, that the same minister in an article eight years earlier had praised Said Nursi, the founder of the Light (*Nur*) sect: "If at the beginning of the republic [1923], the officials had listened to Bediuzzaman [Said Nursi] the present conditions in the country could not have existed."

Alkan added that this minister of education was expecting help from the sheiks of the Islamic sects and was criticizing the estrangement of the republic's ideology from religion. On *takiyye*, Alkan wrote:

> I do not believe that anyone is fooled by their words—we swear by God that we have changed.
> Their mask of takiyye is so inharmonious on their faces that it gives the impression it may fall down at any moment."

He accused the Justice and Development Party of trying to give the general impression of being both Islamic and secular at the same time.

Minister of Education Hüseyin Çelik is known for his attempts to remove the teaching of Atatürk's ideology from the school curriculum. In fact, the regime of the Justice and Development Party in the fall of 2003 was busy pushing three important policies for the benefit of the religious front—control of the universities, acceptance of imam-cleric school graduates into the universities, and legalizing the use of the turban at the universities and in government offices.

The Kemalists and the army brass, keeping in mind how the ayatollahs in Iran took over control of the Iranian state, followed these developments with deep concern. The powerful military publicly displayed its displeasure with the government appointments of religious radicals to important positions in the bureaucracy. Chief of General Staff Hilmi Özkök told journalists in May 2003 that there was concern at all levels of the armed forces.

Living in anxious times, the generals were wary about reforms required by the Copenhagen criteria, despite their support for joining the European Union. The reforms include Kurdish cultural rights, civilian control of the military, reducing the influence of the army brass in the National Security Council, and parliamentary regulation of the defense budget.

The realization of the reforms required for European Union membership was the Islamists' dream of opportunity come true to expand their base. The generals, however, regarded some of the reforms for the EU criteria as potential weapons to subvert the state. They feared that these reforms could change the state's ideology based on the Kemalist reforms and weaken their role as the guardians against separatist and fundamentalist movements.

In July 2003, while the regime of the Justice and Development Party, known as the party of *din ve iman* (religion and faith), kept seeding the state bureaucracy with Islamists, the nightmare of the generals became a reality. The parliament voted to curb the political power of the military. The most important target of a landmark bill was the powerful National Security Council, created after the 1980 military coup and composed of military leaders and senior politicians. Parliament voted to abolish the council's executive powers and to reduce it to an advisory role. The council's secretary general, a four-star general whose power in the past had rivaled that of the prime minister, was to be replaced by a civilian after one year. The secret military budget that had been rubber stamped by parliament in the past would now be exposed to parliamentary review. The reforms included the repeal of some legislation restricting freedom of expression and assembly and amnesty to the members of the Kurdistan Workers Party, or KADEK.

Not too long ago, the far-reaching reform package might have been cause for a coup d'etat by the army brass. A regime with Islamic roots had shown the determination and guts in the eighty-year history of the republic to pass the most liberal reform packages, putting the previous government of Bülent Ecevit to shame. Erdoğan clearly believed that his target, membership in the European Union, was the right way for the success of his regime and for the survival of the Islamist revival. Achieving EU membership would secure the future of the Justice and Development Party and save it from the fate of the Welfare and other Islamic parties.

This time, the generals, having run out of options, waited on the sidelines, intensely following the developments that enhanced the power of the pro-Islamic regime. Prime Minister Erdoğan and Minister of Defense Vecdi Gönül even went so far as to enter their reservations on a decision of the Supreme Military Council to dismiss eighteen fundamentalist army officers.

The leaders of the ruling Justice and Development Party are determined that graduates of the *imam-hatip* (imam-cleric) high schools should be able to enter military academies to become regular officers in the armed forces.

During the Supreme Military Council's meeting in August 2003, three retiring four-star generals—Tuncer Kılınç, Çetin Doğan, and Tamer Akbaş—directly addressed Prime Minister Erdoğan. They said that the government leaders were using the nation's desire to be a member of the European Union as an excuse to advance their own pro-Islam agenda. General Çetin Doğan accused Erdoğan of undermining the armed forces and of trying to change the secular regime: "We know the changes you are aiming to make," the generals said. "The Turkish nation won't allow it. Nobody is so blind as not to see the developments."

Soon after that, a report by a parliamentary commission, dominated by the Islamists, investigating cases of corruption shocked everyone. The commission claimed: "The source of the corruption is the secular morality."

The Chief Justice of the Supreme Court of Appeals, Eraslan Özkaya, expressed the secularists' deep concern. At a ceremony in Ankara in September 2003, to mark the start of a new judicial season, Judge Özkaya implied that the Justice and Development Party was using the European Union's call for greater religious freedom in Turkey as an excuse to lay the ground for a theocratic state. Judge Özkaya added that the country had already done enough to start the EU accession negotiations and that the EU should not demand any more political reforms.

His statement brought an angry response from Prime Minister Erdoğan: "It's an ugly and negative approach. Defending freedom of religion and conscience never amounts to setting up a religious state, and it is very wrong to look at this as such."

Still, there was no end to Erdoğan's faux pas. He dropped a bomb during a meeting with European representatives. Questioned by Wolf-Ruthart Born, the German ambassador in Ankara, about the turban and conditions that allow a man to have four wives, the prime minister said: "A man can have more than one woman if his wife is sick, old, or disabled."

The resistance by the presidents and professors of the universities to Erdoğan's and his party's plans to control higher education brought about systematic attacks against them by the Islamists. Often the attacks turned ugly. Erdoğan used the word *edepsizler*, meaning rude or ill-mannered, to describe university officials. Some of his statements—such as "It's obvious who in Turkey conducts the affairs of the government," and "If we said legal, it is legal"—raised eyebrows.

The Justice and Development Party would like to replace the secularist leaders of the universities with Islamists. The Islamists have been pressuring the universities to accept graduates of the imam-cleric schools for higher education. The universities resisted a related draft law in the fall of 2003, considering it an interference with their authority, which is recognized by the constitution. The qualifications for entering universities of graduates of imam-cleric high schools are not considered to be equal to those of graduates of the secular high schools. Professor Ayhan Alkış, chairman of the Council of Inter-universities, said that the draft law if approved "will transform our educational system into a system of education that does not conform to the present age." Professor Aysel Çelikel, a member of the Foundation of Higher Education (YÖK) and chairman of the Association of Women Jurists, said that the draft law was against the constitution, the understanding of the law and order state, and the principles of secular education. All hell broke out when Professor Kemal Alemdaroğlu, the president of the University of Istanbul, stated in September 2003, "Turkey will not become a country of imams."

The Labor Union for Religious and Pious Affairs (Diyanet-Sen) came out slugging. Hüseyin Demirci, the union's local chairman in the Konya province, declared: "We will not wash Kemal Alemdaroğlu's body when he dies." Other imams soon supported him. Yakup Sözen, the chairman of the Union's Istanbul branch, said: "We will not wash Alemdaroğlu's corpse, we will not perform *namaz* [ritual prayers at a funeral]. There won't be any funeral. We will not remove [to the cemetery] his corpse. ... We have taken much offense at Alemdaroğlu's words, 'Turkey will not become the country of imams.' There are 72,000 imams in Turkey. If these 72,000 imams bother him, then he should choose [to live in] a place where there are no imams."

"The imam-cleric schools ought to be closed," Kemal Gürüz, the chairman of the Foundation of Higher Education, said. The state-funded imam-cleric high schools, meant to educate clerics for religious services, had mushroomed during the premiership of Süleyman Demirel. There were about six hundred imam-cleric schools in 2003, a number much higher than other vocational schools. Demirel opened 233 of these schools and Tansu Çiller another 130. The present yearly need for religious services is fifty-five hundred imam-cleric graduates. During the 1998–99 school year, there were nine hundred thousand imam-cleric students, many of them girls. Still, there can be no female imams in the Islamic religion. In 2002 that figure fell down to 71,000. The regime of the Justice and Development Party was aiming in October 2003 to increase the present twenty-five thousand yearly graduates of imam-clerics.

Columnist Bekir Coşkun wrote in *Hürriyet*:

> An imam state. . . . You must get used to it. The imams will manage the state. There will be an imam governor, an imam district official, an imam judge, an imam prosecutor, an imam head doctor, an imam general manager, and an imam official.
>
> Years ago when I wrote "The imams are coming," everyone was upset, and they accused me of making up things.
>
> Who is prime minister now?
>
> He is an imam. . . .
>
> They [the government of the Justice and Development Party] do not want imams to conduct their business as religious functionaries.
>
> They want an imam governor, an imam district official, an imam director, an imam chief, imam police, an imam nurse, an imam judge, an imam prosecutor and an imam state.

Deputy Chief of General Staff, General Ilker Başbuğ, expressed "serious concerns" about attempts to change the qualifications for acceptance to the universities. He added that it was hard to understand why the regime still sought to increase the number of twenty-five thousand graduates of imam-cleric schools a year when the need in the field was only fifty-five hundred. Finally, the matter was discussed between Prime Minister Erdoğan and Chief of General Staff General Hilmi Özkök, and Erdoğan agreed to put the plans on hold.

Still, the controversy was kept alive when the University of Ankara and the Kemalist Thought Association organized a march named "Respect for the Republic." A huge banner was carried behind the presidents and professors of universities during the march, calling the army to do its duty. The word *Ordu* (army) on the banner were interpreted as call for a coup d'etat to overthrow Erdoğan's government. The university presidents said they had nothing to do with that banner.

Necmettin Erbakan, the ultra-Islamist, had to resign in January 2004 from the Felicity Party. He had been sentenced earlier to a jail term of two years and four months for some missing funds from the closed Welfare Party. Due to claims of ill health, he was not jailed.

Islam's Perfect Man

Oh, my heart, it is impossible to daub the sun with mud,
Perfect Man shines even if he is mute.

Levni

Islam, influenced throughout the centuries by deviationist Arab and Iranian fundamentalists, is an unbending, hard religion that rejects change. This is one of the reasons why I think it is difficult to reform or modernize it or to turn it into an institution based on the rules of democracy. Throughout its history, Islam's strict Canon Law, often misinterpreted by the ulema, has played a dominant role in the Arab and Iranian cultures. The Ottomans adopted its reactionary form from the Arabs, which has survived to this day in Turkey despite the Turkish secular reforms.

During Ottoman times, reactionary Islam rejected change and was often used to force the state to implement political and economic demands. The histories of the Ottoman Empire and Turkish secular republic are replete with murders and assassinations committed by reactionary Islam. In fact, fundamentalist Islam already used terror in the

Ottoman Empire as a means to achieve its objectives. Centuries later, on September 11, 2001, a terror greater than ever seen before in such magnitude in the history of mankind carried a clear political message of reactionary Islam's ruthlessness to the world. That terror, however, gave an undeserved bad name to Islam, while proving at the same time that some people or groups motivated by politics and angry about the tragedy in Palestine and later in Iraq abuse this great religion.

This is the primary reason why a just solution to the Palestinian crisis and the one in Iraq are so interconnected with the urgent reforms needed in Islam. Islamists do not like the word *reform*. They believe that Islam, the perfect religion, does not need reform, but rather a renewal. Such a renewal, in my view, can best be pioneered in Turkey because of the Turks' eighty-two-year experience with secular life.

Kemal Atatürk had realized the need for change in Islam in the 1920s and 1930s. He made no great effort, however, to reform the Islamic religion itself. Instead, he replaced the Shariah with Western laws. In order to make the message of the Qur'an understood by everyone, he had the holy book translated into Turkish from its original Arabic and printed in the new Latin alphabet. Atatürk saw the need to separate the mosque from the state and did so. Eighty-two years after his reforms, Arabic, the language of the Qur'an, is still dominant in the Turk's prayers, and the secularity of the state is under an obsessive and hostile encroachment.

Atatürk levied his reforms on the Turk to save him from the Arabs' traditional interpretation of the Islamic religion. He wanted to change the country's image, which had gradually taken on an Arabic semblance during the Ottoman Empire. He changed the Turk and created a Westernized, secular man and a Westernized, secular country. The Kemalist was his creation.

The Kemalist differed greatly from *Insan-ı Kamil*, the Perfect or the Complete Man of the old Sufi dervish brotherhoods. The dervish orders were divided over the meaning and restrictions of the Shariah. The mainstream Sufis remained strictly loyal to orthodoxy and considered the observance of the Canon Law as essential. To other mystics, however, the separation of the externalities of the law from personal theology was not satisfactory. They sought a personal union with God, often fervently reciting the word *Allah* in their rituals in a state of trance and overwhelming emotion. Truth (*hakika*) was their goal, and the path (*tarika*) led them to truth to become the Perfect Man. The Perfect Man or the Complete Man was someone who had freed himself from imperfection and who had severed the bonds to his lower self.

The Kemalist that Atatürk molded was secular but not an atheist and received his inspiration from the West. As such, he found enlightenment in European culture and wrote the Turkish language not in Arabic letters but in Latin. The modern laws that replaced the Shariah freed him in particular from the outmoded rules of the Ottoman mentality. And so we believed—until the specter of fundamentalist Islam returned with a vengeance and shocked us all.

If Islam ever needed a Perfect Man, a man free of religious bigotry, a man of enlightenment, the time is now. The influence of reactionary Islam is expanding. We are living in an era in which the eternal struggle of good versus evil is at a particularly high pitch. We may even be at the beginning of a reactionary movement hellbent to destroy civilized life. Radical and often ignorant clerics, as they have always done throughout history, are using the Qur'an schools, medreses, and mosques in the Islamic world to recruit young men and even children to use in a kind of jihad against the enemies of Islam. In order to fight such presumed enemies of Islam, these Islamic bigots advocate the denial of goodness and happiness in this world in exchange for the Islamic paradise, where the eternal, real and happy life begins in truth.

What and who are the enemies of fundamentalist Islam? The West's advanced civilization, improved social life? Or is it the West's domination in scientific research, its technological advancement? Is it its booming economy and superior educational and research institutions? Or is it the West's decadent, hedonistic ways? The politics of Israel and its major ally, America? The tragedy imposed for decades upon the Palestinians? The invasion of Iraq and disasters, misfortunes, and killings brought upon the people of that country? Is it Kemal Atatürk, who introduced secular reforms into the heart of Islam and abolished the caliphate? Is it Christianity?

It is all of the above, and you can add still more.

This is why the call for reform of Islam is so urgent in order to prevent worse polarization between two great religions in the future. How could such a reform be accomplished first in Turkey, a secular state since 1923? In order to understand this point of view, let's take a look at the mentality and traditions of the Bektashi sect, the most liberal of Islam's Sufi brotherhoods.

Hacı Bektashi Veli, a thirteenth century Alawite Sufi dervish leader, studied physics, philosophy, and literature. He was born in Nishabur in Iran and arrived in Anatolia at a time when the Seljuk state had deteriorated into political and economic chaos. Hacı Bektashi Veli, known as the founder saint of the Janissaries, was highly instrumental in Turkish unity and had a great impact on Anatolian culture. He settled in Sulucakarahüyük, known today as Hacı Bektaş, near Cappadocia, and died there in 1337. This founder of the Bektashi Brotherhood recognized all gods as God, all prophets as one with Prophet Muhammed. He raised the status of women in social life: "Educate all women; a nation that does not educate women cannot achieve progress."

The word *bektashi* means "freethinker, dissolute." The Bektashis were quite lax in observing Muslim laws, such as the five daily prayers. They drank wine despite its religious prohibition. Hacı Bektashi Veli's views, written in Turkish seven hundred years ago, are telling:

"Find in yourself all that you seek."

"A road without science leads to darkness."

"Do not do to others what you do not wish to be done to yourself."

His legacy is alive today in the stories of the Alawites in Anatolian towns. In addition, the Anatolian Turk, despite his attachment to Islam, has a spirited mind that often takes pleasure in seeing the humor in his own religious traditions. Professor Hüseyin Yalçın and Miyase Ilknur have collected Anatolian anecdotes, including some Alawite-Bektashi humor. Two of those are good examples to show the religious views of the moderate Anatolian.

The man named Deli (Mad) Ahmet from the village of Isa (Jesus) in

Arguvan County, in the province of Malatya, could not find paper to roll his tobacco during World War II. When he could no longer resist the overwhelming desire for a smoke, Mad Ahmet would tear a page from the Qur'an, roll his tobacco in it, and smoke. One day his wife, Yeter, caught him in the act.

"What are you doing?" she asked. "You shall meet with divine punishment for blasphemy."

"Hush, wife, hush," he answered, seemingly indifferent to her concern. "I am filling my inside with inspiration."

On another occasion, Mad Ahmet builds a dike in the stream with earth and stones in order to water his field. The dike leaks, so he takes off his clothes and uses them to plug the leak. When this too is useless, he takes off his long johns and pushes them into the hole.

The pressure on the dike builds up, the wall collapses, and the water carries away his clothing, including the long johns. Mad Ahmet's wife, bringing his lunch, is shocked to see him stark naked.

"What's going on?" she asks. "Where are your drawers?"

"Oh," Mad Ahmet answers, "they are going to Kerbela."

"What are you saying?"

"Look here, woman, doesn't this stream join Tohma? And what river do you think Tohma joins? Is it not the River Euphrates? You know that the river Euphrates leaves Anatolia and flows to Kerbela before going down to Basra, don't you? I couldn't go to Kerbala to pay my respects, but my drawers did!"

The tomb of Hüseyin ibn Ali, the Shi'ite Muslim hero and grandson of Prophet Muhammed is located in Kerbala, in central Iraq. The tomb, a great Shi'ite and Alawite shrine, is an important destination for pilgrims. The members of the Alawite-Bektashi sect, the most enlightened among the Islamic brotherhoods, support Turkish secular reforms.

I remember the following humorous anecdote from my childhood years in Isparta. One Anatolian asked another, "Do you drink *rakı*?"

He answered, stretching the first word *akşam*, evening: "Akşamdaaaan akşama."

By stretching the word *akşam*, evening, he was pretending that he drank rakı only in the evenings and that the time from one evening to the next was too long.

He was asked again, "Do you go to the mosque?"

This time, his answer was a speedy *"Bayramdan bayrama, bayramdan bayrama,"* meaning, from one religious holiday to the next. With such a rapid answer, the Anatolian was attempting to impress upon the other Anatolian that he attended the mosque frequently.

These anecdotes are good illustrations of the difference between moderate Islam and the sour-faced, often ruthless, radical Islam. Yet the Kemalist Turk these days is highly concerned about the influence of the Islamic reactionary in the state itself.

According to President Necdet Sezer, Islam needs to be reformed. Other secular Turkish leaders, concerned that the country is severely divided on the issue of religion, believe Islam has to change in order to catch up with the Christian world in science, technology, commerce, and social development. If not, they reason, a political *din ve iman* (religion and faith) ideology supported by reactionary Islam at the top of the state is bound to destroy the secular state and its democracy.

The chairman of Turkey's Department of Religious Affairs, Professor Ali Bardakoğlu in October 2003 bluntly called for the creation of a "Modern Muslim." He said that there were discussions over the interpretation of religion and that Islam in Turkey needed to be removed from the geographical influences of other cultures, meaning the Arab and Iranian cultures. Ali Bardakoğlu said that the September 11 attacks in New York and Washington hurt the image of Islam: "If we wish to save this society from ignorance, we can achieve this with well trained teachers and religious employees."

During a talk with reporters in his office, Bardakoğlu complained about TV programs that held discussions among speakers who were not well informed on religion. He said such discussions were damaging to Islam and used the word *yobaz* for the speakers. The word *yobaz* means "Islamic bigot or reactionary."

Bardakoğlu said that his department was developing a program in order to create the "Modern Muslim," to fit him with "a new religious suit," and to form Islamic academies—similar to the staff academies of the army—to educate "staff imams" in order to reform the education of the religious employees. There would be a qualifying scale for imams in accordance with their educational achievements: a chief imam, a specialist imam, and an imam. He also said that his department is planning a countrywide "Modern Muslim" campaign with booklets.

Bardakoğlu's statements sparked immediate reaction.

In a statement to the press, Professor Zekeriya Beyaz, the theology dean of Marmara University, said that the present-day culture and lifestyle of the Arabs are damaging the image of Islam. He said the conditions call for a return to Atatürk's teaching and that Atatürk is a "ready prescription" for solving Islam's problems.

In another statement to the press, Professor Niyazi Öktem of the Law Faculty of Bilgi University said that it was time for the Turks to settle the score with the hard traditions of the Arab culture: "This means both a return to essential Islam and to contemporary times. In the Anatolian's understanding of Islam the elements of wisdom weigh heavily while in the Islam of the Arabs dogmas are dominant."

Lütfi Kaleli, the Chairman of the Foundation of Alawi Education and Culture, said: "Islam definitely needs reform. This reform has to be carried out with wisdom and in a way suitable to the traditions of our times."

It is this wisdom, however, that the Turks lacked in the winter of 2003. While a radical faction tried to impose the devout women's Islamic symbol, the turban, into the state's protocol, the Kemalist faction tried to keep it out. The leaders of the Justice and Development Party, despite clear warning signs, doggedly followed a policy of establishing a state dominated by mullahs and imams. Many who call themselves Kemalists, however, found advantage in switching sides hoping for personal benefits from the Islamist regime. They were called turncoats.

The suicide attacks during morning Sabbath prayers at two synagogues in Istanbul on Saturday November 15, 2003, were proof once again that terror was a global problem. The attacks by Turkish Islamic reactionaries connected to Hizbullah and al-Qaeda with two trucks loaded with explosives caused the deaths of twenty-five Turkish citizens and injured another 303. Prime Minister Erdoğan, shocked by this terrible bloodshed in the name of Islam, said: "I curse them [the perpetrators]." He described the attacks as inhuman.

Five days after the attack against the two synagogues, Istanbul was shaken again on November 20, 2003, by two more suicide bombings with trucks loaded with explosives. Once again, the suicide attackers were Turks who had connections to the synagogue bombings, and their victims were mostly Muslim Turks. This time, the targets were the British Consulate and the London-based HSBC bank. Thirty people, including the British consul-general Roger Short, were killed and 461 injured. The number of dead from the attacks in November later reached ninety-one. Because the suicide attacks occurred during the Islamic holy month of Ramadan, Erdoğan said, "Those who bloodied this holy day and massacred innocent people will account for it in both worlds. They will be damned until eternity."

His religious-toned reaction to the terror attacks was interpreted as referring to the terrorists' punishment in the hereafter as well as in the real world. Erdoğan said that the expression "Islamic terror" was part of an effort to identify the terror with the Islamic religion. He said the expression hurt his feelings: "When I hear the words 'Islamic terror,' I cannot put up with it and find it unbearable." Erdoğan named the terror religious. His words were controversial. Bekir Coşkun wrote in *Hürriyet*:

> So what are we supposed to do?
>
> How on earth will this prime minister, who himself used religion as a tool for politics and adopted the expression of "Democratic Muslim," be able to prevent the use of the words "Islamic terror." There are people who abuse our religion as a tool for terror.
>
> If you deny the existence of this terror, its aim, purpose, and its source, how do you plan to find and stop it?
>
> This is the first time I hear of someone who doesn't like the name of the terror and desires to change it.

Its name is religious terror and its target is all of us.
That's all.

Hasan Pulur wrote in *Milliyet* that it is easy to say "I have changed."
He added that Erdoğan, who in his past used clear images and expressions
of pro-Islam views, now finds that it's not really so easy to change.

Özdemir Ince of *Hürriyet* wrote, "This is a government that is unable
to find a name for a nest of evil."

The Directorate of Religious Affairs, however, advised the imams of
the mosques to preach the following sermon on the first day of the
Ramadan holidays: "Terrorism, violence, and anarchy have nothing to
do with Islam. Our duty is to love one another and to live like brothers
in unity."

Despite all those sermons, contradictions existed. How could a
regime with powerful Islamist roots and a political party based on support
of reactionary Islam effectively fight Islamic terror and protect the secularity of the state? Turkey's Islamic media went so far as to blame Israel,
the United States, and Britain for the suicide bombings. It was common
knowledge at the time that Erdoğan's regime was supported by a section
of the media known as the *Şeriatçı Basın*, meaning a press that promotes
the reinstatement of the Shariah.

President George W. Bush, visiting Britain at the time, called Turkey
"a new front" in the war of terror.

The militant Islamic Great Eastern Raiders' Front, or IBDA-C, jointly
with al-Qaeda's Abu Hafz al-Masri Brigades claimed responsibility for
the suicide attacks on the synagogues, the HSBC Bank, and the British
Consulate. According to the police, other radical Islamic organizations,
such as Beyyiat al-Islam and Hizbullah, also had connections to the terror
attacks. The attacks were aimed against Turkey's friendship and alliances
with the United States, Britain, and Israel as well as the country's
Kemalist reforms and secular traditions. The reactionary Islamists consider the secular Turkish state a dangerous model for other Islamic countries and a bridge between moderate Islam and Western democracy, and
they would like to see it destroyed.

Al-Qaeda and other Islamic militant groups were believed to be receiving help from about one thousand radical Turks who had earlier fought in Bosnia as volunteers against the Serbs and in Afghanistan and Chechnya against Russian forces. According to former interior minister Sadettin Tantan, the Turkish intelligence services were having difficulty for a year in placing agents inside radical Islamist groups. According to Tantan, speaking right after the bombings in Istanbul: "Intelligence [from the radical Islamist groups] is no longer being received." His meaning was clear enough—since the election of the Justice and Development Party on November 3, 2002, the reactionary Islamist groups had been left alone.

The bombed synagogues in Istanbul were named Beth Israel and Neve Shalom, which in Hebrew means "Oasis of Peace." The bombings were a new wake-up call that the prospects of peace were few in this time when radical Islam's terrorism was holding sway and that reform in Islam was an absolute necessity.

In the winter of 2004, most Kemalist Turks wondered how much truth there was to Recep Tayyip Erdoğan's and his political team's claim that they have changed. I have to admit that an interview published in the *Radikal* newspaper on February 23, 2004, had been very impressive. The interview was conducted by Neşe Düzel, with writer Mehmet Metiner, who had been Recep Tayyip Erdoğan's counselor when Erdoğan was the chairman of Welfare Party's Istanbul branch and later Welfare's mayor in Istanbul.

Metiner explained how this change came about: "Before the 1980s, we believed that it was a sin for a man to shake a woman's hand. Our thoughts were the same as Taliban's. Islam was to be the state, and the people were to be Islamized by force if necessary."

Of Necmettin Erbakan's Islamist National Order and National Salvation parties, Metiner said: "We were young then. Our view was that the return of the Shariah would bring an end to atrocities and destroy the atheistic state. I have been in the Islamic revival since I was fifteen. We believed that the republic was aiming to make the people irreligious in the name of secularism. We considered secularism the same as atheism."

Metiner added he and his friends began to change at the end of 1980s, and that change was accelerated after February 28, 1996, when the military forced the political leaders to sign a decree prohibiting the activities of all Islamic orders and brotherhoods. That decree also caused the collapse of Necmettin Erbakan's Islamist government on June 18, 1997. Metiner told Neşe Düzel: "I began to defend democracy and democratic secularity and some of my friends believed that I was no longer a Muslim. The Islamists considered the defense of democracy was to abandon Islam."

Metiner said that the reactionary *Milli Görüş*, or National View, politics of Necmettin Erbakan, which considers secularity as atheism, lost its importance among the moderate members of Erbakan's Islamist Virtue Party. As a result, he said, Recep Tayyip Erdoğan and the majority of the founders of the Justice and Development Party realized that it was wrong to conduct politics using religion as a base. "Thank God," Metiner said, "we were unable to establish a state based on Shariah."

Prime Minister Recep Tayyip Erdoğan said that the Islamic religion was used for political gains. On a *Kanal 7* TV program on March 2, 2004, Erdoğan said: "Unfortunately, in the past we, too, made the same mistake."

I think a remarkable analysis of the Turkish situation, regarding religious revival versus the secularity of the state, was made in August 2003 by a retiring general. General Cumhur Asparuk, commander of the air force, spoke following the ceremonies that transferred his command to General Ibrahim Fırtına: "We, as the Turkish Nation, having gone back one hundred years, are spinning inside a sterile circle. We are struggling with the Blue Stream, the plundered banks, the imam-cleric schools, concealing women's figures, the Islamic brotherhoods, and the dress styles of the cultures of other countries while the developed nations dominate the world from space."

General Aytaç Yalman, the commander of the land forces, was blunt about the Turkish situation and democracy. Expressing his personal views to reporters on August 30, 2003, in Ankara during the Victory Day celebrations of the Independence War, General Yalman said, "If there is democracy in Turkey today, it is thanks to the Turkish armed forces, who are the guarantors of not only the republic but also of democracy." General Yalman added: "This is a country where the average national income is $2,580 and its average education level is the fourth grade of elementary school. A very small part of the population is living in the twenty-first century, and the rest are still in the nineteenth and twentieth centuries. Is there a similar country in the world ruled by democracy? This has been possible here thanks to the armed forces."

For many this truth was a bitter pill to swallow, for Turkey had lost great opportunities to continue its reform movement. To catch up and not to skip another century of progress, I thought the Turks needed to change their mentality and reform Islam by modifying it with Kemal Atatürk's ideals. To accomplish such a modification, the Kemalist and the Islamist have to understand that unless a solution is found and accepted by both sides, a conflict will be unavoidable.

President Necdet Sezer stated that to describe Turkey, a secular country, as an "Islamic republic" is meaningless and to think that such an "Islamic republic" would be practicing, in effect, moderate Islam, is inappropriate and unacceptable. President Sezer added, "Moderate Islam may be an advancement for other Islamic countries, but for the Republic of Turkey, it represents a model of an incredible reversal. And frankly speaking, it would be a 'model of fundamentalism.' In other words, to compare a state based on religion, whether moderate or fundamentalist, as equal to democracy is contrary to history and science." Prime Minister Recep Tayyip Erdoğan's Islamic-rooted Justice and Development Party is convinced that Islam is compatible with democracy.

One of the greatest gifts of Kemal Atatürk to the Turkish nation was the Westernization of the education system in order to open the way for people's enlightenment. The military understood this, and the military schools continued in general to graduate officers loyal to Atatürk's legacy and the secularity of the state. The Kemalist of my youth, who remained loyal to Atatürk's ideals and principles, was a patriotic, Westernized man; yet he remained a Muslim, albeit an enlightened Muslim with liberal views. It took fifty years to turn the clock back. Reactionary Islam entered politics, the school system, and the Turkish home in the 1950s, expanded rapidly in later years, and reversed the reform movement. Some of the Kemalists extended a helping hand to change the nation's destiny.

Times changed, and so did my country. Not many people, who, like I, lived through the times of modern reforms in the 1920s and 1930s, are alive today. For decades the new generations have been left ignorant about the meaning of these reforms—that the leadership of Kemal Atatürk saved the Turkish heartland from foreign domination, united the country, and exposed the Turk to secularity and Western knowledge and know-how. In addition, Atatürk's reforms never promoted or caused the practice of atheism. One of the principal targets of Kemal Atatürk's reform movement was to elevate the backward and ignorant peasant to contemporary times. Atatürk's death at the age of fifty-seven in 1938 caused the eventual failure of his objective.

The Turks favored socialism following the coup of 1960 and a powerful Islamist revival after the coup of 1980. Even the coup leaders of 1980, to their profound regret later, had encouraged the Islamist movement as a counterforce in the struggle against the extreme left. Meanwhile, Kemalism stayed rigid, refused change, made no attempts to educate the peasant masses, and neglected to transform itself into a force of the future. A decade after Kemal Atatürk died, the spread of disunity, poverty, greed, callousness, and corruption led to national disheartenment and a depressed state of mind for the people, presenting a boon of opportunity for the pro-Islam movement.

The army brass, highly disappointed with the civilian regimes, attempted time and again to stave off the fundamentalist trend and corruption while acting as the guardian of the secular reforms. The army failed because Turkey's old elite civilian class, determined to protect and adapt the secular reform movement to the requirements of the times, no longer existed. The next civilian regime, led by opportunists flipping between Islamic and Kemalist ideologies, was no better than the one just departed—and often worse. Compassion for the have-nots had been replaced with insensibility. The susceptibility of the elite class to such emotions as disgrace, shame, impropriety, and humility had vanished. The Young Turk, having seen the dollar sign, set his mind on get-rich-quick-schemes no matter what, even if it meant robbing the treasury of the state itself. No governments, including the present Islamist regime, dared to remove the members' of parliament immunity accused of corruption because of thick corruption files on their own backs.

Strong opposition to the principles of the Kemalist ideology appeared. Bülent Arınç, the speaker of parliament, declared that there was a difference between being a Kemalist and pro-Atatürk, meaning yes to Atatürk and no to Kemalism. It was seen as an attempt to devaluate the meaning and value of the Kemalist secular reforms.

The slogan of Atatürk that united the nation in the 1920s and 1930s, *Ne mutlu Türküm diyene*—"How happy is he who can say, I am a Turk"—had been classified as outmoded. The Justice and Development Party adopted a new slogan to replace it: *Türkiyeliyim*, meaning "I am from Turkey." This differs greatly from Atatürk's understanding of *Laik Millet*—"Secular Nation"—and promotes *Ümmeti Müslüman*, a Nation of Muslims. It is also in contrast to the American expression of identity: "Proud to be an American."

Prime Minister Erdoğan said, "If you say 'How happy I am to be a Turk,' the other guy will say, 'How happy I am to be a Kurd.' We must replace the consciousness of being a Turk with the sense of belonging to Turkey."

It is worth mentioning here that Americans often describe themselves as German-American, Chinese-American, or, for that matter, Turkish-American.

Özdemir Ince, a columnist for *Hürriyet*, commented that the words "How happy is he who says I am a Turk" are the ideal of Turkish nationhood and reflect the spirit of the republic. Ince added that a politician who does not like the meaning of these words and wants to replace them with the mentality of the Islamic faithful is now prime minister. He wrote that a political party in constant contradiction with the *raison d'être* of a state would be unable to come to power. If it did, Ince added, it must either destroy that *raison d'être*, or it will have to yield to its authority.

November 10, 2003, was the sixty-fifth anniversary of Kemal Atatürk's death. As usual, there were ceremonies all over the country, and at 9:05 a.m., millions of Turks stood still for a moment in remembrance. The newspapers' bold headlines announced: "We Remember You with Longing" and "We Did Not Forget You."

It is true that the Turks, Kemalists or Islamists, have not forgotten Kemal Atatürk. There is deep hatred as well as great love for his memory. I personally think that Atatürk was an extraordinary leader with a great vision and that his sickness and untimely death was a misfortune for the Turkish nation. His death sixty-five years ago retarded the reform movement.

I remember how journalist Falih Rıfkı Atay in his book *Çankaya* described the last years (1937–38) of Atatürk's life. Atay, who was among his companions, wrote that Atatürk's nerves in 1937 were bad, and he was easily offended. Nobody realized at the time that this was caused by cirrhosis of his liver. Atay wrote, "It all started with a weakness in his memory. Later frequent nose bleeds and itchings began." Finally, the disease was diagnosed.

"We had gone to the railroad station in Ankara to welcome him from the south," Atay wrote. "He had difficulty descending from the train and walking to the station's waiting room. He couldn't stay standing, so he sat down. Şükrü Saracoğlu was next to me. 'Falih, look at Atatürk's skin color. It's the color of death,' he said."

Before he slipped into a coma in Dolmabahçe Palace in Istanbul, Atatürk's spoke his last words: "What time is it?" Was the time important to him as he lay dying? Did he realize that his death would turn the Turkish clock back years later to the Ottoman times? We will never know. What we can be certain of is that Kemal Atatürk himself would have difficulty now recognizing his beloved country.

So this has been my own shocking experience after returning to the country following a twenty-nine-year exile abroad. And, I say, this is not the country I had known, and that nation is not made up of the young, compassionate, reform-minded people I had known when I was a young Kemalist. This is a nation greatly increased in population without planning and divided between the promoters of women's turbans and the enemies of the turban!

And this is a nation whose foreign minister complains about his country in the European Union on the subject of women's headscarves. Foreign Minister Abdullah Gül complained in November 2003 that Turkish laws restricting women from wearing the turban in government and educational institutions was not included as a violation in a EU report that dealt with human rights, despite his party's repeated appeals for it. This happened while EU member countries, particularly France and Germany, were establishing rules against girls wearing headscarves in schools.

In this age, why would a prime minister, a foreign minister, or the speaker of parliament of a secular state desire to hide his wife's hair from other men and consider a woman's handshake with a man immodest? Why do women accept such discrimination? Does a turban help its wearer to be a better Muslim, or is the turban used for promotion of political gains and for the personal satisfaction of men?

More importantly still, is the turban one step away from the harem, the imprisonment of women?

In his message to mark International Women's Day on March 8, 2004 President Necdet Sezer said, "The headscarf issue is invoked in the name of democracy, but it has no meaning other than to cast a shadow over Turkey's democratic advances. . . . In the name of democracy and social peace, we cannot allow the exploitation of freedom of religion and conscience by certain political groups using human rights as excuse. The real guarantee of freedom of religion and conscience is the principle of secularism."

This is also the country where Minister of Justice Cemil Çiçek made the following statement in January 2004: "There are thieves in every professional group including politicians. . . . And each professional group protects its own thief."

And this is the country where professor and doctor Ömer Dinçer, the councillor of the prime ministry, a graduate of an imam-cleric school, has declared his opposition in the past to the basic principles of the secular republic. It is his view that it is time to change the republic to an Islamic state. Oktay Ekşi wrote in *Hürriyet* on December 30, 2003, that in a democracy an individual has a right to freely express his views. In an open letter to Prime Minister Erdoğan, Ekşi added, "A councilor to the prime minister, however, as a top bureaucrat, cannot oppose the state's basic principles, and if he does, he cannot stay at his post." Ömer Dinçer remained the councillor of the prime ministry. He denies that he is antisecularist.

All these developments bring many questions to my mind.

Does Recep Tayyip Erdoğan, whose surname *erdoğan* means a born soldier, represent Islam's Perfect Man? If so, will he be able to blend Islam's moderate views with the secular republic without causing further damage to the Kemalist reforms? Will he be able to control the fundamentalist base of the Justice and Development Party?

Only time will tell, and using his time wisely is crucial for this maverick politician. Erdoğan is aware that he and other leading members of the Justice and Development Party are under close scrutiny. The pashas, the guardians of the secular state, are watching his and his party's every move, analyzing each act and word with the utmost care. If the military brass decides that the basic reforms of Kemalism—such as the secularity of the state and the unity of the nation—are in danger, then, I believe, regardless of world opinion, they may not hesitate to intervene. This intervention might take the form of toppling Necmettin Erbakan's Islamist regime.

The fact is that regardless of the policies of Erdoğan and his Justice and Development Party, Necmettin Erbakan's reactionary Islamic dogma *Milli Görüş*—the National View—is supported with an aggressive campaign. *Milli Gazete*, the newspaper of the Felicity Party, represents the nucleus of this fundamentalist doctrine. Mehmet Şevket Eygi, the lead writer of *Milli Gazete*, wrote on February 27, 2004:

"An Islamic *tarikat* [brotherhood] is not possible without the *Şeriat* [Shariah]."

According to Eygi, the Ottoman Empire during its glory days had reached the summits of excellence on the two wings of Shariah and Islamic brotherhoods. Eygi added, "If Sufism (*tasavvuf*) and Islamic brotherhood (*tarikat*) break down, we will collapse with a great booming sound." Eygi also believes that some Muslim clerics lack the cultural ability to preach the message of Islam effectively to the believers. Eygi's messages, richly interspersed with Arabic religious terms (such as *Mahkeme-i Kübra*, or Judgment Day, and *Melhame-i Kübra*, or Armageddon), carry a clear message to the conservative Anatolian. He had been in trouble with the law in the past for his article titled the "Terror of Religious Hatred." Eygi is also known for his systematic criticism of widespread corruption, mischief, disorder, and debauchery in public life.

Ahmet F. Gün wrote in *Milli Gazete* on December 1, 2003,

> The imperialists, Zionists, and occupiers are now pillaging the geography of Islam. Look at Palestine, Afghanistan, Eritrea. Look at Iraq.
> The infidels of America, Britain, Israil, Italy, and Spain have broken the doors of Islam's lands and trampled on the Islam's sacred places and honor.

I believe that the invasion of Iraq by the US-led coalition forces was a grave mistake because it created more hatred against the United States and Western values in the Islamic countries, including Turkey. Once the daily tragic killings began and Iraq became a nest for al-Qaeda terrorists, the American officials had a hard time explaining what they really had in mind. Any explanation, in fact, was unacceptable to radical Islam. Ismail Müftüoğlu, commenting in his article titled "Attack of the Deccal" in *Milli Gazete* (*National Newspaper*) on December 11, 2004, called America a *deccal*, an evil being that will appear at the end of times:

> Where are you, government of the AKP? How about you, followers of Atatürk? The Army of Deccals of the United States of America first attacked Afghanistan and then Iraq, causing the death of thousands of Muslims. The idea was supposed to bring an end to the systems in these countries and replace them with democracy. It is the United States, however, that caused those who ruled these countries to become Frankenstein monsters. When [the Americans] first lost control of the

Taliban and then of Saddam [Hussein], they became greedy
for revenge.

Müftüoğlu, blaming the United States for arming Saddam once,
added that Saddam became a vampire and used these arms first against
Iran and then in Halabja against his own people. Müftüoğlu continued,
"Iraq is destroyed. The Muslims now have been massacred. The places of
worship demolished. The roaring noise of the bombs dominate Iraq,
replacing the muezzin's call to prayers. The Turkish government too
appeared to favor the cruel. The lands and their peoples that were once
under our rule were left to their fate."

Müftüoğlu then reprinted a speech of Atatürk delivered on July 27,
1937, in the Grand National Assembly: "Nobody else knows as much as
we do about the disorder and unhappiness among the Arab peoples."
Müftüoğlu brought notice to Atatürk's words in the same speech that
Turkey would not allow Islam's sacred places to become a playground for
European imperialism. Müftüoğlu asked, "Is there anything else to say?
Followers of Atatürk, Kemalists, where are you? How about you, Mus-
lims, where are you?"

Radical Islam's unhappiness over the events in Afghanistan, Palestine, and Iraq caused meetings and demonstrations in Turkey against the
United States at the end of 2004 and in early 2005. Mass meetings called
"Curse the Tyrants" were organized by the Islamist Felicity Party in several cities. Necmettin Erbakan, the leader of *Milli Görüş* (National View),
wholeheartedly supported the meetings and declared, "Your sincere stand
will get rid of the crusader of the cross that the Zionist forces have hurled
onto the geography of Islam."

It seems that, despite Prime Minister Erdoğan's belief that Islam is
compatible with democracy, we observe that combining Islam with the
Western understanding of democracy is a difficult issue. According to
Cemil Çiçek, Turkey's justice minister, "Democracy, human rights, and
rule of law are very urgent needs for the Islamic community."

Often I wonder, what happened to the Turkish nation? What happened to Kemalism and the Kemalists? What made that nation lose that

lively spirit of the reform years, the years when we sang our song: "We, fifteen million young have come out of ten years of struggle with pride, heads held high . . ."?

It is true, we were only fifteen million then; we were dirt poor, but free at last, an enlightened, united, civilized, and proud nation. We were confident in ourselves and obsessed with the idea of catching up with the rest of the world. The date was October 29, 1933, and the occasion, the tenth anniversary of the proclamation of the secular republic, the birth of a nation.

That anniversary meant for us the young Kemalists the beginning of still greater efforts in our ongoing progress. Seventy-two years later, it is shocking to see seventy million Turkish citizens divided, in search for a new identity and hoping salvation not from the true legacy of Kemal Atatürk but from reactionary Islam.

The legacy of Atatürk has been the teaching of Western knowledge and the protection of his reforms, not to idealize his image. This is where the Kemalists made their worst mistake. They have ignored his legacy and lost the initiative to continue his reform movement by not creating a unifying national culture. As we have seen earlier, some politicians who masqueraded as Kemalists often supported pro-Islam for personal or political advantages, and others used Atatürk's name to enhance their objectives.

And this brings the inevitable query, even though it is painful.

Who really are the Kemalists today?

The moderate leftists, or the Communists who adopted capitalism with incredible greed after the collapse of the Soviet Union? The reactionary Islamists, or the Islamists of the Justice and Development Party? The corrupt old-guard politicians, robber barons of the media and business world, or the members of Kemal Atatürk's own Republican People's Party? That party used to blame *Hassos* and *Memos*—meaning the uneducated, ignorant, backward peasants—for supporting Adnan Menderes's Democratic Party. The same Republican People's Party, having lost its true calling for reforms and vacillating between left, right, Kemalist, and Islamist ideologies since the 1950s, was in November 2003 trying to redefine the Kemalist ideals—how to merge social democracy, Kemalism, and Islam into a tailor-made suit to fit the Turk, and with any luck win the next election.

These efforts came a bit late, for pro-Islam, having taken over the state, was busy passing reform laws through parliament to gain the country's membership in the European Union. It is a strange reflection of our times that a pro-Islam party has seized the opportunity of this membership for its own survival and expansion. It is clear that Turkey's EU membership is a life jacket for Erdoğan's Justice and Development Party.

I think the following argument between Erdoğan and Deniz Baykal, the leader of the opposition Republican People's Party, during the local elections in March 2004 exemplifies the Kemalists today. Prime Minister Erdoğan, speaking at an election rally in Bolu, western Turkey, said about the opposition, "Their root is not Atatürk; the Republican People's Party is not a party supporting Atatürk's ideals. If they were, they would not have eliminated Atatürk's pictures from the state's money and postage stamps. The Republican People's Party is abusing Atatürk's ideals. Ours is the party [the Justice and Development] that supports Atatürk's vision."

Erdoğan had earlier angered Baykal by saying that the roots of the Republican People's Party are neither productive nor blessed. Speaking at an election campaign, Baykal said that Prime Minister Erdoğan's mouth is corrupted: "I feel like saying, 'May a stone as big as the Republican's People's Party fall on your head. Why are you troubled about the roots of the Republican People's Party? Don't meddle—just give an account of the photographs that show you sitting by the knees of that Taliban. The Prime Minister must learn to keep his mouth's zipper shut tight."

Erdoğan then complained about his salary. The prime minister said that because his monthly salary (about $4,500) was not enough for his family to live on, he also continued to be involved in commercial activities. When Chancellor Gerhard Schröder visited Turkey, Erdoğan asked him what his monthly salary was (over $15,000). The opposition attacked him for being prime minister and a merchant at the same time and for complaining about his salary to the German leader when millions of Turks could not find a job that paid $200 a month.

Having closely observed this incredible transformation that settled over my country, this Turkish Motherland, this heaven for scoundrels, mafia godfathers, and impostors of religion, this land where the justice system is suspect, I now often remember Orhan Veli, the poet who once wrote:

> For this Motherland
> What have we not done for this Motherland!
> Some of us have died,
> Some of us gave speeches.

I, too, remember those speeches. Adnan Menderes used to tell the people at election time half a century ago, "If you so desire, you may even bring back the caliphate." His speeches still echo in Turkish streets in the shouts of the Islamic fundamentalists: "We want the caliphate! We want the Shariah!"

It is this paralyzing fear that the Shariah and the caliphate might return and destroy the secular reforms completely that hangs like a bogey over Turkey's future. General Oktar Ataman, commander of the 3rd army, warned the public about a serious plot by the reactionary Islam on this very subject. On February 16, 2004, during a military exercise in Erzurum in eastern Anatolia, General Oktar Ataman said that traitors inside the country are attempting to sow "seeds of discord" between the nation and its armed forces by spreading untrue and malicious rumors about the army. "Their insidious aim," the general said, "is to replace the eighty-year-old republic's secular system with the Shariah. . . . Because they see the army as an obstacle for their goal, these reactionaries try their best to put a wedge between the nation and its army."

Three important fears have been dominant in the last four decades— the effects of high inflation, corruption, and terrorism carried out by the Kurdish separatist movement; radical Islam; and Communist extremists. These fears helped to bring about undemocratic rules, slowed the reform movement, and led to the present crisis of identity. Most importantly, the fear of reactionary Islam is very real, and it will play a decisive factor in the outcome of the struggle between the secular and the pro-Islam Turk. Consequently, its resolution will not just shape Turkey's future—a transparent, secular, democratic country with a liberal economy, equal justice, and opportunities for all, or a country hoping to achieve greatness by imposing the rules of reactionary Islam.

This resolution will bring profound changes to other Muslim countries in the Middle East and the Caspian Sea region. The United States, Russia, and the countries of the European Union will feel the effects of this transformation. The reason, among others, is that Turkey is the new frontier state in the development of the Greater Middle East Reform Initiative and the fight against terror. The project aims to change the cultural and economic lives and improve the standard of education in the countries involved and to create a region dominated by moderate Islam and not by reactionary forces. It is a huge and difficult job because of poverty, ignorance, and religious bigotry.

General Ilker Başbuğ, deputy chief of the Turkish General Staff, speaking in March 2004 with journalists in Washington about the Greater Middle East Reform Initiative, said that Turkey can be a model state for other countries only as a secular, democratic, law-and-order state: "There can be no such state claiming to be both Islamic and secular."

A statement in April 2004 on this very subject by Secretary of State Colin Powell caused a political storm in Turkey, upsetting the Kemalists. Powell told Maybrit Illner of ZDF TV's *Berlin Mitte* program that Iraq was going to be an Islamic republic similar to other Islamic republics, such as Turkey and Pakistan. *Milliyet*'s banner headline on April 3, 2004, read *Vay Cahil Vay*—meaning "Oh, What an Ignorant Man." Turkish foreign minister Abdullah Gül, speaking about Powell's statement, said he didn't understand what the furor was all about and asked, "Is it not a fact that Turkey is a Muslim country?"

Although Colin Powell later said that his words had been misunderstood, the damage was done. Commenting on the same speech in *Hürriyet*, Bekir Coşkun wrote that Turkey's image has changed, and mirrors don't show a secular republic. Coşkun added:

> The media called Powell's words blunders.
> "Yet they are not.
> "Now we do look like an Islamic republic."

The local elections of March 28, 2004, were like hammer blows to the opposition and the secular image of the country. Prime Minister R. T. Erdoğan's Justice and Development Party swept the elections across the country and took 41.9 percent of the votes, compared with the opposition Republican People's Party's 18.1 percent. Erdoğan said, "Our party has expanded its support base," which was true. In fact, the party gained two million new supporters. The Republican People's Party had lost 500,000 supporters, suffering another political humiliation. The Justice and Development Party had capitalized not only on the party's Islamic character but also on its good governance of municipalities.

Kemalism, too, had received a severe blow once again, perhaps by way of a last nail put in its coffin.

Ertuğrul Özkök of *Hürriyet* likened the victory of the Islamists to a political and social tsunami: "It is impossible to stand against these gigantic waves with an out-of-fashion leftist demagogy, and with only a notion of secularity."

On April 5, 2004, the newspaper *Radikal* printed Neşe Düzel's interview with Professor Baskın Oran of the Faculty of Political Science in Ankara. Professor Oran commented on the Kemalists' resistance against the United Nations sponsored negotiations on Cyprus: "The Kemalists of 1930s say we won't give up [Cyprus]. Is it possible for them not to give up? Cyprus was delivered [to the Allies] in Lausanne. Lausanne [the final treaty in 1923 concluding World War I] is a perfect example of *ver kurtul* [washing one's hands of a thing]. . . . By giving up incredible concessions in Lausanne, Mustafa Kemal [Atatürk] had made it clear that the empire [Ottoman] was done. Now, the nation-state established by Mustafa Kemal [Atatürk], which has completed its mission, is also coming to its end. . . . Kemalism of 1930 in 2000 means going backwards, but for the 1930s it was progress."

These diverse opinions over Kemalism and secularity of the republic bring back the question of what role Turkey should play in the Greater Middle East Reform Initiative. Is this role to be carried out as a secular, democratic, law-and-order state with a Muslim population, or an Islamic country in which secularity of the state remains only a symbolic token in its constitution?

Whatever the outcome, the role of the country in the future development of that huge area will be crucial. Still, the dangerous conditions that have developed in Iraq, in addition to the problems in Afghanistan and Palestine; the horrific activities of al-Qaeda and other religion-based terror organizations; and the strong opposition to the Greater Middle East Initiative in Iran, Pakistan, and several Arab countries, and also Turkey, stand as formidable obstacles in the way of a realization of the project.

I believe one of the foremost hurdles that face the Greater Middle East Initiative not only in Iran, Pakistan, and Arab countries but also in Turkey is this widespread belief that the United States is the leader of a new crusade against the world of Islam. And that the United States and the other Western nations, that is, the Christian world, aim to colonize the region in order to control its rich oil resources and destroy the religion of Islam.

Epilogue

*T*he Associated Press reported the following news item on July 14, 1997, and a number of newspapers in the United States printed it:

Demirel Defends Jailing Journalists

ANKARA, TURKEY—Turkey's president promised a Western media group Sunday to ease government controls over the press but defended the jailing of some 80 journalists.

"I am sure that they are not in jail only because they are journalists," President Süleyman Demirel told former hostage Terry Anderson and other members of a delegation from the New York–based Committee to Protect Journalists.

The delegation made it clear the current situation is unacceptable.

"It is a basic principle of democracy that a person should not be punished for expressing his or her view," said Anderson, who was chief Middle East correspondent of the Associated Press when he was kidnapped by Muslim extremists in Beirut in 1985. He was held for nearly seven years.

Turkish Cat-and-Mouse Game

1923—Kemal Atatürk establishes a secular republic and, until his death in 1938, modernizes legal, social, and educational systems with sweeping reforms and adopts a European way of life.

1950—The Democratic Party wins a landslide victory in free elections, and its leader, Adnan Menderes, relaxes the secular laws of Kemalism. The Democrats permit the establishment of religious schools, reinstate Arabic for the call to prayer, and allow readings of the Qur'an on the state radio. Following a coup d'etat in 1960, Menderes is hanged on the Island of Imralı.

1969—Necmettin Erbakan organizes an Islamic-oriented party and calls it the National Order Party. This party is outlawed in 1971 on charges of acting against the secularist constitution.

1970—The Justice Party of Süleyman Demirel, the premier and former builder of dams for the Menderes regime, uses Islam to gain public support and to fight Communism inspired by the Soviet Union. Left-wing and right-wing extremists clash in the streets. The newspaper *Hürriyet* calls for Demirel's resignation on June 19, 1970, and in March 1971 Demirel is ousted by the armed forces.

1972—Necmettin Erbakan's aides organize a new Islamic party, the National Salvation Party, which delivers to Erbakan an opportunity to join weak coalition governments through the 1970s.

1980—The armed forces stage the third coup d'etat in the republic's history to stop the Times of Chaos and the bloodshed between the extreme right and left. All the political parties are banned and the party leaders jailed.

1983—The military once again returns power to the civilians, and Erbakan founds the Islamic Welfare Party, becoming its leader as soon as the political ban is lifted in 1987.

Anavatan Partisi (ANAP, the Motherland Party) wins the parliamentary election of 1983, and Nakshibendi, the oldest and most powerful Sufi *tarikat* (religious brotherhood), gains a crucial foothold in the Turkish state. Turgut Özal, ANAP's leader; his brother, Korkut Özal; and some ANAP cabinet ministers were members of the Nakshibendi Sufi Order.

The Nakshibendi Sufi Order plays an important role in government by helping Islamist Necmettin Erbakan's own efforts to change the secular face of Turkey.

1995—In December the Welfare Party comes first in general election, and in 1996 Necmettin Erbakan forms a coalition government with secularist Tansu Çiller's True Path Party, angering the secularists, including the army brass. Prime Minister Erbakan promotes an Islamist agenda, proposes an Islamic NATO and an Islamic common market, and pledges to lift the Muslim headscarf ban in government offices. He announces plans to build mosques in secularist strongholds. The generals demand that the government halt Islamist policies. On June 18, 1997, following pressures from the generals, the Islamist-led government collapses.

1998—The Constitutional Court outlaws the Welfare Party on charges of attempting to subvert the secularist constitution. Erbakan is banned from political leadership for five years. Former Welfare deputies in parliament join the new Islamic party, the Virtue Party. Erbakan controls the party behind the scenes.

1999—In April, the Virtue Party suffers losses in the general elections while Bülent Ecevit's Democratic Left Party and Colonel Alparslan Türkeş's ultranationalist and pan-Turanist Nationalist Action Party increase their seats in parliament. In May, the Islamists, upset because of the losses, create a headscarf crisis in parliament. One week later, Vural Savaş, the chief prosecutor, asks the Constitutional Court to ban the Virtue Party for antisecularist activities. Later in May, Ecevit's Democratic Left forms a majority coalition government with two other political parties—the Nationalist Action Party and the Motherland Party.

On August 17, 1999, a major earthquake measuring 7.4 on the Richter scale destroys an industrial area in the northwest of Turkey, killing at least seventeen thousand people. The Turkish government is ill prepared to cope with the disaster and does too little to save lives. The quake eases the strained relationship between Greece and Turkey.

April 2000—Parliament rejects heavy-handed pressure by Bülent Ecevit's coalition government for a constitutional amendment to allow Süleyman Demirel a second term as president. The move is hailed as a victory for democracy. "The Game Is Over," said newspaper *Radikal* following parliament's rejection. Other newspapers declared the career of seventy-six-year old Demirel over, but he stated, "I won't sit still, raising chickens and twisting my thumbs."

May 2000—Parliament elects Necdet Sezer, fifty-eight, the president of the Constitutional Court, as Turkey's president.

February 2001—The Turkish lira collapses against the dollar as a result of a row between President Necdet Sezer and Prime Minister Bülent

Ecevit over the government's inability to deal with corruption. A severe economic crisis follows.

June 2001—The Constitutional Court bans the Virtue Party, and the Islamists later split into two separate parties—the traditional Islamist Necmettin Erbakan's Felicity Party and the moderate Islamist Recep Tayyip Erdo an's Justice and Development Party.

November 3, 2002—The Justice and Development Party snags an overwhelming victory in general election, opening the way for Recep Tayyip Erdo an to become the prime minister. The secularists claim that the Justice and Development Party with strong Islamist roots won the election because of poverty and through *takiyye*, a hidden agenda of pro-Islamic ambitions and plans against the secularist state.

Index